THE **CELL**

THE CELL

INSIDE THE 9/11 PLOT, AND WHY
THE FBI AND CIA FAILED TO STOP IT

JOHN MILLER AND MICHAEL STONE,
WITH CHRIS MITCHELL

HYPERION NEW YORK

Library of Congress Cataloging-in-Publication Data

Miller, John

    The cell : inside the 9/11 plot and why the CIA and FBI failed to stop it / John Miller and Michael Stone.—1st ed.

    p. cm.

    ISBN 0-7868-6900-3

    1. September 11 Terrorist Attacks, 2001.   2. Terrorism—United States—Prevention.   3. Terrorism—Government policy—United States.   I. Stone, Michael. II. Title.

HV6432 .M54   2002

973.931—dc21

2002027322

FIRST PAPERBACK EDITION

PAPERBACK ISBN 0-7868-8782-6

10 9 8 7 6 5 4 3 2 1

ACKNOWLEDGMENTS

There are many people without whom this book could not have been written. Former FBI Supervisor Neil Herman was our early guide through the complex web of the first Islamic terrorist cells discovered in the United States and also helped us understand the alternately admirable and often abysmal culture of the FBI's bureaucracy. Special thanks go to former NYPD Detective Thomas Corrigan, whose incredible memory for detail served to bring vivid detail to some of the most important first steps in the war on terrorism. Special Agents Joe Valliquette and Jim Margolin of the FBI's New York Office helped get us clearance to speak to many of the active agents who were still working on the hunt for bin Laden and his men. Those agents and detectives like Lou Napoli, Kenneth Maxwell, Frank Pellegrino and Chuck Stern were key in keeping us on track. There are many others in the New York Police Department, the FBI, CIA and other federal agencies we agreed not to name, because many of them are still working undercover, overseas or just wanted to speak freely about controversial issues raised in this book. They know who they are. We thank them. Baltimore Police Commissioner Ed Norris, an old friend who speaks the truth in his own name and without hesitation, deserves special credit for opening our eyes to some early failures.

Much of the reporting in the field and a great deal of the confidential source information contained in these chapters come from the work of the best news team in the business, ABC News. Terri Lichstein, who oversees John Miller's team and keeps copious records, lent a great deal of support to the project. Chris Isham and the ABC News Investigative Unit ran the effort that uncovered so much detail about bin Laden and his al Qaeda network. Len Tepper, one of the "I-Teams" key players, would have made a great detective. Many of his notes have been woven into this book. Chris Vlasto, whose sources are always impeccable, also contributed. Eric Avram and the team at the ABC News Law & Justice Unit also delivered key perspectives on the missed signals leading up to 9/11. ABC News President David Westin has our gratitude for allowing John to spend time and use the incredible world-wide resources of ABC News to tell this story. John Miller's assistant Aliza Davidovit deserves a medal, for helping Michael Stone and putting up with John. We also thank Polly Blitzer and Tara Rich-LaTerra, tireless researchers for Michael Stone, as well as Hannah Clever and Hoda Abdel Hamid, who provided valuable reporting from Germany and the Middle East.

Thank you to Richard Emery and Mark Reiter, the lawyer and the agent who found this book a home.

Leigh Haber, our editor at Hyperion, was right there during the most difficult times, waving us toward the finish line and making a very complex story readable at the same time.

AUTHORS' NOTE

A decision was made to publish the first edition of *The Cell* on schedule rather than delay its release for the weeks that would have been necessary to complete endnotes. With the paperback edition, we are able now to give due credit to all the primary and secondary sources from which the book drew, including those journalists whose work had contributed to the available public knowledge about the September 11 attacks.

We wish to apologize to Terry McDermott, the author of a superb *Los Angeles Times* profile of Mohamed Atta. McDermott's reporting and observations about Atta's formative years provided essential material for our Chapter 16, yet in the first edition there was only a single attribution to the *Los Angeles Times* in that chapter and none to Mr. McDermott. Our true debt to his work is reflected in both the new endnotes and in attributions we've added to the chapter.

THE CELL

PROLOGUE

September 11, 2001, started out as such a nice day—no, a *beautiful* day. Then it all turned.

ABC News/Good Morning America, 9:05 A.M.

DON DAHLER

Well, we see—it appears that there is more and more fire and smoke enveloping the very top of the building, and as fire crews are descending on this area, it—it does not appear that there's any kind of an effort up there yet. Now remember—Oh, my God!

DIANE SAWYER

Oh my God! Oh my God!

CHARLES GIBSON

That looks like a second plane has just hit . . .

How many times have you heard someone say, "Well, things will never be the same." It is rarely true. Things *always* go back to being the same. But not this time. Before the day was out many of my friends were dead. Many had just barely escaped. Many of them were badly hurt. Many who got out without even a scrape will be emotionally scarred for years if not forever. Many of them don't even know it yet, or just won't admit it.

Things will never be the same.

I have been a crime reporter since I was a teenager.* I have seen or heard everything that a crime reporter could. Or so I thought, until September 11, 2001. I was listening to the citywide radio frequency of the NYPD when I heard Joe Esposito, the NYPD chief, yell into his radio: "Car 3 to Central, advise the Pentagon New York City is under attack!" Been around a long time. Hadn't heard *that* one before.

I sat with Peter Jennings at the anchor desk in New York watching the flames when a plume of white smoke appeared where the South Tower had stood.

DON DAHLER

The second building that was hit by the plane has just completely collapsed. The entire building has just collapsed . . . it folded down on itself and it's not there anymore.

PETER JENNINGS

We are talking about massive casualties here at the moment and we have—whoo—that is extraordinary.

---

*For the natural flow of storytelling, John Miller has written about the events he was present for in the first person.

• • •

Don Dahler

There is panic on the streets. There are people screaming and running from the site. The gigantic plume of smoke has reached me and I'm probably a quarter of a mile north of there.

By the time the Towers collapsed in a cloud of metal and dust and humanity, I knew this was the work of bin Laden. No one told me. No one had to. It had been a long time coming. I was part of the small club, regarded by many as alarmists, who had been predicting a major attack on U.S. soil since just before the millennium. Even so, I never imagined this result. Nor, do I think, did anyone else.

Things will never be the same.

Those of us who had studied terrorism in general or bin Laden in particular knew that the most reliable way to predict future behavior was to examine past behavior. Truck-bombs, murders, yes—even airplane hijackings. But no one had ever used a huge jetliner as a projectile—a missile—against a skyscraper before. No one had ever committed mass murder on this scale in a set of coordinated acts of terrorism in a single day. Not until September 11, 2001. That was the day my crime story turned into a war. Or had it been one all along?

We all asked, how could this have happened, how could we not have known, why were we not prepared? This book will answer many of those questions. No doubt years will be spent parsing every memo and intelligence report to see what little clues might have been missed. We will deal with that in this story too. But if there is any true value to this narrative, it is not the little picture of the single clue passed over; it is the big picture, the one you have to stand back from, to appreciate its shape and detail.

How did this happen to us? To find the answers we had to go back more than a decade and follow the thread forward to September 11, 2001. As we did, a recurring pattern emerged. It raises questions: Was the FBI fully up to the job of countering terrorists? What about the CIA? Was terrorism a priority in the Bush White House or in Ashcroft's Justice Department prior to September 11, 2001?

This is not a book about how the FBI agents or the CIA's officers on the front lines screwed up. Quite the contrary. Successful cases and captures were made. A number of horrific terrorist plots were disrupted. We found in almost every case that the cops, agents and spies who followed their instincts were usually in the right place and on the right trail. But we found a recurring pattern. Over and over again the investigators were waved off the right trail. The reasons ranged from risk-averse bosses to bureaucratic structures that seemed designed to ensure that the left hand would never know what the right hand was doing.

What struck us was the remarkable stories of those investigators. What we learned is that for more than a decade, the very system they worked for seemed to conspire against them as often as it supported them.

In many ways it seems like America was the sleeping giant. Every time the terrorism alarm went off, the giant stirred to consciousness, hit the snooze button and went back to sleep. Each time it sounded the alarm was a little louder. The Kahane murder, the World Trade Center bombing, the plot to blow up bridges and tunnels, the East Africa embassy bombings, the USS *Cole* attack.

In 1998, I sat with Osama bin Laden in a hut in Afghanistan as he told me he was declaring war on America. His words at the time may have sounded hyperbolic, but read them now.

"We are sure of our victory. Our battle with the Americans is larger than our battle with the Russians. We predict a black day for America and the end of the United States."

•   •   •

From the moment bin Laden declared war on America, one of his frustrations seemed to be that he couldn't get America to declare war back. Not until the loudest and bloodiest alarm sounded on September 11 did the giant finally awake.

CHAPTER 1

SEPTEMBER 11

On the morning of September 11, 2001, Michael Wright, a 30-year-old sales executive, woke at 6:30. Stocky, with a broad Irish face and an easy manner, he rolled over to hug his wife, then remembered she'd gone with their four-month-old son to visit Michael's parents in Boston. With the place to himself, Wright thought about sleeping in, but heard his grandfather's voice barking at him from the grave: "Get your lazy butt to work."

Outside his apartment—a brownstone floor-through facing Prospect Park in Brooklyn—it was a brilliant end-of-summer day, bell-clear with a hint of coolness in the air. Wright was looking forward to work. He had two deals pending and with plans to buy his apartment, he was eager for the commissions. Showered and dressed, he made the subway commute into Lower Manhattan in 20 minutes and exited on Broadway and Dey Street, two blocks due east of his office, a telecommunications equipment company headquartered in the World Trade Center.

Looking up, he marveled at the familiar Twin Towers massed against the sky. Sunlight glanced off the steel rails running up the buildings' sides, making them shine. But what really impressed Wright was their size, their head-snapping height, the sheer, unholy dimensions of their heavenly reach. They embodied, as no other buildings did, the economic muscle he wanted his company to project each time he handed out his business card or told someone where he worked. He walked briskly across the plaza and took the elevator to the 81st floor of the North Tower, getting to his desk by 7:45.

While Wright got started on paperwork, Mayor Rudy Giuliani was bullying midtown traffic in his official car, a white SUV familiarly known as the ice-cream van. He was headed for a breakfast meeting at the Peninsula Hotel on West 55th Street with his counsel, Dennison Young, then back uptown to the Richard R. Green School in Harlem to vote in the elections that would determine his successor. It was Primary Day in New York and the city's political nerves were twitching.

As Giuliani entered the Peninsula's starched dining room shortly after 8:00 A.M., American Airlines Flight 11 was making its ascent over Boston's Logan Airport. En route to Los Angeles, the wide-bodied jet carried 81 passengers and a crew of 11. About 10 minutes later, a second Boeing 767 took off for LA. This flight, United Airlines 175, carried 56 passengers and a crew of nine. Both flights departed without incident, and control tower workers were settling into their early-morning routines when at 8:14, the American plane failed to respond to an air-traffic controller's instruction to increase its altitude. The controller tried to raise the pilot on the radio, without success. Then at 8:24, he overheard a strange communication originating from the plane's cockpit. "We have some planes," an accented male voice announced. "Just stay quiet and you will be okay. We are returning to the airport. Nobody move. Everything will be okay. If you try to make any moves, you'll endanger yourself and the airplane. Just stay quiet."

Moments before, an American Airlines reservations supervisor had received a call from Betty Ong, a flight attendant on Flight 11, describing a hijacking in progress. According to the *Wall Street Journal,* the supervisor had patched the call through to Craig Marquis, the veteran manager-on-duty at American's operations center in Fort Worth, Texas. Nearly hysterical, Ong told him that two flight attendants had been stabbed and that one was on oxygen. The hijackers, she said, had also slit one passenger's throat and stormed the cockpit.

While Marquis verified Ong's employee number and gleaned details about the hijackers' seat assignments, air-traffic controllers tried to track the hijacked plane's flight path. It had turned south over Albany in the direction of New York City and begun flying erratically—apparently while the hijackers were overcoming the pilots—but the hijackers had then turned off the flight transponder, a device that allows controllers to distinguish a plane's radar image from among the hundreds of other blips on a screen. The controllers had no idea where the plane was heading.

As the controllers made last-ditch efforts to communicate with AAL 11, Madeline Amy Sweeney, a 35-year-old attendant on the flight, called Michael Woodward, an American flight services manager at Logan, and went on to calmly describe the hijackers as four Middle Eastern men, some wearing red bandanas and wielding box cutters. "This plane," she said, "has been hijacked."

Suddenly, she reported, the plane swerved and began descending. "What's your location?" Woodward asked her. Sweeney looked out a window and told him she saw water and buildings.

"Oh my God," she said then. "Oh my God."

About 8:45 Michael Wright visited the men's room, located near the elevator bank at the center of the 81st floor of the North Tower. On his way out he ran into a coworker, Arturo Gonzalez, and stopped briefly to chat with him. Suddenly the building shuddered and Wright heard a crash—a screeching, metal-on-metal jolt—and was thrown back against the wall.

The lights blinked and for a moment, the whole building seemed to teeter. Wright waited for the room to settle and adjusted his vision. Everything had changed. The marble façade on the opposite wall was shattered and a huge crack had opened up in the drywall behind. The floor had buckled and Gonzalez was propped up against the broken vanity. The sinks themselves had moved out from the wall. "What the fuck was that?" Wright asked.

"Holy shit," Gonzalez intoned.

Smoke threaded through the air between them.

They headed out to the hallway, where the devastation was horrendous. Chunks of roof were falling, the facing wall was ripped open and the elevator doors to their right had blown out. The whole building, Wright realized, had shifted on its foundation. Every joining surface was awry; every hinge was twisted or bent. A crater had opened in the floor ahead of him exposing wires, pipes, girders and beams at least ten floors below. Acrid smoke poured out of the elevator shafts.

Wright's instinct was to get the hell out of there, but instead he turned back toward his office to check on his coworkers. As he ran past the elevators, he heard screaming from the ladies' room. The jamb above the door had caved, trapping whoever was inside. Gonzalez and another colleague began kicking down the door.

Wright's 30 or so officemates were pouring out into the hall. Some were calm, others terrified or in tears. He directed them to the stairwell. Flaming chunks of material were falling around them and Wright could smell burning fuel, though he had no idea where it was coming from.

John O'Neill, the World Trade Center's 49-year-old chief of security, dashed out of his South Tower office to assess the situation. A brusque, larger-than-life New York character, O'Neill had spent all but a few days of his professional life at the FBI, the last eight years as one of its top counterterrorism officials. Ironically, he'd retired from the Bureau two weeks before in order to take what friends called a cushy private-sector job, and former colleagues still regarded him as the nation's most knowledgeable counterterrorist. Only the night before, over dinner with friends, he'd expressed a fear that New York was ripe for an attack like the one he now found himself in the midst of. He made a quick damage inspection, placed a call on his cell phone, and then sprinted back inside to help coordinate the rescue effort.

Joe Lhota, Rudy Giuliani's chief of staff, felt the explosion in his office at City Hall almost a half mile from the World Trade Center. He dashed out onto the steps, saw the flames engulfing the tower and called Giuliani at the Peninsula. An aide answered the phone. "Tell the mayor a plane has hit the Trade Center," Lhota said.

Back downtown at One Police Plaza, anxious aides pounded on Bernie Kerik's bathroom door. The 46-year-old bullet-shaped police commissioner had worked out earlier in the vest-pocket gym attached to his office and was taking advantage of a break in his busy schedule to shower and change. He answered the door wearing nothing but a towel, a beardful of shaving cream, and a "this better be good" expression.

"A plane just hit the World Trade towers," several staffers said at once.

"All right, relax. Calm down," Kerik said, noting the worry in their faces. He was thinking small aircraft, an accident.

"You don't understand, Boss," John Picciano, his chief aide, said. "You can see it from the window. It's enormous."

Kerik realized that every phone on the floor was ringing.

Still wrapped in a towel, he followed Picciano through the outer office to a conference room at the southwest corner of the building and looked out at the Trade Center. Then he ran back to his office to call the mayor, who was already headed downtown, and got dressed.

He was out of the building within four minutes, at the scene in eight. Pulling up in his black four-door Chrysler at the corner of Vesey and West Broadway, he saw people jumping out of windows 90, 100 stories up, one after another. For the first time in his 25-year law enforcement career, he felt totally helpless.

More than a thousand miles away, at American's operations center in Fort Worth, top executives were experiencing similar feelings. With the assistance of the Federal Aviation Administration (FAA), the center's technicians had finally managed to isolate Flight 11's radar image on Aircraft Situation Display—a big-screen tracking device used for just such emergencies—and stunned officials watched as the blips approached New York, froze and then vanished. Still no one knew what had happened. Even when a ramp supervisor called from Kennedy Airport several minutes later to report that a plane had crashed into the World Trade Center, they couldn't believe that it was Flight 11.

Meanwhile, air-traffic controllers back east were scrambling to make contact with two more rogue planes, according to a *New York Times* report. Even before the first World Trade Center crash, United's Flight 175 seemed to be in trouble. At 8:41, one of its pilots had radioed them that he'd heard a suspicious transmission emanating earlier from Flight 11. "Someone keyed the mike and said, 'Everyone stay in their seats,'" the pilot told the controllers. Minutes later, Flight 175 swerved off course and shut down communication.

Almost simultaneously, air-traffic controllers lost contact with a second American flight, AAL 77, a Boeing 757 en route from Washington's Dulles International Airport to Los Angeles with 58 passengers and 6 crew on board. At 8:56, just moments after the first World Trade Center crash, that plane doubled back toward Washington, shut off its transponder, and didn't answer repeated calls from a controller out of Indianapolis.

Airline executives were finding it impossible to keep abreast of developments in the air. Officials at United's operations center outside Chicago had just gotten news of the first Trade Center crash, when Doc Miles, the center's shift manager, received an alarming communication from United's maintenance department in San Francisco. Moments before, a mechanic had fielded a call from an attendant on Flight 175 saying the pilots had been killed, a flight attendant stabbed and the plane hijacked.

Miles questioned the report; it was an American Airlines jet that had been hijacked, he pointed out, not a United plane. But the mechanic confirmed that the call had come from United Flight 175 from Boston to LA and frantic efforts by a dispatcher to raise the cockpit were met with silence. Meanwhile, executives watching CNN on an overhead screen in United's crisis room saw a large, still unidentified aircraft crash into the Trade Center's South Tower.

I had just walked out of *Good Morning America*'s Times Square studios and when I'd got to my car all hell had broken loose. My pager went off. My cell phone rang, and so did the car phone. I know from experience, this is never good news.

"A plane crashed into the World Trade Center," Kris Sebastian, the ABC News's national assignment manager, told me.

"I'm on my way," I said. I calculated the routes to the scene. I could get there in 12 to 15 minutes if I drove a smart, back-road route and ran some lights. But a network crew starting out from the office would take longer, and a satellite truck, which is what I would need to "go live," would take an hour to be ready for broadcast. I really wanted to go to the scene. That's what I had done my whole life. I was a "street guy." But I also realized that the news choppers would already be broadcasting live pictures from the scene.

I could hear information pouring out of the police radio in my car. When I finally got to the corner of 44th Street and Eighth Avenue, I called the news desk and told them: Change of plans. I'm coming in and will help with live coverage from the set of the ABC News Desk.

Not much more than a minute later, police radio still in hand, I was sitting down next to Peter Jennings. We watched with astonishment as the second plane crashed into the other tower. Peter, never one to rush to conclusions—especially on the air—looked at me. "Whatever we thought this was, we now know what it is," I said. "This is a terrorist attack."

● ● ●

Back at the site, Kerik was patrolling the plaza's uptown boundary, making calls on his cell phone and shouting instructions at chief aide John Picciano to set up a command post a few blocks north, when he heard the explosion of the second crash. He looked up and saw a massive fireball shooting out of the South Tower straight at him. But he didn't see the plane itself, which had banked low across the harbor and slammed into the south side of the building. "How the hell did the fire leap from one tower to the other?" he wondered.

There was no time to figure out what happened. The crash was sending debris flying toward Kerik and his men. For a moment they stood transfixed, watching the deadly shrapnel make its descent. It looked like confetti, it was so high. Then someone yelled at them to get out of there and they took off up West Broadway.

As Kerik ducked around the corner into a garage on Barclay Street, someone told him that a United Airlines plane had hit the building. Instantly he realized they were being attacked by terrorists. He thought, "How many more planes are up there? What are the other targets?" He began calling for a mobilization and ordered his chief deputy commissioner to evacuate police headquarters, City Hall, the UN, and the Empire State Building.

Within minutes, Giuliani arrived at the corner of Barclay and West Broadway, and Kerik, joining him, reported that the city was under attack. "We've got to cut off the air space," Giuliani said.

Kerik relayed the order to Picciano, adding, "Get us some air support. We need F16s."

Picciano was looking at him like he was crazy. "What the fuck are you talking about?" he said.

Kerik realized how surreal the situation had become. He was a police commissioner, not a general in the army. Who the hell do you call to get an F16, anyway? Is there a number for that?

• • •

In fact, the FAA had already notified the Northeast Air Defense Sector in Rome, New York, at 8:40, about ten minutes after controllers began to suspect that they had a hijacking in progress. At 8:46, Otis Air National Guard Base near Falmouth, Massachusetts, had gotten a call from NORAD, the North American Aerospace Defense Command, and scrambled two F15s, 1977-vintage fighters equipped with heat-seeking missiles. The planes were dispatched immediately, and were airborne by 8:52, but they were still some 70 miles—eight minutes—away when the second plane, UAL 175, crashed into the Trade Center at 9:03.

By then, Michael Wright had fallen in with his coworkers on the stairs and was being joined by people from the floors above and below. They descended the narrow stairs slowly, two abreast.

Twenty floors down, the mood lightened. Wright heard tones of relief, trails of nervous laughter. "I don't care what time it is," someone said. "I'm going to get a drink at John Street [bar and grill]."

Conversation turned from what people had seen to what might have actually happened. Wright initially thought that a gas main had exploded; now people around him speculated it was a bomb. Nobody knew for sure. They'd been frantically trying their cell phones, but service was down. At length, a stranger with a BlackBerry, a wireless email device, informed them that a plane had crashed into their building and that the tower next door had also been hit.

Wright knew at once that terrorists had attacked them. One crash might be an accident, two had to be intentional. But he assumed they'd used small planes, Cessnas maybe—the kind of light commuter craft he'd seen routinely winging past his office window.

Another 20 floors down, Wright's sense of relief turned to dread. Firefighters, rescue workers and police shouldered past him on their way upstairs. Most of them were stern-faced, but some were clearly frightened. Many of them, he realized later, had been about to die.

Arriving at the fire department's makeshift command post on West Street in the shadow of 1 World Trade Center, the mayor and the police commissioner witnessed a scene of almost unimaginable horror. Hundreds of office workers were streaming out of both towers under a rain of glass, steel and airplane and body parts; the air was choked with smoke and ash; the street awash in blood.

Surrounded by aides, Giuliani met briefly with the fire department's top commanders—Thomas Von Essen, the commissioner; Bill Feehan, his first deputy; Pete Ganci, the chief of department; and Deputy Chief Ray Downey. Giuliani listened to their plans to evacuate the buildings, while Kerik consulted with police. One familiar face on the scene belonged to John Coughlin, an Emergency Services Unit (ESU) sergeant who had once saved Kerik's daughter from choking.

About 9:40, Giuliani and Kerik, now joined by the fire commissioner and other top administration officials, trooped a few blocks north to set up a forward command post. "God bless you," the mayor said to Ganci on leaving.

"Thank you," Ganci said. "God bless you."

"Pray for us," Giuliani then said to Mychal Judge, the department chaplain, who was standing nearby.

"Don't worry," Judge told the mayor. "I always do."

Informed that another one of their flights was lost after the first World Trade Center crash, officials at American's operations center began to realize that the morning's events were more than an ordinary hijacking. Gerard Arpey, American's executive vice president of operations, immediately grounded every plane in the Northeast that wasn't already airborne. Moments later, when he heard that United also had a plane hijacked, he ordered all American flights grounded nationwide.

United was taking similar actions. Andy Studdert, United's COO, froze all international flights on the ground at 9:20. At 9:30, he ordered all domestic flights out of the air. By then, however, United had another plane in trouble.

Thirty-eight-year-old former flight attendant Deena Burnett had risen in her family's modest Bay Area home at 6:00 A.M.—9:00 EDT—to get her three daughters ready for school. While she prepared breakfast—pop-up cinnamon waffles, milk—Deena's attention was drawn to the TV, then airing reports of the first World Trade Center crash. Her husband Tom was flying home from Newark that morning and she felt a twinge of worry. She thought about calling Tom's mother to find out what flight he was on, but decided not to.

Fifteen minutes later, Deena's mother-in-law called her, expressing the same concern. Deena tried to calm her. The airlines had hundreds of flights up each morning and those were just the commercial jets, she said. The plane in the reports might have actually been private. They were still talking at 9:20 EDT when another call came in on the other line. It was Tom. "Are you okay?" Deena asked.

"No," he said. "I'm on United Airlines 93 from Newark to San Francisco. The plane has been hijacked." He was speaking quickly and quietly, as though he were afraid of being overheard. Deena understood the hijackers must have been close by. "We are in the air," he went on. "One guy knifed a guy. They're saying they've got a bomb onboard. Please call the authorities."

The line went dead.

Michael Wright reached the 20th floor of 1 World Trade Center at about 9:30, nearly 40 minutes after he'd begun his descent. Emergency workers there were asking for volunteers to escort the elderly and infirm the rest of the way. Wright, who knew CPR, made several runs up and down, and then, satisfied that there were no stragglers, exited onto the mezzanine, heading east toward the plaza on his way back to his subway entrance. But when he rounded the elevator banks he had to alter his route. With its central fountain, flowers and statuary, the plaza had always been a refuge for Wright, a place to meet friends, picnic at lunchtime and listen to the bands that played in the warm weather. But this morning it was a war zone. There was debris everywhere—chunks of metal, shattered glass, burning material. Wright made out the fuselage of one of the jumbo jets, his first realization of the enormity of the catastrophe. But it wasn't this that riveted his attention. It was the human wreckage, the bodies and parts of bodies—limbs, torsos, entrails—strewn amid the rubble. Facing him, perfectly intact, was the severed head of a woman. Pert, blond, the same age as him, her eyes were still open. Reflexively, he lifted a magazine he'd been carrying—he'd brought it with him to the men's room—and shielded his eyes from the carnage.

That carnage had now spread beyond the Trade Center. As Wright had been walking down the stairs of the North Tower, AA 77—the LA–bound flight out of Dulles—was racing back across Pennsylvania toward Washington. At 9:24 NORAD ordered Langley AFB in Hampton, Virginia, to scramble three F16s together. They were in the air by 9:30. Though they still didn't know Flight 77's precise location, they headed toward New York at their top speed. Just after 9:30 a controller at Dulles observed a "fast-moving primary target" about to move into restricted air space above the Capitol. An airport supervisor immediately alerted the Secret Service, who evacuated the White House. At 9:36, the plane was identified as a Boeing 757, the same model as the missing American aircraft. By then, the plane had crossed over the Pentagon and begun a 360-degree turn that would bring it nearly to ground level. NORAD rerouted the F16 fighters west to Ronald Reagan Washington National Airport, but they were too far away to intercept, and two minutes later, at 9:38, AA Flight 77 slammed into the west side of the Pentagon, obliterating itself and killing everyone on board.

Meantime, United officials were frantically attempting to communicate with UAL 93. The San Francisco–bound flight had been traveling over western Pennsylvania when, just before 9:30, air-traffic controllers had heard someone in the cockpit say, "Hey, get out of here," then someone else with a thick Middle Eastern accent addressing the passengers: "This is your captain. There is a bomb on board. Remain in your seats. We are returning to the airport."

Almost simultaneously, Tom Burnett called his wife a second time. "They're in the cockpit," he announced.

In the ten minutes since Tom's first call, Deena Burnett had contacted the FBI and was still trying to explain to a series of agents that her husband's flight was not one of the planes that had already crashed into the Trade Center. She put them on hold and told Tom about the earlier attacks.

"Were they commercial planes?" he asked.

"I don't know. They're speculating on the news that they might have been private or cargo planes. There's no visible identification."

"Do you know who's involved?"

Deena couldn't answer. Tom's first call had been brief, businesslike, his way of conveying the facts efficiently. Now he was trying to get information from her, assess the forces he was up against. After nearly ten years of marriage, Deena knew what her husband was planning.

Tom Burnett was the ultimate can-do guy. At 38, the muscular six-foot-two former college football player was the head of a medical equipment company with more than 700 employees and $80 million in sales, a man used to making executive decisions. He wasn't ever rash, but he never flinched from a challenge either. Here he was in the middle of a hijacking—there was a man lying wounded in the aisle just a few feet from him—and yet he was coolly debriefing his wife about his attackers' MO, the nature and targets of their threats.

"The guy they knifed is dead," he said then. "They're telling us there's a bomb onboard. Do you think it's true?"

"Have you seen a bomb?" Deena asked.

"No." He paused. "I gotta go."

The call had lasted no more than 30 seconds. Deena had the sense that Tom was already moving around the airplane, conferring with other passengers, formulating a plan, enlisting support. Deena got back on the phone with the FBI. A policeman, perhaps alerted by her earlier 911 call, showed up to sit with her. She shooed the children upstairs to dress and make their beds. One of her five-year-old twins, Madison, started crying. She'd heard her father on the phone and was upset that she couldn't speak to him. "Daddy's on an airplane," Deena told her. "He's having a little problem. You can speak to him when he comes home."

It never occurred to Deena that he might not come home. At one point she even thought, "If Tom's plane is on time, he'll be back by seven. What do I need to get for dinner?"

Just then, the news was reporting that the Pentagon had been hit. Deena thought it was Tom's plane. She'd been so busy with the children, fielding calls—the FBI's, her in-laws', Tom's—so used to her husband's confidence she had perhaps mistaken it as her confidence. She realized that in spite of her training and experience as a flight attendant, she hadn't considered the implications of what was happening. And so now, without warning, when she thought Tom might be dead, she began to wail, a long, high-pitched keening sound that she'd never heard before and couldn't seem to control.

The children had never heard it either, and it sounded so strange that at first they thought she was laughing, and they began to laugh too. But then they realized there was something wrong and they gathered around her, hugging her, and she knew she had to stop it, and then Tom called again.

"Tom, are you okay?" she asked.

"No, I'm not," he answered, a hint of impatience in his voice.

"They just hit the Pentagon," she said, composing herself. "It looks like they're taking planes and hitting designated landmarks up and down the East Coast."

"How many are involved?" he asked.

"I don't know," Deena said. "Three have already crashed and they're speculating two more have been hijacked. I've already called the authorities. They didn't know about your plane until I called."

"We can't wait for the authorities," he said.

"Is there anything else I can do?" she asked.

"Pray, Deena, just pray."

Then he said, "I think we're going to have to do something. [The hijackers are] talking about running the plane into the ground." Before they'd lost control of the cockpit, the pilots had switched on the intercom to the cabin. Passengers could hear the hijackers discussing their plans in fragmented English.

"What is the probability of their having a bomb onboard?" Tom asked. "I don't think they have one. I haven't seen a bomb. They're just telling us about that."

"I love you," Deena said.

"Don't worry. I'll call you back."

Emergency workers in the mezzanine of 1 World Trade Center directed Wright down the east escalators to the main lobby. From there he made his way through the mall underneath the plaza to another bank of escalators leading up to the lobby of 5 World Trade Center, a smaller building facing Church Street at the northeast corner of the complex.

Wright had his arm around two women coworkers. In just minutes they'd be out of the Center altogether. But when they were nearly at street level, Wright heard a thunderous noise above them, like the roar of an F16 directly overhead. He clambered up the last few steps of the escalator to check out its source and froze. In the mirrored glass front of the Millennium Hotel across the road, he could see the South Tower's one million tons of steel and concrete collapsing behind him. Instinctively he knew it was too late to make a run for it; debris was already raining onto the street. He ran back into the lobby and threw himself and his coworkers headlong against an interior wall.

Everything went black. The roar had reached a crescendo and he was inundated with falling material: drywall, wood splinters, plaster. He tucked his head into his chest and, thinking he was about to die, shouted the names of his wife and baby.

• • •

"The building's coming down!" someone yelled. "Hit the deck." A detective guarding the mayor shoved him under a desk in the ground-floor offices that Giuliani and his aides had commandeered as part of a temporary operations base at 75 Barclay Street. Moments before, Giuliani had been talking to Vice President Cheney, who had called from a bunker underneath the White House. Within seconds, the phone had gone dead. Then the building started to tremble and someone noticed that the South Tower, just a few blocks away, was collapsing. Seconds more, and the windows in the building started popping and a column of smoke and dust poured through the door.

Giuliani and his aides had to get out fast. Several doors leading to the street were locked and they trekked down to the basement and then back up to the lobby before building workers guided them out. They exited onto Church Street—which was as dark as night under a cover of smoke, dust and debris—and, swept up in a tide of office workers, began running north until they reached daylight, some three blocks uptown.

Wright lay on the ground for a full minute after the collapse, stood up slowly and felt his body. He wasn't hurt, but he was gagging. His nose, mouth and ears were packed with dust. He tried to spit out the grit and vomited instead, clearing his airway. His eyes hurt and he still couldn't see. He thought he might be blind, then realized somehow he was in a small, enclosed space, buried under rubble. He knew there were others with him. He could hear their cries and moans. But his attention was fixed elsewhere. The space was filling quickly with smoke; in a matter of minutes, they would all suffocate.

He ripped off his shirt, soaked from the overhead sprinklers, wrapped it around his head, dropped to his knees below the blanket of noxious smoke and began crawling through the flooded enclosure.

A light blinked on. He scrambled to its source. A firefighter, trapped along with the others, was probing the perimeter with a flashlight. Wright was uncertain how far down they were buried and was still entertaining thoughts of asphyxiation when the firefighter unsheathed the axe he was carrying and began hacking at a store-size window so caked with dust that Wright had mistaken it for a cement wall. The glass shattered easily and Wright's spirits soared as he escaped down into a deserted bookstore and from there into the dust and smoke-filled air of Lower Manhattan.

Not long before 10:00 A.M. EDT, Tom Burnett called home a fourth time from UAL 93. "Have you heard anything else?" he asked.

"No."

"Well, a group of us are going to do something."

"No," his wife said, her flight attendant reflexes kicking in. "Sit down. Be still and be quiet and don't draw attention to yourself."

"No, Deena. If they're going to run the plane into the ground, we have to do something."

Deena couldn't say anything. He kept repeating. "We're going to do something. If we're going to die, we're going to have to do something.

"Pray, Deena."

"Okay," she said.

He hung up. The call had lasted under a minute.

Since her mother-in-law's call 45 minutes earlier, Deena had not put down the phone once. Even as she fed and dressed her daughters and herself, mimicking her husband's competence and confidence as best she could, she clung to the portable receiver.

As Tom hung up from her the fourth and last time, a number of like-minded passengers were wrapping up calls to friends and loved ones, announcing their intentions to take back the plane.

Seated across from Burnett in the fourth row, Mark Bingham, 31, called his mother to tell her that he loved her. He was so upset and flustered that when she came on the line, he announced, "Mom, this is Mark Bingham."

Farther back in the plane, Jeremy Glick, a 31-year-old Internet sales manager and former judo champion, managed to reach his wife using his seat-back phone. Having described the hijackers—three Middle Eastern men wielding knives—he told her the passengers had taken a vote and decided to storm the cockpit.

"Do what you have to do," Lyzbeth Glick told him.

Sandy Bradshaw, a flight attendant forced back to the rear of the plane, told her husband in Greensboro, North Carolina, that she was boiling water to use as a weapon against the hijackers.

Todd Beamer, a 32-year-old account manager for Oracle Corp., concluded a 13-minute conversation with Lisa Jefferson, a GTE Airfone supervisor who'd come on the line after Beamer had punched "0" on his seat-back phone.

Beamer had passed along as many details about the hijacking as he could think of. He'd asked Jefferson to tell his pregnant wife and two sons how much he loved them and to recite the Lord's Prayer and the 23rd Psalm with him. Then he'd informed her of the plan to rush the hijackers. "I'm going to have to go out on faith," he'd said.

A few minutes before 10:00, Jefferson heard him ask another passenger: "Are you ready?" Then she heard Beamer say, "Okay, let's roll."

Meanwhile, to the south, the three F16 fighter pilots from Langley were also receiving a series of troubling communications. First they heard an FAA transmission grounding all civilian aircraft. Then they picked up a squawk on their transponders putting them on near emergency wartime status. Finally, after confirming the Pentagon crash, they were radioed a chilling instruction from a Secret Service official: "Protect the White House at all costs."

Now, as they patrolled the capital's skies, the three pilots, two of whom also flew for commercial airlines, were faced with the prospect of having to shoot down a civilian plane with U.S. passengers and crew aboard.

That possibility never arose.

At approximately 10:00 A.M., Flight 93 crashed in an uninhabited field near Shanksville, Pennsylvania, 80 miles southeast of Pittsburgh and 163 miles from the White House, its putative target.

The cockpit recorder picked up the sounds of a violent struggle. Investigators speculate that a group of passengers wrested control of the plane from the hijackers and crashed it into the field. Tom Burnett, along with 33 fellow passengers, 7 crew and 4 hijackers, perished in the crash.

Sitting next to Peter Jennings in the ABC News studio, I heard a cop yell that the second tower was coming down. I interrupted Peter to point to the monitor. As the tower was going down, I was tempted to say something—anything—just out of shock. But as the plume of smoke rose into the skyline, Jennings looked at the monitor, knowing our mikes were live, and held up his hands preempting any comment. He had the good sense to know that this was such a profound moment that words would be superfluous, even inappropriate.

Giuliani and his aides had regrouped on Church Street and were slowly walking uptown when, at about 10:30, the North Tower imploded with count-less people still trapped inside. Once again a black cloud of smoke, dust and debris mushroomed over Lower Manhattan, menacing the mayor's contin-gent. A detective threw his arm around Giuliani, shielding him as best he could, and they took off up Church Street. "Just keep going north!" Giuliani shouted, according to New York 1 News reporter Andrew Kirtzman.

Giuliani and his aides began searching for a new base of operations. Several suggestions—the First Precinct house, the Fire Museum—were nixed in favor of the nearby Tribeca Grand, a trendy downtown hotel. But the hotel's chic décor and well-heeled clientele seemed to clash with the gravity of their mission, not to mention the Mayor's populist style. After a quick tour through the lobby, they poured back out on the street and headed uptown toward Greenwich Village.

Their wanderings led them to Engine Co. 24 at Sixth Avenue and Houston, where they decided to encamp. Still they had to wait precious minutes while someone jimmied the lock; the entire company had gone down to the Trade Center. Finally, at 10:54, Giuliani, ensconced in a small, glass-enclosed office, gave his first interview over the phone to local TV news anchors. He told them that he'd been in touch with White House officials who had secured the city's airspace. He said that he'd talked to Governor George Pataki several times and they'd agreed to postpone the primary. Then he addressed the people who'd lost loved ones in the disaster. "My heart goes out to [you]," he said. "I've never seen anything like this. I was there from shortly after it happened and saw people jumping out of the World Trade Center. It's a horrible, horrible situation, and all I can tell [you] is that every resource that we have [is being used in] attempting to rescue as many people as possible. And the end result is going to be some horrendous number of lives lost. I don't think we know yet, but right now we have to just focus on saving as many people as possible."

The mayor's intent was to reassure the public, and he'd sounded candid, human and clearly in charge. But later that afternoon, after moving uptown to more commodious quarters at the Police Academy on East 20th Street, Giuliani held his first televised press conferences, and as he spoke he struck that uncanny balance between grief, anger and calm resolve that gave New Yorkers—and many in the nation—a voice with which to address the unfolding tragedy. "We will strive now very hard to save as many people as possible," he said. "And to send a message that the City of New York and the United States of America is much stronger than any group of barbaric terrorists. That our democracy, that our rule of law, that our strength and willingness to defend ourselves will ultimately prevail . . .

"New York is still here," he went on. "We've undergone tremendous losses, but New York is going to be here tomorrow morning, and this is the way of life that people want throughout the world."

•   •   •

Perhaps no one who'd been at the site that morning—civilians and officials alike—escaped unscathed. Even the most fortunate survivors, it seems, left friends and coworkers behind. The men whom Giuliani had visited at the fire department's forward post on West Street—chiefs Ray Downey and Pete Ganci, and Deputy Commissioner Bill Feehan—all died in the collapse of the North Tower. Mychal Judge, the department chaplain, died in the lobby of 1 World Trade Center, the victim of falling debris or possibly a heart attack, after he administered the last rites to a dying firefighter. John Coughlin, the ESU sergeant who once saved Bernie Kerik's baby daughter, is still missing, buried no doubt beneath the rubble that was the Trade Center.

CHAPTER 2

THE GOOD GUYS

Neil Herman had just come home to his Westchester apartment with his morning papers and coffee. The phone was ringing.

"Are you watching?" asked a familiar voice.

The caller was a supervisor in the FBI's New York office, where Herman had served as chief of domestic terrorism for most of the 1990s. In fact, September 11 marked the third anniversary of a retirement party that had been held in Herman's honor at the Windows on the World restaurant atop the North Tower of the World Trade Center.

"Am I watching what?" Herman asked.

"Flip on the TV," his old colleague told him. "It will bring back memories."

Louie Napoli, another of Herman's old coworkers, was afforded much less time for reflection that morning. Standing at the window of the terrorism unit's Lower Manhattan office, Napoli briefly had had the wherewithal to connect the sight of the two burning towers to a suspect: Osama bin Laden. But then he and the rest of the unit had hit the streets, and by the time he found himself running a second time from an avalanche of thunder and dust, his mind had gone blank. The towers were gone, the world was white; when the noise finally subsided, he couldn't see ten feet in front of him. He was, though, still within shouting range of most of the other members of the task force. What to do next was a question no one's experience or training could answer. Where to go was easier: Napoli's unit commander chose to convene in a park about six blocks away in Chinatown. They'd get a head count of their survivors there, and somehow launch an investigation.

Tommy Corrigan figured the busy signal at Michael Seaman's Long Island home was a good sign: The line had been tied up for a while, so maybe Michael had finally found a way to get a call through. Not that Corrigan had anything new to report to Michael's wife. He'd reached a couple of his old colleagues in the terrorism unit before the second tower came down, but in their stunned, dust-covered state, they'd only strengthened his worst fears about the number of casualties. John O'Neill, they said, had disappeared, along with a few other of Corrigan's old coworkers. Maybe Michael, he thought, had a better chance. Eight years earlier, the Cantor Fitzgerald securities trader had been one of very few civilians who'd set foot inside the 70-yard-wide crater blasted into the Trade Center's underground garage by a van bomb. From that day on, Michael had had one more reason to dial up his old Queens College basketball teammate. "Am I safe in the building?" Michael would ask. It was a way of wrapping humor around a twinge of true fear.

"Yeah, you're safe," Corrigan would say.

"You sure?"

"You'll be the first to know if I hear something."

Now, when Corrigan needed a reason to hope, he told himself his closest friend wouldn't have stayed at his desk on the 104th floor for long if he'd survived the first plane's impact. Another busy signal at the Seaman house: *Please let it be Michael calling in.*

• • •

While no one who watched the September 11 assault on the U.S. was prepared for the horrors that unfolded that day, Neil Herman, Louie Napoli and
Tommy Corrigan were among a select group who saw the attacks as something other than bolts out of a blue sky. The three men, as veterans of New
York's Joint Terrorism Task Force, or JTTF, had a history with the enemy
that dated back more than 12 years, and even in their shock they each experienced the instant recognition when the second plane struck that they were
witnessing a painfully logical escalation in a war that had consumed a large
part of their careers. The memories were vivid: A sallow-skinned assassin
who had kept files on the New York landmarks he planned to bomb. A blind
and portly sheik, or religious scholar, who spoke in riddles but had radicalized Muslims from Cairo to Jersey City. A pencil-necked explosives expert
who foreign authorities put on the run just as he was preparing to blow 11
airliners out of the stratosphere simultaneously. For sure, glasses of whiskey
were raised when that globe-hopping jackal was finally captured, but the
celebrations of plots disrupted hadn't lingered in the mind like the images
left by the plots that slipped through.

Some of those grim memories were on my mind too as I sat with Peter
Jennings at the ABC News Desk and tried to find words worth speaking
on the morning of September 11. In 1993, I had been down in that
crater under the Trade Center. In 1994, I joined the New York Police
Department as a deputy commissioner and for two years witnessed horrific crime scenes on an almost daily basis. In October 2000, I had
watched forensics specialists gathering "DNA material" from a gutted
U.S. Navy destroyer in a port off the Arabian Sea. But putting the pieces
of the puzzle together that morning was beyond me, so I attempted to
get hold of the one man I thought might be able to make sense of it all. I
wrote Neil Herman's name and number on a slip of paper and handed it
to a desk assistant. His line was busy, I was told, but Neil later admitted

that he had turned down all media requests that day. He had felt incapable, he said, of setting the day's events into a larger framework, the kind that points firmly to a logical response to the challenge at hand.

I can't remember another moment, in the two decades I've known Neil Herman, when the same could have been said.

Beginning in 1990, and for several years after, Neil Herman's domestic terrorism unit at the JTTF represented the best hope America had of preventing a new international form of Islamic militantism from metastasizing into a potentially implacable threat. A few dozen New York police detectives and FBI agents couldn't do that alone, of course. And really, they weren't asked to. But this malicious movement's first moorings in the U.S. happened to be dropped on turf that belonged to Neil Herman, Louie Napoli, Tommy Corrigan and the rest of the terrorism task force. Dutifully, they followed the leads, sometimes arriving tantalizingly close to the kind of break that might have smothered in its infancy the network that became al Qaeda. Eventually, most of the agents, including Herman, came to see that the threat had grown too big for the JTTF, or even for all the U.S. law enforcement agencies put together. At that point, when the guys from the New York office were trying to hunt down bombing conspiracies halfway around the world, the battle they saw and the one they were asked to fight had become two different things. They tried, but they were unable to make their superiors at the Justice Department, or in the White House, adequately appreciate why that was so.

If there was any one man or woman the higher-ups should have listened to, it was Neil Herman.

By the time he eased into private industry in 1998, the 51-year-old St. Louis native had spent well more than half his life in counterterrorism. Just 27 when the FBI assigned him a desk on the ground floor of that fledgling enterprise, Herman would spend his entire career in the Bureau's New York office, leaving a formidable legacy that was built entirely on real achievements in some of the Bureau's biggest cases—because whenever a little apple polishing was called for, big, rumpled Neil Herman just left bruises. From the time he took over JTTF's domestic terror unit in 1990, he wore his bosses out with his Cassandra-like warnings and constant requests for more resources and manpower.

The son of a St. Louis sportswriter, Herman first arrived in New York in August 1974.

It was a good place for a smart 27-year-old agent to be. The 1970s were turning out to be a period of great change in the Bureau. The top positions were still held by old Hoovcrites—Cold War warriors who tended to see the world in black and white. But recruitment efforts were bringing in a new generation of agents who had come of age in the turbulent 1960s, and—because the Young Turks were better positioned than family men to cope with the expenses of city living—a disproportionate number of them ended up in the New York office.

A lot of the best work was in New York too. The domestic terrorism unit in particular would emerge as a talent magnet, a place where an ambitious young agent could expect plenty of action and plenty of chances to earn promotions.

"It was an exciting time," Herman recalls. "Terrorism was in its infancy. It had never before had the dimension it had then." From 1974 to 1978, a bomb was going off every month, it seemed, with the culprits ranging from anti–Castro Cubans to Croat nationalists to the FALN, the Puerto Rican pro-independence group. "There was no foundation or history for what was happening. We were responding from one crisis to the next, learning on the job as we went."

The sandy-haired Midwesterner soon gained a reputation as a relentless, methodical investigator. Which is not to say he lacked imagination. Once, in fact, he had a parrot hypnotized and interrogated because it was the only eyewitness in a thorny murder case. Unfortunately, the bird refused to talk.

The young agents worked hard, and (what else?) they played hard too. The New York office of the FBI was located at the time in a converted ten-story shoe factory on the trendy Upper East Side. Most of the young guys lived nearby, and they spent many of their nights roaming Second Avenue's bars and cafes, making the most of the hedonism of that too-short era before the AIDS crisis hit. The older generation lived in another universe entirely. "When there were snowstorms," Herman notes, "we took over the office." Because the older agents all lived out in the suburbs, they couldn't get into town.

> At joints like Omelias or the Hudson Bay Inn, the young agents drank Budweiser and traded war stories into the night. As a young reporter I drank with them, and in fact was one of very few reporters who were allowed into their world. I got to know guys from the Bank Squad and the Foreign Counterintelligence Squad besides the crew from the JTTF. And sometimes, late at night, a bomb would go off, and we'd all roll out together.
>
> Only when my police friends were at the scene did these excursions get sticky—and not because of the drinking and driving. (This was, of course, years before the Bureau imposed stringent no-second-chance rules against mixing cars with alcohol.) A fierce rivalry had developed between the NYPD and the FBI on these cases. Cops and agents would almost come to blows over witnesses, crime scenes and evidence collection.

The competition eventually became so charged that in 1978, when police raided a bomb factory in Queens run by Willie Morales, a central figure in the FBI's investigation into FALN, the cops barred Herman and his colleagues at the door.

A truce was needed. New York, with its vast financial and media resources, had become a theater for every group with a political axe to grind: FALN, the anti-Castro Omega 7, the Croats, the Serbs, the Jewish Defense League and various remnants of the Radical Left. The crisis begged law enforcement to put aside petty factionalism.

In 1980, a solution was finally hammered out. Following the model of a bank-robbery unit that had been created a year earlier, the FBI and NYPD agreed to create the nation's first Joint Terrorism Task Force. The original plan called for 20 investigators—10 agents and 10 NYPD detectives—a small, nimble unit whose investigators would be able to work with minimal supervision. Herman was among the first agents drafted.

The task force's first big case grew out of a 1981 botched armored-car robbery that left two police officers and one guard dead in Nyack, New York, a town 15 minutes north of the George Washington Bridge. The perpetrators, who netted $1.6 million from the Brinks holdup, turned out to be holdovers from the Black Liberation Army, the Black Panthers, the New Africa Republic and the Weather Underground, groups thought to have been defunct. JTTF investigators also were able to link the defendants to numerous other robberies, as well as the prison breakout of a cop killer named Joanne Chesimard.

Over a six-year period, Herman and his colleagues apprehended, and ultimately convicted, a virtual Who's Who network of radical domestic terrorists. Cathy Boudin and Marilyn Jean Buck, from the Weather Underground, were both JTTF collars, as were Mutulu Shakur (Tupac Shakur's stepfather) and Eddie Josephs of the Black Liberation Army. For the Brinks robbery, both radical groups had supplied guerilla fighters.

The Brinks convictions put JTTF on the map. But the case also pointed up a problem that continually plagues law enforcement. Many of the crimes enfolded into JTTF's case had once been under investigation by the Bank Squad, so when those cases were taken and JTTF ended up with the credit for solving them, bad blood broke out between the two units. The ill feelings would come back to haunt JTTF.

A second, related investigation on which Herman was the case officer exposed another problem. This problem was systemic to law enforcement in general, and it would come back to haunt everyone.

The New Afrikan Freedom Fighters, or NAFF, was a successor group to the Brinks gang. In fact, NAFF was plotting the jailbreaks of two individuals who had been convicted in connection with the Brinks robbery when JTTF smashed the ring in October 1984.

NAFF had been planning a virtual crime wave of its own, but the problem with these crimes, the ones that Herman was charged with investigating, was that they had never left the drawing board. Though the investigation was one of the FBI's largest to date and used every technique then known to law enforcement—from wiretaps to informants to old-fashioned stakeouts—a single shot had yet to be fired when eight suspects were arrested and accused of plotting another armored-car robbery.

The defendants, all of whom were well educated and black, referred to themselves as the New York 8, and their 1985 trial convened in a charged political atmosphere. In the end, though the evidence of conspiracy that JTTF collected was overwhelming—videotapes, witness testimony, diagrammed plans and a cache of high-powered weapons—the eight defendants were acquitted of all serious charges.

The verdict was the low point in Herman's career. The investigation alone had taken more than two years—a lifetime by law enforcement standards—and the resources expended had been enormous. Legally, the case presented by prosecutors was built on solid ground. But the jury had delivered a very different message: If it hasn't happened yet, it's not a crime.

That message reverberated through the Bureau for years, though its effect would have no immediate impact on the safety of the American public.

Before the JTTF's first decade was out, there would be one more horrendous act of terrorism carried out against a U.S. target—the downing in 1988 of Pan Am Flight 103 over Lockerbie, Scotland. After that, however, the FBI's terror watch went quiet, and counterterrorism became less of a focus for the Bureau than it had been.

New York's JTTF, along with imitators that had sprung up around the country during the 1980s, had largely succeeded in tamping down home-grown terrorism. And the international picture was equally encouraging: By the early 1990s, many in government felt that the selective application of economic sanctions and diplomatic pressure had ended, or at least suffi-ciently curbed, the threat of state-sponsored terrorism. In the upper realms of the Bureau, no one was interested in spending a lot of time and resources on trying to guess what was coming next. Apparently, the bosses had taken to heart the message from the jury in the NAFF trial.

A new cycle of terror was about to begin, however. The first harbinger was a stocky Egyptian janitor who took it upon himself to assassinate a rad-ical Jewish leader in a New York City hotel ballroom. Herman and his JTTF investigators understood almost immediately that the gunman belonged to a larger movement, and as the years passed, leads crossed and the movement's violence escalated, the task force came to see that this terrorist organization was unlike any that had come before it.

As Tommy Corrigan saw it, this international conglomerate gave new resonance to the term "umbrella organization." It had spokes all over the world—in New York and in the Southwest; in capital cities throughout Europe; in East Africa, the Philippines, Upper Egypt and Malaysia. Investigations that ate up years took out only a spoke at a time, and when the true shape of this adversary became clear, the guys doing the investiga-tions realized they were trying to bring down an entrenched global army with nothing but their badges and a pile of court papers.

On the day Corrigan left the task force in early 2001 to fulfill a long-time ambition of starting a business, he confessed to a few colleagues his worry that he was bailing out on them at a critical moment in one such al Qaeda investigation. The contest, though, had gone beyond critical moments. "This is not gonna end," one of his colleagues told him. "Whenever you leave, there will always be something on the table."

Six months later, on the morning that his best friend, Michael Seaman, died, Corrigan realized that even the notion of a global army didn't accurately represent what the American people were up against. Until September 11, al Qaeda had seemed to limit its targets to government sites or military installations. True, the group had shown little concern about killing civilians in the process, but none of Corrigan's speculations about the next escalation in the confrontation had prepared him for the image of dozens of airline passengers being strapped to a weapon of mass destruction.

"I felt, watching that second plane hit the tower, that it was the most barbaric act that any human being could do to another human being," he says. "As much as I thought I understood the people in that world, this was . . . this was mind-boggling."

Now, sitting in his living room watching the Towers collapse, Neil Herman was overcome with emotion. For more than three years, he had investigated the first attack on the Towers, the 1993 bombing of the World Trade Center, and hunted down its mastermind, Ramzi Yousef.

"This was Ramzi Yousef's dream. His goal had been accomplished. It was eerie. Here it was, eight years later, and I remember thinking: 'Jesus, you know, they really did succeed.'"

The phone began ringing: friends, the media. Through it all, Herman felt a bone-deep sadness. "A sense of failure," he says. "This is what they wanted to do and it had taken them a long time, but they did it. They'd won, we lost."

But as the day wore on, Herman began to feel angry. "One after another, commentators who really should have known better came on the TV saying, 'This is unprecedented. No one's ever attacked us on our soil like this,'" Herman recalls. "It was like 1993 had never happened. It was the same target, for God's sake. Maybe even the same group. It was eerie, sort of like a flashback. I felt like it was happening all over again."

CHAPTER 3

THE FIRST TERRORIST

Rabbi Meir Kahane finished his speech to rousing applause. The fiery orator had touched on lifelong themes: the immigration of Jews to, and expulsion of Palestinians from, Israel.

As he stepped down from the podium and into the ballroom of the Marriott Hotel in midtown Manhattan that evening, Kahane, the 58-year-old founder of the Jewish Defense League and a former member of the Israeli Parliament, was surrounded by followers.

It was November 5, 1990.

Opposite Kahane, at the back of the hall, a 35-year-old Egyptian-born militant named El Sayyid Nosair met with his friend, Bilall Alkaisi. "It looks okay," Nosair told him. "I think we can do it."

Alkaisi glanced nervously around the room. A wiry Palestinian with a trim black beard, he was armed and, like the stocky, sallow-skinned Nosair, was wearing a yarmulke for disguise. The two men had had similar conferrals in the past. For more than a year, they'd been attending Kahane's speaking engagements with the understanding that if his security seemed lax, they'd kill him. "Relax," Bilall said. "I'll be back in a moment."

Maybe Alkaisi didn't believe Nosair would actually shoot Kahane. Or maybe he didn't want to be involved if he did. Whatever his motivation, Alkaisi left for the men's room.

Nosair draped a coat over his arm, drew a .357 Magnum revolver from his waistband and ambled to the front of the hall.

A young man was videotaping Kahane as the rabbi chatted with his circle of admirers. Nosair paused at the fringe of the crowd until the camera stopped rolling. Then, aiming the revolver from his hip, Nosair slipped back the coat and fired twice, hitting Kahane in his neck and chest.

As Kahane slumped to the floor, Nosair dashed for the rear exit. The room was in chaos. People were screaming. Nosair began screaming too. "It's Allah's will," he yelled.

At the door, Irving Franklin, a 70-year-old Jewish activist, grabbed Nosair in a bear hug. Nosair shot him in the leg and continued fleeing. Outside the hotel, he clambered into a waiting taxi on Lexington Avenue and banged on the divider, expecting to see the face of his friend Mahmoud Abouhalima, the giant red-headed Egyptian who some investigators thought was supposed to drive the getaway car. Instead, he saw the fear-stricken face of a Hispanic man from the Bronx. Hotel security had shooed Abouhalima from the entrance.

Nosair ordered him, "Just go." But the taxi barely made it to the next corner south before traffic, and a red light, halted their progress. A crowd from the hotel was now coursing through the lines of cars, searching for Kahane's shooter. Nosair hunched down in the backseat of the cab, but one of his pursuers spotted him and began banging on the window. In the confusion, the taxi driver jumped out from behind the wheel, while Nosair slipped out the other side of the cab in front of the Grand Central Station Post Office.

Carlos Acosta, a uniformed U.S. postal police officer, was standing in the entrance. Assuming he'd stumbled onto a livery car hold-up, he ducked back into the doorway and reached for his gun. Nosair, determined to keep heading downtown past Acosta, edged along the building façade, hoping to get a shot off as he ran past the doorway. But Acosta popped out and confronted him first.

Both men fired at once.

Nosair got off two shots. The first bullet hit Acosta in the chest, but was deflected into his shoulder by the bulletproof vest he was wearing. The second whizzed past his head. Acosta fired just once. But it was enough. The bullet hit Nosair in the neck and chin, rupturing his jugular and knocking him to the ground.

Nosair's accomplice, Bilall Alkaisi, meanwhile, had exited the hotel. He jogged a few blocks south to Nosair's parked green sedan and slid in behind the wheel, shouldering the driver, a Palestinian named Mohammed Salameh, into the passenger's seat. Alkaisi didn't wait to find out what had happened to Nosair before flooring the accelerator. Witnesses later reported seeing two bug-eyed Middle Eastern men in the front seat of a green sedan careening the wrong way down Park Avenue.

As the sedan disappeared into traffic, Nosair was rushed downtown to Bellevue Hospital. He arrived in the emergency room moments after Kahane had been carried in from another ambulance.

As all this unfolded, I was sitting with Captain Sal Blando and a bunch of other Manhattan homicide detectives at Campagnola, an Italian restaurant on the Upper East Side. Blando, the Detective Bureau commander for midtown Manhattan, had starved himself all day, even skipping lunch so he could better savor the restaurant's classic Sicilian bracciole. The rest of us had followed his lead when it came time to order, and the plates were just being set on the table when all of our beepers went off at once.

A flash from the Operations Unit at Police Headquarters: "Shooting on Lexington Avenue, federal officer down, perp shot, rabbi seriously wounded." I dialed my news desk for details, as the cops used their cell phones to call the police operations desk. "Holy shit, the rabbi is Meir Kahane," I said to the table. "And it looks like he's going out of the picture at Bellevue."

We all hurried out the front door as our confused waiters placed the last plates in front of our empty chairs. There would be no dinner.

Car doors banged shut, red lights were clapped onto the roofs and sirens began to scream. We sped down Lexington Avenue in a caravan to the crime scene. But the chaos at the hotel didn't hold much promise for a reporter, so I stayed only a moment before jumping back in my car to head to Bellevue, where Kahane had just been pronounced dead.

Nosair, who would survive his wounds by some miracle of modern medicine, would claim years later that he had coated the bullets with cyanide. Whatever the truth his other two victims that night—Irving Franklin and Carlos Acosta—would both survive too.

As I raced downtown, I called an old friend, Barry Slotnick, who had been Kahane's lawyer for the past 20 years, and filled him in on what had happened. "Meir Kahane is dead," I told him. "He's at Bellevue."

There was a pause at the other end of the line. "I'm on my way," Slotnick said.

For many, Meir Kahane was not a sympathetic victim. As leader of the Jewish Defense League in the 1960s and 1970s, he'd been linked to bombings and sniper attacks on the Soviet Union's Mission to the United Nations. The JTTF had a huge file on Kahane and his associates. Even in the 1990s, his rabid anti-Arab views and terrorist tactics had made him a pariah among Jews and Arabs alike. Israel had outlawed his ultra–right-wing Kach party, and New York's Jewish establishment shunned him.

At a lunch we'd had together a few weeks before at Schmulky Bernstein's deli on the Lower East Side, Kahane had told me that the Arabs could never assimilate as citizens of Israel. "It's not meant to be a melting pot, like America," he explained. "If the Arabs were given full rights as citizens of Israel, then soon they would outnumber the Jews there."

Then it would not be a Jewish state, which was, he pointed out, the very reason for Israel's formation. "I know it's not a popular position to take in a place like America," he said. "But that is the way it has to be."

As Kahane's lifeless body lay in a trauma room, Bellevue was swarming with cops, television crews, rabbis and Jewish leaders. Kahane's following in New York may not have been wide, but it was deep.

Slotnick was negotiating with the Mayor's Office and police brass to have the body released to the family immediately. Under Orthodox Jewish law, Kahane had to be buried within 24 hours of his death, and Slotnick was making a persuasive argument that an autopsy would not tell the police a lot they didn't already know. Kahane had died of gunshot wounds in front of dozens of witnesses, many of whom saw the gunman. Nothing was immediately known about Nosair's accomplices—if there were accomplices—but the cause of death didn't look like a case Quincy would have to crack.

Slotnick was an influential member of the bar who had close ties to the city's Jewish community, which itself had and still does have plenty of political clout. The cops and the chief medical examiner may have wanted an autopsy, but it was not to be. Mayor David Dinkins's office interceded, and the body was released to the family and flown to Israel.

I left the hospital and sped across the river to Jersey City. On a tree-lined street, I found the address the police thought was home to the shooter, El Sayyid Nosair. It was well past one in the morning, though, and there was no sign of life. I knew I'd be back at daybreak to talk to the alleged killer's neighbors, but I also knew that if I were going to get a jump on the rest of the media, I would have to keep working while my colleagues went to sleep.

It had to be 2:30 by the time I got to Melon's, a great old Upper East Side watering hole, and found Steve Davis at one of the front tables. Davis, a longtime friend, had been one of the cops I had started the night with at Campagnola. Now Davis began telling me an important story. Nosair, the NYPD had already learned, had apparently not acted alone.

"So when the detectives get to Nosair's apartment, it's like one in the morning," Davis told me. "They knock on the door hard, because they figure, if anyone is home, they're gonna be asleep. But no sooner do they knock three times than the door flies open and there's a giant Arab guy with red hair standing on the other side like he was waiting there all along." Davis said that two men were in the apartment. One of them, the redhead, was Mahmoud Abouhalima, the New York taxi driver. The other was Mohammed Salameh.

Both admitted not only that they knew Nosair, who no longer lived in the building, but also that they had been at the hotel when the murder occurred. They were hauled in for further questioning at the 17th Precinct stationhouse on East 51st Street.

A little later that morning, Lieutenant Eddie Norris was contemplating the vicissitudes of fate. Norris, just 30 years old, was a very sharp cop. He had the build of a baby bull, the suits of an investment banker and talents that would carry him, within the decade, to the top of the department. But November 5 was his first day as commander of the 17th Precinct Detective Squad, the unit that was assigned the Kahane case. It was not the way to ease into the job: Not only had he caught a highly charged murder case, he seemed to be looking at a conspiracy involving three and possibly more assassins.

As dawn approached, Norris gathered his case notes and headed downtown to One Police Plaza for a meeting with the department's chief of detectives, Joe Borelli. Norris may have been a newly minted squad commander, but he had been a cop long enough to know there was more to the case than a simple shooting. That, however, was not the position the brass at headquarters had decided to take.

Borelli, a tall, balding man in his late 50s, kept his 13th-floor office lined with pictures of the best-loved sleuths of fiction: Sherlock Holmes,

Inspector Clouseau, Lieutenant Columbo. In the real world, Borelli qualified as a legend himself. Avuncular in manner, he patrolled the 13th floor
wearing a frayed cardigan and smoking a Holmes-style pipe. Arguably, he'd
earned that latter affectation. Back in 1977, he had been the commander of
the task force that hunted down the famous "Son of Sam" serial killer.

Along with Norris, Borelli had summoned his own top aides to the
meeting, as well as a small team of agents and detectives from the JTTF.
Norris had begun giving a brief overview of the case when Borelli posed a
question.

"Can you tell me this was the work of one man?" the chief asked.

"Absolutely not," replied Norris, and he began telling Borelli about the
two suspects he was holding at the precinct.

"You, shut up," Borelli snapped. "You do murder cases. They," he said,
pointing at the surprised FBI agents, "do conspiracies."

Norris was then told he didn't have enough evidence to hold
Abouhalima and Salameh. He was instructed to let them go.

Later, at a packed news conference, Borelli announced that Kahane's
murder appeared to be the work of a "lone, deranged gunman" with no ties
to known terrorists or Middle East conspiracies.

Now this may come as a surprise, but I consider Joe Borelli to be a
friend of mine. He was one of the great detective chiefs, and he helped
transform the Detective Bureau into a proactive investigative force
when a new regime shook up One Police Plaza in 1994. But back in
1991, he was a loyal general, not a revolutionary, and the prevailing theory in the NYPD was, "Don't make waves." That is why a commander
in those days who uncovered corruption was blamed for causing scandal rather than rewarded for cleaning house. And why a commander
who called the media's attention to a serial rape suspect was rebuked for
bringing pressure on the department instead of being applauded for
warning the public. So in the Nosair case, when Chief Borelli turned a
blind eye to the obvious, he was merely remaining true to the culture of

the NYPD. The thinking was, Don't take a high-profile homicide case that could be stamped "Solved" and turn it into an unsolved conspiracy. To do so would create a lot of extra work. Instead of getting the press and the Jewish community stirred up about the bad guys still out there, it was just so much simpler to say, the bad guy got Kahane, we got the bad guy, and it's all over. No pressure, no panic, no more headlines.

On the ground, of course, to Eddie Norris, the assassination was looking an awful lot like a big, fat conspiracy.

Before the day was out, Norris's detectives had tracked down Nosair's real address. Nosair had been living in a small rented house in Cliffside Park, New Jersey, a bedroom community just off the George Washington Bridge. I waited in front of the house as the detectives and some FBI agents from JTTF carried out 16 boxes of files. Those files would raise a hell of a lot more questions than answers. There were training manuals from the Army Special Warfare School at Fort Bragg. There were copies of teletypes that had been routed to the Secretary of the Army and the Joint Chiefs of Staff. (How had Nosair come up with those? Clearly, he had a source in a sensitive position in the U.S. military.) There were also bomb-making manuals, as well as maps of landmark locations like the Statue of Liberty, Times Square, Rockefeller Center and the World Trade Center, with notes written in Arabic. The papers were all carted to the 17th Precinct stationhouse, where Norris's squad could go through them to prepare for Nosair's murder trial.

The next day, Barry Slotnick told me, "You know, Nosair had a hit list." I checked it out with my sources. Yes, they confirmed, the names of local Jewish leaders and of politicians who supported Israel had appeared on notes in Nosair's files, and there were newspaper photos of many of these individuals as well. The official position of the NYPD, however, was that the evidence didn't constitute a hit list per se. That didn't slow down the story. It got heavy play on TV and in the papers, and prominent New York Jewish leaders were soon demanding police escorts and bodyguards. Even leaders whose names weren't found in Nosair's files were asking for police protection. Being on the hit list had became a status symbol, and suddenly the NYPD was burdened with exactly the kind of headaches Borelli was trying to avoid when he had downplayed the whole conspiracy angle.

On the third day after the shooting, while Norris was out to lunch, the FBI removed Nosair's 16 boxes of files from Norris's squad room. Unfortunately, that evidence was about to enter a black hole. The FBI now says it turned the files over to the Manhattan District Attorney's Office, after it was decided, following a series of meetings and phone calls, that the local prosecutor and the NYPD would have exclusive jurisdiction over the murder case. The Manhattan DA's office won't comment on what was done with the files before Nosair's trial, though Norris was never informed they were available. But this much is certain: The bulk of the material remained untranslated and unread for nearly three years.

Many officials, Norris among them, have since claimed that the files provided a virtual road map to future terrorist acts, including the 1993 World Trade Center bombing. Along with the military documents, the bomb manuals, and the diagrams and photos of New York landmarks, the Nosair papers contained a manifesto exhorting his associates to topple the "tall buildings of which Americans are so proud."

What's more, says Norris, his squad would have had the files translated as a matter of procedure if they had remained in the NYPD's possession. "If we'd kept the files, we'd have had to translate them," he says. "We couldn't go on the witness stand in a murder trial and say, 'Yeah, we had all this material, but we didn't read it.'"

Of course, even without the files, Eddie Norris never believed Kahane's assassination was the work of a lone gunman. Just given the little he had learned during those first few days after the shooting, Norris felt that Nosair was involved in something much larger, something that would come back to haunt law enforcement—hell, even the whole city.

And Eddie Norris didn't know the half of it.

I can't say I stayed on the story very long myself. There was a crack war going on in the streets of New York City. There were six or seven murders a day, and battles for drug turf being fought in the five boroughs by Colombian drug cartels, the Mafia and ethnic street gangs. I was busy most of the rest of that month conducting surveillance of mob boss John Gotti, trailing him from place to place and collecting videotape of his movements for a series of stories I had planned. By December, I rarely thought about El Sayyid Nosair or the clues many of us felt had been brushed aside. Of course, like everyone else involved, I vastly underestimated the significance of Nosair. Nosair turned out to be the pioneer of a new kind of terrorism, the first to act out the malicious ideology of a rogue strain of Islam that would eventually seek to eviscerate the American way of life. More than a symbol, he would prove to be, even as he sat behind bars, an instigator and source of inspiration for other like-minded militants. In fact, in any attempt to understand the events of September 11, 2001, it makes sense to begin with El Sayyid Nosair. That's where the law enforcement aspect of the September 11 story began, and where American law enforcement agencies first revealed themselves to be institutionally ill-equipped for the war this new enemy had brought to U.S. shores.

When Nosair arrived in America nine years before the Kahane shooting, there was little in his background to distinguish him from countless other Middle Eastern men who had come to the U.S. in the 1970s and early 1980s. Born in 1955 near Port Said, Egypt, he was the oldest son in a family that was displaced when Israel humiliated the Egyptian military in 1967's Six-Day War. He thus spent his adolescent years in Cairo, where he would go on to study industrial design and engineering at the Helwan University Faculty of Applied Arts.

In July 1981, three years after his college graduation, he immigrated to America and settled in Pittsburgh at the home of a close family friend. He soon found work as a diamond cutter, and those who knew him say his goal at the time was to make his fortune and return to Egypt a wealthy man.

Nosair at 25 years of age was not particularly religious, and whatever lingering resentments he harbored about Israel and her Western allies did not dampen his enthusiasm for American culture. "He loved everything about this country," Barbara Ausman, his work supervisor, later told reporters. "He'd go to the zoo, museums, nightclubs. He really got into fast food. And he was very intrigued by young women."

Eager to acquire a green card, Nosair began courting Caren Ann Mills, an American he'd met through a matchmaker at a local mosque. Mills had recently converted to Islam in the aftermath of a stressful divorce, and she married Nosair in June 1982, just 11 months after his arrival in the U.S.

Around this time, Nosair embraced Islamic fundamentalism, which in a sense was not unusual. Many young Arab émigrés rediscover their religious roots after leaving home. "Religion was a part of everyday life for Nosair growing up," says Roger Stavis, who later became Nosair's lawyer. "It was nothing special for him to be a Muslim in Egypt. But when he came here, his religion defined him."

Behind the trappings of his renewed faith, however, Nosair's life began spiraling out of control. He quarreled with his host, and he and his wife had to find a new home. In 1983, he was fired from his job, in part, Ausman says, because he failed to develop his craft, but also because he began hectoring his coworkers about religion. Soon he had his first brushes with the law. In 1985, a woman from the mosque, a recent convert who had been boarding at Nosair's home, filed rape charges against him. Two weeks later, a second woman he knew from the mosque lodged a similar complaint. Both women dropped their charges after the imam intervened, but the following year, Nosair, now with three children in tow, moved his family to New Jersey, to the apartment complex in Jersey City that New York detectives would visit in the first hours after the Kahane murder.

Commuting to New York, Nosair found work as an electrician's aide, but he was laid up in September 1986 by a power-plant accident in which he was nearly electrocuted. His injuries left him impotent—and depressed. But 18 months later, using the Brooklyn address of an older cousin, Ibrahim el-Gabrowny, Nosair obtained a job with the city working as a heating and air-conditioning repairman in the Criminal Courts Building.

It is clear that from the time he arrived in the New York area, Nosair's life revolved around his religious and political activities. In Jersey City, he worshipped at the Masjid al-Salaam, a radical mosque whose founder, a Palestinian named Sultan el-Gawli, had been recently convicted of conspiracy for his role in a terrorist plot to blow up targets in Israel. In addition, Nosair became a fixture—and virtually the only full-time worker—at the Brooklyn office of an organization that proved to be the headwater of jihad in America.

Located in a remodeled tenement in a dingy section of downtown Brooklyn's Atlantic Avenue, the al-Kifah Refugee Services Center was the main U.S. branch of the Pakistan-based Office of Services, the organization that would later become al Qaeda. Throughout the 1980s, al-Kifah functioned chiefly as a recruiting post, propaganda office and fund-raising center for the mujahideen fighting the Soviet army in Afghanistan. But the office, located in a suite of rooms on the ground floor of the al-Farooq Mosque, was also a hotbed of radicalism, a place where Muslim men from the area came together with militant religious leaders to exchange ideas and rally to Islamic fundamentalist causes.

At the Services Center, Nosair came under the spell of Abdullah Azzam, the charismatic founder of al-Kifah. Scholar, soldier, orator, organizer, prophet and propagandist, Azzam frequently traveled from his base in Peshawar to raise funds in the U.S. and to preach his message of global jihad. "Every Muslim on earth should unsheathe his sword and fight to liberate Palestine," he told a crowd of about 200 followers at the First Conference of Jihad, held in 1988 at the Farooq Mosque. "The Jihad is not limited to Afghanistan. Jihad means fighting. You must fight in any place you can get to. Whenever Jihad is mentioned in the Holy Book, it means the obligation to fight. It does not mean to fight with the pen or to write books or articles in the press or to fight by holding lectures."

Nosair longed to go to Afghanistan to fight. But neither his family situation nor his weakened condition permitted his enlistment. Instead, taking Azzam's message to heart, he had, by 1987, assembled a group of like-minded associates—Abouhalima, Salameh and Alkaisi among them—to wage jihad in the U.S. Training came first. Beginning in 1987, Nosair had begun organizing weekend paramilitary camps in upstate New York, day trips to rifle ranges on Long Island and in Connecticut, and survival and surveillance courses with an Army Special Forces instructor in the Nosair family's Jersey City apartment.

Some of the men had already been to Afghanistan—Alkaisi had even served as a trainer in bin Laden's camps—but the outings instilled the mostly ragtag group with a sense of mission and taught them special skills. As early as 1988, for example, Nosair began practicing the hip shot—a technique designed to thwart security guards and eyewitnesses—that he would employ against Kahane.

Nosair also sought the imprimatur of higher-ups in the jihad movement. Around 1988, he began to ingratiate himself with a blind Egyptian sheik named Omar Abdel-Rahman, arguably the most influential cleric among Islamic extremists worldwide. Certainly, Abdel-Rahman ranked as the foremost religious leader among Islamic militants in Egypt, where the government was keeping him under house arrest due to his links to various terrorist acts.

Abdel-Rahman nevertheless was planning to immigrate to the U.S., and by early 1989, Nosair was in regular contact with him. In fact, some of their conversations, recorded by Nosair and played in mosques in Jersey City and Brooklyn, were among the personal effects that would be retrieved by police when they searched Nosair's home in November 1990. The tapes suggest that Nosair had been assembling an Islamic terror cell, arguably the first in the U.S., with Abdel-Rahman's blessing and encouragement. "We have organized an encampment," Nosair informed Abdel-Rahman in the summer of 1989. "We are concentrating here."

Tommy Corrigan's unit actually witnessed several of the Nosair group's training sessions. Acting on a tip that a group of Palestinians who frequented the al-Kifah Refugee Services Center were planning to set off bombs in Atlantic City casinos, the FBI in July 1989 dispatched a JTTF surveillance squad, Corrigan among them, to keep an eye on the Center. On weekdays, the JTTF team tracked Mustafa Shalabi, al-Kifah's emir. On weekends they followed Nosair and a dozen or so subjects from the Center to a shooting range in Calverton, New York—a town on eastern Long Island—where the group engaged in small-arms training. According to a posting on al-Kifah's bulletin board, Nosair had organized the small-arms exercises. The instructor, who would play a part in later investigations, was a tall, sinewy African American who wore a beard and had a large mole on his cheek.

Corrigan and his colleagues observed and photographed the Calverton group on four successive Sundays. But it was an "open secret" within law enforcement that the mosques were sponsoring paramilitary training for recruits to the war in Afghanistan, an exercise that the U.S. government supported. Few officials at the time were concerned that the subjects might turn that training against American targets. So once the casino threat subsided in August, the Bureau dropped the surveillance, and Corrigan's team returned to other duties without having identified any of the trainees or their instructor.

Knowing nothing of the Bureau's near miss, Nosair and his associates continued throughout the summer and fall to train and plan for jihad against the U.S. Unlike the disciplined, self-sufficient coterie who carried out the September 2001 hijackings, however, the first U.S. cells were unstable alliances characterized more by boast and squabble than action, and there was no guarantee that the fiery anti-Western rhetoric coming out of the mosques would ever be translated into actual violence. "It was hard getting some of these guys motivated once they got over here," Tommy Corrigan recalls. "It's one thing hating the U.S. when you're running around barefoot in Sudan or you're actually living under repression. But a lot of these guys, the worst thing they could say about their lives here was they couldn't find a parking space."

Nosair, however, seemed to be driven by different demons. "He was always pushing people to do things," Corrigan says. "He was constantly coming up with plans for bombings, assassinations, you name it. He was like a jihad machine."

Janitor by day, jihadi by night, Nosair was beginning to convert some of his plans to action by the end of 1989. On December 8, for example, when Soviet Premier Mikhail Gorbachev was being swept out of the city in a motorcade, Nosair was among the mostly admiring crowd who lined the Soviet leader's route through Manhattan. A short while before, Mustafa Shalabi, al-Kifah's militant emir, had supplied Nosair with a Pepsi can filled with explosive. As the line of cars approached, Nosair lobbed the grenade at Gorbachev's limousine. It failed to detonate.

A nearby police officer witnessed the attempt and grabbed Nosair as he walked away. But the cop figured Nosair was just another angry protestor tossing an empty soda can, and Nosair was slapped with nothing more than a warning. Only years later did investigators learn, from an informant, about the can's lethal contents.

Nosair next began experimenting with explosives in a workshop he'd set up at work, in the basement of Manhattan's Criminal Courts Building. By spring, he was ready to test his concoctions.

For his target, he chose Uncle Charley's, a gay bar in Manhattan's West Village. On a warm Friday night in April, he mingled briefly with the customers at one end of the crowded bar before planting one of his "homemades" in a metal garbage pail filled with empty bottles.

The bomb exploded just after midnight. It was a crude device, a six-inch pipe filled with M-80 firecrackers. It didn't have a timing mechanism and had to be lit moments before detonation, but it did send shards of glass flying everywhere. Fortunately, only minor injuries were recorded, though, once again, Nosair got away undetected.

Throughout the spring Nosair hatched one scheme after another. At one point he ran surveillance on a top United Nations official; at another, he put a tail on Egyptian President Hosni Mubarak. Officials never concluded what his intentions were in those cases, but he simply may have been working his way up the scale of misdemeanors and felonies, building confidence with each act.

Nosair's jihad plans got a boost at about that time, when his spiritual mentor, Sheik Abdel-Rahman, arrived in New York from Egypt. Short and portly with a pillowy gray-white beard, dark glasses and a crimson-and-white fez that denoted his Cairo alma mater, the blind cleric looked less like a terrorist than a hip Santa. But Abdel-Rahman was a world figure in jihad, a man whose writings, preachings and political savvy had helped create an international network of armed militants devoted to the re-creation of an Islamic empire.

Over the next three years, JTTF agents would get to know him well.

Born in the Nile Delta in 1938 and blind since infancy, the young Abdel-Rahman was a precocious student of Islam. By age 11, he had memorized the Koran, and before he was 30, he was elevated to the rank of sheik by Cairo's prestigious al-Azhar University, even though he had yet to complete his doctorate in Islamic jurisprudence. Interestingly, he was radicalized almost overnight following 1967's Six-Day War, the clash with Israel that drove the Nosair family out of Port Said. Leaving Cairo for a smaller city to the south, Abdel-Rahman created for himself a provincial political stronghold, then capitalized on his growing reputation when Egyptian President Anwar Sadat briefly encouraged the spread of right-wing Islamism in the early 1970s. The blind cleric toured Upper Egypt, and his calls for the overthrow of Egypt's secular state inspired the creation or growth of several radical groups—one of which, the Egyptian Islamic Jihad, carried out Sadat's assassination in 1981.

Charged with issuing the fatwa that unleashed Sadat's killers, Abdel-

Rahman was tried two times and eventually cleared of all charges. But he spent the early 1980s in custody, and the torture he was thought to endure at the hands of the Egyptian government only increased his leadership stature.

In 1985, Abdel-Rahman visited the front in Afghanistan for the first time and formed or renewed several important friendships. One old acquaintance, Afghan warlord Gulbuddin Hekmatyer, was able to provide the sheik introductions to U.S. intelligence officials. That was because, despite his virulently anti-Western views, Hekmatyer was receiving roughly half the arms that the CIA was funneling through Pakistan to help the Afghan fighters turn back the Soviet invasion.

A former university mate, Abdullah Azzam, meanwhile hooked the sheik up with a young millionaire named Osama bin Laden. In the years to come, that alliance would become increasingly important to both men's burning ambitions.

Abdel-Rahman spent the remaining war years traveling the globe raising money for the Afghan jihad, and soon after he returned to Egypt, he was placed under house arrest once more. Supporters armed with stun guns engineered his escape, however, and from the Sudan he immigrated to the U.S. in May 1990. Why Abdel-Rahman, a known terrorist and fugitive, was even allowed to enter the U.S. remains a mystery.

Abdel-Rahman's visa was signed by a CIA officer stationed at the Sudanese consulate, and one theory advanced by FBI agents is that the Agency sponsored his immigration. The CIA, in that scenario, may have wanted to nurture its ties to Egyptian fundamentalists in order to avoid a replay of Iran in 1979, when the overthrow of the Shah left U.S. intelligence out in the cold.

However Abdel-Rahman gained entry to the U.S., his arrival served to galvanize Nosair's band of wanna-be terrorists. Al-Kifah's emir, Mustafa Shalabi, arranged for the Egyptian cleric to preach at the al-Farooq Mosque and helped provide him a place to live. But before long, the two leaders fell out over money, and Abdel-Rahman moved to Jersey City, where Nosair, who was also feuding with Shalabi, had set up his own Refugees Center.

Beginning in the fall, Nosair began stalking Kahane in earnest. He attended several of Kahane's speaking engagements—to case Kahane's security and perhaps to get up his courage.

His behavior was becoming increasingly erratic. He even squabbled with Abdel-Rahman. On November 5, he reportedly tore up a locker room at work after he was told that he was being transferred out of the Manhattan Criminal Courts Building to another borough. That afternoon, he picked up Salameh and Alkaisi and drove to the Marriott ballroom, more determined than ever to strike a blow against the enemies of Islam.

In the first hours following Kahane's murder, JTTF agents began pursuing a conspiracy investigation. Louie Napoli and his partner, John Anticev, hauled out the July 1989 surveillance photos taken at the Calverton rifle range and immediately recognized Nosair as one of the subjects, though it would be months before they got around to identifying any of the other faces in the pictures.

Within days of the assassination, Manhattan DA Robert Morgenthau, known for having sharp elbows when it came to headline cases, claimed jurisdiction over Kahane's murder, meaning the investigation would belong to the NYPD, not the FBI. Napoli and Anticev did do some digging into Nosair's associations and the cells forming around Abdel-Rahman, but the Bureau rarely puts its resources or reputation behind a case it doesn't own completely. Bureau officials sent the 16 boxes of Nosair's papers over to the DA and agreed to "monitor" the investigation, which in effect meant to do nothing. And somehow, no one ever informed Eddie Norris that the files were no longer under federal jurisdiction.

The Kahane assassination was exactly the kind of thing Neil Herman, the JTTF supervisor, had been warning his bosses about, and even then—

when it seemed obvious that Nosair had been part of a larger group—he couldn't get them to mount a more aggressive assault on terrorism. The deal with the DA's Office was worked out way above Herman's pay grade, so the door was closed to making a conspiracy case against Nosair's jihad-minded pals.

"This was exactly the time you needed to crack down on these guys," Herman says. "But you couldn't get anybody to take terrorism seriously. Even after Kahane, nobody felt it could happen here, nobody wanted to believe it could happen here.

"I've always thought that the 26-month period between the Kahane assassination and the first WTC bombing was a key period—a time when we could have really made a statement. But that time was just lost. I'm not saying we could have prevented everything that followed. But it would have given us a fighting chance."

A few months after the Kahane assassination, Louie Napoli asked Tommy Corrigan to look over the surveillance photos that had been taken at the Calverton, Long Island, firing range. Napoli, who was monitoring the DA's murder investigation, had by then made some progress in identifying the Arab men who had joined El Sayyid Nosair for those July 1989 training sessions. He had nothing, though, on the two black men who seemed to be the group's instructors.

Had Corrigan crossed paths with either of them?

A month earlier, the answer would have been no. But now, just a few weeks into 1991, a face did jump out of the first photo Corrigan picked up. The mole on one cheek left no doubt that the man who caught Corrigan's attention was the same character Corrigan and his FBI partner, Tom McNally, had been chasing around the outer boroughs since the new year had arrived. His name was Richard Smith. He was a central suspect in a gun-running case Corrigan and McNally were developing in Brooklyn's Black Muslim community. And if Corrigan's sources were correct, this tall, powerfully built firearms expert had a more than accidental interest in fostering armed revolution.

The JTTF had, in that moment of recognition, broken into a fertile new field for investigation, and Corrigan and McNally were eager to charge into it. Their instincts told them that the apparent alliance between black militants and Arab militants might lead to serious violence if left unattended, and, ultimately, time would prove that hunch right.

But hunches and legwork wouldn't write the story of the FBI's counterterrorism efforts in the decade leading to September 2001. In spotting the Black Muslim connection, Corrigan had located a convenient side entry into the first Middle Eastern terrorist cell that would target America. Time would tell if the efforts of a few detectives would be enough to avert disaster.

Corrigan and McNally had gotten wise to Richard Smith by following a simple premise: Terrorists need guns. Herman and his men figured that if they could crack the right gun rings, they would most likely run across a Baskin-Robbins assortment of revolutionary baddies, and the gun charges would protect against a repeat of the NAFF fiasco, where all eight defendants were cut loose because none of the prosecutors' conspiracy charges had stuck.

The initial focus of the probe had been a Brooklyn-based gun dealer named Edwin Ransom. Ransom served on the security force, or *sutra*, at al-Taqwa, a radical mosque located about a mile from the Farooq Mosque, in Brooklyn's Bedford-Stuyvesant section. JTTF had known for some time that Ransom was providing black militants with paramilitary training, and Corrigan suspected that he was also supplying them with weapons.

As part of the investigation, Corrigan and McNally began checking area gun shops in the fall of 1990 to try to identify if the black militants were buying their own weapons. At the T & T Gunnery in Seaford, Long Island, none of the customers' names matched Corrigan's suspects or their aliases. But a salesman did recall a tall black male dressed in a flowing Muslim robe who visited the store regularly and bought .223 rounds, the kind of ammo used in assault rifles.

Corrigan and McNally checked back at T & T two more times. On their third visit, the salesman had news for them. The customer—who they would soon learn was Smith—had been in a few days earlier with a friend. This time the salesman had snuck outside and recorded the license plate on Smith's car, a black Lincoln Continental. While showing the agents Smith's receipts, the salesman related a chilling little detail about Smith's visit. A battle scene from a Vietnam War movie had been playing on a TV set in the store, and as Smith was leaving, he pointed at the screen and said: "Someday, that's going to happen here."

Corrigan traced the Lincoln Continental's plate number to an address near Kennedy Airport in Queens and, circling the block, spotted the car parked nearby. Two days later, Corrigan was sitting in front of Smith's house in the back of one of the JTTF's surveillance vans. McNally was parked farther up the block in a Chevy Lumina with tinted windows. When Smith finally emerged a little after 10:30 that morning, he gave Corrigan's van a long, hard look, then jumped into the Lincoln and sped off. Corrigan called McNally on the radio. "He's on the move, headed your way." Corrigan also warned McNally that he would have to take the lead, since Smith might have spotted the van.

Like an old married couple who knew a favorite ballroom dance, Corrigan and McNally moved gracefully, invisibly through the traffic behind Smith. They had done this a thousand times together, yet there was a certain excitement that came with a fresh target on the move. Who was Richard Smith? Why was he buying heavy munitions? Where would he take them? And would he be connected with Edwin Ransom's gun-running conspiracy?

They followed Smith locally for an hour or so and then were going to drop him. They were sure to be "made" if they stayed with him any longer.

But as the partners waited in their separate vehicles at a gas station on Rockaway Boulevard, they saw Smith's car pass them. "Fuck it," Corrigan said, "let's see where he goes." Rolling out, McNally called back to Corrigan over the radio: "Looks like he's headed for the Belt Parkway." Smith's black Lincoln led the way out of Queens and into Brooklyn before heading down Atlantic Avenue into Bed-Stuy. As Smith arrived at his destination, McNally picked a location a few blocks away and told the trailing Corrigan they'd meet there. When Corrigan pulled up, McNally said, "You're not going to believe where this guy just took us."

"Where?"

"Al-Taqwa."

Bingo. Al-Taqwa was the mosque frequented by Edwin Ransom and his radical crew, which suggested Richard Smith had to be tied to Ransom. That supposition would quickly be confirmed. Several days later, in mid-January 1991, Corrigan and McNally would photograph Smith and Ransom together outside al-Taqwa.

Seeing Smith in Napoli's surveillance photos seemed to raise the stakes. What was Richard Smith, a Black Muslim and suspected gunrunner, doing with a bunch of Arabs from the al-Kifah Services Center? Corrigan and McNally began pressing their informants. Black Muslims, they were told, were becoming increasingly sensitive to the plight of their Arab brothers, and some had even joined the mujahideen in Afghanistan to wage jihad. Moreover, with the U.S. military engaged in driving the Iraqi Army out of Kuwait, many black and Arab Muslim militants suspected that Washington, fearing terrorist reprisals, would soon move to lock them up, much as the federal government had interned Japanese Americans during World War II. Some militants, with the help of men like Ransom and Smith, were already arming themselves for an American guerilla war.

At first, Corrigan didn't know how much of what he was hearing was real, how much of it rhetoric. But his investigation into Smith would soon indicate there was more to the threats than just talk. One of Corrigan and McNally's informants who'd begun asking around about Smith eventually reported back that Smith was not only training Arabs, he was also teaching urban guerilla tactics to a robbery crew. Further working their sources, Corrigan and McNally learned the members of the gang, who called themselves the Forty Thieves, were affiliated with a mosque located around the corner from al-Taqwa. Led by a 22-year-old ex-Marine named Marcus Robinson, the gang started knocking off post offices around March before moving on to other targets. They were unusually proficient, remarkably well equipped, and more than ready to use violence—even against police officers.

On May 8, for example, Robinson and two crew members, posing as police, forced their way into the Queens home of Thomas Bey, the owner of a small check-cashing business. In an effort to get their victim to turn over his receipts, they tied up Bey's family and placed a pipe bomb in the lap of his six-year-old son. Moments later police, acting on a neighbor's tip, surrounded the house and called for the bandits to surrender. Instead, Robinson and his accomplices grabbed Bey's teenage daughter as a hostage and charged the police, tossing the pipe bomb at them and shooting one officer in the face. Guns blazing, they made it to the street, stole a car and led police on a frantic chase down the Cross Island Parkway, eventually shooting an innocent driver to secure their getaway.

The gang would shoot two more police officers during a spree that lasted another five months, but its key players were finally taken down in October during another bloody shootout.

Marcus Robinson himself didn't last that long. In July, he was collared in Chester, Pennsylvania, on a gun charge, prompting Corrigan and McNally to make the 75-minute drive a couple days later to visit the Forty Thieves' "Ali Baba" behind bars.

Robinson came across that day as an uncommonly earnest young bank robber. He told Corrigan and McNally that he considered himself not a stickup man but a soldier in the worldwide Islamic jihad then taking root in Brooklyn. He characterized his crimes, always staged against "unbelievers," as "appropriations of funds," an expression Corrigan had heard many times before investigating Black militant groups like the BLA and NAFF. Apparently, Robinson had been building a war chest for the revolution ahead.

The interview with Robinson was essentially a meet-and-greet exercise, and Robinson spoke mainly in generalities. Nevertheless, while driving back to New York, Corrigan felt optimistic that future conversations would be more productive. For years, he'd been hearing about cells like the Forty Thieves gestating inside Brooklyn's most radical black mosques—fed, and in some cases run, by a Black Muslim prison network. Perhaps Robinson would be able to throw light on the backroom activities of at least some of these mosques, and connect them to their Middle Eastern counterparts.

Corrigan and McNally had the impression that Robinson, despite his religious zeal, was looking to make some kind of deal; and in October 1991, facing more than 100 years in prison, Robinson did indeed sign a cooperation agreement with federal prosecutors in Brooklyn. But the Forty Thieves case was assigned to another FBI-NYPD joint enterprise, the Bank Robbery Task Force, and Corrigan and McNally were barred from talking to him again.

There followed the usual reasons. The Brooklyn-based U.S. prosecutors who were trying Robinson's crew didn't want Corrigan and his pals repositioning their chief witness as the centerpiece of a large conspiracy case involving terrorists. The fact that the JTTF investigators were working on their terror case with prosecutors from the U.S. Attorney's Office in Manhattan, the Brooklyn Office's bitter rival, did not make things any easier.

But JTTF's investigators never doubted the real reason that a firewall had been placed between them and Robinson: The bosses at the Bank Robbery Task Force had never gotten over losing the Brinks case to JTTF years before, and the bank squad wasn't about to let the JTTF now steal a key witness or worse, take over the whole Forty Thieves case. Thus, despite several entreaties by JTTF boss Neil Herman, his investigators never got the chance to find out what Robinson had to share.

How valuable Robinson would have been to JTTF is a matter of conjecture. But one thing the JTTF would soon need to know was the identity of a black militant, known as "Dr. Rashid," and Robinson could give it to them. Robinson had supplied Rashid with guns, bombs and detonators, and Rashid had tried to recruit Robinson during the spring of 1991 for a private jihad army he was sending to fight in Bosnia. A shadowy figure with close ties to black and Arab Islamic extremists, "Rashid" would turn out to be a pivotal figure in the 1993 World Trade Center bombing and a subsequent plot to blow up four New York landmarks.

Robinson also might have saved the JTTF years in establishing how closely linked the black and Middle Eastern militants had become. Corrigan didn't learn until much later, for example, that members of the Forty Thieves had attended some of Sheik Abdel-Rahman's sermons and had worked on the blind cleric's security detail. Nor was Corrigan then aware that Abdel-Rahman, only months after finding asylum in the U.S., had issued a fatwa bidding his followers to rob American banks and kill Jews anywhere they were found, including America. Nor did Corrigan know that Abdel-Rahman had preached that a Muslim who robs from the enemies of Islam may rightfully keep 80 percent of his plunder if he kicks back the other 20 percent to his mosque.

Corrigan never did, in fact, learn if the Forty Thieves had tithed to Abdel-Rahman or any of the Brooklyn mosques, but Robinson had made clear in his one meeting with the JTTF investigators that the "appropriations of funds" served a higher purpose than pure greed.

The first half of 1991 proved to be even more eventful on Louie Napoli's turf, the Middle Eastern side of the Brooklyn investigation.

Napoli and his partner, John Anticev, had learned early on, while monitoring the NYPD's murder case against Nosair, about the rift that had opened up between Sheik Abdel-Rahman and Mustafa Shalabi, the emir of the Refugee Services Center in Brooklyn.

Well before Abdel-Rahman's May 1990 arrival to the U.S., Shalabi's autocratic style and arbitrary spending had alienated many of al-Kifah's hard-core militants. In fact, from the moment the Egyptian cleric arrived at Kennedy Airport, Nosair and Mahmoud Abouhalima had begun lobbying the sheik to help effect a change in al-Kifah's leadership.

At first, Abdel-Rahman sided with Shalabi. But eventually the sheik came to feel that he was being exploited by al-Kifah's longtime emir, that he was trotted out at fund-raisers and sent out on tour for the Center but was never allowed a say in how the donations were spent. Shalabi wanted the funds directed to helping Afghan refugees, but the sheik and other Egyptians, including Nosair, contended that with the Afghan war over, at least some of the money should be spent on new fronts—like the toppling of the secular regime in Egypt.

Curiously, the Brooklyn fight mirrored a debate that had taken place among top-ranking al-Kifah officials in Peshawar as the war was winding down. Shalabi's mentor and al-Kifah's founder, Abdullah Azzam, had wanted al-Kifah's substantial resources to remain dedicated to the mujahideen until a pure Islamic state had been established in Afghanistan. Others, including Azzam's friend Abdel-Rahman, the Azzam protégé Osama bin Laden, and Gulbuddin Hekmatyer, the virulently anti-Western warlord who had received the lion's share of U.S. war aid, wanted al-Kifah's funds to be used for global jihad. A meeting was held in which Azzam was asked to account for his finances, and shortly afterward, in November 1989, Azzam and two of his sons were killed by a car bomb. Some U.S. intelligence officials believe bin Laden ordered the assassination.

In early 1991, Shalabi met a similar fate. Top al-Kifah officials had sent Abdul Wali Zindani, a Yemeni who would succeed Shalabi, to investigate the Brooklyn office's finances. Shalabi balked at the intervention, and was last seen alive on February 26, the day before he was scheduled to leave for Egypt. A few days later, he was found bludgeoned, shot and strangled at his home near Coney Island. Nosair's pals, Bilall Alkaisi and Mohammed Salameh, are the prime suspects, but they have never been charged.

The murder sent two clear messages to investigators. In executing one of their most powerful leaders, Abdel-Rahman's followers had demonstrated a willingness to use extreme violence to achieve their goals. More important, Shalabi's demise signaled a shift in those goals. No longer would the jihad begun in Afghanistan and supported by the U.S. target the Soviets and their proxy government in Kabul exclusively. The U.S. itself was now a potential target, and the files found in Nosair's home suggested it might even be near the top of the list.

Early in the summer of 1991, Napoli and Anticev found troubling evidence of the extremists' new intentions when they paid a routine visit to Mahmoud Abouhalima to question him about his association with Nosair. Abouhalima wasn't at home, but the building janitor was eager to chat about the tall, red-headed tenant. "I was wondering when you guys were going to get here," he told the investigators.

"What do you mean?" they asked him. The janitor then explained he'd seen boxes full of bomb material in Abouhalima's apartment.

By the time Napoli and Anticev returned with a search warrant, Abouhalima had removed the material. But the janitor had shown the investigators a sample that he'd filched from Abouhalima: a silver, disklike blasting cap capable of detonating a powerful bomb.

With the help of an energetic informant, Napoli and Anticev would penetrate Abdel-Rahman's circle before the end of the year. In the meantime, El Sayyid Nosair was preparing to stand trial for the murder of Rabbi Meir Kahane.

A common criminal in the eyes of most of the public, Nosair had, as the first among his group to take definitive action, become the star of the nascent jihad movement in the U.S. In the months following the assassination, his old friends visited him regularly in Lower Manhattan's house of detention and consulted him about future operations. The El-Sayyid Nosair

Defense Fund became a cause célèbre among Arab extremists around the world. His cousin Ibrahim el Gabrowny, acting as Nosair's executor, traveled as far as Saudi Arabia and was granted an audience with Osama bin Laden, whose reputation as a supporter of radical Islamic causes was already legendary in the Brooklyn and New Jersey mosques. Bin Laden contributed $20,000 to the fund.

Trial proceedings began in November 1991, and each morning Kahane's militant Jewish supporters and Nosair's militant Muslim friends squared off in front of Nosair's former place of employment, the Manhattan Criminal Courthouse. FBI agents, sent to observe the trial, saw the same Middle Eastern faces among the crowd that they'd photographed at the Long Island shooting range in July 1989. Black Muslim security forces protected their Arab brethren and Richard Smith himself, the Calverton group's trainer, made regular appearances as the bodyguard of one of Nosair's three lawyers.

The carnival atmosphere invaded the courtroom as well. Nosair's lead attorney was William Kunstler, then in the last stages of a long, illustrious career as the American dean of lost-cause defense lawyers. Kunstler had originally reviewed the facts of Nosair's case and begun laying the foundation—in the press, as well as in briefs—for an insanity plea. No doubt, he intended to include a political component to his defense: that some combination of Israeli aggression, Egyptian repression, and U.S. wrong-headedness had contributed to his client's psychosis. Still, insanity it was. Nosair had no other chance, he reasoned. He'd shot and killed a man in front of sixteen eyewitnesses, and if that weren't enough, he'd shot and wounded two others while making his escape.

The only trouble was that Kunstler hadn't yet consulted with his client, who had a different plan. Not only was Nosair refusing to plead insanity, but he also claimed that he hadn't even fired a gun at the JDL founder. According to Nosair, Kahane had actually been shot by one of his own people, a JDL member disgruntled over finances. In explaining his flight and the two other shootings to Kunstler, Nosair pointed out that he was the only Arab in the room and that he'd been afraid others would think he was the shooter. How he happened to be carrying a firearm was never made clear.

The story was, of course, ludicrous. What's more, Kunstler never established a legal basis for Nosair's "grassy knoll" assertion that there was a second gunman. Nevertheless, the seasoned attorney argued with his customary panache, and in one of those shocking moments that seem to punctuate American jurisprudence—when all the system's safeguards of reasonable doubt conspire to obscure the obvious—the jury returned a verdict on December 21 acquitting Nosair of the Kahane murder but convicting him of shooting the two men who tried to block his escape. Also the last count, criminal possession of a weapon, resulted in a conviction.

Critics would quibble with the District Attorney's strategy. The prosecutors, for example, had decided not to make an issue of Nosair's motive since nothing in New York State law requires that a motive be established and leaving the subject untouched would prevent Kunstler from injecting politics into what looked to be an open-and-shut case. But there were factors beyond the prosecution's control. The mayor's decision to release Kahane's body for burial before the medical examiner could perform an autopsy had meant there was no physical evidence linking Nosair's gun and the bullet that killed the rabbi. And though more than a dozen witnesses testified that Nosair shot Kahane, none of them had actually seen the defendant pull the trigger.

Still, it was a gross perversion of justice, and the trial judge, Alvin Schlesinger, would say as much at the sentencing, when he handed Nosair the maximum allowable term—7½ to 22⅓ years—for shooting Franklin and Acosta with the illegal gun.

The verdict, though, had given Nosair's supporters ample reason to celebrate. After the jury's decision came in, a group of them, including Abouhalima and Salameh, hoisted Kunstler on their shoulders and marched him down the courthouse steps in triumph.

Any reporter watching that procession could read their thoughts as they passed. America really was a spineless nation, just as the imams had been preaching. Here, you could murder your enemy in public. Here, you could run amok in the streets, shoot a federal officer, and receive nothing more than a slap on the wrist. Here, the jihadi will be victorious.

CHAPTER 5

EMAD SALEM, RAMZI YOUSEF AND THE
FIRST TRADE CENTER BOMBERS

E mad Salem always needed to be one of the good guys. That may have been, in fact, the ex-soldier's defining trait, though he had, at least when Louie Napoli worked with him, both a stubborn streak and a useful talent for deception that sometimes obscured his better intentions.

Born in Cairo at mid-century, Salem had joined the army as a young man and served as an officer until he decided that maybe the Egyptian Army wasn't the side the good guys were on. In the late 1980s, when he immigrated to the U.S., he sought out the FBI and soon was working for them as an informant, penetrating elements of New York's Russian community that had links either to the KGB or the "Russian Mafia." (Sometimes it was hard to tell them apart.)

After the fall of the Soviet Union, there was much less of a market for Salem's Russian connections. But Salem was a useful commodity to the

FBI. He was a known quantity. He already knew how the Bureau operated. And his handler recommended his work. Indeed she believed Salem might be just what the JTTF was looking for: a Middle Easterner who could penetrate the underground organizations in New York that were raising money for international Islamic terrorist groups.

Salem's file fell on Napoli's desk in mid- to late 1991. It was a fortuitous pairing. Even sitting in the climate-controlled JTTF offices high above Federal Plaza, with the kind of sweeping views usually reserved for Wall Street bankers, Louie was still the quintessential tough-talking New York detective he'd been before he was plucked from the grimy quarters of the Manhattan South Narcotics Division. He had a leathery face that wouldn't have drawn a second look in the streets of Southern Italy, a taste for flashy sport jackets and a bit of a gut cinched by a belt laden with cell phone, beeper, 9 mm pistol and handcuffs. Many of the agents in the New York office, drawn from the heartland, could come off square and buttoned-down with street people the first time out. But Napoli, like most city detectives, could talk to just about anyone from anywhere and make them feel comfortable.

From his first meetings with Salem, Louie found common ground with the ex-soldier. Salem said he'd have no trouble with the new assignment and soon began visiting the mosques Napoli suspected were terrorist breeding grounds. Salem also began haunting the Nosair trial, where he befriended Ibrahim el-Gabrowny, Nosair's cousin and chief fund-raiser. Before the trial had even ended, el-Gabrowny brought Salem to visit Nosair in jail, introducing him as "a new member in the family." Another time, el-Gabrowny invited Salem to join him for dinner at his Brooklyn home. Confiding that he feared the apartment was bugged, el-Gabrowny turned up the volume on the television in the dining room and broke the news that he and some friends were assembling materials for a bomb. He was vague about the target, but he impressed Salem that the plan was serious and its intent lethal.

There was one problem with these reports: Carson Dunbar, JTTF's overseer in the FBI's National Security Division, was reluctant to trust too much in the man who was providing them. Dunbar was no older than Neil Herman, but his inherent caution reflected an organizational mentality more suited to the Khrushchev era than the post-Soviet 1990s. In fairness, the FBI of a generation earlier wouldn't even have opened the door to Salem. Back then, spies were culled from the ranks of disgruntled Soviet diplomats and scientists. Double agents wore trench coats and low-brim hats and made existential decisions about life and loyalty before they demanded, or after they were courted with, large, discreet sums of cash. They carried files, microfiche and aerial photographs. They were serious people.

Salem, by contrast, had arrived on the FBI's doorstep unannounced and unemployed. True, he wanted only piddling compensation to continue his undercover work on a more formal basis—$500 per week and expenses. But that just made him seem more ludicrous and unreliable. He was also chatty, unctuous, boastful and by turns ingratiating and pigheaded. Napoli himself dubbed his prize informant "the Colonel," an appellation that recognized Salem's military background as well as his propensity for self-promotion.

Some in the Bureau were also legitimately concerned about Salem's possible ties to Egyptian intelligence. Naturally, Salem couldn't disprove such suspicions, but he seemed to some of his handlers to possess genuine passion about Nosair's brand of extremism; he professed that it was bad for Islam, that terrorism would provoke a backlash around the world against his fellow Muslims. Even so, Egypt had ample reason to monitor Abdel-Rahman, and Dunbar didn't want the FBI to become the unwitting sponsors of an Egyptian government operation against its political opponents here.

There were other problems, as well. Salem appeared to have an aversion to gathering evidence that would be admissible in court. He constantly asked the agents to take his word on things—he said wearing a wire would be too dangerous. (Salem was no fool; he knew that if there were tapes, he'd be asked to testify and that would be the end of working undercover, which he seemed to enjoy.) Lie detector tests also rubbed him the wrong way. At first, he simply refused to take one. It was an insult. Then, when he gave in, the results were inconclusive.

Still, Nosair's acquittal of Kahane's murder in December 1991 had gal-vanized the Bureau. On the one hand, they were shocked and angered. On the other, they now saw an opportunity to make the larger conspiracy case against Nosair and his pals that the NYPD brass had deliberately shied away from. For all his liabilities, Salem was a direct pipeline into Nosair's inner circle. Dunbar wasn't exactly thrilled about it, but he eventually authorized Napoli and Anticev to run Salem.

A few weeks after Nosair's acquittal, Salem accompanied Abdel-Rahman and his circle to an Islamic conference in Detroit. Hoping to gain Abdel-Rahman's approval, Salem confided that he'd served in the Egyptian military and fought against the Israelis in the 1973 October War. The cleric responded that Salem had been paid to fight by infidels, that his war could not be considered a jihad. However, Abdel-Rahman had a remedy: Salem could redeem himself, Abdel-Rahman said, by assassinating Egyptian President Hosni Mubarak, who was nothing but a "loyal dog to the Americans."

Nothing new there, one of Abdel-Rahman's cronies told Salem after-ward. The sheik asked anyone who would listen to take on that mission. But within weeks, Abdel-Rahman had fully welcomed Salem into the jihad fam-ily and Salem was offering to restart the paramilitary training that had lapsed in the year since Nosair's arrest. Abdel-Rahman was appreciative. There will come a time, he told the group, when that training will be needed.

Meanwhile, the FBI kept close tabs on Nosair, who continued to play an active role in the group's operations, the way a Mafia don runs his family's business from prison. Part strategist, part cheerleader, Nosair actually had a threefold agenda. First, he felt the group should be doing more. He'd risked his life and his freedom striking a blow for jihad; now it was time for his brother Muslims to step up and take direct, violent action. Second, he wanted revenge on those he felt were responsible for his imprisonment. Toward that end, he had a hit list: Alvin Schlesinger, the judge who'd sen-tenced him to the maximum possible prison term on the assault and illegal gun charges; U.S. Senator Al D'Amato, a staunch supporter of Israel; and Dov Hikind, a state assemblyman from Brooklyn who'd been a friend of

Kahane's and who had rallied against Nosair during the trial. Finally, he wanted out, a prison break. He concocted a steady stream of schemes—having his mates kidnap former president Richard Nixon and former Secretary of State Henry Kissinger and hold the two icons hostage for his release, for example. (Perhaps Nosair had been misinformed about how most Americans felt about Nixon.)

In early spring, Nosair's cell hatched a different, Hollywood-style plan to free Nosair from prison. It involved storming the walls of Attica prison in upstate New York, where Nosair had been held since his sentencing on the gun charge. Salem asked el-Gabrowny about the plan and el-Gabrowny sensibly counseled patience, at least until after a judge had ruled on Nosair's pending appeal.

According to Salem, el-Gabrowny was much more interested in talking about the bomb plot he'd first mentioned in December. With summer approaching and Nosair pressuring him to take action, he told Salem he was in contact with "underground people" who were helping with the construction of the bombs. He needed Salem's help. He needed remote control detonators, some kind of radio device that could set off the bombs from a distance.

In mid-June, at el-Gabrowny's urging, Salem and another plotter, Ali el-Shinawy, visited Nosair in Attica. Nosair berated them for not making more progress on a certain bomb plot—Salem assumed it was the same plot el-Gabrowny had first spoken about back in December—and instructed el-Shinawy to obtain a fatwa from Abdel-Rahman that would legitimize their plans. On their return to New York, el-Shinawy confided those plans to Salem. The group intended to set off bombs at twelve "Jewish locations." The details were not worked out yet, but the targets included temples, banks and Jewish centers around Brooklyn and Manhattan.

El-Shinawy also told Salem that they still needed handguns and the remote detonators, and that they could obtain them through a "Dr. Rashid." Louie Napoli made a note of that: *Who is Dr. Rashid?* Salem had not heard the name before and, as far as Napoli knew, neither had the FBI.

The new information definitely got the agents' attention. Salem had been passing Napoli and Anticev hints of some kind of bomb plot for more than six months, but nothing as ambitious or as evolved as blowing up a dozen Jewish targets in New York City. Two days after el-Shinawy first confided the plot's outline to Salem, they visited el-Gabrowny, who approved the idea of their meeting with Dr. Rashid, but said he would also try to get the detonators from sources in Afghanistan. Salem and el-Shinawy meanwhile agreed to secure a warehouse in which to build the bombs.

A few days later, el-Shinawy took Salem to meet the mysterious Dr. Rashid. The chosen location was the Abu Bakr, another Brooklyn mosque that was well known to JTTF investigators because of its links to militant Arab Muslim groups. Rashid turned out to be a wiry African-American Muslim with clear-rimmed glasses and a stiff leg he'd injured fighting in the Afghan War. He'd earned the name "Dr. Rashid" working as an emergency medical technician in Brooklyn, though the discussion that afternoon had nothing to do with saving lives.

Dr. Rashid told his visitors he couldn't get the remote detonators they requested (his usual source, Forty Thieves leader Marcus Robinson, was in FBI custody), but he could get them "ready-mades"—already assembled pipe bombs—at $900 to $1,000 apiece. He also said he could acquire "clean" guns—firearms that hadn't been used in the commission of any crimes.

A few days later, el-Shinawy handed Salem a handgun that Salem assumed was from Rashid.

Meanwhile, Louie Napoli and John Anticev briefed their bosses at the FBI. Build a case that can be taken to court, the two investigators were told. Dunbar also informed Napoli that the time had come for his informant to get with the program and wear a wire. Without recordings of the conspiracy, the Bureau would have a very weak case. Either Salem wired up and agreed to testify, Dunbar said, or the Bureau would have to drop him.

Salem, however, wouldn't bend. Throughout June and into July, Napoli used every trick of persuasion known to New York detectives short of a smack on the back of Salem's closely trimmed head. Nothing seemed to work. They met him in cars, parking lots, diners. The discussions went from reason to yelling to begging. Salem was unmoved. No wire. No testifying in court.

According to Napoli, the Bureau had been able to corroborate the core of Salem's information through their own surveillance and with tapes of Nosair's phone calls from prison. What's more, for all their reservations, Napoli and Anticev trusted Salem. He was easily their best source of intelligence on Abdel-Rahman and his followers. Though Napoli had other informants in the militant Middle Eastern community, none of them had access to the sheik's inner circle.

Nevertheless, in early July 1991, Napoli fired Salem.

Louie was very Sicilian about relating all this. Sitting in an FBI office high above Manhattan, with the World Trade Center gone from view, he looked across at Michael Stone and me and said, "Carson and I didn't agree on a lot of things, but he didn't drop Salem. I did." That is typical Louie. He would not let anyone else take the weight for what happened with an informant he had controlled. Yet many people in the Bureau, especially street agents, blamed Dunbar for dropping Salem. It was to many of them "typical Bureau," meaning follow the rules to spite your face. They blamed Dunbar because it smelled like a decision that was meant to insulate the bosses from problems even though a serious source of information was being cut off. Louie ultimately may have given Salem his walking papers, but it seemed clear to anyone who examined the handling of Salem that the bosses at the Bureau acted very shortsightedly in holding to a standard that mandated Salem's firing. Especially when the cell he was informing on was apparently planning a dozen bombings.

The "Jewish locations" plot did not develop in any recognizable form, at least not over the next several months. The jihad group was active throughout the summer, but indecision and internal feuds pushed any plot of such complexity beyond their capacities for the moment. Had Salem been available to fill them in on that trend, the JTTF investigators might have felt relieved. As things stood, the investigators simply were in the dark.

A different faction of the group was trying to pick up the slack. Using a fraudulent check-cashing scheme, three of Nosair's closest associates—Mohammed Salameh, Nidal Ayyad and Bilall Alkaisi—had raised a war chest of $8,500, and they started stockpiling small amounts of chemicals that summer at Alkaisi's house. But they had yet to settle on their target, and with Nosair in prison, they began squabbling among themselves as to who was going to be emir. Alkaisi seemed the natural choice: He was the only one among them with actual jihad experience, having served as a trainer at bin Laden's camps. But the others questioned Alkaisi's commitment. After all, he had backed out of the Kahane shooting at the last moment, and had fled in the escape car, leaving Nosair on his own.

Salameh, on the other hand, was obsessed with jihad. And as Nosair's protégé, he was especially sensitive to Nosair's increasingly abrasive appeals for action. Unlike the others, he had no job or family to divert him from the cause.

The three men continued to dicker through August. At one point they drew straws to decide who would be emir and Salameh won, which alienated Alkaisi. Inevitably, their animus spilled over into money issues, and a battle for control of their joint account ensued. Finally, in October, Salameh and Alkaisi confronted each other during a car ride in New Jersey. The argument became heated, and Salameh pulled a gun, causing Alkaisi to back down and quit the group.

Alkaisi's departure solved the cell's leadership issues. Salameh had become the group's only full-time member. But this created another problem. Alkaisi, who had once studied explosives in bin Laden's camps, had been the cell's bomb maker. They needed someone to replace him.

Enter Ramzi Yousef. A shadowy figure whose background is still veiled in myth and controversy, Yousef was about to become the world's most wanted terrorist. He was an expert bomb maker with a genius for the dramatic strike. He was also cunning and charismatic, despite his unimposing appearance. Tall with a long skinny neck and face, he had a large, bulbous nose and flared ears. To many who knew him, he looked like a horse.

On September 1, 1992, a month or so before Alkaisi's exit, Yousef had arrived at Kennedy Airport from Pakistan with a friend named Ahmad Mohammed Ajaj. Both men were stopped. Ajaj's bags contained fake passports—including one belonging to Yousef; several bomb-making manuals; a guide to surveillance training; and four instructional videos on weaponry. What did Ajaj in, though, was the sloppy craftsmanship on his stolen Swedish passport: He was charged with passport fraud and soon sentenced to six months in prison.

Yousef, who was dressed in traditional peasant garb and carried an Iraqi passport without a U.S. visa, was a remarkable sight.

"Yousef was dressed in these Ali Baba–type pants and a shirt with balloon sleeves," recalls FBI Agent Chuck Stern. Apparently, Yousef was trying to look like a poor Arab refugee wearing his only good clothes. Yousef told the immigration inspector that he was fleeing from the oppressive regime of Saddam Hussein in Iraq and needed asylum in the U.S. After Yousef was questioned and fingerprinted, an INS inspector recommended that he be detained. But there was not enough room in the INS lockup, so he was released with the promise that he would turn up at a hearing later.

Yousef later claimed that when he left the airport, he took a cab to a mosque in Manhattan's East Village and there met Mahmoud Abouhalima. Yousef either knew the towering, red-haired Egyptian from the camps in Afghanistan or had been instructed to contact him. Abouhalima, in either case, greeted Yousef warmly and brought Yousef around to meet all of his friends. Abouhalima's social circle boiled down to Nosair's co-conspirators and Sheik Abdel-Rahman. Abouhalima brought the newcomer to Ibrahim el-Gabrowny's home in Brooklyn. At el-Gabrowny's, Yousef says, he met Mohammed Salameh, who immediately offered to share his Jersey City apartment.

Given all the socializing Yousef did on his first day in America, he almost certainly had come to New York for a reason—to carry out an operation.

There may always be a debate about Yousef's intended purpose, but the more pressing question is: Who sent him?

Did Yousef actually stumble into Nosair's pals upon arriving in New York? Was it a coincidence that he, a highly trained master bomb maker, met them as they struggled to pull off the Twelve Jewish Locations bomb plot? Or is a more likely scenario that Yousef was sent to America by bin Laden's organization, the parent group of the Afghan Services Office in Brooklyn, to aid them in that plot?

In fact, investigators can't even agree on his name, much less his provenance. Though popularly known as Ramzi Yousef, his real name appears to be Abdul Basit Karim and he seems to have been born in 1968 in Kuwait, where his Pakistani father worked as an engineer for Kuwaiti Airlines. Descended from Palestinians on his mother's side, he was raised in an immigrant community outside Kuwait City that was nearly half Palestinian. Yousef excelled at school, especially in math and science, and was popular among his classmates, but Kuwait had a tradition of treating its so-called guest workers as second-class citizens or worse, no doubt planting grievances that would emerge later on.

When Ramzi was still a teenager, his father embraced fundamentalism and moved his family to his native Baleuchistan, a rugged, lawless province in southwestern Pakistan. Ramzi, however, traveled overseas to complete his education, landing eventually at the West Glamorgan Institute in Swansea, Wales. At Swansea, as the institute is now known, Yousef studied engineering and fell in with a local chapter of the Egyptian Muslim Brotherhood, a fundamentalist organization that has stopped just short of endorsing terror. But Yousef got his advanced degree in bin Laden's terrorist training camps, where he spent several months in 1988 honing his bomb-making skills.

Some speculate that Iraq was behind Yousef's role in the World Trade Center bombing. According to author Laurie Mylroie, the chief proponent of this theory, Yousef arrived almost simultaneously with an Iraqi government employee who took up residence in Salameh's Jersey City apartment building and became intimate enough with the plot that he was able to name the bomb-making location when the FBI questioned him days after the explosion. Within 24 hours of being questioned, that source flew back to Baghdad. Yousef secured a new temporary passport during his six-month stay in New York using ID Mylroie claims belonged to a man who disappeared from Kuwait in 1990 during Iraq's occupation. It was using that passport, and the name Abdul Basit, that allowed Yousef to flee to Pakistan following the bombing.

A second camp sees bin Laden's handiwork behind the Trade Center operation. They point out that Abouhalima and other members of the conspiracy had trained in bin Laden's camps, where they would have either met Yousef or others who were in contact with him. What's more, Ibrahim el-Gabrowny had met with bin Laden a year before the bombing and investigators believe that at least a portion of the $20,000 bin Laden gave el-Gabrowny during that meeting—ostensibly for Nosair's defense—was spent on materials used in the World Trade Center bomb.

Supporters of the bin Laden theory say the World Trade Center bombing plot was consistent with other bin Laden operations at the time. With U.S. troops still occupying the Saudi peninsula more than a year after the end of the Gulf War, al Qaeda had begun issuing fatwas against the Americans and American targets. In December 1992, three months after Yousef's arrival in New York, bin Laden's men bombed a hotel room in Yemen, targeting U.S. servicemen who were on their way to Somalia. (The servicemen had departed and two Austrian tourists were blown up instead.) Also at about that time, bin Laden had begun sending trainers to Somalia to help tribal militias oppose U.S. forces there.

Tommy Corrigan feels the original Trade Center plot was homegrown, in the New York area, and that after the rift between Salameh and Alkaisi, a member of the jihad group—perhaps el-Gabrowny or Abouhalima—sought help overseas, probably through contacts in bin Laden's camps.

Whoever bears responsibility for Yousef's coming to the U.S., the terrorist's effect on Nosair's ragtag battalion is indisputable. For one thing, he helped professionalize the largely inept, undisciplined soldiers. For another, he radically changed the scale of their mission. Before Yousef's arrival, even the Twelve Jewish Locations plot was based on classic terrorist strategy: a series of small, local explosions whose primary objective was to terrify, not kill or maim. Yousef had much bigger plans—to build a bomb powerful enough to topple the World Trade Towers, one into the other, with a potential death toll in the tens of thousands—many levels of magnitude beyond anything the others had previously imagined.

Yousef was also different from his amateurish cell mates in another respect, one that presaged problems for law enforcement in dealing with future generations of terrorists. The original group around Abdel-Rahman seemed to revel in their Islamic-ness. They wore beards, dressed in *kofis*, socialized in their mosques and communities, and made no secret of their sympathies and hatreds. Recall Nosair haranguing his coworkers about religion or Abouhalima hoisting Kunstler on his shoulders. Yousef, by contrast, was discreet. His charade at Kennedy Airport notwithstanding, his appearance was relatively Western. In his few contacts with U.S. officials, he was low-key and invariably polite. He moved through the city as a sylph, slipping in and out of aliases, boarding with cell members, using phone cards, paying in cash and planning his escape weeks before the scheduled strike. It would be days after the Trade Center bomb exploded before the authorities even knew of Ramzi Yousef, much less his critical role in the plot.

But Yousef's precautions may have been unnecessary. Having cut Salem loose, JTTF's agents were lurching about, feeling for answers. Toward the end of September, Napoli and Anticev had summoned el-Gabrowny and members of the suspect mosques to FBI headquarters for questioning and fingerprinting, ostensibly in connection with the Nosair and Shalabi murder cases. Their real motive, however, had been to rattle the Arabs' cages, in the process possibly prying loose an informant or two. But no one ever came forward.

I n mid-November 1992, Tommy Corrigan's Black Muslim investigation came back from the dead.

The jolt to the case arrived by way of a phone call from a trusted informant, and this time, the trail didn't just brush up against a Middle Eastern terrorist cell, it led straight to the heart of a plot intended to kill thousands and to bring New York City to a standstill.

The informant, Garrett Wilson, was a six-foot-tall, 300-pound former Army Ranger who worked as a military police officer at a naval base in Philadelphia. A friendly, outgoing man, Wilson ran his own security business on the side, and back in the mid-1980s, while attending martial arts conferences in the New York area, he had gotten to know a number of militant New York Black Muslims, including Edwin Ransom, Richard Smith and other members of al-Taqwa Mosque. Al-Taqwa had been engaged at that time in a war to rid its neighborhood of drug dealers, and over the next several years, Wilson provided them with paramilitary training and helped them procure surplus military equipment.

But beginning in the early 1990s, Wilson's Muslim clients had begun asking him to acquire material that, while legal, seemed peculiar for the security needs of a religious organization. Wilson ran the requests by John McGuire, an officer in the Naval Intelligence Service (NIS), who was also taken aback. McGuire, in fact, sent a Teletype to law enforcement agencies asking if anyone knew why members of a small mosque in Brooklyn were interested in obtaining rappelling equipment. Months passed before John Liguori, an agent in Corrigan's squad, remembered that NIS query while mulling over Corrigan and McNally's gun-running investigation. Liguori had then contacted McGuire, who in turn hooked Corrigan and McNally up with Wilson.

In the beginning, when Wilson was first funneling information to the JTTF about the mosques' paramilitary activities, Corrigan figured his unit had stumbled into another nest of felons, much like Marcus Robinson's crew.

But on October 3, 1992, events took a strange turn.

On that date, Wilson received a call from Abdul Wali Zindani, Mustafa Shalabi's successor as the emir of the al-Kifah Refugee Services Center. Zindani said that friends at al-Taqwa had recommended Wilson and that he wanted Wilson to supply commando-style training and equipment for an elite unit of about ten men. Zindani then put his security chief on the line to handle the details. The security chief, a man named Yaya abu Ubaidah, told Wilson that the emir was especially interested in hostage-rescue training.

Corrigan and Liguori were intrigued. What did Zindani want with a squadron of elite guerilla fighters? The war in Afghanistan had been over for three years. True, Zindani's uncle was a powerful sheik in Yemen, a nation then at war with the communist government in South Yemen. But the whole enterprise was suspicious. With Nosair's people known to be plotting a prison break, Corrigan was especially troubled by the hostage-rescue aspect of the training. Corrigan and Liguori told Wilson to keep the lines of communication open.

Wilson followed their advice, and in mid-November, the strategy paid an unexpected dividend. Corrigan got the news from Wilson: A friend of Ubaidah, a "Dr. Rashid," had also begun calling for training. Did Corrigan want Wilson to meet with him?

Wilson didn't need to ask twice. Napoli and Anticev had been trying to track down and identify Rashid since the mysterious medicine man had met with el-Shinawy and Emad Salem on June 16 and offered to get them bombs and guns.

Using the number Rashid had left on Wilson's beeper, Corrigan ran some background on this cipher. His given name turned out to be Clement Hampton-El; he was 54 and worked in the dialysis unit of a Long Island hospital. More important, toll records showed that he had made recent calls to Abdel-Rahman.

On December 20, Wilson met with Hampton-El and Ubaidah in an apartment in Jersey City. Hampton-El wanted Wilson to train eight to ten men for an international jihad battalion that he was forming separate from Zindani's. He said that he would provide AK-47s for the training sessions, but that he was also looking for remote-detonator caps and clean guns, the same equipment Shinawy had requested from him during the June 16 meeting attended by Emad Salem. The group would be shipped off to Bosnia, according to Hampton-El. But it occurred to Wilson that the type of instruction requested—sniper firing and frontal assaults on buildings—was also compatible with terrorist operations in a U.S. city. "It sounds to me like they either want to kidnap or kill someone," Wilson told Corrigan.

Corrigan was alarmed. Everything seemed to be converging: Kahane and Shalabi's murders, Nosair and Abdel-Rahman's increasingly blatant calls for jihad against the U.S., el-Gabrowny and el-Shinawy's plan to bomb 12 Jewish locations, the search for detonator caps and assault weapons, and now this new round of paramilitary training. "Until then we were seeing things from the black side of the house," Corrigan recalls. "The talk about jihad, the gun deals and the robberies. It was serious stuff. But now with Zindani and Hampton-El, we were seeing the crossover to the Arabs. Back in 1988–89, we'd seen black Muslims training Middle Easterners. Then those guys went out and killed Kahane and Shalabi. I suppose you could plausibly say that this time they were training to go to Bosnia or someplace else. But you could also make the case they were planning to do something here. All I know is we were looking at each other and saying: 'No good can come out of this.'"

The irony of the situation was that just that past summer, the chief of New York's Criminal Division had called Corrigan and McNally into his office and told them that "terrorism was dead," that from then on they would be working urban gang investigations. Neil Herman had objected, of course, and had even tried as a last resort to talk his NYPD counterpart, Deputy Inspector Dennis Cunningham, into assigning more detectives to the unit. Cunningham had at least been sympathetic; he agreed that JTTF was stretched too thin. But when Herman asked for more manpower, Cunningham balked. The NYPD didn't have enough detectives, period.

Herman, seated across a table from Cunningham in a Lower Manhattan restaurant, didn't swallow this news without one last protest. "What happens when the big one goes down?" he asked.

"When the big one goes down," Cunningham said, "I'll send you five hundred detectives."

There's no telling, of course, how much more JTTF may have known in mid-December if Herman had been granted all the resources he'd requested over the previous year, or if Louie Napoli had been encouraged to hold on to Emad Salem.

But the opportunities were there.

On December 19, just a day before Wilson's meeting with Hampton-El and Ubaidah, Mahmoud Abouhalima called Salem's cell phone. Salem, still simmering over his firing at the hands of Carson Dunbar, didn't return the call or report it to Napoli and Anticev. So one can only speculate as to its purpose. Still, that day, Ramzi Yousef and his fellow plotters were dealing with the problem of how to ignite the bomb they were building. Components of the main charge had already been purchased and secreted in a rented storage shed. On December 19, Yousef and Mohammed Salameh began calling chemical companies in search of initiators, and Abouhalima actually bought smokeless powder, material that could be used in a fuse if they chose to go with that option. It could be that the reason Hampton-El asked Wilson for detonators on December 20 was because Abouhalima had just put in that request. It could also be that detonators were the reason for Abouhalima's call to Salem. Had Salem still been working as an informant for JTTF at the time of the call, the World Trade Center bombing plot might well have been cracked before Salem had hung up the phone.

Obviously, the cell had moved rapidly from disarray to action that fall, and Ramzi Yousef seems to have made all the difference.

Though Nosair remained the group's figurehead and Salameh its nominal leader, Yousef learned quickly after his September arrival how to use the old allegiances to power the ambitious plot he had in mind. In Yousef's mind, the bomb the cell started building in October was always destined for the World Trade Center. Though Yousef had apparently signed on to the "Twelve Jewish Locations" plot at first, and though at least some of the cell members initially argued that the Trade Center plot put too many civilians at risk, no other target was seriously considered once Yousef got down to business.

As the cell reshuffled its hierarchy, Salameh fell in as Yousef's chief aide, reviving the role he had played in support of Nosair. Salameh's close friend Nidal Ayyad, who worked for the chemical company Allied Signal, and Mahmoud Abouhalima, the red-headed cab driver, handled crucial logistics as well. A fifth man, Abdul Rahman Yasin, provided some observers with evidence that the bombing may have been sponsored by Iraq. Yasin is the Iraqi government employee who landed almost simultaneously with Yousef in Salameh's Jersey City apartment building. Most investigators, however, feel that Yasin was more a lackey than a wily ground commander: He ran errands for the operation and helped on the grunt work of mixing the explosives, but he wasn't giving anyone else their marching orders.

El-Gabrowny's role was more difficult for investigators to pin down. Corrigan now views him as a kind of a group elder, a universally respected figure called on to dispense counsel and mediate disputes. He also represented a conduit to Nosair, of course, and his apartment provided a Brooklyn meeting place and mail drop for the rest of the group, most of whom resided in Jersey City.

Using the $8,500 they had socked away in a bank account that October, the group had started spending with a purpose in mid-November. Salameh bought a 1978 Chevy Nova for $553 on November 18; that same day, he and Yousef began calling chemical companies. Shortly afterward, Salameh withdrew $4,400 from the group's account and on November 30 rented a shed at the Space Station storage facility on Mallory Avenue in Jersey City under the name Kamal Ibrahim. Yousef, using the same alias, purchased the first large batch of chemicals for the bomb—including 1,000 pounds of urea and 1,500 pounds of nitric acid—from City Chemicals, a Jersey City company. Yousef's order was delivered to the storage shed December 1.

Meanwhile, JTTF was still in the dark. Neil Herman's squad had gotten close to the Trade Center plot through their work with the informant Garrett Wilson, but the two plotlines were running along parallel tracks. Clearly, there was some crossover between Hampton-El and the al-Kifah faithful, but Wilson wasn't yet in a position to see it. Moreover, since Wilson was known among Brooklyn Muslims as a straight shooter—he'd turned down Hampton-El's request for remote-detonator caps on the spot, for example— he would have created suspicion if he had begun showing too much interest in the mosque's extralegal activities.

Corrigan and Liguori suggested the alternative of bringing in an undercover to deal with Hampton-El. Wilson could introduce him as, say, a military buddy looking to make some extra cash training jihadis, as someone with a looser moral code. But Dunbar nixed the idea. He was concerned that one of the trainees might later commit a crime.

This reservation seemed peculiar to the investigators, because the subjects were going to get training whether or not the FBI provided it. Corrigan understood the heat the Bureau would take if it turned out it had assisted a future terrorist. But what was the Bureau's responsibility, he wondered, if it ignored an opportunity to get information on that same terrorist and thus disrupt his plans? How else could you a stop a terrorist, for that matter? Wait until he's already murdered and maimed? If you weren't willing to get close to the action, to get your hands a little dirty now and then, how would you ever know what he's plotting to do?

When the FBI refused to authorize an undercover, Corrigan and Liguori persuaded John McGuire, Wilson's handler at Naval Intelligence, to "loan" them Wilson for the training operation. In fact, McGuire was just as keen as the investigators to find out what Hampton-El was planning.

On January 7, Wilson met with Hampton-El and Ubaidah at the India House, a restaurant in downtown Brooklyn, to firm up the arrangements. The training was set to commence that Saturday at a shooting range in New Jersey that Wilson had access to, and would run for five days. Wilson, who told Hampton-El he had a federal firearms license, would pick up the AK-47s Hampton-El was supplying from Brooklyn and transport them on Friday night to New Jersey. The terms of the deal were straightforward: Wilson was to receive $5,000—$1,500 in advance—for his instructional services and some surplus military equipment Wilson had agreed to procure for Hampton-El.

The operation was set to go on January 13. Herman's squad would run surveillances on the exchange of weapons between Wilson and Hampton-El in Brooklyn, and Wilson would meet with Corrigan and Liguori en route to New Jersey, allowing the investigators to run a check on the guns. Then

JTTF, subject to court approval, would bug the hotel rooms Wilson had booked near the range for his trainees, and surveil the actual training exercises in New Jersey.

On the afternoon of January 13, Dunbar got wind of the plan and called Corrigan and Liguori in for a meeting. (Normally, the squad reported to Herman and Don Clark, the head of the Criminal Division, but since most of the surveillance subjects were foreign, the job fell under the jurisdiction of the National Security chief.) Once again, Dunbar was concerned that the Bureau was training potential terrorists, holy warriors who may not be breaking the law now, but who might one day turn the skills they were acquiring against the U.S.

Dunbar began bartering with Corrigan and Liguori about what types of exercises should be excluded from the training. He didn't want Wilson actually handling the weapons during instruction. He didn't want bow-and-arrow instruction. He wanted to excise rappelling from the training menu. With each request, Corrigan paged Wilson, who was getting ready to meet Hampton-El, to see if he could comply. "We were taking so much out of the package, we were afraid they were going to kill him," Corrigan remembers.

Finally, Dunbar decided to shut the whole operation down. Don Clark had already told Corrigan and Liguori that if the guns Wilson was transporting turned out to be "dirty," he was going to confiscate them and arrest Hampton-El, thereby exposing Wilson as the likely informant. Now, as Dunbar ticked off his objections, it became clear to Corrigan and the others that he was uncomfortable with the entire mission. Corrigan called Wilson to tell him to abort just as Wilson was getting in his car to drive to the meeting place.

The next day, Corrigan and Liguori met with John McGuire, Wilson's NCIS handler, in the back room of Smitty's seafood restaurant on Pearl Street in Lower Manhattan. McGuire was furious. JTTF had involved his man with dangerous, heavily armed people, then left him hanging without a cover story. What the hell was Wilson supposed to say to them now? In fact, Dunbar had already come up with a plausible alibi. Earlier that week, Iraqi war planes had violated the no-fly zone and U.S. fighters had engaged them. Wilson, whose military background was well-known to Hampton-El, could tell him that his base was on heightened alert. As a result, he hadn't been able to contact Hampton-El the night before and now wouldn't be able to go through with the training.

McGuire was somewhat mollified, but he was still angry at the way the Bureau had handled the case. Mostly, though, he was disappointed at not being able to follow through on Hampton-El. Was there something they could still do?

Corrigan and Liguori suggested a Plan B. They pointed out that Wilson would still have to give Hampton-El the equipment he'd purchased for him. Why not set up a meeting, run surveillance on the exchange, then follow Hampton-El, or whoever shows up—and see where the trail leads? McGuire liked the idea, but after their last experience, the investigators were reluctant to go back to Dunbar. Instead, they explained the situation to Herman.

"Do it," Herman said.

Wilson called Hampton-El for a meeting and was paged to the Sandman Motel in Bordentown, New Jersey, on January 15. Herman's squad preceded Wilson to the location and set up surveillance outside. Hampton-El wasn't there. Ubaidah and two unknown Middle Eastern men were waiting. The exchange went smoothly and Wilson departed. Herman's squad and several agents from the Newark office then tailed Ubaidah and his two associates, who were driving in a black station wagon, to Ubaidah's aunt's home in Newark, where they unloaded the equipment—plastic knives, cannon fuses, military manuals and blow guns. The subjects then split up. Some of the surveillance team followed Ubaidah, now in a second car, back to the al-Kifah Center in Brooklyn. The rest of the team, including Liguori and Corrigan, followed the two unknown subjects to an apartment on Fairview Avenue in Jersey City. "Do you believe where these guys are taking us?" Liguori asked Corrigan.

Liguori was driving a block behind the "eye," or lead car, but Corrigan recognized the address as soon as it crackled over the radio. The apartment belonged to Omar Abdel-Rahman, the blind sheik and the jihad group's spiritual leader.

The circle was closing. Hampton-El, already connected to the "twelve targets" plot through his meeting with el-Shinawy and Emad Salem, was forming a jihad group whose members were linked to the al-Kifah Refugee Center and Abdel-Rahman, mentor of Nosair, enemy and rival of Shalabi and a preacher of violence and terror against the U.S. "The whole thing was just screaming at you: violence," Corrigan recalls.

The honchos at the Bureau didn't hear it quite the same way; however, they authorized round-the-clock surveillance on Ubaidah for the rest of the week. The day after the weapons exchange, he led investigators to Jersey City's Lincoln Park, where he held exercises for a group of Sudanese and Middle Eastern men. Then, on the weekend, the investigators followed the same group to a farm near Harrisburg, Pennsylvania, where the militants attended a full-blown training camp. Investigators observed the men practicing martial arts, sniper firing, and rappelling.

Meanwhile, the Bureau began running plates of cars they picked up on their surveillance. The black station wagon Corrigan and Liguori had followed to Abdel-Rahman's from the Sandman Motel came back to Abdo Haggag, a 35-year-old Egyptian national who served as the blind sheik's speechwriter and confidant. His passenger was identified as Siddig Siddig-Ali, the sheik's Sudanese translator. Both men would figure prominently in later investigations. Also among the trainees was a tall, red-haired Egyptian whom the investigators mistook for Mahmoud Abouhalima, but who turned out to be Mahmoud's brother, Mohammed.

The chase was heating up. The JTTF was just a whisper away from the World Trade Center plot. But once more Dunbar lost patience with the operation. The surveillances were already eating up manpower from other cases. Having a squad the whole weekend outside Harrisburg was the final straw. On Sunday he called them back to New York, preventing them from following their subjects home later that evening. Herman's squad was pissed. "Bedding down" the subjects, they were certain, would have generated a cluster of new identifications and leads. More troubling, however, were the implications for the future of the investigation. With much of the action now taking place in New Jersey and Pennsylvania, Dunbar wanted to transfer the entire case to the Newark office. Herman's squad would continue to monitor Hampton-El and Ubaidah, but Abdel-Rahman and his acolytes would no longer be in New York's jurisdiction. At that point, JTTF's jihad investigation would effectively be dead in the water, killed by an administrative stroke of the pen.

The Trade Center plotters were about to make the issue of jurisdiction moot, however. On December 29, Yousef had reached out to his traveling partner, Ahmad Ajaj, who was still in an Immigration and Naturalization Service lockup in Lower Manhattan. As he had done previously, Yousef avoided leaving a phone trail connecting him with Ajaj by making the contact through Ajaj's lawyer. That evening, Ajaj rang Ismail Najim—a boyhood friend of Yousef's living in Texas—who patched the call through to Yousef in Jersey City. Yousef told Ajaj he wanted to get hold of the bomb-making manuals that had been in Ajaj's luggage when INS stopped him. Ajaj replied it would be too dangerous for Yousef to try to retrieve the material, so he should send someone else. The call was taped by the prison recording system, but apparently not reviewed until much later.

Almost ready to begin assembling the bomb, Yousef and Salameh moved in early January into a new apartment on Pamrapo Avenue, close to Jersey City's border with Bayonne. By then, they were in daily contact with Mahmoud Abouhalima, who visited the apartment three to four times a week, and Nidal Ayyad, who used his position at Allied Signal to acquire "restricted" chemicals like lead nitrate, phenol and methylamine for the operation. Yousef and Salameh also kept in close contact with el-Gabrowny and Abdel-Rahman, calling them repeatedly at their homes.

Later that month, speaking at an Islamic Conference in Brooklyn, Abdel-Rahman issued a virtual fatwa against the U.S. Being called a terrorist is fine, he said, as long as one is terrorizing the enemies of Islam, in particular the U.S. and its allies.

Around this time, el-Gabrowny began arranging for the World Trade Center conspirators to visit Nosair as a kind of homage in the months before the bombing. Abouhalima visited Attica on January 2 and February 7. Salameh would make the trek upstate on February 13.

On January 24 the plot was nearly derailed when Salameh and Yousef got in a car accident while driving home from Abouhalima's apartment. Salameh's Nova was totaled, and Yousef, who had been riding in the passenger seat, was hospitalized with lacerations.

But Yousef didn't miss a beat. Still using the alias Kamal Ibrahim, he continued calling chemical companies from his hospital bed, arranging for deliveries of aluminum, magnesium, ferric oxide and more nitric acid to the storage shed. A few days later, Abouhalima—a more dependable driver than Salameh—picked him up at Rahway Hospital and drove him home.

On February 15, using a contact from Allied Signal, Ayyad rented another car for Yousef and Salameh. The next day, Salameh drove into Manhattan to scout the World Trade Center bomb location. He entered the B-2 level of the parking garage in the early afternoon, checked out his surroundings for about a half hour, then headed back for New Jersey. On his way to the storage shed, he was involved in another accident on Jersey City's West Side Avenue. The police wrote a report of the incident and let him go.

Things were coming to a head. Almost every day, the conspirators were transporting the chemicals they'd kept at the storage facility to Yousef and Salameh's apartment and were mixing the liquid center of the bomb they were about to plant in the garage of the Trade Center. For weeks the plotters had been searching for a bomb vehicle. Abouhalima had pestered the boss of the taxi and limousine company where he worked to let him borrow an old van that was sitting neglected on the lot, and even offered to register it in his name. But his boss refused. Finally, on February 23, the accident-prone Salameh walked around the corner from his apartment, put down a $400 cash deposit at a Ryder rental office on Kennedy Boulevard and drove out of the lot with a yellow cargo van.

On February 24, Salameh made a last surveillance of the World Trade Center.

On February 25, Salameh, posing as Kamal Ibrahim, took delivery of three tanks of compressed hydrogen—to be used as an accelerant in the explosion—at the Mallory Avenue storage shed. Forbidden to bring them inside the facility—storage workers felt they were too hazardous—Salameh called on Yousef to help transport the tanks back to their apartment, where they completed assembly of the bomb that afternoon.

Later that evening, Salameh drove to a ShopRite on the west side of Jersey City to establish a cover story for the following day. He bought a few items, then called the police to report the Ryder van stolen from the parking lot. However, he gave the police the wrong license plate number to ensure the van wouldn't be stopped the next morning as a stolen vehicle.

By then, the van was loaded with a 1,500-pound bomb. Yousef and Ismail Najim, who'd flown up from Texas for the occasion, drove the van to the Harbor Motor Inn in Brooklyn and spent the night there. Perhaps they wanted to avoid the Jersey traffic into the city the next morning. More likely, they didn't want to be seen in their own neighborhood driving a Ryder van the next morning. In any event, they were set to go.

CHAPTER 7

WORLD TRADE CENTER I

The Ford Econoline van is parked. It is white, with a long window on the side. You are looking at it from far away, but you can see it clearly. Now the explosion. First the fireball, white, then yellow and orange. You are watching it in slow motion. The noise— the *boom*—hasn't happened yet. Light travels faster than sound, so the actual flash and the force of the blast happens before you hear the *boom*, but already, pieces of the Ford van are flying at you. Now you hear the sound of the explosion. The shrapnel is coming at you at thousands of feet per second, flying like giant, jagged bullets. In real time it has only been a second or two, but now, in slow motion, black smoke is shooting upward. When it begins to clear, the van is gone. All that is left is a chassis, four wheels and most of the engine block.

You press "pause" on the VCR. The tape came from the Explosives Unit of the FBI Lab. They have re-created the World Trade Center bombing by building its twin and detonating it on videotape so the jury can see.

Now you close your eyes. You are no longer in an empty field at the FBI Academy in Quantico, Virginia. You are in the B-2 level of the World Trade Center at exactly 12:17 P.M., on February 26, 1993. This van is yellow. It's a Ryder rental van parked against a concrete wall in the garage. The force of explosion goes to the point of least resistance. So when this flash happens, the fire is shooting away from the wall, trapped above and below by the floor and ceiling where it has no place to go but forward—toward you. You don't know what's happening. Only a fraction of a second has gone by, but you already know this thing is moving faster than you can run. It is scorching everything in its path, igniting anything that will burn. The debris is also on this forward path and so is the energy of the blast, traveling at thousands of feet per second with a pressure of 150,000 pounds per inch. It will crush anything in its path. The *boom*, when it comes, is so much louder, and longer, the sound trapped by the confines of the garage, echoing, reverberating. Now, what was once the B-2 level garage is a much bigger place. It is a crater that spans downward to a train station several floors below and upward to a hotel ballroom three stories above. The concrete floors that once separated each level are gone, blasted into dust. The bomb was a mix of fuel oil and fertilizer with a nitroglycerin booster. It has served its purpose. It is not yet 12:18, but six people who were in the garage area are dead, or near dead. And now the fires are roiling. Gasoline from the tanks of many cars are fueling it. The smoke is filling the basement and climbing up through the elevator shafts, stairwells and ventilation systems. Below it all, in the PATH train station, a 200-foot section of the ceiling has blown down and injured several commuters.

Now you open your eyes again.

You remember that the Towers don't exist anymore. But they didn't fall that day in February 1993. No, that would come later. But make no mistake. They were supposed to fall that day, one toppling into the other, knocking them both on their sides, killing everyone inside and everyone in the path of their collapse.

That had to disappoint Ramzi Ahmed Yousef as he stood on the New Jersey side of the Hudson River watching for the towers to fall. He had come a long way and worked very hard to make that happen. Either way, he must have thought, the explosion would say plenty to America: We are here. You can't hide anymore. Be afraid. Ramzi Yousef watched a little longer, but all he could see was smoke and the flashing lights in the distance. He got back in his car. He had a plane to catch.

There were very few strangers to law enforcement among the men who blew up the World Trade Center. Mohammed Salameh and Mahmoud Abouhalima had been collared by Eddie Norris's detectives after the Rabbi Kahane murder, but then let go under pressure from the NYPD brass. JTTF's people had surveilled a number of the other bombers at the shooting range in Calverton, even before the Kahane case. Emad Salem had become a trusted member of the group's larger circle, with close links to Abdel-Rahman, Nosair, Abouhalima and el-Gabrowny. He'd been in the thick of the original "Twelve Jewish Locations" plot and a hair's breadth away from the actual World Trade Center bombers. Tommy Corrigan's colleagues had tailed several more of their associates to the training camp in Harrisburg just a month or so ago. In fact, the last of the surveillances had run up until just a few weeks before the bombing, when one group seemed to be asking the other if they knew how to get detonators.

One could suggest that, had those investigations gone forward, the JTTF surveillance team would have followed the suspects as they met, and maybe even trailed them as they unloaded the chemicals at the storage shed they rented. Would they have been observed in the house where they were making the bomb? Would the FBI have stopped the rented Ryder van after the blasting caps were attached to the huge drums in the back, just as it was pulling out of the driveway in Jersey City?

We'll never know. The two cases were both shut down based on a series of FBI management concerns that were more administrative than exigent.

On February 26, 1993, the FBI was caught by surprise. Neil Herman was in his office at the JTTF when the bomb went off. Special Agent Chuck Stern had just walked out to get a sandwich. He got as far as Varick Street and North Moore when he heard a rumble that shook the ground beneath his feet.

"What was that, thunder?" Stern asked himself. He had no idea that rumble would change his life. Soon, Stern saw the fire engines going by. They seemed to just keep coming. Even as he walked back into 26 Federal Plaza, back to the JTTF offices, police cars and ambulances streamed south. Any explosion in New York City is automatically reported to the NYPD Bomb Squad and to the JTTF. Neil Herman wandered out of his office into the JTTF bullpen. Agents were listening to the police radio. Frantic calls for more ambulances and Police Emergency Service Units were still coming in. The preliminary reports said that it was a transformer explosion in the PATH train station beneath the Towers.

Uptown at NBC's studios, in a darkened video editing room, I was working on cutting a story together: part two of a three-part investigative series about pedophiles working in the public schools. It was going to be a big story.

Bob Dembo, the managing editor, called the edit room. "Can you head down to the World Trade Center?" I had already received a message on my pager about the explosion and made a call. A cop at the Bomb Squad told me that it was a transformer explosion. I told Dembo, who said, "Please, just head down there. I have a really bad feeling about this one." The pedophiles would have to wait.

Racing down the West Side Highway in my blue Mercury, I fell in with a caravan of Police Emergency Service Unit vehicles heading toward the Twin Towers. It was bitter cold and the rain had turned to snow. I threw a spinning red light onto the dashboard to keep up with the speeding police cars and trucks. Sirens were screaming. We darted in and out of traffic over the slick pavement until we passed the first roadblock at Canal Street. All I could see ahead of me were the Towers, the smoke and a million flashing lights. The police radio was jumping with calls about hundreds of people inside the Towers, complaining of smoke inhalation. I jumped out of the car across from the North Tower. People, choking, coughing, were streaming out into the snow. When I got across the street, I heard glass breaking. People in the Towers were trying to let the smoke out. The shards fell around me on the street like daggers. I backed away from the building and literally walked into an old friend from the NYPD Bomb Squad. "Hey, what is this?" I asked, not letting go of his arm.

"It looks like a bomb," he said. I asked him why.

"I've gotten down there to look at it. It's on the B-Level of the garage. I got the top building engineer from the Port Authority and asked him about transformers, gas mains, whatever. He says there is nothing down there that could generate an explosion like this. It's just a big crater now."

"Holy shit," I said. "So it's a car bomb?"

"No, bigger. A van or a truck, packed with explosives." I loosened my grip on his raincoat. The meaning of this was just sinking in.

"Who else knows this?" I asked.

"Right now, just the chief of detectives, the police commissioner and you."

I ran to find the NBC Live Truck. I already had plenty of news to report. Smoke was pouring out of a garage door at the bottom of the Towers. People coming from the garage were covered in soot and gasping for breath. An hour had probably passed since the blast, and the people coming out of the Towers from the upper floors had fear in their eyes and little black mustaches from breathing the acrid smoke. They were carried by New York cops, Port Authority cops, firefighters, Emergency Medical Service medics and Samaritans who took the arms of the dizzied workers who streamed from the buildings.

Neil Herman and his men had listened to the police radio traffic and called the Bomb Squad's duty officer. They now had reports from the scene that it had been a massive explosion that left a giant crater in the subterranean depths of the Trade Center. Neil gathered a team of agents to go take a look. He made sure to bring a couple of the JTTF trained bomb technicians.

When Herman and his small team of JTTF cops and agents got to the scene they found Lt. Walter Boser, commanding officer of the NYPD Bomb Squad. Boser, a tough German, led them as close to the damage as they could get. Neil Herman is a hard guy to get a rise out of, but on that day, at that moment, he admits he was shocked.

"I was thinking at that moment of the horrific crime scenes I'd witnessed," he recalls. "The LaGuardia Airport bombing where eleven people lost their lives. The Fraunces Tavern bombing, which I thought was the worst I'd seen. But nothing—nothing on the scale of this. It was a miracle that only six people lost their lives."

> I located the NBC Live Truck. It was still snowing and windy. My cameraman, Tom Bear, gave me the signal. I was "on." My report described the scene, an account of how massive the damage was. I said that, because there was no physical or logical explanation for the level of force from the blast or the amount of damage, police suspected it was a truck-bomb. I was the first to report that line of thinking, and for a couple of days officials would go to great length to downplay that possibility. But it was what it was, and my sources were sure it was a bomb.

Neil Herman knew he would need a command post at the scene to coordinate the FBI's work. The nearest big building was the headquarters of Shearson Lehman across the street. When Herman went in to look for space, the face that greeted him was a godsend. Pat Murphy, the chief of security for Shearson, was the retired NYPD chief who had been cofounder of the JTTF 13 years before. "He told me, 'Neil, anything you need, just let me know,'" Herman recalls.

Herman knew there were some real priorities. First, they had to establish a perimeter around the crime scene. Any trace of the bomb could be a vital clue. Still, that would have to wait until the fires were out and the rescues complete. Then they would need to trace every car and truck down there to their owners, to see if any of the car owners could be linked to the bombing.

At 26 Federal Plaza, the Command Center on the 26th floor was already up and running. Special Agent Chuck Stern, who had felt the thunder of the blast as he was walking back with his sandwich, now sat down to compose a Teletype to FBI Headquarters in Washington. It was sent under the heading NON MIDEAST TERRORISM because, at that point, no one thought that Middle Eastern terrorists would strike on U.S. soil. Terrorist organizations like Hamas and Hezbollah availed themselves of America's political freedoms and wealth to set up bases of operation and raise funds for their compatriots overseas. No one thought they wanted to jeopardize their status by targeting their neighbors. Stern was designated as the "case agent," making the investigation his primary responsibility. The case would need a designation in the FBI's files, so it was code-named simply TRADEBOM.

In the Command Center, leads were coming in from the public, the police and other agencies. An anonymous man taking responsibility for the bombing in the name of a Bosnian terrorist group had made a call to the NYPD's First Precinct stationhouse. At the FBI, in the first few days, there were two theories that seemed dominant. One, the bombing was related to the Balkans, where the U.S. was just beginning its involvement. Or two, it was indeed Middle Eastern terrorism, a delayed payback for the Gulf War from Saddam Hussein.

Friday night, just before the eleven o'clock news, I took a camera crew and found a side door to the Trade Center. Winking at a couple of fire marshals who were old friends, I managed to bypass the lines to get a shot of the damage. Lights and generators were running. The crater went up and down. Each level had its own spaghetti-like mess of wires and pipes and rebar hanging down. Water was dripping from the ceilings from fire hoses and busted pipes. In this business, you think after 10 or 20 years, you've seen everything. I had never seen anything like this. It was total devastation. Of course, looking back, I now realize that was nothing.

The next morning—Saturday—Dave Williams, the FBI's top bomb expert, arrived on the scene. He knew this was the biggest "post blast" scene he or any other team had ever processed in the U.S. Williams was a legend in the bomb business. Known as "Super Dave," he was partial to wearing an Australian bush hat and a long black duster. Williams took a good long look at the damage. He knew they would have to find the "seat" of the blast to locate critical evidence. He and other agents from the lab took stock of the massive job ahead of them.

Williams realized there was already a problem with the post-blast investigation: too many investigators, too many agencies, too little coordination. He called all of the bomb technicians from the FBI, ATF and NYPD into the Grand Ballroom in the Vista Hotel, situated between the two towers. The hotel was badly damaged. The explosion had blown out a large section of the ballroom floor. Looking down into the hole, you couldn't see the bottom of the crater. A plan was hatched. A small exploratory team would go down into the crater and try to swab for explosive residue, take photos and document evidence. The team included a chemist, a crime-scene photographer and bomb techs from each agency. As they descended, they saw a ledge of concrete with crushed cars. It appeared to be a piece of the B-2 level. It was still being held up by rebar. Most of the B-2 level had been blown down into the hole. This remaining piece seemed like a good place for the team to try and reach. It was near the seat of the blast and it didn't appear that any firefighters or rescue workers had gotten to it. It would be a pristine, uncontaminated place to gather evidence. It took a long winding route to reach the ledge. The investigators began to take swabs from the demolished cars and debris.

NYPD Bomb Squad Detective Don Sadowy spotted a piece of the thick metal housing of a differential case from a car. Sadowy knew a thing or two about cars. The 39-year-old detective had grown up in Brooklyn, in

Greenpoint's Polish neighborhood. He attended the high school nearest to his home, which happened to be Automotive High School, one of the few trade schools run by the city. At Automotive High, Sadowy had gotten to know cars inside and out.

Suddenly, Sadowy's mechanic's courses came rushing back to him. So did his Bomb Squad experience. Sadowy had investigated a number of car bombs, but had never seen one of these heavy metal cases shattered. Farther ahead, he noticed gears that had been blown out of the shattered case. Next, he recognized a piece of the frame of a vehicle. He and Joe Hanlin, a bomb tech from ATF, began to dig the piece out. It was a four-foot-long section. "My ex-partner works in the Auto Crime Squad now," Sadowy told Hanlin. "He taught me that there are hidden VIN numbers on the frames of some cars." Sadowy took off his glove and ran his fingers down the inside of the metal frame. Then he felt it: little dots, raised like braille. "I just knew this was from the vehicle that carried the device, it was just so totally decimated," Sadowy recalls.

Just then, a call came over the radio. The FBI was pulling everyone out of the hole in ten minutes. Train service was going to resume in the subway, and they were worried about the rumble causing more collapses in the crater. Sadowy called out and got a wire mesh stretcher and a body bag to put the twisted auto frame in. When he climbed out he and Hanlin snuck the evidence into the back of a Crime Scene Unit station wagon and the driver, Crime Scene Unit Detective Anthony Lombardo, rushed it to the police lab.

At the NYPD lab, located in the police academy on East 20th Street, FBI agents and NYPD lab technicians tried to read the numbers, but without twisting the metal and cleaning the piece off, there would be no way to see them. The FBI was firm. The evidence had to stay in its original form. No twisting, no scraping. No one could make out what the number was. It looked like a lot of dots.

NYPD Detective John Sardone, an expert from the Documents Section of the police lab, said he'd like to take a crack. He took the piece into his lab, and either didn't know about or simply ignored all warnings about how to handle this piece of evidence. He bent the metal back, used an acidic cleaner to wipe off the section and came up with a clear set of numbers. He took a photo and handed it to the agents.

The number still didn't mean anything to any of the cops and agents looking at it. It wasn't conformed the way a vehicle identification number would be. But if it wasn't a VIN, what was it?

On Sunday, Dave Williams assembled all the bomb techs who would be working the crater. Williams was furious. He told the techs that the day before, a team had gone into the hole and removed evidence against strict instructions. Furthermore, Williams said, evidence had been taken to another agency's lab. Don Sadowy had already been privately dressed down by Williams and was avoiding eye contact with everyone as he laced up his work boots at the back of the room. "I was trying to be invisible, because I knew I was very close to being thrown off the case," Sadowy remembers. Sadowy still felt he was right about the auto parts. He was sure they had come from the vehicle that had carried the bomb. But he knew he was in big trouble for moving the parts out of the hole without clearance from the FBI.

Neil Herman, whose domestic terrorism unit comprised about 50 agents and cops, was now running a major FBI conglomerate: Seven hundred agents nationwide were to follow any leads of TRADEBOM. One hundred of them would be directly under his full-time control in New York. The Command Center at 26 Federal Plaza would run 24 hours a day. A team of 30 bomb technicians from the FBI, the NYPD and the ATF would work in shifts at the blast site looking for clues.

By Wednesday the NYPD lab people had reached out for the FBI's Auto Crime Task Force. Special Agent Jaime Cedeno arrived at the lab, took one look at the number and knew it was a C-VIN, a confidential VIN hidden on parts where a car thief or chop-shop might not think to look. He went back to the office, opened a manufacturer's manual to decode the C-VIN, and then ran the correct VIN through the FBI's National Crime Information Center computer. NCIC spat out the answer. The VIN belonged to a Ryder rental van, Alabama plate XA70668. It had been reported stolen in Jersey City on February 25, one day before the bombing. Cedeno called Jimmy Lyons from the JTTF to give him the lead.

Quickly, Lyons learned that the Ryder truck was rented by DIB Leasing in Jersey City to a man named Mohammed Salameh. In fact, DIB Leasing told JTTF that Salameh had been calling them every day since he reported the van stolen, trying to get his cash deposit back.

Neil Herman knew he had his first real break.

Herman called Corrigan and other members of the squad into his office. The name Mohammed Salameh meant nothing to Neil Herman or any of the other investigators, but the address he read out sent chills down their collective spine: 57 Prospect Park Southwest, Brooklyn. Apartment 4C.

Ibrahim el-Gabrowny's place.

El-Gabrowny was Nosair's cousin, the man who'd been telling Emad Salem (the informant the JTTF had been ordered to drop) about the plan to blow up 12 Jewish locations.

Instantly, Corrigan realized it was their guys—the guys they'd been tracking for the past three years, right up until the surveillance in Harrisburg—and that one way or another they were connected with the people who were responsible for the WTC blast. The key, of course, was el-Gabrowny, who was linked both to the Brooklyn mosques and to al-Kifah as well as to Nosair and the blind sheik; to the Twelve Jewish Locations bomb plot; and to the nefarious Dr. Rashid, AKA Clement Hampton-El.

Neil Herman knew he and his JTTF men would have to move quickly. He ordered Corrigan to write out everything they knew about el-Gabrowny and Nosair so the U.S. Attorney's Office could get a search warrant for el-Gabrowny's apartment. Neil Herman and Chuck Stern, the case agent, sat down with the U.S. Attorney's Office to devise a plan on how to get the most information they could from Salameh without tipping their hand. The plan was elegant in its simplicity. When Salameh returned to DIB Leasing they would tell him he had to complete a special Ryder form before they could return the cash deposit. That night, the agents and prosecutors invented a form that would ask most of the questions they needed answers to. Where was the van stolen? Where were you coming from when it was taken? Where were you going? Where are you living now? They joked it would be nice to add a question like: At any time did the van contain a giant bomb? But there was little time for joking.

By Wednesday morning JTTF had called the Newark office of the FBI and had them detail a surveillance team to the DIB rental agency. If and when Salameh returned, tailing him could lead to safe houses and maybe even other suspects. Newark FBI also inserted Special Agent Bill Atkinson, wired with a recording device, as a sales agent to help Salameh with the "special questionnaire" they'd devised the night before.

Herman's original impulse to have the surveillance team follow Salameh for a day or two was aborted when word of the FBI's big break began to leak out. On Thursday, March 4, with the surveillance team in place and a SWAT team hidden in a truck, a local TV crew showed up at DIB to ask if the "bomb truck" had been rented there. With some fast talking, agents convinced the TV reporter he was at the wrong rental agency. Not long after the "live truck" pulled out of DIB's lot, Mohammed Salameh showed up. The DIB manager, Pat Galasso, introduced Salameh to Bill Atkinson, who was posing as the "Loss Prevention" man from Ryder. He helped Salameh complete the form. Salameh said the van had been stolen from the parking lot of a ShopRite supermarket and he'd had friends pick him up. He haggled for his $400 deposit back, but Atkinson told him $200 was the best Ryder could do. Salameh thanked Atkinson warmly and stepped out into the parking lot, where the FBI SWAT team descended on him, cuffing him and tossing him into one of the Surveillance Unit cars that drove him to the JTTF in New York.

Just after noon, my pager went off. I called back the number. It was an old friend who filled me in on the case.

"Holy Shit. Holy SHIT!" I thought. I had to find a way get on the air. This was a giant scoop. Odds were, it wouldn't hold until the six o'clock news. I called Bob Dembo at NBC and told him what I had. I was in Brooklyn. The nearest Live Truck was at the World Trade Center, where the noon news conference had just concluded. Traffic near the Towers was still backed up, so I jumped the sidewalk, and raced down the last two blocks, using the horn to scatter pedestrians. When I got to the corner of Vesey Street, I drove over a jagged piece of metal sticking up out of the sidewalk blowing out both tires on the driver's side. When I got out of the car, my colleagues were howling with laughter at my dramatic entrance and two flat tires. They all thought it was hysterical, until I picked up the mike and began my live report. It was 1:16 P.M.

"Sources tell us there has been an arrest in the bombing of the World Trade Center . . ."

Some of them later told me they thought I was not really "on," that I was playing out a practical joke, pretending to have the scoop. That changed when their bosses started paging them, screaming. Most of them had just completed their live shots reporting that there were no new developments in the case. Needless to say, before I finished my report, there was a lot of scrambling for telephones. Several minutes went by and then the White House confirmed my report.

That afternoon, NYPD Detective Don Sadowy was still working deep in the crater looking for more clues. He was trying to stay far away from Dave Williams or any other heavy hitters from the FBI, because he knew he was still in trouble for acting on his hunch. He had no idea that a suspect had been arrested.

"I came up the ramp, just to get some air and clean myself off and at the top of the ramp, all the cops and agents were clapping and cheering," Sadowy recalls. "I looked behind me, and there was no one else there. I thought they were making fun of me because everyone knew I was in hot water over the auto frame." But when Sadowy reached the top of the ramp, they were all high-fiving and back-slapping him. Over and over, they kept saying, "You broke the case, man! You did it!"

The investigation was taking off. In a stark interview room on the 25th floor of the FBI's New York office, the case agent, Chuck Stern, sat uncomfortably across from Mohammed Salameh, trying to make non-incriminating small talk as he waited for a translator. Stern had been told not to attempt to take any statement until Salameh had been given his Miranda warnings in Arabic. When Stern asked him if he wanted anything, Salameh had only one request. He wanted time to pray.

But without saying a word, Salameh had already provided clues. In his wallet, agents found a business card for Nidal Ayyad. A search warrant was executed at Salameh's apartment at 34 Kensington Avenue in Jersey City. There they found Ahmed Yassin, who said he could not believe that Salameh was involved in such a terrible act. Yassin told the agents he had just taught Salameh how to drive the Ryder truck a few days before. He led the agents to another address, 40 Pamrapo Avenue, the place where the bomb was built. The agents thanked Yassin and he agreed to stay in close touch.

After a warrant was obtained to search el-Gabrowny's apartment just off Prospect Park, Detective Tommy Corrigan and another JTTF member, ATF agent Mike Burke, set up surveillance outside the building. Then the signal was given for a team of JTTF agents and an NYPD Emergency Service Unit to hit the building. Just before the caravan of cars came rolling up, Corrigan and Burke saw el-Gabrowny. Tall and square-shouldered, with a broad, olive face made studious by rimless glasses and a trim beard, he exited the building and walked north. At the corner, el-Gabrowny took one look at the caravan of police cars pulling up at his apartment and turned into the path of Corrigan and Burke, who were following behind him. The investigators grabbed him to make sure he wasn't armed. "Freeze, police," Corrigan said as he and Burke spun el-Gabrowny around to frisk him.

Corrigan felt a thick plastic package in el-Gabrowny's pocket. "Plastic explosives," he thought. Whatever it was, el-Gabrowny sure didn't want him to find it. Corrigan felt a stab of pain as el-Gabrowny's elbow slammed into his cheek. Reeling, he glimpsed the sidewalk, his assailant's face, the sidewalk again, then el-Gabrowny's broad, muscular back straining against the material of his jacket, as he began swinging wildly at Corrigan's partner. Corrigan regained his footing and the two lawmen brought the taller el-Gabrowny down and cuffed him.

With el-Gabrowny incapacitated, Corrigan carefully removed the envelope from his pocket and slid out the contents: five Nicaraguan passports with false names and photos of El Sayyid Nosair, and Nosair's wife and three children.

Since Nosair was doing 20 years in prison, his need for a passport was limited—unless, of course, he planned to escape. A search of el-Gabrowny's apartment revealed a few items that might be useful in a jailbreak: a licensed 9 mm handgun and several stun guns. El-Gabrowny was charged with assault, resisting arrest and fraud for possessing the forged passports.

Back at the JTTF, they were sorting through the clues found at Salameh's apartment and the safe house where the bomb was made. That is where they discovered the first clue that would point them in the direction of the mastermind, Ramzi Ahmed Yousef. It was a letter from Wilkie, Farr & Gallagher, a white-shoe law firm that was representing a man named Ahmed Ajaj, pro bono. When the FBI ran Ajaj's name through its database, the screen lit up: Agents learned how Ahmad Ajaj and Ramzi Yousef had arrived together at JFK International Airport from Pakistan on September 1, 1992.

They would later discover that Ajaj—using his free lawyer from one of the nation's top law firms—petitioned the federal court in Brooklyn, arguing that he needed his reading material back. The judge agreed, returning to him all of his bomb-making manuals and videos so he could give them to Ramzi Yousef. One reason America is a great country—especially if you are a terrorist.

Within a few weeks, Neil Herman and his JTTF team had done the impossible. They had either arrested or identified most of the World Trade Center bombers. On Wednesday, March 10, cops and agents from the JTTF grabbed Nidal Ayyad as he left his New Jersey home. Ayyad was the engineer from Allied Signal who had helped Yousef obtain some of the harder-to-get chemicals for his bomb. The day of the bombing, he'd borrowed a coworker's radio to listen to the news, something he'd never done before, and his computer contained the draft of a note claiming responsibility for the bombing that was sent to the *New York Times*.

Chuck Stern had tracked Abouhalima around the world. After the bombing, Abouhalima had flown to Saudi Arabia and then on to Egypt, where his family lived. At the FBI's request, the Egyptian Intelligence Service captured him and questioned him using some of the more indelicate techniques known to the trade. When they were finished, they notified the FBI that they could pick up their suspect.

A small team of FBI agents was directed to a far corner of an airport where the Egyptian government had arranged for them to land a U.S. Air Force plane. A couple of agents and a handful of FBI SWAT people waited. From far off they saw a cloud of dust coming toward them. It was a car. As it neared, it slowed down, but not much. A body was dumped out. It was blindfolded. The FBI agents picked up Mahmoud Abouhalima. When he heard their voices, he began to hug them and kiss them. He may have hated America enough to help blow up the World Trade Center, and he probably still hates America now, but according to the agents who were there, he sure seemed to appreciate America at that moment. He couldn't wait to get on the plane. During the flight, he asked the agents if they had captured Ramzi Yousef, referring to him by one of his aliases. It was now clear that Yousef had been running the show. Abouhalima needed medical treatment upon his return. It seemed that during his interrogation in Egypt he had suffered second-degree burns to his testicles.

A few months later, Abouhalima's brother Mohammed was arrested for helping his brother escape the U.S. The FBI now had Salameh, who had rented the van, Abouhalima and his brother, Nidal Ayyad, and others. But Ahmed Yassin, who had been so helpful to the agents when they found him in Salameh's apartment, had fled to Iraq before the FBI had learned he knew much more about the plot than he'd admitted. And then there was the mastermind, Ramzi Yousef. He was long gone. Still, solving such a huge crime in just six days was a remarkable feat. The break had begun with Detective Don Sadowy's hunch about the car frame down in the hole, but since then, using the Rapid Start database and their own instincts, the cops and agents were closing in on the remaining members of the cell.

Still, there were questions. Who sent these people? Who was paying for all this? Who was benefiting from it? Since Yousef appeared to be Iraqi, many of the agents thought this was an Iraqi government operation. Add to that the fact that Ahmed Yassin had fled to Iraq. But others on Neil Herman's team saw that many of the suspects in the TRADEBOM case were tied to Nosair. Abouhalima and Salameh had been with Nosair the night he killed Kahane. El-Gabrowny, Nosair's cousin, had turned up in this case too. Many of them were Egyptian and followers of Omar Abdel-Rahman, the blind sheik. Was this a homegrown plot from Jersey City inspired by Abdel-Rahman?

For Neil Herman, one thing was now different. He finally had the Bureau paying attention. He was no longer fighting to keep agents from being pulled from his squad. He had more than he could handle. He had all the money and resources he needed. And he had two big jobs ahead of him. He had to find Ramzi Yousef, and he had to find out if there were more terrorist attacks in store for the U.S. And he had to do both in a hurry.

To that end, Herman detailed a small part of his Domestic Terrorism squad to the International Terrorism squad. Finally, Detective Tommy Corrigan, from Domestic, and Detective Lou Napoli, from International, would be working together. That was ironic, since before TRADEBOM, both were working parallel investigations and both were shut down. Corrigan had the Black Muslims who had been asked by the Arabs to get detonators. Napoli was working on the Arabs, who were *asking* for the detonators.

The first thing Napoli was told was to re-recruit his old informant, Emad Salem. It was not a hard sell to either man. Salem was outraged at the death and destruction caused by the bombing. Napoli wanted a man on the inside again. Salem's anger, and the promise of a big payday, helped him overcome his resistance to being exposed as a witness. In fact, he was gung ho. He would wear a wire, and would testify before the grand jury and in open court when the time came.

Corrigan and Napoli began to combine their cases. Napoli had Salem reach out to his former friends around the blind sheik. In fact, it was Salem's information that first alerted Chuck Stern that Abouhalima was hiding out in Cairo. Corrigan, meanwhile, contacted Garrett Wilson, the informant who had been asked to give commando training to a small group of men by Clement Hampton-El. Wilson reached out to Hampton-El on the pretext that he still owed him equipment. On March 24, Wilson got a message that Hampton-El didn't need training or equipment, but might want to hire Wilson to do security sweeps for an office safe house he'd just signed a lease for that day.

In the middle of all this, the CIA passed on some information to the Bureau that changed the direction and timing of Corrigan's investigation. Egyptian Intelligence told CIA officers that its informant in New York had reported that a cell affiliated with the blind sheik was planning to assassinate Hosni Mubarak during a scheduled visit to New York in early April. What's more, they said the cell members were being trained by Black Muslims, two of whom he identified. One, the informant said, was known as "the Doctor," clearly a reference to Dr. Rashid or Hampton-El.

Until then, Corrigan felt he was investigating the World Trade Center bombing conspiracy, if only from a different angle than the rest of Neil Herman's unit. He felt they had established that Nosair's followers—Salameh, Abouhalima and el-Gabrowny—had been in on the plot to blow up the World Trade Center. But he needed to learn what the connection was between those Arab suspects and the Black Muslims he'd been investigating for gunrunning and robbery—especially now, because it seemed they were working together in a plot to kill a world leader in the streets where Corrigan was a cop.

Corrigan's first priority was to disrupt the assassination plot. One approach was to find a weak link and try to pry him loose as an informant, or at least let him and his co-conspirators know that the Bureau knew about their plan. Their chief candidate was Abdo Mohammed Haggag.

Haggag, an Egyptian, had turned up in several of Corrigan's surveillances and had been identified as Abdel-Rahman's speechwriter and confidant. He'd traveled with the blind sheik on his 1990 exodus out of Egypt. Lately, however, the word was that Haggag had soured on the sheik. Apparently, Haggag felt that Abdel-Rahman treated him like a servant. In one story, the self-absorbed cleric had barely offered Haggag condolences after the recent death of Haggag's mother. In another, Abdel-Rahman had failed to invite Haggag to his wedding, especially galling to Haggag because Haggag had brokered the marriage.

Haggag was not likely to overlook these slights. What investigators didn't know was that Haggag was the informant who'd tipped off Egyptian Intelligence to the assassination plot in the first place.

On March 20, Corrigan and Special Agent Dan Coleman confronted Haggag as he was leaving his Pearl Street office, where Haggag worked for Prudential Bache as a data processor. Tall and stocky, with an infectious smile, Haggag appeared boyish despite his full, black beard. The agents told him that they were aware of the plot to kill Mubarak and that it would be in his interest to cooperate with them. They'd also learned that he was trying to arrange for his wife and children to come to the U.S. and they indicated they could help him with INS in exchange for his assistance.

Haggag was polite but noncommittal. He said he'd think about the agents' offer. At a second meeting several days later, however, he explained that his religious beliefs made it impossible for him to work for the Americans.

Corrigan and fellow case officer Chris Voss continued surveillance on

Hampton-El and Ubaidah, and stepped up efforts to locate Hampton-El's new safe house. Finally, a hand search by Con Edison of their billing records—they were too new to show up in the computer—turned up the address.

Corrigan, Voss and their squad went right to work. An undercover posing as a building inspector checked out the interior as a first step toward bugging the place, and Corrigan and Liguori installed a long-distance video camera on a building across the street. But it was too late to insure Mubarak's safety, and the New York leg of his trip was canceled.

The taps did yield some interesting tidbits, however. In early April, the investigators listened in on an overseas call from Hampton-El's right-hand man, Yaya Abu Ubaidah. He was in Vienna picking up cash for Hampton-El's jihad group from the Third World Relief Agency, a European counterpart to Brooklyn's Afghan Services Office said to be backed by Osama bin Laden. Throughout the spring, Ubaidah made several trips to Vienna collecting an estimated $100,000.

Then Detective Louie Napoli got a big break. His informant, Emad Salem, had some very troubling information. On April 23, a tall, elegant Sudanese man Salem knew as Abdel-Rahman's translator had approached Salem in the Abu Bakr Mosque in Brooklyn. He said he was planning a series of bombings and that he'd heard from the sheik that Salem was a good and trustworthy man with bomb-making experience. Corrigan had also run across the Sudanese translator. He had been the second man in the car with Haggag when Corrigan's team tailed the two Abdel-Rahman aides to the sheik's home from the meeting with Garrett Wilson at the Sandman Motel. His name was Siddig Siddig-Ali.

What was so troubling about Siddig-Ali's plan was the breadth of its conception. It called for the simultaneous bombing of four major New York City landmarks: the Lincoln and Holland tunnels, the United Nations and 26 Federal Plaza, the location of the New York offices of the FBI. If Siddig-Ali's plan were executed, it would not only result in an incalculable loss of lives and property, as well as the destruction of highly symbolic targets, but it would also demolish vital city lifelines, triggering unprecedented fear and panic among New Yorkers.

The small team working in the shadows behind the larger TRADEBOM case now had an urgent mission: to stop the next wave of attacks. The case became the top priority in the New York office of the FBI. Like all cases, it would have a code name: TERRSTOP.

The TERRSTOP investigators might have noted the irony that an informant whom Bureau heads judged to be not worth $500 a week had just tipped them to the most horrific conspiracy ever directed at the city. But there was too much to do. They outfitted Salem with a body recorder to capture incriminating statements from cell members. In fact, Siddig-Ali shielded Salem from the other conspirators at first, but he did seem willing to take him into his own confidence. On several occasions, he drove Salem to the target areas and videotaped the locations he'd chosen as possible bomb sites. During one of those trips, he confided to Salem that he had friends in the Sudanese embassy who had approved the plan and would provide diplomatic plates and credentials that would enable them to bypass security and gain access to the UN's underground garage. Siddig-Ali said he also had safe houses lined up in the Sudan where they could hide out after the attack.

Within weeks, Siddig-Ali mentioned to Salem that they'd need a safe house in which to build the bombs, and Salem offered to find one. Siddig-Ali accepted the offer and JTTF, acting on Salem's behalf, rented a garage in Queens that they equipped with video and sound recorders.

Through May and most of June, Salem met a number of the conspirators, many of whom had been trainees at the paramilitary camp JTTF had surveilled outside Harrisburg. Then, as the plot evolved, they began conducting strategy sessions, developing targets and defining their various roles in attacking them. The group determined that they'd need to assault the guard booth at 26 Federal Plaza and kill the guard in order to gain access to the underground garage. They acquired an Uzi submachine gun for this purpose.

Hampton-El re-entered the scene. His role seemed to be supplying logistical support—training, weapons and tactical advice. JTTF surveillance, wiretaps and Salem's body recorder captured him contracting with the group to obtain C-4 or hand grenades to use as an accelerant for their fertilizer bombs.

On May 21, with the group's plans proceeding apace, el-Gabrowny brought Siddig-Ali and Salem to Attica to visit Nosair and have their operation anointed. Nosair was delighted with the plan and suggested additional acts. In particular, Nosair enjoined them once again to kidnap Richard Nixon and Henry Kissinger and hold them as ransom for his release.

Salem also tried to get Abdel-Rahman's blessing on tape, but this proved to be somewhat trickier. After his years of imprisonment and torture at the hands of the Egyptian police, the sheik had developed a reflexive wariness about his involvement in, or even knowledge of, actual jihad operations. When Salem questioned the sheik in his home about Siddig-Ali's plan, the sheik steered him into the kitchen. He felt parts of his apartment were bugged. Even then, he was vague and not very responsive to Salem's insistent questioning. Yes, the UN was a legitimate target, but he didn't think that blowing up the UN would be good for Muslims. The UN was regarded by the rest of the world as a symbol of peace.

Abdel-Rahman then told him to attack military bases in the U.S.

"What about the FBI?" Salem asked.

Yes, the FBI was an appropriate target, the sheik told him, but counseled patience. "The one who killed Kennedy, he was trained for three years," he said cryptically.

Still, Siddig-Ali assured Salem that the sheik had issued him a fatwa for all U.S. targets, including the UN.

Other complications arose. Siddig-Ali confided to Salem additional plans to assassinate political figures sympathetic to Israel. U.S. Senator Alphonse D'Amato and Brooklyn Assemblyman Dov Hikind—both on Nosair's hit list—were also at the top of Siddig-Ali's list. They had to be informed. Only a few core members of Abdel-Rahman's jihad group knew about the list, however, and if the threat were made public, Salem would most likely be revealed as the informant. JTTF agents explained the predicament to both officials on May 21. D'Amato kept the report quiet. However, the story of the threat on Hikind ended up in the papers. On May 25 the *New York Post* ran headlines announcing a second terrorist plot.

Salem should have been exposed. But Siddig-Ali was so convinced of his group's fidelity that he assumed the FBI had picked up the information through some kind of surveillance. Moreover, he didn't seem concerned that the agents were onto them. Allah, he told the others, will protect us.

Meanwhile, the Landmarks plot was accelerating. JTTF agents followed cell members traveling to Philadelphia to acquire explosives, timers and fertilizer. Conspirators also led investigators to Mount Vernon, just north of New York City, where Mohamed Saleh, a gas-station proprietor and Hamas agent, supplied them with free fuel oil for their bombs.

Finally, in the early morning hours of June 24, the Bureau decided to act. Several members of the cell were busy in the garage mixing the witches' brew that would make their bombs. Because Salem had set up the safe house, the FBI already had a key. The SWAT team came in so quickly and so quietly that hardly anyone in the room realized they were there until they told everyone, "GET ON THE GROUND, NOW!" Five men dropped to the floor. The ringleader, Siddig-Ali, lay there in shock with a gun pointed at his head. The NYPD Bomb Squad moved in and began removing the explosives.

During simultaneous raids, investigators collared three more cell members, including Hampton-El, at their residences.

In July, U.S. prosecutors superseded the original indictment to include charges of seditious conspiracy, a rarely used statute that covers the crime of waging a war of urban terrorism. Five more defendants, including Abdel-Rahman, Nosair and el-Gabrowny, were either arrested or rearrested under the expanded charges, bringing the total number of defendants to thirteen.

• • •

On September 14, 1993, with Ramzi Yousef and Ahmed Yassin still at large, the first World Trade Center bombing trial against the remaining four defendants began in the U.S. Courthouse in Lower Manhattan. Almost five months later, the jury returned a verdict convicting Mohammed Salameh, Nidal Ayyad, Mahmoud Abouhalima and Yousef's traveling companion, Ahmad Ajaj, on all 38 counts against them. On May 24, 1994, each defendant received a 240-year sentence.

But there was still unfinished business: Ramzi Yousef was still out there.

CHAPTER 8

THE HUNT FOR RAMZI YOUSEF

T he bomb on Philippines Airlines Flight 434 was so small and ingeniously designed that airport security didn't have a chance to detect it. On December 11, 1994, Ramzi Yousef, traveling with an Italian passport that identified him as Armaldo Forlani—he told travel agents he was a Roman senator—passed through the X-ray machines at Manila Airport carrying liquid nitroglycerin in a contact-lens case and a nine-volt battery, perhaps in the heels of each of his shoes. Once on the plane, he'd assembled the device in the bathroom, using a Casio watch as a timer, then concealed it in the pouch of the life-jacket vest under his seat just moments before landing at Cebu's Mactan Airport. The bomb was so powerful that when it exploded two hours later on the flight's next leg to Tokyo, it ripped through the aileron cables that controlled the plane's wing flaps and gutted Hiruki Ikegami, a 24-year-old Japanese engineer who'd taken Yousef's seat in Cebu. Conscious for just a moment after the blast, Ikegami raised his index finger—a plea signaling "Wait" or "Help"—then slumped over and died.

Ikegami's final gesture was not lost on Neil Herman. For the past 21 months, he and his men had been locked in a race against time, tracking Yousef around the world, trying to capture him before he acted again. As soon as Herman heard about the explosive device used on Flight 434 and the flight's port of origin, he instinctively felt that Yousef was involved. Even more troubling to Herman was his suspicion that this had only been a test, a prelude to the real thing. Though the bomb had nearly downed a plane with 272 passengers and 20 crew members aboard—only the pilot's skill and cool head averted a greater tragedy—Herman was certain that Yousef was planning a more powerful device, something catastrophic.

Herman couldn't understand why it was taking so damned long for the U.S. authorities to corral Yousef. Within weeks of the World Trade Center blast, Herman had understood Yousef's role as ringleader of the conspiracy, and had quickly gained an appreciation for the bomb maker's technical skills. He had then launched an urgent manhunt to locate and arrest him, assigning six full-time investigators to the task. He got the Bureau to place Yousef on its Most Wanted List and to post a $2 million reward for information leading to his capture, which the State Department then had printed on matchbooks and distributed throughout Pakistan and Central Asia. Finally, he reached out to the CIA and the FBI's own system of legal attachés or "legats," agents posted to embassies around the world to investigate crimes against U.S. citizens abroad. But Yousef not only remained at large, he also stayed active, recruiting cells, planning and executing operations, and moving around the globe with seeming ease.

The search had begun slowly. The task force had started without any background information on Yousef. They didn't even know his real name—his confederates knew him only as Rashid—much less where he'd gone after leaving the U.S. However, a few days into the TRADEBOM investigation, Herman's men learned from an informant that several weeks before the Trade Center bombing Yousef had obtained a new passport from the Pakistani consulate in New York, claiming his original had been lost or stolen. It was a terrorist's trick, Yousef's way of expunging the record of his past travels. But in this case, the gambit almost backfired. JTTF investigators got hold of Yousef's application form from the consulate and tracked him to Karachi through a computer program that contained the passenger manifests from all the flights leaving the U.S. around the date of the World Trade Center explosion. A search of Yousef's telephone records indicated that he had family in Quetta, a Pakistani town in the mountainous Afghan border region. But once he decamped in Karachi, his trail went cold.

Herman later learned Yousef had gone to Islamabad, where he'd resumed his terrorist activities. After news of his role in the World Trade Center bombing spread, Yousef's reputation soared, and he had no trouble raising money for his next project: a plot to assassinate Benazir Bhutto, then a candidate for Pakistani prime minister. He joined with an old friend, Abdul Hakim Murad, in two abortive attempts against Bhutto. (In one, he was hospitalized after he nearly blew off his face assembling a bomb he was planning to plant in front of her residence.)

According to some reports, Yousef's next stop was Bangkok, where he was thought to have headed up a plot to bomb the Israeli embassy. On March 11, 1994, the theory goes, Yousef, together with a cell of young militants he'd recruited from the city's thriving Muslim community, hired a small truck, strangled the driver and stuffed his body in the back of the truck along with a powerful bomb that he'd assembled. Only a road accident on the way to the embassy—the replacement driver panicked and fled—prevented a disaster.

Back in Pakistan a few months later, Yousef reportedly mounted another attack, this one against the Imam Reza Shrine, Iran's holiest Shiite site. Crossing the border on June 20 with a small band of commandos that included members of his family, he is said to have placed a bomb in the women's section of the mausoleum, killing 26 and maiming hundreds more.

• • •

As reports of Yousef's supposed whereabouts came in, Herman was becoming increasingly frustrated. By mid-1994, Yousef was the World's Most Wanted terrorist, the bin Laden of his day, and foreign police, bounty hunters and ordinary civilians were quick to connect him to any suspicious action. There were Yousef sightings all across Asia, many of them conflicting, none of them timely. Investigators now feel that Yousef hadn't even been in Bangkok the previous spring, much less been the leader of the plot to bomb the Israeli embassy. Nevertheless, they had to track down every lead.

More troubling to Herman was the government's apparent inability to conduct an investigation on the global scale necessary to catch a fugitive as cunning and well-connected as Yousef. The CIA was of no help whatsoever, apparently with few, if any, contacts in Yousef's surprisingly wide orbit. Ditto the National Security Agency (NSA) and other intelligence services. And the FBI's corps of foreign agents seemed woefully understaffed to Herman. With just a handful of legats in the main capitals, and hundreds of leads pouring in each week, there simply weren't enough agents to follow through on them all. "I didn't blame those guys," Herman says. "Often you'd have one legat covering 20 countries. In Rome, there were four agents for 38 countries, including all of Africa, which included trouble spots like Egypt. The legat for Pakistan was stationed in Bangkok, a seven-hour plane trip away. And you couldn't just walk into these places and do what you wanted. Each one had their own laws and protocols, not to mention language, politics and culture."

Even when Herman was able to contact a legat, there was no guarantee he would be able to do what Herman was asking. Stationed in places like London and Paris, a lot of them seemed to be still fighting the Cold War, mingling at cocktail parties with diplomats or other law enforcement types on the "wine-and-cheese" circuit, as one of Herman's colleagues put it. "You'd think once they're there, they'd be able to handle things," Herman says. "But the reality was, they couldn't. Even when they were able to check something out, it would often take them three or four months to get back to you."

Herman himself was working 16-hour days, rarely catching more than a few hours of sleep in his office. He'd just wrapped up the first World Trade Center trial and was still managing a full roster of cases, including the Ted Kaczynski Unabomber investigation. But Yousef was a ticking bomb and the Bureau's deliberate procedures ate at him. Early on, Herman had sent a Teletype through headquarters to all the Bureau's foreign offices expressing the urgency he felt. The cable stressed that the leads in the Yousef investigation were of the highest priority and had to be immediately addressed, or acts of terrorism could and would continue to happen. But far from yielding results, it caused Herman even more headaches. "I received a lot of criticism for that," Herman recalls. "I was thought to be bashing policy and I caught a lot of shit. My supervisor called me into his office and instructed me to write another cable saying that I wasn't speaking for the New York Office."

Meanwhile, Yousef was continuing his rampage. He spent part of the summer of 1994 off the coast of Malaysia on the island of Basilan giving sophisticated explosives instruction to members of Abu Sayyaf, a brutal, bin Laden-backed guerilla army intent on carving an Islamic state out of the southern Philippines. Then in the fall, he was in Manila, where he was joined by Khalid Shaikh Mohammed, Yousef's uncle from Qatar. Short and heavyset, with a trim beard that he sometimes let grow as a disguise, Mohammed was the physical opposite of his gangly, clean-shaven nephew. But in other respects, the two men were kindred spirits: westernized, sociable and brash. Mohammed had first caught the FBI's notice as a donor who wired about $600 into WTC plotter Mohammed Salameh's account a few months before the bombing. Now he was bringing money and support, perhaps from al Qaeda, for Yousef's boldest plan to date.

Yousef's main project was the so-called Bojinka plot. Serbo-Croat for "big explosion," Bojinka was a complex, breathtakingly lethal operation intended to blow up as many as twelve intercontinental flights at roughly the same time. The linchpin of the plan was Yousef's design for a micro-bomb—like the one he would plant on the Manila-to-Tokyo plane—small enough to evade airport security, yet this time powerful enough to bring down a large jetliner. Yousef first tested the device in November 1994 in a generator room underneath a shopping mall in the Philippines. The explosion sparked a small fire and little damage. Then, on December 1, Yousef, along with a bin Laden operative named Wali Khan Amin Shah, planted one of the tiny bombs in a Manila movie theater. It went off under a vacant seat, causing only minor injuries. The last test took place on Flight 434 and claimed the life of Hiruki Ikegami.

In the midst of these activities, Yousef was toying with at least two other plans, either of which would have shaken the world. Earlier in the fall it was known that President Clinton would visit the Philippines on November 12, and Wali Khan had devised several assassination strategies. Ultimately, they were abandoned because of the extremely tight security surrounding the president. Instead, Yousef began working on a plot to kill the Pope, who was planning to visit the Philippines in mid-January and would provide a softer target.

How close Yousef might have come to achieving his objective no one knows for sure, but what is certain is that Yousef was quite serious. On December 8, using the alias of Naji Owaida Haddad, he signed a one-month lease for an apartment overlooking a route that the Pope was expected to travel. He bought priest's vestments to enable himself or, more likely, an emissary, to get close enough to the Pope to effect a suicide bombing. He may even have enlisted the help of his old friend and fellow Benazir Bhutto plotter, Abdul Hakim Murad, to stage an aerial attack on the Popemobile. Murad, who arrived in Manila in December, was an experienced pilot. Yousef reportedly tried to charter a small plane, scrapping the plan only when he learned that the airspace over Manila would be cordoned off—a routine precaution—during the Pope's stay.

According to Murad, Yousef hatched two other plots involving planes. One called for Murad to fly a small plane loaded with explosives or just a full tank of fuel into CIA headquarters at Langley. A second version had Murad hijacking a large commercial jet and crashing it into a Washington landmark.

All of Yousef's plans became academic, however, on January 6, when he and Murad accidentally started a small chemical fire in their apartment while mixing the ingredients for a bomb. They managed to extinguish the fire and escape before police and firefighters were called in, but they left behind a trove of incriminating evidence. After the firefighters departed, Yousef persuaded Murad to go back to the apartment to retrieve the incriminating laptop. But the police—on high alert with the Pope about to visit—had also come back and were searching the apartment when Murad returned.

After arresting Murad, the police found pipe bombs, bomb-making manuals and chemicals, a photo of John Paul II, a priest's robes, a map of the Pope's route through the city, the aborted plans for a phosgene gas attack on Clinton and, of course, Yousef's computer. A cursory examination of the laptop's files spelled out the chilling dimensions of the Bojinka plot, now worked out in scrupulous detail and scheduled for January 21, just two weeks from the date of the fire.

Upon his arrest Murad insisted that he was Ramzi Yousef, perhaps better to cover his friend's escape. The police knew better. Their search had turned up documents identifying Yousef and his accomplices. With a flourish of gallows humor, Yousef had activated one of his ID cards on February 26, 1993, the date of the World Trade Center bombing.

As soon as he got news of the raid, Herman dispatched a team to Manila, where they bumped up against the CIA. A scrimmage over control of the investigation ensued, and Herman, who had asked the Agency for help in finding Yousef earlier in the case, now found himself trying to get them out of his agents' way.

The issues were fairly mundane, but illustrate the agencies' different, often conflicting, approaches to investigations, sometimes characterized as string them up versus string them along. Both agencies' priorities were to capture Yousef as quickly as possible, but Herman's agents had also come to Manila to collect evidence and build criminal cases against him and his accomplices, while the CIA was there chiefly to extract intelligence about Yousef's contacts and activities. The last thing the Agency wanted to do was to get involved in a big, splashy trial in which its officers might have to testify in open court and reveal information about their identities and procedures. But Yousef had already been indicted in New York on the World Trade Center bombing charges and any new evidence turned up in Manila was, ipso facto, part of a criminal investigation. That meant there were chain-of-custody concerns: whoever handled the evidence or debriefed the suspects was going to become a witness, subject to examination. "I kept telling [the CIA], 'If you keep getting involved, you're going to be involved,'" Herman says.

Within a year, the agencies would begin working together. Lacking an enforcement hammer, CIA officers would come to rely on their FBI colleagues to make cases against terrorists they'd tracked down. And JTTF investigators would soon be traveling to Langley, where they were allowed access to the Agency's voluminous terrorist database. But through 1995, relations between the agencies were marred by rivalry and mistrust. The CIA felt the Bureau's doggedly legalistic approach to cases was getting in the way of their intelligence gathering, and worse, the Bureau was withholding vital information under cover of grand jury secrecy. Meanwhile, Herman didn't want the Agency messing about with his witnesses and getting in his investigators' way. But his real objection to working with the CIA had nothing to do with procedure. He just didn't think the Agency was going to be of any help in finding Ramzi Yousef. "Back then, I don't think the CIA could have found a person in a bathroom," Herman says. "Hell, I don't think they could have found the bathroom."

Herman called Gil Childers, the lead prosecutor in the Ramzi Yousef case, to discuss what to do. Childers was also wary of the Agency. Six months earlier, he'd gone to Langley at the CIA's behest with colleagues from the U.S. Attorney's Office in New York's Southern District. The first World Trade Center bombing trial had just ended and Childers, who'd grown up with the Hollywood myth of an all-knowing CIA, thought that the Agency was going to provide him with background and leads on Yousef to facilitate his office's search for the fugitive.

At the meeting, however, Childers got questions, not answers. "They started out asking us, 'What can we do to prevent this kind of thing [the World Trade Center attack] from happening again?'" Childers recalls. "I remember thinking, 'My God, that's what *you're* supposed to be telling us.'"

Things did not improve. "We talked in generalities for about an hour or so, but it was clear to me that they didn't have a clue," Childers says. "Afterwards, when we got outside the building, [my colleagues and I] just looked at each and shook our heads. It was obvious if we had to rely on these guys to find Yousef, we were in trouble."

Herman had a similar experience when he visited the Agency a few months later. "They brought me into one of their secure rooms. I think they called it the Bubble," Herman recalls. "Well, no wonder it was secure. They didn't have any information."

In the end, Herman and Childers decided they were better off without the CIA's help and Childers persuaded the Agency to back off from the investigation. "It just wasn't worth the hassle," Herman says.

Childers and Herman were not alone in their disenchantment with the Agency. Through the late 1980s and 1990s, a growing number of dissident officers—some with outstanding reputations—left the CIA and, unlike previous generations of alumni, spoke out publicly against the Agency. Their criticism focused on a wide range of issues—from a perceived lack of imaginative leadership to creeping bureaucracy and low morale within the ranks. But their greatest concerns were reserved for the CIA's once-vaunted Directorate of Operations (DO), the division responsible for collecting intelligence and planning covert operations. In the view of the dissidents, mounting government regulation and an internal culture of careerism and risk-aversion had shackled a field officer's ability to develop agents—Agency-speak for paid informants—or even interact with the populations they were supposed to monitor.

How these factors played out in the hunt for Ramzi Yousef may never be known. But it was clear to Childers and Herman that the CIA had few, if any, reliable on-ground sources in the regions and milieus where Yousef operated. "They'd send us information, but I'd say at least 99 percent of it turned out not to be credible," Herman recalls. "Either it was dated or just plain wrong, and they'd never tell you where it came from, so you'd have to spend time and resources checking each lead out. In the end, Gil and I decided we were better off without them."

The reasons for the Agency's human intelligence meltdown were mainly twofold. The first stems from the CIA's Cold War mindset and dates back to its founding mission. Set in 1947, it instructed the newly formed agency to raise the nation's intelligence quotient so that it would never again be vulnerable to a surprise attack like Pearl Harbor. Since it perceived the Soviet Union to be the only country capable of carrying out such an attack, the Agency concentrated all of its efforts on the Russians. "The Third World was just a theater in the Agency's eyes, a stage on which to play out their conflict with the Russians," says Vince Cannistraro, a former top-ranking CIA official. "In 1979, Afghanistan was an officially neutral, landlocked Asian nation without any significance to our vital interests. The CIA didn't give it much strategic importance before the Soviets invaded; and once they'd departed, I think they gave it even less."

The second reason dates to the mid-1970s, a period of national introspection in the wake of Vietnam and Watergate. With many U.S. institutions under review, Congress held a series of hearings on alleged CIA abuses. The results were more damaging to the Agency than even its critics had anticipated. Witnesses recounted a string of follies and excesses ranging from Agency-backed assassination attempts involving poison cigars and Mafia hitmen to the overthrow of democratically elected governments in Chile and Guatemala. Outraged legislators censured the Agency and enacted guidelines restricting its covert operations. Most important, then-president Gerald Ford issued an executive directive outlawing politically motivated murder.

In addition, the CIA was changing via attrition. Many of its old hands were retiring. They'd served in the OSS, the CIA's forebear, during WW II, and inculcated the Agency with its wartime ethos, its vital sense of mission, and its impulse to action. And they'd recruited the nation's best and brightest, culling the campuses of the Ivy League and other top schools, to carry on those traditions as a duty, if not a birthright.

Now all but a handful had left, along with many of their progeny, replaced by a new generation of officers who'd come of age in Washington's careerist peacetime bureaucracy. Perhaps it was inevitable that the Agency's culture would become more corporate and risk aversive, but the congressional hearings accelerated the process, triggering more than 800 resignations from the Directorate of Operations, gutting the Agency's elite field division. Morale plummeted.

In 1980, Ronald Reagan appointed William Casey, an OSS veteran and Cold War warrior who'd made millions on Wall Street, to run the Agency, and he succeeded in reinstating the CIA's budget and at least some of its former swagger. But the Agency never recovered the élan that had characterized it in its salad days, before the Bay of Pigs and the 1960s campus antiwar movement.

In 1979, with the fall of Iran, the CIA's reputation bottomed out. Once again, its officers had been focused on Russia, peering so avidly into the Soviet mists across Iran's northern borders that they'd missed entirely what any child on the streets of Qom or Tehran could have pointed out to them: A religious fervor had gripped the populace and threatened the stability of Iran's secular government. In fact, the Agency took pains to stay out of Iran's internal affairs for fear of upsetting the shah.

Of course, even if the CIA had been paying attention, it's hard to say what it might have done to avert the coming tidal changes. Even Ayatollah Khomeini's close advisors were surprised at how easily the shah's government toppled. Nevertheless, the Agency's intelligence was shockingly poor: In August 1978, just months before Khomeini's triumphant return, the CIA was reporting, "Iran is not in a revolutionary or even a pre-revolutionary situation."

More troubling, the Agency failed to adapt to the lessons it should have learned from Iran. It continued to overlook, or at least underestimate, the breadth and power of the fundamentalist Islamic reform movement sweeping through the Middle East. And it failed to upgrade the competence and suitability of the agents it sent into the area. Bob Baer, arguably the most effective case officer in the Near East Division during the 1980s, recalls that there were relatively few Arabic-speaking field officers in the region at the time.

What's more, the Agency had plenty of warning of the fundamentalist threat. In 1983–84, agents of Hezbollah, the Iranian-backed terror organization based in Southern Lebanon, drove truck-bombs into the U.S. embassy in Beirut, killing 63, including six CIA officers; and into a Marine barracks outside Beirut, killing 242. Throughout the 1980s, the group kidnapped numerous Americans and Westerners, including the CIA station chief in Beirut, James Buckley, whom they tortured and beat to death over the course of a year. They also launched international operations, the hijacking of the *Achille Lauro* among them.

In 1986, the Agency did try to respond to the growing threat by founding the Counter-Terrorism Center (CTC), a 100-man section aimed at breaking down bureaucratic walls inside and outside the Agency. The CTC was the idea of its first director, Dewey Clarridge, a legendary field officer frustrated by the government's reactive posture in dealing with terrorists. His new strategy was to hunt down terrorists before they struck, and to help achieve that goal, Clarridge recruited 25 of the Agency's most aggressive field officers, Baer included. For Baer, the first year at CTC was the high point of his career with the CIA—the only time he felt he had total access to the Agency's intelligence base, as well as a clear, no-holds-barred mission. Within two years, however, the mission had already begun to bog down in turf battles and the culture of risk-aversion that made station chiefs reluctant to authorize any operation that wasn't a slam dunk. Clarridge left in frustration.

•   •   •

On the day after Christmas 1979, barely a month after Khomeini's followers deposed the shah, the Soviets marched into Afghanistan, once again catching the Agency off guard. President Carter ordered the CIA to provide covert aid to the Afghan resistance over the objections of some of the Agency's top officers. CIA officials reasoned that despite the opportunity to help mire the Russians in a Vietnam-style guerilla war, their support of the rebels, if discovered, could escalate the conflict and expose the Agency to another round of criticism.

Against that background, the CIA arranged for the purchase of Soviet-bloc weapons, mainly from Czechoslovakia, and had them funneled to the mujahideen through neighboring Pakistan's Inter-Services Intelligence Agency (ISI). The plan had the virtue of deniability, but some top officials felt it also made the Agency too dependent on the Pakistanis, who had their own agenda. With a large population of Islamic fundamentalists, Pakistan, these officials say, favored the most extreme, anti-Western warlords, thereby arming America's enemies to the tune of billions of dollars and slighting their potential allies. "Of course, the Pakistanis denied any favoritism," recalls Vince Cannistraro, who visited the area on numerous occasions. "The Pakis were always giving chalkboard presentations meant to show that they were distributing weapons on the basis of efficiency. It was just a pack of lies, but we didn't have enough intelligence on the ground to dispute them. In effect, we'd become clients of Pakistan's foreign policy."

Milt Bearden, the officer who ran the Pakistan station and oversaw the war effort, disputes Cannistraro's claim. Pakistan's help was necessary in some instances, Bearden says, but he was personally in contact with the key Afghan commanders and made sure that each one got his due. Moreover, Bearden says, the Agency had a network of in-country agents—CIA-speak for paid informants—who kept it abreast of the war's progress.

If so—and there seems no dispute that the Agency had at least some agents inside Afghanistan—it makes what happened next seem even more inexplicable. In 1989, when the defeated Soviet forces withdrew from Afghanistan, America abruptly cut off aid to the mujahideen and made no effort to help rebuild the war-torn nation.

The issues were not black-and-white. Some government officials justified U.S. withdrawal under a theory of "negative symmetry"—a fancy way of saying to the Russians, "You step down and we'll step down." What's more, civil strife continued in Afghanistan for another five years after the Americans packed up and before the Taliban took command. No relief organization, Bearden points out, was going to fight their way into the country in order to administer aid. Finally, a series of cataclysmic events were taking place in other parts of the world, from the fall of the Berlin Wall to the collapse of the Soviet Empire.

But nothing explains or justifies the speed and completeness with which the U.S. extricated itself from Afghanistan. Not only did the Agency pull its support of the mujahideen, it also severed its ties to the network of agents it had developed throughout the nation, a loss that would cost the U.S. dearly.

At the time, however, there was little second-guessing. Just the opposite: The CIA, which hadn't particularly wanted to get into the war in the first place, now celebrated a victory over the Russians that many in government viewed as leading to the end of the Cold War. It also seemed to reinforce the notion among CIA administrators that it was possible to achieve difficult objectives without the risks and hard work of direct, hands-on intelligence, but with technology and the assistance of "friendly" third-party agencies.

After the Soviet Empire collapsed, field office staffs around the world were slashed and became increasingly reliant on foreign police and intelligence agencies for information. Without the need to expend its resources on Russia, the CIA was awash with money and personnel, and so it set out to redefine its mission. For a while, it focused on the "war on drugs" and expanded its investigations into state-sponsored terrorism. But it never recovered the clarity of mission its officers had known during the Cold War years. "We'd been trained to believe there was no action too extreme, no expenditure so large that it wasn't justified by the recruitment of a Soviet diplomat or military officer," says Bob Baer. "What drug informant could alter the balance of power among nations? What political terrorist threatened the world with nuclear annihilation?"

Baer recalls trying to recruit a Russian colonel on an early assignment. "I got him drunk one night, let him drive my car and crash through the gates of the embassy," Baer remembers. "Nobody said a word. My station chief never said a word. And if he'd tried to stand in my way, he'd have gotten himself into trouble."

Serving under the same station chief 12 years later, this time in Ankara, Baer asked permission for what he thought was a routine surveillance mission in northern Iraq to observe the fighting between the Kurds and Iraqi regular army forces, but things had changed and the station chief ordered him not to cross the border. "He wanted me to monitor the war from Ankara," recalls Baer, who ultimately finessed his instructions. "If he'd had his way, I'd have spent my days in the local Sheraton eating peanuts, watching CNN and reading two-day-old newspaper reports from Reuters."

Some of the changes within the Agency were shaped by changes within the larger political culture. Clinton focused on the economy and domestic issues in contrast to his two predecessors. James Woolsey, Clinton's first-appointed CIA director, resigned after two years in large measure, he says, because he couldn't get a private audience with the president. Shortly after his departure, when a small plane crashed into the White House, West Wing staffers joked that it was Woolsey, still trying to get in to see the president. "When I first heard that, I wasn't very happy," Woolsey recalls. "But now I suppose it's a fairly accurate representation of the way things were."

In fairness, Clinton was a voracious reader who devoured briefing papers and often sent them back annotated with questions and comments. But the absence of face-to-face meetings surely limited his dialogue with the CIA. More important, since Agency directors are esteemed in proportion to their access, he undermined Woolsey and sent a clear signal to Langley that the Agency's activities were not a priority.

Also in the mid-1990s, two events rocked the Agency and called into question its competence and ethics. In 1994, Aldrich Ames, a mid-level case officer in the Russian Division, was discovered to have been operating as a mole for nine years, during which time he may have been responsible for the deaths of dozens of CIA agents. How, critics asked, could someone like Ames, a heavy drinker who lived well beyond his means, have gone undetected for so long? Indeed, how could he have been promoted into such a sensitive position in the first place?

Then, in 1995, Congress learned that the CIA had on their payroll as an informant a Guatemalan army officer who may have been involved in the murder of another Guatemalan married to an American woman. The case, which was championed by U.S. Senator Robert Torricelli of New Jersey, triggered congressional hearings, and once again, the Agency found itself the target of unwelcome publicity and criticism.

What the probers uncovered was what every law enforcement officer already knows: You have to get into bed with bad people in order to get even worse ones. Local cops depend on a network of petty thieves and dope peddlers to know what's going on in the criminal worlds that exist in every precinct. Federal prosecutors made a deal with Sammy "the Bull" Gravano so they could take down John Gotti. Why, Agency officers ask, expect the CIA in pursuit of national security to adhere to a higher standard?

Nevertheless, new rules that required case officers to vet shady informants through a series of special committees were imposed on the Agency, causing many officers to just stop trying, either cutting loose potentially embarrassing agents or not bothering to recruit new ones.

Worse, according to dissident officers who resigned from the Agency in the mid-1990s, the scandal ushered in an era of introspection and re-engineering during which the leadership hunkered down, the bureaucrats and paper-pushers held sway, and the Directorate of Operations felt rudderless. In fact, the entire Agency underwent a series of civil-service-type reforms in this period that emphasized political correctness and career tracking.

In 1992, for example, Baer was made station chief of Tajikistan, a posting he'd requested. Sandwiched between the former Soviet Union and Afghanistan, Tajikistan offered an opportunity for action. But nearly every initiative Baer proposed was rejected by his overseers at Langley. They did, however, offer to send a four-person sexual harassment team to lecture Baer's office on etiquette. Baer sent a cable back to Langley declining. Neither he nor the other male officer at the station—the only CIA personnel in Tajikistan—felt it was a priority.

But the new regulations, while onerous, were not in themselves prohibitive, the dissident officers point out. It was their tone, the spirit behind them. "Nobody actually said you can't do recruitments," recalls Bob Baer. "What they said was, 'If you recruit someone and he goes out and does something—you know, whacks someone—you're responsible. Your career's over.' So of course no one did anything."

Baer himself, then engaged in coordinating Iraqi opposition forces, was called back to Washington and investigated for plotting the assassination of Saddam Hussein. "Probably not a bad idea," Baer muses. "But totally untrue." In fact, Baer was cleared of the charges and awarded a career intelligence medal instead. But even Baer had finally had enough. He resigned his commission in 1997, reducing the number of Arabic speakers in the Agency's Mideast field division by a sizeable fraction.

The long, slow decline of the DO was coming to a head. It had not been a straight line, but the twin preferences that had determined its course—the preference for technical collection over human collection of intelligence, and analysis over action—was now unmistakable and perhaps best articulated by a sign that hung for years over a case officer's desk in the Agency's Rome station. It read: BIG OPS, BIG PROBLEMS. SMALL OPS, SMALL PROBLEMS. NO OPS, NO PROBLEMS.

Ramzi Yousef's career as a terrorist ended with a whimper, not a bang. On January 11, 1995, five days after the fire in Yousef's Manila apartment and the arrest of Ahmed Hakim Murad, Philippine police apprehended their accomplice, Wali Khan Amin-Shah. (Amin-Shah, who was carrying passports from four different countries at the time of his arrest, bribed his way out of custody, but was rearrested in Malaysia and extradited to the U.S.) Now without his two closest associates, Yousef, who had gone back to Pakistan the morning after the fire, was forced to rely on new recruits, one of whom proved to be his undoing.

On January 23, 1995, Yousef summoned Istiaque Parker to the Pearl Guest House, a bin Laden hotel in Islamabad, and outlined his latest scheme: a plot to kidnap the Philippine ambassador and ransom him for Hakim Murad's freedom. Parker, who'd already backed out of an earlier Yousef plan to plant bombs on two transcontinental flights between Bangkok and London, was both appalled and afraid for his life. On February 3, he contacted the U.S. embassy with information on Yousef's whereabouts, and on the morning of February 7, a pick-up squad of American officials and Pakistani police surrounded Yousef at the Su Casa Guest House on the outskirts of Islamabad and arrested him.

On the flight to the U.S., Yousef couldn't help boasting to agents about his exploits, even drawing a diagram of where he placed the bomb underneath the South Tower in the garage. He'd hoped, he told the agents, that it would topple "like a tree" into its twin, resulting, he'd calculated, in 125,000 deaths.

The flight landed at Stewart Air National Guard Base in Newburgh, New York, and the detail continued on to FBI headquarters in Lower Manhattan by helicopter. As they flew over Battery Park City, at the southern end of the island, Special Agent Chuck Stern lifted the hood they'd placed over Yousef's head for the final leg of their journey and pointed at the downtown skyline. It was past midnight, but the buildings below shone in the darkness, none brighter or more imposing than the towers of the World Trade Center. "They're still standing," Stern said.

Yousef's expression caught between a smile and a grimace. "They wouldn't be," he said, "if I'd gotten a little more money."

CHAPTER 9

DISCOVERING BIN LADEN

If the World Trade Center bombing had been a wake-up call for Neil Herman, revelations about the Bojinka plot and Ramzi Yousef's other terrorist activities were more like a siren blast. Herman had known there'd been something out there, but whatever that something was, it had been large and amorphous. He still couldn't put a face on it, couldn't locate it on a map. But now he knew for certain it was targeting U.S. interests—hell, it was targeting U.S. cities—and he knew when it next struck, it would make the World Trade Center blast look like a walk in the park.

Herman was not an alarmist; his pulse rate, colleagues say, lowered in a crisis. Nor did he see conspiracies behind every crime; rather, he often debunked them. He considered himself a criminal investigator, a skeptic who built cases on a bedrock of facts, by the slow accretion of physical evidence, circumstance and witness testimony.

But the clues had been there from the beginning, gathering in the margins of the TRADEBOM and TERRSTOP investigations: the manifestos and Special Forces documents in Nosair's files; the $20,000 el-Gabrowny had solicited from bin Laden in Saudi Arabia for Nosair's defense fund; the payments bin Laden made to underwrite Abdel-Rahman's expenses; the letters Nidal Ayyad had sent to the *New York Times* and other newspapers in the wake of the World Trade Center blast claiming responsibility and warning there was an army of cells ready to strike at America; the links to Afghanistan; the many phone calls made to the same number at an al Qaeda Services Office in Peshawar, Pakistan, and much more.

Those clues and others snapped into focus once Herman got hold of the files taken off the laptop from Yousef's Manila apartment. From them, he learned about the Bojinka plot, as well as about Yousef's sundry other projects. "The real eye-opener for me, the thing that brought it all together," Herman says, "was the ease with which Yousef was traveling around the world. I mean, he wasn't hiding in a cave in Afghanistan or in some hut in Somalia. He was getting on airplanes in European and Asian capitals, flying first class, recruiting more terrorists, and we never could get ahead of him. That's when I realized he had to have a sizeable organization behind him."

U.S. Attorney Gil Childers was also troubled by Yousef's travel patterns. No matter how far afield Yousef went—Malaysia, Hong Kong, Thailand, the Philippines—he always returned to Pakistan, and from there, Childers could only speculate, to Afghanistan. Childers didn't know what Yousef was doing in that part of the world. But he was aware of the many links between the World Trade Center conspirators and the same region, and he felt there must be some sort of organizational infrastructure there. "We didn't think Yousef kept going back because he was homesick," he says.

Other evidence emerging from the Philippines increased Childers's suspicions, suggesting a possible link to the scion of one of Saudi Arabia's wealthiest families. Osama bin Laden was best known to U.S. intelligence, to the extent he was known at all, as a former fund-raiser for the Afghan war. Milt Bearden, the CIA station chief in Pakistan during those war years, recalls him as having been a peripheral figure in Peshawar, a kind of mujahideen-wanna-be floating around the edges of the big power players. U.S. law enforcement knew he'd made a token donation to Nosair's defense fund and was rumored to be underwriting Sheik Abdel-Rahman's living expenses in America. Now, however, as Yousef's activities and associations became better known, bin Laden's name was popping up with increasing frequency.

Investigators had heard reports, for example, that Yousef had spent part of the summer of 1994 as an explosives trainer in guerilla camps on Basilan, the island stronghold of Abu Sayyaf. Abdul Rajak Janjalani, the head of Abu Sayyaf, had fought with the Afghan rebels and spent the early 1990s in Peshawar raising money for Abu Sayyaf. It's not known whether he met with Osama bin Laden there, though it's likely. What is known is that he developed close ties with bin Laden's old schoolmate and fellow freedom fighter, Mohammed Khalifa.

A trusted bin Laden aide, Khalifa was married to bin Laden's sister and acted as an agent for bin Laden's many Islamic "philanthropies." Childers likens his role to that of Michael Anthony in *The Millionaire*. "He'd go to terrorists and say, 'My employer likes what you're doing and wants to present you with a check . . .'"

Khalifa began traveling to the Philippines in the late 1980s as an officer of the International Islamic Relief Organization (IIRO), a benevolent or non-governmental organization (NGO). Bin Laden had begun using NGOs like the IIRO or the Refugee Services Center in Brooklyn as fronts for his subversive activities in cities around the world. In addition to their good works, NGOs provided bin Laden's operatives with legitimate employment, identity papers and the infrastructure for moving money and equipment. Khalifa, for example, founded two more NGOs and used them to set up a terrorist training school and to funnel funds into Abu Sayyaf.

The web of connections tying bin Laden to Yousef became more apparent when investigators learned more about Wali Khan Amin-Shah, Yousef's accomplice in the Bojinka plot. Wali Khan had fought alongside bin Laden in Afghanistan and was thought to have pledged bayat—a loyalty oath—to him. Wali Khan was also associated with Khalifa in the Philippines and had served as a trainer for Abu Sayyaf.

Still another bin Laden–Yousef link was Ibrahim Munir. Like Wali Khan, Munir's brother had also fought with bin Laden, but was killed in Jalalabad; bin Laden is said to have become Ibrahim's mentor. Ibrahim arrived in Manila in November, about two months after Yousef had begun planning Bojinka and, according to witnesses, became Yousef's constant companion.

Yousef may have had even more direct links to bin Laden. His uncle, Khalid Shaikh Mohammed, whose name has surfaced prominently in connection to the September 11 attacks, would eventually become one of bin Laden's top financial aides. Mohammed, who was with Yousef in the Philippines in September 1994, is thought to have already had close ties to Mamdou Salim, bin Laden's spiritual advisor. Investigators think that Salim visited Mohammed and his nephew in Manila, perhaps to issue a fatwa to Yousef's Bojinka plot.

But bin Laden was slow to emerge as a full-blown villain. For one thing, he started out as someone whose background and wealth made him easy to dismiss as a dilettante or "Gucci terrorist." Yousef, by contrast, was a larger-than-life figure in the mode of Carlos the Jackal, a dangerous and unpredictable free agent whose stature among counterterrorists easily overshadowed bin Laden's. In their view, a view that has yet to be disproved, bin Laden running Yousef would have been the tail wagging the dog.

Moreover, bin Laden's connections to Yousef and other terrorists and terror groups were largely circumstantial, buried in a complex, poorly understood network of operatives, fundamentalist leaders and wealthy Arab donors. Though bin Laden's significance may seem obvious in hindsight, it was anything but at the time. U.S. investigators needed an informant on the inside who could explain to them what all the associations they were learning about meant.

They had an opportunity to get that inside view in December 1994, when INS officials detained Mohammed Khalifa in San Francisco for traveling under a false visa. The Justice Department wanted to charge Khalifa with fraud and question him about his activities in the Philippines. But INS and the State Department had already agreed to extradite Khalifa to Jordan, where he'd been convicted and sentenced to death in absentia for financing terrorist bombings. With a death sentence hanging over his head, Khalifa may well have cooperated with authorities had he remained in the U.S. But the government handed him over to Jordan, where Khalifa's sentence was eventually overturned and he was set free.

The government did get a peek into bin Laden's affairs through a series of interviews with Ali Mohamed, a soldier-adventurer with known ties to El-Sayyid Nosair and Sheik Abdel-Rahman. With the TERRSTOP case about to go trial, prosecutors subpoenaed Mohamed to see if he could add to their knowledge of the defendants.

Tall, square-jawed and powerfully built, Mohamed was one of the most intriguing figures in the saga leading up to September 11. He embodied the passions and contradictions, the discipline and duplicity that seemed to mesmerize and ultimately frustrate U.S. law enforcement in their long battle against Islamic terrorists. At different stages in his colorful career, Mohamed had worked, or seemed to have worked, for the Egyptian Army, the Egyptian Islamic Jihad, the CIA, the FBI, the U.S. Army Special Forces, the al-Kifah Refugee Services Office, the Afghan mujahideen and Osama bin Laden. Of course, investigators didn't know all this when he arrived in New York for questioning in December 1994. But he was by no means a stranger.

He was born in 1952 in a town near Alexandria. The son of a professional soldier, Mohamed grew up a devout Muslim, attended the Military Academy in Cairo and followed his father into the army. He was a skilled linguist with a degree from Alexandria University and rose quickly through the ranks of the Egyptian Special Forces, serving as an intelligence officer during Egypt's 1973 war against Israel.

During the 1970s, the fundamentalist movement was taking root in Upper Egypt and Sheik Omar Abdel-Rahman was arguably its most radical and popular proponent. Every Friday night, when his duties permitted,

Mohamed was among the crowd of Muslim youths who attended the sheik's prayer meetings. Mohamed adopted Abdel-Rahman as his spiritual mentor and became a member of Egyptian Islamic Jihad (EIJ), one of the many revolutionary groups inspired by the blind cleric's fiery preaching.

In 1981, four Egyptian Army officers from Mohamed's unit, all of them members of EIJ, ambushed President Anwar Sadat during a military parade, gunning him down along with a number of others. Mohamed, who was in the U.S. at the time attending a Special Forces training program for foreign officers at Fort Bragg, was never linked to the plot. But the Army was aware of his fundamentalist sympathies and forced him to resign his commission with the rank of major.

After his discharge in 1984, Mohamed began working as a security advisor to Egypt Airlines, a perfect job for someone who would eventually train terrorists to hijack planes. He also offered his services to the CIA. The Agency hired him on a probationary basis, but when it found out he was making unauthorized contacts with members of a Hezbollah cell in Germany, it cut him loose and placed him on a State Department watch list. But the system failed to pick up on his status quickly enough to flag his visa application, and in 1986 he was allowed to immigrate to the U.S.

Once in the U.S., Mohamed, like many of his fellow militants, married an American, a medical technician nine years older than he was, whom he'd met on the plane trip over. He moved into her house in Silicon Valley, worked briefly as a tech specialist for a computer company and was eventually granted U.S. citizenship, despite his known terrorist links.

Even more remarkably, in late 1986, Mohamed enlisted in the U.S. Army. Not only did the army apparently overlook his watch status, but they assigned him to his old posting at Fort Bragg with many of the same Special Forces troops who were likely to be deployed should the government order a covert mission against bin Laden and his organization. Mohamed served as a supply sergeant, but once on base, he was recruited by Lt. Colonel Steve Neely, an instructor at the JFK Special Operations Warfare School, to help as an assistant lecturer on Islamic culture and politics.

By all accounts, Mohamed was an exemplary soldier—cooperative, well-prepared and highly informative in the classroom. He was also a disciplined athlete who ran two miles in under ten minutes and won several commendations for fitness. His record shows he was trained as a paratrooper and took courses for an advanced degree at a nearby state university.

Mohamed was unabashedly devout. He prayed five times a day and read the Koran, which he was trying to memorize. What's more, he was frank about his views, especially his support for the assassination of Sadat. "He's very articulate, but not an ostentatious kind of individual," Neely says. "He is very modest in his dress. He was modest in the car he drove. He was not a boastful individual at all. [But] he was not shy when it came to telling people what he thought. He was not an agitator, by any stretch, but he was very, very opinionated and if he had a chance to express his opinion about something, he would do that."

Neely recalls numerous instances when Mohamed expressed his opinion, and not always discreetly. "He wanted to make sure that people understood the truth as he saw it," Neely says. "So if anybody deviated with that, like Colonel Anderson [Mohamed's commanding officer] one time took up for Anwar Sadat. Well, here you've got a lieutenant colonel and at that time, Ali was a [sergeant] and he jumped right up and objected. And told him how much he differed with that opinion."

But Neely points out that Mohamed was equally forthright in defense of his religion or a friend. "He was very loyal," Neely says. "He told me at one time that there were two things he would never do. And it stuck with me for the longest time. One was that he would never do anything where he would have to act against his government, at that time, which was the Egyptian government. And as a corollary to that, he would not do anything against the United States. He felt that he had been able to take refuge in the U.S. He had a certain loyalty to the U.S. Even though he didn't agree with them on many things, he said he would not harm the Americans. And that indicated his loyalty to me, which was reinforced time and time and time and time again over the months following my initial conversations with him."

But Mohamed's controversial views were putting him increasingly at odds with his role as a U.S. soldier. He told Neely that he wanted to help his Muslim brothers in their fight against the Soviets, and in 1987, he contacted Mustafa Shalabi, the emir of the al-Kifah Refugee Services Center in Brooklyn. Shalabi transmitted a request from the mujahideen that Mohamed train rebel troops in Afghanistan and Mohamed informed Neely that he intended to use an upcoming 30-day leave to do just that. The army had authorized Mohamed to travel overseas to Paris. Once in Paris, he explained to Neely, he would make his way to Afghanistan using false documents provided him by rebel agents.

Neely was dismayed. Apart from being a highly unusual arrangement, Mohamed's foreign service was potentially embarrassing to the U.S., in the event the Russians captured him. He tried to dissuade Mohamed from going and sent a report up the chain of command informing the army of Mohamed's imminent plans. He never heard back.

Mohamed spent the month before his departure meticulously preparing for his assignment. He made a list of the equipment he would need, wrote out a detailed lesson plan, and got himself into top physical shape. When he reported back for duty—"right on time, like the soldier he was"—he'd lost 25 pounds and looked gaunt, according to Neely. He told Neely that in addition to the training, he'd run several missions with his men and wiped out more than one Soviet patrol. This time Neely was interested from an intelligence perspective. Mohamed's engagements with the Soviet Spiznets (special forces) and his firsthand experience of the CIA-backed Afghan War, a top priority for Washington at the time, should have made him an invaluable resource. Neely duly outlined what Mohamed had told him in a report and transmitted it through the appropriate channels. Once again, though, there was no follow-up, either with Neely or Mohamed.

After he returned from Afghanistan, in the last years of his enlistment, Mohamed began traveling to Brooklyn and Jersey City on his weekends to meet with Mustafa Shalabi and his al-Kifah group and then with his old mentor, Sheik Omar Abdel-Rahman. He told Neely about his renewed association with Abdel-Rahman, but little else about his activities in the New York area. Those activities included training future jihadis, El Sayyid Nosair among them, in self-defense and paramilitary tactics in a New Jersey apartment. In fact, Mohamed stayed with Nosair in Nosair's home when he came up from Fort Bragg. (Mohamed was the source of the "secret" U.S. Special Forces documents police found in Nosair's apartment.)

After his tour was up, Mohamed remained in the army as a reservist, and returned to California. He'd told Neely that he wanted to reapply to the CIA, and Neely feels he may have enlisted in the U.S. military in the first place in order to earn the Agency's trust. (As is customary, the CIA never told Mohamed why he was let go.) But Mohamed's actions made it clear that his loyalties lay elsewhere. "We were all very interested in Ali, and he was a very gregarious kind of guy. Very outspoken fellow. Articulate," said Neely. "But we only saw one side of him. He could have been there with ulterior motives. He certainly had the background that would have trained him to operate in certain ways and certain circumstances for disguising motives that we could have never identified."

Those ulterior motives began to play out as soon as Mohamed arrived in Sacramento, where his wife had moved. In 1990, he seems to have tried to penetrate the FBI as an informant and double agent. He applied to the Charlotte and San Francisco offices for a translator's job and was turned down. During the interview process in San Francisco, however, he told agents about a local document-forging conspiracy that may have involved members of the terrorist group Hamas, and he became an informant for the Bureau. What he did not report, however, were his activities on behalf of Ayman al-Zawahiri, the head of the Egyptian Islamic Jihad (EIJ) terror group, who visited the West Coast twice on fund-raising tours in the early 1990s. In these instances, Mohamed served as host and security guard to al-Zawahiri, who was traveling incognito. (Agents later felt, but couldn't prove, that some of the funds raised by al-Zawahiri were used in the 1995 bombing of the Egyptian embassy in Pakistan.)

Mohamed also didn't mention that his involvement in EIJ led him to bin Laden's jihad organization, which was forming a strategic alliance with EIJ (Al-Zawahiri would become bin Laden's second-in-command). He did tell his interlocutors that in 1991, he'd traveled to Afghanistan to handle bin Laden's security arrangements, when bin Laden moved with his family and followers to Sudan.

Afterward, Mohamed began working for bin Laden in a number of different capacities, though he didn't relate this part of the story until much later. "In 1992, I conducted military and basic explosives training for al Qaeda in Afghanistan," Mohamed would tell U.S. authorities in 1999. "I also conducted intelligence training for al Qaeda. I taught my trainees how to create cell structures that could be used for operations."

In spring 1993, Mohamed was back in California and in touch with the Bureau, this time in connection with an immigration case. One al Qaeda operative who'd helped Mohamed move bin Laden to Sudan had been stopped by the Canadian police in Vancouver attempting to cross into the U.S. with fraudulent papers. Mohamed, who'd traveled to Seattle to meet him, tried to intercede with the Canadians by saying he worked for the FBI. The ploy failed—the operative was barred entry into the U.S.—but the Canadians contacted the Bureau, prompting Special Agent John Zindt to set up an interview with Mohamed outside San Francisco in May 1993. During the course of their conversation, Mohamed gave the FBI its first glimpse of al Qaeda. According to court papers, he told Zindt that bin Laden was determined to drive U.S. forces off the Arabian Peninsula and was "building an army" capable of toppling the Saudi monarchy.

Zindt was troubled enough by Mohamed's information that he called in intelligence officials from the Defense Department to meet with him. But apparently neither the Bureau's New York office nor JTTF were informed about the interviews, even though Islamic terrorists had tried to blow up the World Trade Center only a few months before and the TERRSTOP investigation was ongoing.

Mohamed also told agents about his activities as an al Qaeda trainer in Afghanistan and Sudan. But, perhaps feeling that Mohamed was a helpful informant, they decided not to detain or even monitor him. By the end of 1993, he was in Nairobi on a surveillance mission for bin Laden and he was there a year later, unbeknownst to the FBI, when the Southern District subpoenaed him at his California home in late 1994. Investigators later learned that his wife passed the subpoena on to him and his al Qaeda overseers told him to answer the summons and not return to Africa. No doubt, they didn't want Mohamed drawing attention to their activities in Nairobi. They also wanted him to find out what, if anything, the U.S. authorities already knew about them.

Thanks largely to the prodding of U.S. prosecutor Patrick Fitzgerald, the FBI would eventually investigate and arrest Mohamed, and he would become a government cooperator, providing valuable information about bin Laden and al Qaeda. But that would not occur for another four years. In late 1994 when he was called to New York for questioning by the prosecutors of the TERRSTOP case, Mohamed was a reluctant subject. He had no intention of implicating Abdel-Rahman or, for that matter, himself. Nor did he volunteer much more information than he'd already told the FBI in San Francisco. But this time when Mohamed reiterated his statements about bin Laden, they fit together with the other bits and scraps of evidence coming in from the Philippines. Here was an Islamic extremist with a fortune of tens, if not hundreds, of millions of dollars; guerilla training camps in Afghanistan; a cadre of veteran mujahideen; an anti-Western agenda; and numerous links to Ramzi Yousef, the world's most wanted terrorist.

"By late spring 1995, bin Laden was definitely on our charts," Childers says, referring to the organizational charts federal investigators often draw up of Mafia families. "He wasn't the godfather, yet, more like a *capo regime*. But he was someone we felt needed to be looked at."

But a bin Laden inquiry would have to wait. The feds were in the midst of the TERRSTOP trial, by far their biggest, most demanding case at the time. It was also a case they couldn't afford to lose, given Abdel-Rahman's profile.

The Justice Department had served prosecutors with a narrow mandate: Don't bring charges against the sheik unless you are sure you can convict him.

As Neil Herman learned in the 1985 New African Freedom Fighters trial, pre-emptive cases—cases centered on crimes not yet committed—are extremely difficult to prove. Jurors make a sharp distinction between doing something and just saying you're going to do something. In fact, prosecutors had broadened the scope of the conspiracy to include the Kahane murder and the World Trade Center bombing. But the case hinged on the Landmarks plot. If prosecutors couldn't convince the jury that Abdel-Rahman was connected to the plan to blow up New York's bridges and tunnels, it was unlikely they could link him to the other crimes in the indictment.

Still, the government had acquired some powerful weapons. Abdo Haggag, the blind sheik's speechwriter (whom Corrigan and McNally had tried to recruit as an informant in connection with the Mubarak assassination plot), and Siddig Siddig-Ali, the sheik's translator, both agreed to cooperate, boxing the sheik in. Once, he might have quibbled with the prosecution about the meaning and intent of his writings, his fatwas or his taped conversations with Emad Salem. Now Abdel-Rahman would have to contend with the testimony of his two closest aides.

The trial began in January 1995 and lasted nearly nine months. Emad Salem testified and was instrumental in implicating Abdel-Rahman in the conspiracy, and the government rewarded Salem with $1.5 million for his effort. But the heroes of the case were Corrigan, Napoli and their colleagues at JTTF and the Southern District whose meticulous investigations—dating back years in some cases—connected the dots among 130 government witnesses and more than 1,000 exhibits. On October 1, 1995, the defendants were convicted on 48 of the 50 counts in the indictments, including the most serious charges.

On January 17, 1996, the presiding judge handed out life sentences to the ten defendants who hadn't entered into plea agreements with the government. El-Sayyid Nosair was finally convicted of the murder of

Meir Kahane, as well as other charges, and sentenced to life in prison. Sheik Omar Abdel-Rahman received a sentence of life plus 65 years for his role in the conspiracy.

But as with the World Trade Center trial, the Landmarks trial raised as many questions as it answered. Was the conspiracy homegrown? Or did it have backing from an organization overseas—EIJ, perhaps, or Al Gama'a al-Islamiyya, or perhaps even the suddenly ubiquitous Osama bin Laden, who, Haggag told investigators, had been paying for Abdel-Rahman's living expenses since the sheik arrived in America?

As the trial wound down, the feds drew up a list of 70 to 80 names, people who they felt were connected one way or another to the defendants and needed to be looked at. Bin Laden was among those at the top of the list.

In October 1995, the FBI had officially opened a case on Osama bin Laden and dispatched JTTF agents Dan Coleman and John Liguori to the CIA's Counter-terrorism Center (CTC) in Langley to see what the Agency knew about their subject. They were amazed by the amount of material—some 40 thick files' worth—that they found. The CIA may have come late to the game, but once galvanized their resources were remarkable.

Most of the information consisted of raw, unfocused data: itineraries, phone records, associates lists, investment holdings, bank transfers. "The kind of stuff you'd expect to see at the start of an investigation," according to an FBI official who viewed the files shortly after Coleman and Liguori. Several agents noted that most of the material came as the result of electronic eavesdropping, "the kind of stuff the NSA does." According to these investigators, the problem was much the same as the one that had plagued the feds in their Manila investigation of Ramzi Yousef: The CIA didn't seem to have any agents on the ground who were close to bin Laden and who could explain to them what their data meant.

JTTF investigators were also surprised to discover that the CTC was conducting a vigorous spin-off investigation into another subject on their suspects list, an Islamic fundamentalist named Wadi el-Hage. El-Hage had first come to their attention during the investigation of the Shalabi murder. He'd flown up to New York from his home in Texas to manage the Refugee Services Center during Shalabi's planned trip to Egypt, arriving the day of Shalabi's disappearance. However, no evidence was found to connect him to a crime, and the Bureau lost track of him after 1992.

What JTTF investigators now learned was that el-Hage was a key bin Laden operative who'd moved in 1992 to Sudan where he had acted as bin Laden's private secretary and business agent. More recently, the CIA files told them, he'd set up housekeeping in Nairobi and was running an NGO called Help Africa People. Of course, no one at JTTF thought he'd moved to Nairobi with his family for purely humanitarian reasons. What they did think was that the key to getting bin Laden was to try to make a case against el-Hage and then lever his cooperation.

But bin Laden was still not a top priority at JTTF. For all his resources and rhetoric, for all the rumors of a jihad brigade under his command, he still, as far as U.S. officials knew, hadn't committed an act of terrorism against American interests at home or even overseas. That view of bin Laden, at last, was about to change.

In November of 1995, two men in their mid-twenties drove a beat-up pickup truck into a parking lot outside a U.S. training mission to the Saudi Arabian National Guard in Riyadh. The two men disembarked, fiddled with some-thing in the back of the truck, then left the area. Minutes later, the truck exploded killing five American and two Indian servicemen.

The FBI dispatched a small team of agents to assist with the investigation, but the Saudi authorities held them at bay. Though the Saudi officials claimed at first that the blast must be the work of outside agitators, they were clearly concerned about anti–U.S. extremists within their populace, indeed within their government. In this case especially, the Saudis, who are secretive by nature, didn't want foreign police agencies poking into their internal affairs.

Instead their Ministry of the Interior compiled a list of several hundred suspects culled from nearly 15,000 files of Saudi nationals who'd fought in or supported the Afghan War. By April, prompted by a $3 million reward, a Yemeni man identified two of the suspects as men he'd helped smuggle goods across the porous border between Yemen and Saudi Arabia. With the case broken, Saudi police rounded up four local men, videotaped their confessions and beheaded them before U.S. officials had an opportunity to question them. On the next day, April 23, the FBI investigators watched the terrorists' confessions for the first time on Saudi TV along with the rest of the nation.

But the confessions were interesting just the same. Three of the four men alleged that while they planned and perpetrated the bombing themselves, they were inspired by the faxes and fatwas issued by bin Laden and his organization. There were other links as well. Several of the men had been to Afghanistan and trained in camps built and operated by bin Laden. Though the bombing in Riyadh had little impact in the U.S., and the links to bin Laden were sketchy at best, it changed investigators' views of the Saudi millionaire. Now when they thought of bin Laden, it was not merely as a financier, but as a terrorist.

Apparently, the White House had gotten the message as well. In January 1996, President Clinton signed off on a CIA finding establishing bin Laden as a threat to national security and mandating the FBI and CIA work together to bring bin Laden to justice. The government adopted a law enforcement approach as its main strategy: build a case against bin Laden, apprehend him, and prosecute him in a U.S. court. As a result, the Agency set up Alec Station, a squad of officers, including agents from the FBI and other government departments, dedicated to collecting intelligence and evidence on bin Laden and his organization. At about the same time, JTTF started up a bin Laden desk in New York with about six full-time investigators.

Also, the State Department began pressuring Sudan to disgorge bin Laden. Ruled since 1989 by the extremist National Islamic Front, Sudan had become home to an alphabet soup of anti-Western terrorist organizations, most notably bin Laden and some 300 Afghan-Arabs under his command. In January, however, the U.S. withdrew its embassy staff and the Sudanese, fearing sanctions or perhaps even a military strike, made an attempt to shore up its deteriorating relations with America.

On February 6, Ali Othman Taha, the Sudanese foreign minister, invited newly appointed U.S. Ambassador Tim Carney, a career diplomat who specialized in conflict management, and David Shinn, the State Department's country director for East African Affairs, to dine with him in his Khartoum home. According to Carney, they began the first Sudan–U.S. dialogue about terrorism. What, Taha wanted to know, could his government do to prove they were not a terrorist state?

Carney and Shinn passed on Taha's concerns and interest to the State Department and in March, U.S. officials delivered Sudan a memorandum listing a number of steps they wanted Sudan to take. Getting rid of bin Laden's organization and closing down his suspected terrorist camps were near the top.

At a secret meeting in Washington in March, Sudan indicated it was willing to meet most of the U.S. demands. In fact, they not only agreed to expel bin Laden, but also to turn him over to any responsible authority with legitimate grievances. The Saudis, who'd begun to regard bin Laden less as a prodigal son and more as an enemy of the state, were the obvious choice. Egypt was also brought up as an option. But both countries, fearing a backlash from bin Laden's many sympathizers in the region, refused to take him, and the U.S. reportedly did little to press them.

What happened next is in dispute. Some officials privy to the discussions feel that Sudan's offer to turn bin Laden over had included the U.S., that they would have permitted U.S. authorities to apprehend him much the way they'd allowed French agents in 1994 to arrest Carlos the Jackal. But other U.S. officials say there was never a clear offer on the table and point out that any offers made by the Sudanese, given their troubling history with terrorists, had to be viewed with suspicion. In either case, the administration thought seriously enough of the possibility of getting bin Laden that they made inquiries to the FBI and the Southern District, asking if they had enough evidence to indict bin Laden. Both offices replied that they didn't and the matter was dropped.

The administration appears to have run out of options. America is a nation of laws; U.S. prosecutors were unable to make a case against bin Laden that would stand up in court, and given the political climate, there was no other way the government could justify detaining him. But once again, things were not so clear-cut. The administration was reportedly divided as to whether or not it should treat bin Laden as a war criminal. Bin Laden had effectively declared war on U.S. troops and their allies in the Gulf. He was a suspect in several terrorist acts against the U.S. And he was already deemed to be the world's largest individual financier of radical Islamic causes. By itself, the creation of the Alec Station and its counterpart at the FBI established bin Laden as America's most wanted terrorist. Not even Hezbollah chief Imad Mugniyah, the architect of the deaths of hundreds of Americans, had a dedicated desk at either agency.

What's more, the Sudanese warned the administration at the March meeting that if they simply expelled bin Laden, he'd go to Afghanistan—a place where the U.S. had no presence and little leverage, and where it would be unable to exert any control over bin Laden's activities. Nevertheless, the White House decided to deal with bin Laden as a law enforcement issue, all but ensuring his departure to Afghanistan.

As a final option, the Sudanese recommended leaving bin Laden in Khartoum and offered to keep close tabs on him until the U.S. decided what action it wanted to take. But the White House wanted no part of an extended arrangement with Sudan, and while the administration didn't particularly want bin Laden in Afghanistan, its first priority was getting him out of Sudan and away from his businesses and operational infrastructure.

On May 18, bin Laden left the Sudan and began reconstituting al Qaeda in Afghanistan under the protection of the Taliban. America's last easy chance to put bin Laden out of action before the September 11 attacks had just slipped away.

CHAPTER 10

THE TERRORIST WHO CAME IN FROM
THE COLD

N othing made Jamal al-Fadl stand out as he waited on the long line of visa applicants at the U.S. embassy in Asmara, the capital city of Eritrea. He was of medium height, medium build, dark-haired and dark-skinned. Although it was the start of the summer, June 1996, the hot air inside the crowded entrance hall was already thick as bread. Al-Fadl waited patiently in line and when his turn came, instead of submitting the usual forms, he whispered to the clerk that he had information of vital interest to the security of the U.S.

Within hours, U.S. officials knew that this man was a remarkable find, their first informant with an intimate, comprehensive knowledge of al Qaeda. They would spend the next five years meticulously sifting through the information he offered them on a silver platter. Al-Fadl wasn't a top-ranking member of al-Qaeda but there was something about the ordinariness of his appearance and manner that had apparently rendered him inconspicuous among bin Laden's top people, that made him a kind of Zelig, a background figure at just about every important event in al Qaeda's history from its inception until the year before his appearance at the embassy in Asmara.

Thirty-three-year-old Jamal al-Fadl had been born to a middle-class family in Rufa'a City, Sudan. After high school, he'd immigrated to New York on a student visa, settling in the Arab community along Atlantic Avenue in Brooklyn, just across from the skyline dominated by the twin towers of the World Trade Center. He eked out a living working in a grocery store and took on a second job that wasn't really for money. He helped out at the al-Khifah Refugee Services Office, where his boss was Mustafa Shalabi.

Part of al-Fadl's job was to raise money from other Muslims for holy war in Afghanistan and to recruit able-bodied men to go there and fight. When his time came, al-Fadl went too, ending up in the Khalid ibn Walid camp training for 45 days fighting against Soviet tanks and helicopters. Then he was sent to the Areen Guest House in Pakhita, near the front lines, where he was introduced to a man whose real name, he would later learn, was Osama Muhammad Al-Wahad bin Laden.

Al-Fadl stayed at the guest house for several days, each day listening to bin Laden lecture the departing soldiers about jihad. He then went to the front lines to battle the Soviets in the name of Allah. For all his training, he was not the best battlefield technician. He fired eight rocket-propelled grenades at a Soviet helicopter, missing every time. Two months later, he was settled back in Khost, moving from one training camp to another. At the al-Farouk camp he received religious training and heard more lectures on jihad. At the Jihad Wal camp, he learned about pistols and explosives.

Al-Fadl moved easily among the men in the camps and the guesthouses. He had worked for Mustafa Shalabi, the emir of the al-Farooq Mosque in Brooklyn, had answered the call in Afghanistan and was battle tested, having spent two months on the front lines. Now, as the war wound down, he began to meet the men who would form the backbone of al Qaeda's organization, including Mamdou Salim, the imam of the mosque in Peshawar where bin Laden prayed; Ayman al-Zawahiri, the Egyptian doctor who headed the Egyptian Islamic Jihad and who would become bin Laden's right hand; Abu Ubaidah al-Banshiri and Mohammed Atef, bin Laden's best battlefield strategists; and Abdullah Azzam, bin Laden's erstwhile professor at the University of Jeddah and his mentor. When the Soviets invaded Afghanistan, Azzam had been among the first to go there and bin Laden had followed him. They had cofounded and run the Afghan Service Office, also known as al-Kifah. They had sent Mustafa Shalabi to open a branch in Brooklyn, a sort of U.S. recruiting center, with Azzam providing the fiery inspiration and bin Laden the money and logistical support until their falling out over the direction of jihad and Azzam's subsequent assassination in the fall of 1989.

Around that time, al-Fadl attended a lecture by Abu Ubaidah al-Banshiri, bin Laden's top military aide, at the al-Farouk camp in Afghanistan. There were about 40 people in the room, including bin Laden and his advisors, as well as the core of his fighters and training officers. According to al-Fadl, al-Banshiri told the assembled mujahideen, "We [are] going to make a group and this is the group that is under Farouk, and there's going to be one [leader] for the group and it's going to be focused on jihad, and we are going to use the group to do another thing out of Afghanistan."

After the meeting, the men were asked to sign papers swearing allegiance, or bayat, to the new group, which would be called al Qaeda, Arabic for "the Base." The men who signed that night would become its founding members, and al-Fadl was the third signatory.

In the weeks and months that followed, the pyramidal structure hinted at in al-Banshiri's speech was fleshed out. Bin Laden was of course the emir, or leader, and under him were a number of *shuras*, or councils, to advise him on religious, military, political and media issues.

The first thing al Qaeda needed was a base of operations. Afghanistan had been virtually destroyed in the war, left with no infrastructure and poor communications. In any case it remained remote from the rest of the Arab world. On the other hand, Sudan had just installed a conservative Islamic government, and leaders of its ruling party, the National Islamic Front (NIF), had met with bin Laden several months before. At that time, they'd told him that he and his men would be welcome in Sudan and bin Laden had sent his son, Abu Abdullah, to prepare a survey. In 1990, he sent al-Fadl to Sudan, along with Mamdou Salim, to rent houses for al Qaeda's top command and buy farms that would become its new training camps. Al Qaeda had begun the process of relocating.

Meanwhile, bin Laden had returned home to Saudi Arabia, where he was welcomed as a war hero. Next to the royal family, the bin Ladens, with a construction fortune valued at $5 billion, were the best known and richest in the kingdom. Osama's exploits in the war had made him, in the popular imagination, a cross between a Rockefeller and Che Guevara, and he was invited to speak in mosques and at private gatherings throughout the kingdom.

In 1990, bin Laden set up modest housekeeping in Jeddah and initially went back to work at his family's construction company, Bin Laden International. But bin Laden's true interests remained political. "He said he wanted to continue his work in Afghanistan to help the mujahideen and the refugees," says Turki al-Faisal, then chief of Saudi intelligence.

In fact, the principal themes of bin Laden's speeches, which were recorded and sold throughout Saudi Arabia, involved the U.S. and Iraq. In the first instance, he asked Muslims to boycott American goods to protest U.S. support for Israel. In the second, he warned of Saddam Hussein's military ambitions in the Gulf.

In August 1990, bin Laden's fears were realized when Iraq invaded Kuwait, a move widely viewed as the first stage in a plan to occupy the Arabian Peninsula and take over neighboring Saudi oil fields. Bin Laden immediately went to see Turki al-Faisal and presented him with a national defense plan that would make use of the Afghan–Arab troops who had fought against the Soviets. "He was looking for another struggle," al-Faisal recalled. "He said that the king should not allow non-Muslim troops to come to the kingdom and that if [the king] would allow him—bin Laden—he would collect an army of mujahideen from all over the Muslim world and drive the Iraqis out of Kuwait."

Of course, fighting the Soviets from the caves and mountains of Afghanistan and taking on the Iraqi army and air force in Kuwait City, a city that is about the size of Manhattan, were two different things. The Saudis rejected the plan out of hand and turned to a U.S.-led coalition instead. "The week after [the Kuwaiti invasion], King Fahd [the Saudi ruler] made his most courageous political move, in my view, in calling for support from the whole world to resist the Iraqi invasion of Kuwait," Turki recalls. "This did not sit well with bin Laden."

It's hard to say what rankled most, the fact that bin Laden was sidelined from the big game, or that it was the Americans who had been chosen to defend his homeland. Bin Laden believed that the very presence of American troops in Saudi Arabia was an insult to Islam and he quickly became an outspoken critic of the royal family's policies. "I think the Gulf War may have been a turning point for him," Turki said. "I think at that time, we see the first signs of a disturbed mind."

The story usually goes that after being turned down to defend his homeland, bin Laden broke with the Saudi regime. But in fact bin Laden continued to lobby officials in support of his plans for global jihad. Not long after the Iraqis were driven from Kuwait, for example, bin Laden fashioned a new initiative. "He wanted to instigate a holy war against the then communist regime in South Yemen and to recruit what he called his mujahideen, or volunteers from the Arab world to the Afghan Jihad, and bring them to the kingdom and from there to South Yemen to operate against the communist regime," Turki recalls. "Of course, his proposal was turned down flat by the government."

According to Turki, the Saudis finally had had enough of bin Laden, and placed him under virtual house arrest in Jeddah. Only his family's close ties to the Saudi ruling elite saved him from more severe punishment. "For a while he seemed to be quiet, but then he went back to Afghanistan, where I saw him last in ninety-three, and he never came back to the kingdom," Turki recalls.

Most reports have bin Laden engineering his escape from Jeddah on the pretext of pressing business in Pakistan. But U.S. intelligence sources paint a more complicated picture. The Saudis, they say, wanted to expel bin Laden, or worse, but were constrained by his popularity among the conservative religious community, whom they couldn't afford to alienate. According to ex-CIA official Vince Cannistraro, who was advising the royal family on security issues at the time, the Saudis solved their dilemma by convincing bin Laden that the U.S. forces stationed in Saudi Arabia had been tasked by the CIA to kill him. The Saudis, Cannistraro says, then staged a dramatic midnight "escape," pretending to spirit bin Laden out of the country for his own safety. In any event, by the spring of 1991, bin Laden was back in Peshawar—a man without a country and without a war. Soon he would acquire one of each.

Arriving in Pakistan, bin Laden enmeshed himself in an effort to broker peace among the warring rebel factions in Afghanistan, who were fighting a chaotic battle against the central government as well as each other. A few months later, frustrated by the fruitless negotiations and concerned for his own safety, he embarked for Sudan.

Bin Laden's relationship to Sudan was based on mutual interests. He got along well with the NIF's party leader, Hassan al-Turabi, a Muslim scholar and intellectual who shared his political agenda: the use of jihad, including terrorism, to make Islamic states accountable to shari'ah, or Koranic law.

Bin Laden further ingratiated himself to Sudan's rulers by supplying equipment to the nation's military and pumping investments into its foundering economy. In exchange, bin Laden was given a relatively free hand to set up lucrative monopolistic and duty-free businesses and to import and train his growing army of mujahideen.

Al-Fadl worked under bin Laden's private secretary in al Qaeda's corporate offices, a pleasant nine-room townhouse in Khartoum's busy center. Among other duties, he helped out with office administration and payroll, and in the "delegation," or personnel department, screening the scores of veteran mujahideen streaming into the country each month in the aftermath of the Afghan war.

On the surface, bin Laden seemed like any prosperous, well-connected merchant. His portfolio included investments in banks, agricultural concerns, and trading and shipping companies. Al-Hijira, the construction company he owned in partnership with the state, built a 500-mile highway from Khartoum to Port Sudan. But his businesses also provided cover and infrastructure for his expanding terrorist activities, functioning almost like a state with its own labor, finance, security, transport and communications systems.

By the summer of 1992, with the Gulf War winding down, al Qaeda was firmly established in Sudan. Its businesses were generating a steady stream of income; in fact, they'd become so successful, bin Laden had been forced to move into quarters that were more spacious, a huge three-story guest house in the wealthy Riyadh section. What's more, al Qaeda was supporting a standing army of about 300 men (with many times that number of contacts it could call upon around the world). But its mission was still vague. It didn't have defined targets. And it had yet to execute a major act of terrorism.

That was about to change. After Iraq surrendered to the U.S., ending the Gulf War, and the promised U.S. troop pullout failed to materialize, bin Laden was outraged. Hadn't he predicted this? It mattered not at all to him that the Saudi government itself had asked the troops to stay. This may even have deepened his anger.

Al-Fadl heard rumblings of an increasingly anti-American attitude in the guest house and on the farms, where bin Laden and Mamdou Salim addressed the men. "They say [they have a] fatwa," al-Fadl recalls. "They say we cannot let the American army stay in the Gulf area and take our oil, take our money, and we have to do something to take them out. We have to fight them."

But how? Bin Laden was not in a position to invade his own homeland and begin carrying out attacks on the U.S. military. Nor had he apparently yet developed the bravado or taste for terrorism that characterized al Qaeda's later operations. As late as mid-1993, bin Laden shelved a plan to bomb the U.S. embassy in Riyadh because it endangered civilians. But soon another opportunity arose, one that he thought was within the scope and ability of his troops.

In December 1992, 28,000 U.S. troops landed in neighboring Somalia on a UN-backed humanitarian mission: to break the impasse created by Somalia's warring clans and deliver food supplies to its starving civilian population. But bin Laden believed the U.S. had a hidden agenda. According to al-Fadl, bin Laden and his top aides felt the U.S. Army was trying to occupy Somalia, and from there to strike across the border into the south of Sudan, already the scene of a bloody civil war between the NIF and Christian rebels.

For bin Laden, Somalia was just another version of the Gulf War: the U.S. was exploiting squabbling Muslims to gain power in the region. He began meeting regularly with his commanders and members of al Qaeda's *Shura* council to obtain religious rulings, and soon the council was regularly issuing fatwas against the U.S. occupation in Somalia. It had become clear that the fighting in Somalia would not be like battling the Soviets on an Afghan mountain range. Mogadishu, Somalia's capital city, was a crowded sprawl of huts and hovels, teeming with people. "'It is no guarantee we won't injure innocent people,'" al-Fadl recalls Mamdou Salim saying to bin Laden's troops. "'If [a victim is] a good person, he'll go to Paradise, and if not, he'll go to hell.'"

In the fall of 1993, bin Laden dispatched a team to retrieve Milan and Stinger missiles from al Qaeda's old stockpiles in Afghanistan and transport them to Somalia. According to his plan, al Qaeda would assume a role not unlike that of the U.S. Special Forces, becoming trainers and observers, while the Somali tribesmen fought the U.S. Army. To conceal the operation from the Sudanese, bin Laden hired a Sudan Airways cargo plane ostensibly for the purpose of delivering food to the Afghan people. For the trip to Somalia, however, al Qaeda men loaded the plane with enough military hardware to fight a small war, which was in fact exactly what they intended to do.

At the guest house in Sudan, bin Laden's military advisor Abu Ubaidah al-Banshiri told al-Fadl to keep his workload light; he might be going to Somalia. "[Al-Banshiri] says about the American army, now they came to the Horn of Africa and we have to stop the head of the snake . . ." al-Fadl told U.S. officials. "He said the snake is America and we have to stop them. We have to cut off the head [of the snake] and stop them."

In the end, al-Fadl didn't go to Somalia, but others did. Mohammed Atef, another of bin Laden's top military commanders, led a team of al Qaeda men to advise—and very likely arm—the Somalis. Meanwhile, the U.S. mission there had bogged down into a nasty police action against Mohammed Aideed, a brutal warlord who was blocking U.S. relief efforts. Aideed was stealing American food supplies to sell on the black market, but since he was also the leader of Somalia's most populous and powerful clan, operations against him led to the perception, however skewed, that U.S. troops were killing the very people they'd been sent in to save.

The conflict came to a head on October 3. Under pressure from the administration to wrap things up, U.S. Special Forces launched an operation into the center of Mogadishu aimed at snatching two of Aideed's top lieu-tenants. In the ensuing battle, which spanned 18 hours and involved some of the bloodiest fighting by U.S. forces since Vietnam, Aideed's men shot down two U.S. Black Hawk helicopters and killed 18 soldiers.

Though U.S. officials initially debated bin Laden's actual contribution to the conflict, policy makers regarded the operation as a debacle, a view underscored when a day later, Somalis dragged the naked body of one of the dead American soldiers through the streets of Mogadishu. Though the U.S. forces had achieved their objective—the two top-ranking Somalis had been apprehended—albeit after 500–1,000 of Aideed's men had been killed, the perception was that, once again, as in Beirut, American lives had been lost when the military, acting outside the national interest, had tried to be good Samaritans. Less than a week after the battle, U.S. troops pulled out of Somalia, exactly as bin Laden predicted they would.

Bin Laden was overjoyed. He bragged about the prowess of his fighters in Somalia and he made the rapid withdrawal of U.S. troops a touchstone for his nascent campaign of terror against the West. America, he repeatedly told his followers, had no stomach for war. They were a paper tiger, much like the once-vaunted Soviet army. They had fled Lebanon in 1983 after a lone terrorist had exploded a truck bomb in a Marine barracks, killing 242. They had quit Somalia after just one battle. Now, bin Laden announced, he would launch a holy war against the U.S. that would drive them from the Arabian Peninsula altogether.

But no one in the U.S. government seemed to hear him or, if they did, to take him very seriously. It would be three years before the authorities fully recognized bin Laden's participation in Somalia, nearly five before his name appeared publicly on an indictment. And as late as 1998, despite a series of escalating fatwas ultimately targeting U.S. civilians for death, the government continued to treat al Qaeda like a "fly buzzing around a giant elephant's ear," in the words of a former top-ranking State Department official.

Bin Laden seemed to be saying he had a public relations problem when, a year after the Mogadishu firefight, he founded an al Qaeda media wing under the direction of an old Saudi friend and purported businessman named Khaled al-Fawwaz. Based in London and known as the Advice and Reformation Committee (ARC), the office ostensibly served as an advocate for the peaceful reform of the Saudi government. In practice, according to U.S. prosecutors who indicted al-Fawwaz as a terrorist in 1998, ARC was a communications center and apologist for al Qaeda. Either way, bin Laden clearly wanted to get his message out.

The Saudis apparently heard him loud and clear. Always sensitive to criticism, they stripped bin Laden of his citizenship in 1994, froze his assets, and pressured his family to publicly renounce him. Also in that same year, gunmen wielding AK-47s attacked bin Laden's residence in Sudan, an incident that is widely believed to have been a Saudi-sponsored assassination attempt.

For the most part, though, bin Laden's plans were allowed to unfold without interference. Throughout his time in Sudan, he tried to establish links between al Qaeda and other terrorist organizations, chiefly with Egypt's Islamic Jihad and al Gama'a al-Islamiyya, and with Hezbollah, an Iranian-backed group with bases in Iran and Southern Lebanon's Bekaa Valley. According to al-Fadl, al Qaeda sent agents to the Bekaa Valley, where bin Laden's organization maintained a guest house to cross train with Hezbollah and learn how to make "big bombs." Some U.S. intelligence officials still believe even now that the Iranians were senior partners in bin Laden's organization and that U.S. leaders played down such links so as not to jeopardize diplomatic initiatives within Iran.

More alarming was the willingness of bin Laden, a Sunni Muslim, to put aside longstanding cultural and religious differences with Shiite and secular Muslims in order to unite behind their common enmity toward the U.S., much the way all three groups did when they joined forces to drive the Soviets out of Afghanistan. In 1995, Sudan's al-Turabi hosted an international conference of terrorist groups, an unlikely gathering reminiscent of the early Mafia conventions in New York and Atlantic City that helped previously rival gangs forge a national conspiracy.

Most troubling of all, though, was bin Laden's search for weapons of mass destruction. Al-Fadl told investigators that in the early 1990s he was deputized by bin Laden to approach the Sudanese army about procuring and even developing chemical weapons. Later, al-Fadl used his army contacts to broker a $1.5 million deal for a canister supposedly containing weapons-grade uranium.

The deal turned out to be a hoax, but al-Fadl, who was cut out of the final negotiations, resented missing the chance for a potentially hefty commission. It was not the first time he was disappointed by his relatively low status. Like many within the organization, he'd noted that bin Laden seemed to favor Saudis and Egyptians, who occupied plum command posts and were paid higher salaries, more than Muslims from other backgrounds. Al-Fadl, for example, made about $700 per month, half as much as al Qaeda's top employees.

Al-Fadl decided to do something about it, and began taking unauthorized kickbacks on the purchases he made on bin Laden's behalf. Though he later told investigators that he broke with al Qaeda over ideological differences, al-Fadl went into hiding in 1995 when his superiors discovered he was scamming the organization. He then promised to pay back the stolen funds, estimated to be as high as $250,000, but instead he went to the Saudi authorities. Only later, after the Saudis refused to deal with him, did al-Fadl offer his cooperation to the CIA.

Al-Fadl's walk-in was a crucial step forward in the U.S. government's nascent case against bin Laden. Apart from the sheer bulk of information he provided on al Qaeda—names, dates, locations—he also gave investigators their first appreciation of the size and sophistication of bin Laden's organization, its implacable hatred for the U.S., and the imminent threat it posed. Before al-Fadl's debriefings, U.S. intelligence had amassed thick files on bin Laden and his associates and contacts. But they'd had no idea how the many pieces fit together. "Al-Fadl was the Rosetta Stone," an intelligence official says. "After al-Fadl, everything fell into place."

R E D   H E R R I N G S

J ust one month after Jamal al-Fadl came forward to detail bin Laden's secret war against America, the FBI's focus was abruptly turned elsewhere. In fact, if there was a single moment in time that bought bin Laden an extra year and a half to gain momentum in his war, it came at 8:30 P.M. on July 17, 1996.

That night I was fishing. I had turned my 24-foot Boston Whaler to the west to watch the sun set over Long Island's Peconic Bay. Just then, over my left shoulder and 12 miles out to sea, a Boeing 747-100 jet exploded. The jet was ripped into three pieces. People who were facing south saw the explosion and the flames from the beach.

Though I didn't see it, I have had nightmares about that scene based on what I saw and learned later. Some passengers were cast from the jet, sent flying at hundreds of miles an hour, gaining speed as they fell into the water to an instant death. Others were trapped in their seats, belted in, looking through the gaping hole in the fuselage at the sky, speeding by in flames as if they were on some hellish rollercoaster ride.

Soon my pager was going off. David Bookstaver, a deputy director of New York City's Emergency Medical Service, was telling me that scores of ambulances were being dispatched to the plane crash off the Hamptons. I had just tied up the boat. I still had no idea. When I flipped on the Coast Guard radio, the call was going out for all boats in the area to respond to the site with blankets, life jackets and medical supplies. I ran to the car and grabbed a couple of jackets and sweaters and a case with a handheld video camera and some tapes. Tony Villareale, the owner of the boatyard, was there. I drafted him to come with me. I thought that between rescuing people, shooting video and operating the boat, it would be good to have a second hand on board.

We set out quickly. The water was flat. There was no moon. It took us nearly an hour to get to the site. The first sign was a glow on the horizon. As we got closer the glow became a wall of flames, jet fuel burning in the water. Around it, Coast Guard and police boats, their blue lights flashing. As Tony and I maneuvered past the flames, we could see parts of the plane floating. Bodies in the water. It was now clear to both of us that the blankets and jackets were not needed. There was no way anyone had survived this. A plastic bag floated by with the red-and-white Marlboro logo. It was filled with cigarettes from the Duty Free shop. Letters floated by, one addressed to a man in Paris. As we drifted through the debris, we entered a hellish canal. The water was in flames on either side of the boat. Then the water ahead of us was on fire. Tony executed a tight U-turn and we retreated. I delivered several live reports via cell phone to NBC. I kept shooting video. While Tony steered the Whaler, I used the spotlight to illuminate bodies in the water while we called for a police boat over the radio. One of the bodies was that of a woman. She wore a flowered blouse and dark skirt. We kept the light on her as they pulled her onto a Suffolk County Police launch. The air was thick with mist and the taste of salt and jet fuel. It was trapped in our throats and on our lips. Yet we barely noticed until much later.

We came alongside an NYPD police launch. I had only left the department a few months before. The cops greeted me as I came aboard. Bodies were lined up at the stern. I can still see them. Some were naked and torn. Some were still fully clothed and intact as if they had died in their sleep. And then I thought, "Who could have done this?" There had been no distress call from the plane, no indication of mechanical difficulty from the pilots. Seven-forty-seven jets did not just fall from the sky—unless they were blown up by a bomb. That is what I was thinking that night. That is what the FBI was thinking. It was the only explanation that made sense.

Neil Herman was called in and so was the entire JTTF. Coming off the Ramzi Yousef Bojinka trial, they were aware of the insidious design Ramzi Yousef had developed specifically to bring a plane down. A Casio watch, a cologne bottle filled with nitroglycerin and a blasting cap would have done the job.

A day after the crash, at the Coast Guard station in Moriches Bay, dozens of men and women from the JTTF were fanning out to question witnesses who had seen the plane explode. They were setting up a hangar in Calverton a few miles away to house the wreckage. If anything, the picture of what happened was only becoming less clear. Witnesses interviewed by the JTTF were reporting that flames shot up to the plane from the water, as if it had been hit by a missile. Neil Herman sent teams of agents to every boatyard to find out if anyone had seen anything suspicious or if any boats had been stolen. Was it possible that terrorists had *shot down* a passenger jetliner? The old Afghanistan "blow back" theory quickly reemerged. How many Stinger missiles had we given to the mujahideen during the Afghan War? How many had we recovered when the conflict was over? Hundreds were missing. We all knew that. What would be the terrible irony in that? That a piece of U.S. military hardware was used by former allies to commit a mass murder in the United States? That was not half as troubling as the next theory.

Pierre Salinger, the former press secretary to President Kennedy and a former investigative reporter for ABC News, publicly advanced a theory that the U.S. military had shot down Flight 800. Salinger's theory was buttressed by the fact that a fleet of navy ships had been on a training exercise 200 miles off the coast of Long Island. The JTTF was then faced with questioning navy personnel, having them account for every piece of ordnance on each ship. It was time-consuming and frustrating.

As months passed it was becoming increasingly evident that what had caused Flight 800 to explode was not terrorism but a catastrophic mechanical failure. The 747-100 had been plagued with electrical problems involving wiring in and around the fuel tanks. The National Transportation Safety Board theorized that a spark from a bad wire had set off a spontaneous combustion of fumes that had built up in the nearly empty center fuel tank. By the fall, it was the prevailing theory among investigators that the TWA Flight 800 case was the result of a tragic accident. But with conspiracy theories now the fodder for radio talk shows and Internet chat rooms, the answer needed to be supported with evidence. If the FBI walked away from the case, leaving it to the NTSB, it would only fuel the conspiracy theories: Of course the plane was shot down by the U.S. Navy, the skeptic would say. Why else did the FBI just walk away from the case?

Kenny Maxwell, a JTTF veteran, was assigned to the hangar at Calverton to supervise the collection of evidence and of testing during the reconstruction of the plane. Incredibly, 95 percent of the wreckage was recovered over a yearlong period by divers and robots working from navy salvage ships. The wreckage told a large part of the story. The area around the center fuel tank was scorched and torn. There was no damage or residue consistent with a missile strike. There was no sign of a bomb. Yet for months, many in the airline industry, at Boeing and even in the FBI still believed it was a bomb. One of the last to convert from that theory was Jim Kallstrom, then head of the FBI's New York office.

Naturally, the FBI can't be faulted for vigorously investigating a possible terrorist act as horrendous as the bombing of a passenger jet. But Herman still bristles at the mind-numbing length of the process, the day-in, day-out detail work of trying to prove a hypothesis that in the end could not be proved, but about which virtually everyone involved in the inquest felt confident.

In the end, the investigators would require the intervention of someone with a fresh perspective on the case just to bail them out.

That someone became a good friend of mine. His name was John O'Neill.

John P. O'Neill was born in 1952 in Atlantic City, New Jersey, where his parents ran a small taxi business. For many teenagers in Atlantic City, the cadre of tough guys from North Georgia Avenue were role models. This was before Atlantic City was flush with legalized gambling dollars. Mobsters like "Little Nicky" Scarfo and the Merlino brothers were some of the very few in town who drove new cars and seemed to have a supply of fresh cash. But from the time he was a boy, John O'Neill wanted to be an FBI agent. He got his first job out of high school as a fingerprint technician. While in college at Washington University in 1976, he finagled an assignment as a tour guide at FBI headquarters. Then John P. O'Neill's boyhood dream came true. Upon his graduation from college, he became a Special Agent of the Federal Bureau of Investigation, assigned to Baltimore.

Twenty years later, as the Assistant Special Agent-in-Charge of the Chicago office, O'Neill had built a reputation as a guy who got things done. He was respected by the Chicago cops and by the Chicago Mob. "I went to all the police retirement parties," O'Neill told me once, "but the part I was proudest of in Chicago was every time we put a wise guy away, I was invited to his going-away [to prison] party." O'Neill attributed the seemingly high level of détente to the fact "they knew we'd gotten them fair and square, and they respected that."

One of John O'Neill's qualities was that he could hold forth at a drinking party for a departing Chicago hood and be equally at ease as the FBI's representative to the National Security Council during a White House meeting. He was full of self-confidence, tall and handsome, with black, slicked-back hair that came to a peak above his forehead. He favored dark double-breasted suits, and often wore those silky, almost see-through black socks. "Gangster socks," he called them. But O'Neill's knowledge of gangsters went deeper than style. He understood the way they thought, their arrogance and ambition. He understood their will to power, not just as a concept, but as a raw, animating force. It's what had made him a good street agent and maybe an even better executive. He never lost sight of what the other guy was after—in the streets of Chicago, in the corridors of Washington, in the caves of Afghanistan.

At times, O'Neill even seemed to embody the traits of the Southside hoods he'd once hunted down. He possessed fabled appetites, a lust for the good life, an excess of energy and ego that could put him at odds with his colleagues. He'd almost come to blows with Kenny Maxwell, another big personality, over whose town New York was. But he also had a reservoir of charm, a knack for making men and women love him, if only because he so transparently needed them to love him. He'd turn on an agent, if he thought the agent was derelict or, worse, disloyal. But he was also the first one to offer his support if the same agent suffered an illness or other setback.

After Chicago, O'Neill transferred to Washington as the chief of the FBI's Counterterrorism section just in time to help coordinate Ramzi Yousef's capture in early 1995. Two years later he moved to New York as head of the National Security Division, putting him in charge of espionage and terrorism. Jim Kallstrom was his boss, but O'Neill came to the job well educated. In Washington, his job had been to coordinate the FBI's efforts on terrorism within and outside the U.S. Most of his time had been spent trying to keep all the other agencies on the same page. O'Neill had forged alliances with everyone from Richard Clarke, the White House deputy national security advisor, to O'Neill's counterparts at the CIA and at the Pentagon.

O'Neill would need all his skills when he got to New York. The JTTF agents and supervisors like Neil Herman were beginning to feel that the

TWA 800 case had become an anvil chained to their feet. O'Neill knew it too, but he also understood the politics involved.

"A year into the investigation, John O'Neill told us we needed an exit strategy," Herman recalls. "I remember thinking, 'My God, what the hell is an exit strategy? We get out of cases when they're over. Since when do we need a strategy to get out of them?'"

But it wasn't that simple this time. Scores of witnesses had seen what appeared to be a missile trail going from the water to the plane, causing them to believe the plane had been the victim of a missile attack. Anything short of an exhaustive inquiry would have met with the same kind of public skepticism that attended the Warren Commission hearings.

Finally, O'Neill prevailed on the CIA to produce a computerized simulation of the crash, which demonstrated the effects of a fuel tank explosion on Flight 800. The animation showed how, as a flaming stream of fuel fell, it would extinguish itself as it mixed with the air. That would create the visual effect—the *illusion*—that the fire was traveling upward. Thus the "missile trail." It was finally a scientific explanation that matched what the witnesses saw.

Justified or not, the investigation cost JTTF 17 months, nearly a year and a half, during which many of the nation's most experienced terrorism investigators were effectively sidelined from the task of hunting the nation's most wanted terrorist. Even in the two years before TWA 800, the JTTF was working on the trials of the suspects in the World Trade Center case, the TERRSTOP investigation, and then the Ramzi Yousef trials. Each trial lasted months and tied up dozens of agents.

The JTTF had also been bogged down helping out with other frontline terrorism investigations, including the 1995 Oklahoma City and 1996 Atlanta Olympics bombings; as well as with routine duties such as protecting Pope John Paul II during his fall 1995 visit to New York. TWA 800 topped a three-year period during which the FBI had made little progress in combating militant Islamic terrorism. In fact, Herman says, it lost the investigative momentum it had gained in the wake of the World Trade Center and TERRSTOP arrests.

"We were stretched too thin," Herman recalls. "It got to be that we were responsible for all kinds of chicken-shit events, from the Goodwill Games to visits from foreign dignitaries. If a bag was left outside the UN, we'd dispatch our people on a moment's notice just to show who's in command. We were trying to be everything to everyone."

JTTF was growing to meet its expanded mission, not just in manpower, but also in complexity. The small, supple, close-knit unit that Herman had grown up with in the 1980s and early 1990s was now saddled with layers of bureaucracy, liaisons to other agencies, public relations. "You could not do another TERRSTOP investigation [by 1997]," Herman says. "You could not penetrate a group, do physical and electronic surveillance and translate the information over a long period of time the way it was done. You couldn't hold on to the information. There were too many leaks, too much potential access, too many agencies, too many politicians who wanted to be briefed."

Toward the end of his tenure, while still mired in TWA 800, Herman was asked to look into the Taliban's activities in the U.S. "It was almost like an afterthought," he recalls. "Nobody cared much about the Taliban back then. It was just another bullshit thing. The government hadn't recognized them, but they had a kind of legation—two guys in a residence in Queens. Somebody wanted to know what they were up to, so we tried to penetrate them, put a wire up. But then what was the point? We couldn't get any translators. We tried to borrow some from the DOD, but there was a problem with clearance. So we went to the CIA, and they didn't have any translators at all. No wonder bin Laden fell through the cracks."

O'Neill was keenly aware of bin Laden. When he had been the chief of the Counterterrorism Division in Washington, O'Neill had overseen the FBI's efforts to investigate two bombings targeting U.S. military personnel stationed in Saudi Arabia. The first was the 1995 Riyadh attack that killed five U.S. advisors. The Saudis charged three men who gave videotaped confessions saying they had been inspired by bin Laden. In 1996, a second bombing had collapsed a U.S. Air Force housing complex in Dhahran called Khobar Towers, and bin Laden had been an early lead suspect. O'Neill traveled to Saudi Arabia with FBI Director Louie Freeh to inspect the damage and jump-start the stalled case. In both instances, the damage was done. Nineteen U.S. servicemen were killed and 550 people were injured. The Saudis had no intention of turning suspects or evidence over to the FBI. O'Neill began to believe the work had actually been carried out at the behest of Iran. He believed the Saudis had figured that out too. O'Neill thought a tacit agreement had been reached between the Saudis and the Iranians, that the Saudis would overlook the whole thing as long as there were no further attacks on Saudi soil. O'Neill walked away from the two bombings with a fresh understanding of international politics. It was observed that the Saudis had long been America's best friends in the Arab world. "Yeah," O'Neill commented one night at a Manhatten watering hole, "except when it's inconvenient."

Once the Flight 800 investigation was over, O'Neill's focus turned back to bin Laden. A secret grand jury sitting in the federal courthouse in New York City was hearing testimony from Jamal al-Fadl about bin Laden's clandestine war on America. U.S. Attorney Mary Jo White felt she had enough to indict bin Laden for conspiring to kill Americans. When the sealed indictment was handed up, Osama bin Laden could be arrested at any time by any federal law enforcement officer. Still, it was a little more complicated than that.

CHAPTER 12

MEETING BIN LADEN

A fter covering TWA Flight 800 for a year, I left NBC, taking a job with ABC News in its newly formed Law & Justice Unit. The concept was that LJU would be a group of specialists who could tackle any major crime story, from the outset to the trial. Terri Lichstein was the senior producer in charge. She had put together a team, which included former defense lawyers, prosecutors and investigative producers, that would give ABC News an edge over any competitor on any major crime or legal story. To get started, I began to canvass my sources to figure out who might be the biggest criminal in the world. The Colombian drug lords had all been jailed or killed. Most of the Mafia bosses had met the same fate.

One night in early 1998, a friend summoned me to a bar on Manhattan's Upper East Side to introduce me to a new name: Osama bin Laden.

My friend told me the FBI had just learned an awful lot about bin Laden. They believed he was behind the attacks on the U.S. military in Somalia. They believed he had financed and supported Ramzi Yousef's plot to blow airliners out of the sky, the so-called Bojinka plot. He said there was a bin Laden plot to kill President Clinton and even the Pope. Some of this they knew from Wali Khan Amin-Shah, who had been with Ramzi Yousef in Manila and was cooperating with the FBI. Wali Khan knew a lot about bin Laden. He had trained in bin Laden's camps, he had been bin Laden's friend. They had fought side by side in the trenches against the Russians.

I began to look into bin Laden the next day. The only place he appeared in any of my files was in a single notation. It was just after the al Khobar bombing. I had written his name down on a short list of suspects. After that, I forgot about him. Now, I met with Terri Lichstein and briefed her on what I'd been told. She suggested I meet with Chris Isham and Len Tepper from the ABC News Investigative Unit. Both had extensive backgrounds in covering Islamic terrorism. Isham reached out to Vince Cannistraro, the former CIA officer who worked very closely with us as an ABC News consultant. Vince suggested we meet with an acquaintance of his, an Iraqi who could afford us an introduction to bin Laden's underground public relations apparatus. It would not be a simple process. Soon he sent word back: We would have to travel to London and meet with some of bin Laden's people. Bin Laden, it seems, has people all over. So investigative producer Len Tepper and our Iraqi translator, whom I'll call Ali, set off for London. We were to meet there with Khaled al-Fawwaz.

Al-Fawwaz had once been stationed in Afghanistan in bin Laden's camps. Then he was dispatched to Kenya to set up the bin Laden cell in Nairobi. Soon he was asked to set up the bin Laden propaganda machine from London. It was an ideal place from which to operate. It was a city with a large Arab population, it offered access to all forms of communication and every media organization in the world had a bureau there. At al-Fawwaz's Tudor-style house, Len and I took off our shoes, sipped cider and made our case for interviewing Osama bin Laden. Next we were asked to meet with Dr. Saad al-Fagih, the leader of a Saudi dissident group. We told him we would raise the issues that concerned bin Laden, about both the Saudis and the U.S. "We'll tell his side" and enough about his background so people would get a broader understanding of him.

"Instead of just pounding on the 'terrorist on the mountain' theme," I said to Dr. Saad, "we could frame his issues about America in such a way that people might find his arguments reasonable."

Saad smiled. "It may be better if he does not appear to be too reasonable," he said. It made sense in a perverse way. Bin Laden hadn't gone this far to be portrayed as reasonable. Scary was actually what he was going for.

From London, we were to move on to Islamabad and await further instructions at the Marriott. We had made the first cut. After a day in the Pakistani capital, a man arrived and said his name was Akhtar. We would only ever know him as Akhtar. But during the next few days, he would become the most important person in our world, our passport, our safe passage. He was tall, maybe six-two, thin and lanky, and he walked to an inaudible beat, with one hand crooked back, swinging slightly. A rolling strut, the walk of an urban black kid. Where he picked it up I never learned. Akhtar was Afghani and spoke almost no English and only a little Arabic—just enough so that Ali could understand him. Akhtar told Ali he would have to inspect us, our rooms, our gear. He was such a no-nonsense guy, it sometimes just made me want to laugh.

When the knock came at my door early the next morning, it was a surprise. Akhtar and another man, a heavyset guy, came in. "They just want to see you," Ali explained as the two men carefully looked at me in my boxer shorts. They looked at my open suitcase on the bed stand. Akhtar and the other man looked in the bathroom. I was not sure what they were looking for. I assumed just telltale signs that we were CIA agents or something. The two men left for further negotiations in Ali's room. That night, Akhtar called Ali at the hotel.

"It is happening," Ali told me when he relayed Akhtar's instructions. "Be ready at 7:00 A.M., and be dressed like him."

Ali, cameraman Rick Bennett and I immediately took a cab from the hotel to a run-down strip of stores and found the Cash Departmental Store, where we each purchased a suit for about $15. Rick went all out and got the vest. A suit was a knee-length shirt, baggy pants and rope— the white cotton belt with fringe that would hold up the one-size-fits-all pants if you knew how to tie it. We suspected we were going to Afghanistan, but none of us had the necessary visas to get into Afghanistan or back into Pakistan. Akhtar told us that his "people" would handle everything.

The next morning, curt instructions: Get to the Islamabad airport. In time, Akhtar also showed up at the airport. He looked us over. I was wearing the light-brown baggy pants and the oversized shirt that I'd bought the day before. It seemed to be the uniform for millions in this region. The outfit, which was meant to make me blend in at the airport and on the road, was offset slightly by the white socks I wore under the sandals, the Armani prescription glasses, and the Cuban cigars I'd picked up in London. I wasn't fitting in. Rick and Ali wore the same outfit in light gray. Akhtar led us to the gate. We were traveling on sealed orders. As we boarded the plane, we were handed tickets. We were going to Peshawar, the pearl of Pakistan.

It was hazy when we got off the plane—very hazy. As you drive into Peshawar, smoke fills the air and sticks in the back of your throat. Something seemed to be burning almost everywhere—rubbish, wood, tires. We checked into the Hotel Grand, a 1950s Miami Beach art deco affair located down an alley off the main road. Hotel security was a man in a green uniform who wore a red beret and carried a Chinese-made machine gun. The very friendly clerks who signed us in made note of the odd collection of nationalities—American, Canadian, Iraqi and

Pakistani—and they knew enough not to ask any of us what our business was in Peshawar. After we checked in, Akhtar strutted into the night, carrying the plastic bag that held his things.

I went out on the fifth-floor balcony to light up one of my Romeo y Julieta Churchills. Just what Peshawar needed: more smoke. I imagined what this sad, bustling city was like during the Afghan War, when it had been the staging area for the mujahideen. This place had been a world-class hotbed of militant organizers and recruiters, CIA operations officers and KGB spies. Even now, it is the back office of the militant Islamic movement for the region. I looked out at the hovels and junk-yards and watched the moon come up through the smoke.

Akhtar called the hotel in the morning and told us once again to get to the airport. And again, we were handed tickets in the waiting area. We walked across the tarmac to a prop plane headed for Bannu, in northern Pakistan. With each stop, our trip was taking us further back in time, each place getting more primitive in custom and lifestyle. Here, donkeys pulled carts and men and women carried sacks hanging from sticks across their shoulders or baskets on top of their heads.

In Bannu, we waited outside the tiny airport as vans and buses passed by. After an hour, a van packed with locals stopped, and an old man got out and greeted Akhtar. We all crammed into the van, which was already too crowded. We had been told not to speak. The other passengers already knew we were Westerners, but they didn't need to know that some of us were American. The van drove for two hours. People got off; more people got on. At a village that was nothing more than mud huts and thatched roofs, a loud bang came from the roof of the van. A young man with a cloth bag tied to the end of a branch scampered off the roof and ran toward the huts. The van itself was the only sure reminder that we were not 2,000 years in the past.

Minor revelation: For most Americans, me included, experience with the ancients is pretty much confined to the Bible. In the Bible is a world rife with plagues and pestilence, a world where things are worth killing and dying for, a world from a time before kill ratios and collateral damage and unacceptable levels of casualties. A world of huts. A world where there is no such thing as a losing battle. At Bannu, it felt as if we were crossing over into that world, where the ancient texts aren't so ancient, where martyrs are made.

When the van reached a small town, we got into another van, which took us for another hour, farther north through mountains and barren valleys, stopping at the last town before a wilderness that leads to the Afghan border. The old man drove the van into the courtyard of a small house, and metal gates closed behind us. We were to remain unseen in this village. The old man said that this place had been a safe house for mujahideen fighters headed for the Afghan War. The walls were covered with pictures of tanks and grenades. A pair of loaded AK-47s hung from nails on the walls.

Akhtar brought in a stainless-steel bowl filled with meat on the bone, placed it on the floor, and invited us to eat. There was pita bread and Pepsi. We sat on the floor, eating with our hands. In two hours we were on the road again, in the back of a covered Japanese pickup, our gear hidden under bags of flour. Near the Afghan border, the truck stopped.

Most of Afghanistan was, of course, controlled by the Taliban, a Muslim fundamentalist group that believes, among other things, that television is evil and that no living thing should be photographed or videotaped. So sneaking three American television journalists with camera equipment past a Taliban border checkpoint posed difficulties. Akhtar gave us the options: We could (1) don long black veils with narrow slits for eyes and cross into Afghanistan disguised as women or (2) walk over the mountains under cover of darkness and hope to avoid the Taliban's patrols. Ali had strong feelings on the subject. "We are not women," he said indignantly. "We will not wear veils. We will walk, as men."

An hour into the journey, Ali was wheezing and barely able to continue. He had not mentioned his asthma. "I want to go back to truck and be woman now," he said before hauling himself up to walk again. I lagged behind with him while Rick and our two guides led the way. At one point, I noticed that the guides were holding hands. "Ali," I whispered as I nodded in their direction, "you didn't mention that this was a gay terrorist group." Ali, still very asthmatic, patiently explained that among Muslim men it is customary to hold hands while walking. It is a sign of respect and friendship. It is perfectly masculine. "Yeah," I said. "I was joking." A moment passed. We walked in silence, save for Ali's wheezing. "So, wanna hold my hand, Ali?" I asked. "No," he replied.

It was still dark when we finally made it into Afghanistan. A truck was waiting with our gear. We drove for several more hours, mostly through dry riverbeds, before we reached the first of bin Laden's three camps. We were stopped on a dirt road. There we were met by a greeting committee. It was Dr. Ayman al-Zawahiri, bin Laden's right-hand man, and Mohammed Atef, bin Laden's military commander. Atef's men confiscated our camera gear and drove away. We were left with our overnight bags.

We stayed in a hut, sleeping on the floor, which was covered with brown and red flannel blankets. Pillows lined the walls. "You are not prisoners here; you are our guests," said one of bin Laden's aides. "Still, we would prefer it if you stayed inside. We don't want to advertise your presence." Several of bin Laden's soldiers were assigned to guard us. They slept in the hut next to ours. We washed from a bowl. Water came from a spigot just outside. An outhouse was up the hill. We spent our time reading or smoking and bullshitting with bin Laden's men, one of whom spoke pretty good English. We would eat with the soldiers. Bread, meat, tea. It was hot and dry. It had occurred to us that the interview might not be for days, or that after a few days we could be told that there would be no interview at all. That is the way these things go sometimes. Days of waiting, and then nothing. Most of that kind of waiting—for Castro or el-Qaddafi—is done in nice hotels. This was a little downscale, but it seemed to go with the territory.

On the night of the third day, May 28, we were told bin Laden would see us. After being searched again, we were loaded into a four-by-four military-style pickup truck. We left one camp. We were headed for another. An hour into this leg and, suddenly, gunfire. It was rapid-fire, from machine guns; I could see the muzzle flash through the tinted windows. It was coming from up the hill. Four short blasts, about 30 rounds, then another 30 from the opposite side of the road. My mind was racing. Several times during the three-hour drive between camps, men with guns jumped out from both sides of the road and screamed in Arabic for the truck to halt, for the windows to come down. Those men were part of al Qaeda, bin Laden's army. But now who was shooting at us? And why? Were we going to die? I was trying hard to duck my head between my legs, but with three of us stuck together in the backseat, there was no room to get our heads down . . . bam bam bam bam . . . My stomach was in knots. Now I was thinking: *"This is really not worth it."* Remember, at the time, bin Laden was an obscure figure. No one in America had ever heard of him . . . bam bam bam bam . . . I just felt the interview wasn't worth getting killed over . . . bam bam bam bam . . . Then a second wave of thoughts flashed through my head: I was not hearing the sound of metal being hit. No glass breaking. The shots were missing. Wait, our guides were not ducking. If they were not worried, maybe this was okay. Slowly, I raised my head.

The shooters in the road were yelling for us to halt, to open the doors. The gunfire had been warning shots. *"Jesus,"* I thought. Looking at their faces between the blinding beams of their flashlights, I could see they were very young, perhaps 18 or 19. They had apparently not received the radio message from the last checkpoint that the boys from ABC News were coming up. Though it was a little cold out that night, I was wiping sweat off my forehead. After a little tension and much talk, the driver settled the problem and we were moving again. We passed one more checkpoint—without incident—before reaching the camp where bin Laden would meet us.

In the mountaintop camp, generators were rumbling. The smell of gasoline was thick in the air. Rick Bennett was agitated because bin Laden's people had taken his camera days before, and it didn't look as though he was going to get it back. Now they wanted to give him another camera. A Panasonic home-video camera. Bennett had not come halfway around the world to shoot a home video. He wanted his $65,000 television camera back, and he wanted it back now! Just then, gunfire erupted again. Bin Laden's convoy was arriving. Now the show that was being staged for us was in full tilt, and we had no camera with which to record it. Bin Laden's cameraman handed Bennett the Panasonic. Bennett started taping. Dozens of Arab men were firing their rifles into the air. My right ear was pounding. I turned, expecting to see a cannon, but instead it was just a smiling boy—he might have been 15—and he was firing his machine gun an inch from my ear. I assumed that this was some kind of test, a rite of passage. He wanted to see fear. I'd been a reporter, and, for a time, deputy police commissioner of New York City. I'd heard my share of shots fired in anger. I just smiled at the kid and gently pushed the gun away. This was my way of saying, "Nice try, but you didn't make me jump." No matter, the kid was right back an inch from my ear, firing away. Now it wasn't funny anymore. I glared at him, but let's face it, the little prick had an AK-47 with a 30-round clip. How far could I get with hard eyes? One thing I learned in New York during the crack wars of the late eighties: Teenagers with machine guns are best not challenged. So as I watched the man arrive and his loyal soldiers discharged their weapons in ecstasy, this kid was doing his best to make me deaf.

Just minutes before this explosive welcome, I had been told by Dr. al-Zawahiri, "Mr. bin Laden will be here shortly. We have prepared a great welcome. Whenever he comes, there is always celebration."

Yellow trails from tracer bullets streaked at odd angles, crisscrossing the black, star-crowded skies. Fireworks shot up, and sparks fell like orange rain, evaporating before they hit the ground. As the gunfire continued, the motorcade of three four-wheel-drives crossed the flat dirt encampment.

Scores of bin Laden's most devout followers were here, all carrying Chinese- and Russian-made machine guns. Several were posted strategically with rocket-propelled grenades. It was after midnight on this mountaintop. Osama bin Laden was not yet a household name in the U.S., but he was about to be. I knew bin Laden had already been indicted, by a secret federal grand jury sitting in New York, for conspiring to kill Americans. He was already the top target for the JTTF. But I could also see just by looking around that bin Laden was not going to be what my cop buddies refer to as "an easy collar." By now, bin Laden knew that his targets were beginning to wake up to the threat he posed.

Into the din of the gunfire, he walked quickly, surrounded by seven bodyguards. Each had an AK-47. Their eyes darted in every direction for any attacker. This was either merely theatrical or entirely pointless, because with hundreds of rounds being fired into the air, it would have been impossible to pinpoint an assassin. At bin Laden's side was his military commander, Mohammed Atef. Al-Zawahiri had joined them. Bin Laden, with his simple white turban and long black beard, stood six-three and was the tallest man in the group. Despite the chaos of the scene, his eyes were calm, fixed and steady. He walked by me and ducked his head to step into a rectangular hut that had been set up for our meeting. One of his aides waved off the gunfire the way an emcee might quell a standing ovation. Everyone kept shooting. Somewhere, all these bullets were falling back down to the earth.

Osama bin Laden had made his entrance.

After his security detail crowded in behind him, I followed into the hut. Aside from his height, the first thing that struck me about bin Laden was his voice: It was soft and slightly high, with a raspy quality that gave it the texture and sound of an old uncle giving good advice. Bin Laden settled onto a bench covered with red cushions at the head of the long, rectangular room with clay walls painted white. Sitting down, he propped his own gun against the wall behind him. Twenty of his gunmen lined the benches on either side of the long room, leaning in, straining to hear whatever he might say. Bin Laden's clothes told the story of his entangled themes. He wore a green army field jacket with no insignia. Draped over the jacket was a gold shawl, and under the army jacket was the traditional Muslim clothing, basically the same outfit I was wearing.

Osama bin Laden has a firm handshake. We exchanged pleasantries in the polite but stilted manner one uses when speaking through a translator. His aides had insisted the day before that I give them a list of my questions in writing. As bin Laden was getting settled, al-Zawahiri smiled and said to me, "I have very good news. Mr. bin Laden will answer each of your questions." Then he added that bin Laden's answers would not be translated on the spot. "You can take the tape to New York and have them translate it there."

"If the answers are not translated now, how can I ask follow-up questions?" I asked the doctor.

"Oh, that will not be a problem," al-Zawahiri told me. "There will be no follow-up questions."

At this point, Rick, using stronger terms than one might want to with alleged terrorists, demanded his camera back. Suddenly, all his equipment reappeared.

Looking to break the ice, I said to the translator, "Tell Mr. bin Laden that for a guy who comes from a family known for building roads, he could sure use a better driveway up this mountain."

Okay, so admittedly it wasn't much of a joke, but bin Laden answered as if he hadn't quite understood the line. "Yes," he said, "I learned to drive the tractors when I was very young."

As I continued my awkward attempts at small talk, waiting for Rick to get the camera and lights in place, flies kept landing on bin Laden's face and white turban. Sensing that this was undercutting their leader's dignity, his aides asked bin Laden and the gunmen in the room to step outside so that they might spray.

A few minutes later, in a cloud of insecticide, we began.

Why, I asked, would a man of wealth, from a powerful family, have gone to Afghanistan to live in trenches and fight the Russian invaders on the front lines?

"It is hard for one to understand if the person does not understand Islam," he said, patiently explaining his interpretation of Islam for a citizen of his sworn enemy. "During the days of jihad, thousands of young men who were well-off financially left the Arabian Peninsula and other areas and joined the fighting. Hundreds of them were killed in Afghanistan, Bosnia and Chechnya." Of course, by the time of our meeting, the enemy had shifted. The Soviet Union no longer existed. The enemy was us.

"Our battle with the Americans is larger than our battle with the Russians," bin Laden said at one point. And he seemed to hint that whatever he was behind, there was much worse in store. "We predict a black day for America and the end of the United States as united states, and that they will retreat from our land and collect the bodies of their sons back to America, Allah willing."

And when I asked bin Laden if he was worried about being captured in an American raid, he quickly dismissed the possibility, turning instead to the reasons he hates the U.S.

"The American imposes himself on everyone. Americans accuse our children in Palestine of being terrorists—those children, who have no weapons and have not even reached maturity. At the same time,

Americans defend a country, the state of the Jews, that has a policy to destroy the future of these children." Much of what bin Laden said was wrapped in flowery prose and Koranic references.

"We are sure of our victory against the Americans and the Jews as promised by the Prophet: Judgment day shall not come until the Muslim fights the Jew, where the Jew will hide behind trees and stones, and the tree and the stone will speak and say, 'Muslim, behind me is a Jew. Come and kill him.'"

Bin Laden never raises his voice, and to listen to his untranslated answers, looking at what appear to be kind eyes and the trace of a smile, one could imagine that he was talking about something that did not much concern him. He continued, looking down at his hands as if he were reading invisible notes. "Your situation with Muslims in Palestine is shameful—if there is any shame left in America. Houses were demolished over the heads of children. Also, by the testimony of relief workers in Iraq, the American-led sanctions resulted in the death of more than one million Iraqi children. All of this is done in the name of American interests. We believe that the biggest thieves in the world and the terrorists are the Americans. The only way for us to fend off these assaults is to use similar means. We do not worry about American opinion or the fact that they place prices on our heads. We as Muslims believe our fate is set."

His interview technique was formidable. Aside from the advantage of not allowing for simultaneous translation, bin Laden's approach to questions could have been taught by an American public relations adviser: First, get your message out. Then, if you like, answer the question.

Bin Laden pointed out that the U.S., which was so heavily involved in supporting the Afghan rebels, was missing the profound point of that exercise: Through sheer will, even superpowers can be defeated. "There is a lesson to learn from this for he who wishes to learn," he said. "The Soviet Union entered Afghanistan in the last week of 1979, and with

Allah's help their flag was folded a few years later and thrown in the trash, and there was nothing left to call the Soviet Union."

If defeating the Russians didn't wipe out the myth of a superpower's military might, then in bin Laden's view the assault that caused the U.S. military to leave Somalia sure did. "It cleared from Muslim minds the myth of superpowers. After leaving Afghanistan, the Muslim fighters headed for Somalia and prepared for a long battle, thinking that the Americans were like the Russians," bin Laden said. "The youth were surprised at the low morale of the American soldiers and realized more than before that the American soldier was a paper tiger and after a few blows ran in defeat. And America forgot all the hoopla and media propaganda . . . about being the world leader and the leader of the New World Order, and after a few blows they forgot about this title and left, dragging their corpses and their shameful defeat."

I asked bin Laden why he would kill American soldiers whose work was to restore order and allow for the distribution of food to people starving at the hands of despots. "Why should we believe that was the true reason America was there?" he replied. "Everywhere else they went where Muslims lived, all they did was kill children and occupy Muslim land."

During the two days I had waited at the camp for bin Laden, some of his fighters had sat on the floor of our hut and told war stories. One soldier, with a big grin, told of slitting the throats of three American soldiers in Somalia. When I asked the al Qaeda fighter if bin Laden had been with his men in Somalia, he referred to bin Laden by his nickname among the men. "Yes, Abdullah was there." No one, not the CIA, the FBI, or the Department of Defense believes bin Laden was actually on the ground in Somalia, but what the soldier said was indicative of bin Laden mythology: that he is on the front lines of every Muslim battle. When I asked bin Laden about this, he said, "When this took place, I was in the Sudan, but this great defeat pleased me very much, the way it pleases all Muslims."

The Somalia operation, in some ways, made bin Laden. But as I sat there in the hut, I was wondering exactly what he would admit to. So I asked him about the 1993 bombing of the World Trade Center. I asked him if Ramzi Yousef was one of his men. "Unfortunately," he said with a wave of his hand, "I did not know him before the incident." But bin Laden said something else that now rings true with an eerie quality. "Ramzi Yousef, after the World Trade Center bombing, became a well-known Muslim personality, and all Muslims know him. Unfortunately, I did not know him before the incident. I remember him as a Muslim who defended Islam from American aggression on Muslim lands. He took this effort to let the Americans know that their government assaults Muslims to insure Israeli interests, to insure Jews. America will see many youths that will follow Ramzi Yousef."

Of course I knew something bin Laden probably did not: that Yousef's partner from the Manila bomb factory, Wali Khan, was cooperating secretly with the FBI. I was curious—since Wali Khan had told the agents that he and bin Laden were pals—to know whether bin Laden had ever really met Wali Khan. When I mentioned Wali Khan, bin Laden looked up.

"Wali Khan," bin Laden began, "is one of the best youths. We were good friends. We fought together in the same trench against the Russians until Allah sent them away in humiliating defeat. You mentioned that he works for me? We do not have anyone who works for someone else. We all work for Allah and await his reward."

That may be so. But I had my answer. Wali Khan had been Ramzi Yousef's key man. Before that he had been one of bin Laden's key men. The link was there. At least in my mind, it gave what Wali Khan was telling the FBI even more credibility.

In the winter of 1997, Khan, wearing a bright orange jumpsuit, had sat in a closed room in the Metropolitan Correctional Center in Lower Manhattan, patiently explaining to the FBI that the mercury found in his apartment in Manila was not for bomb-making but for placing inside the bullets that would be used to shoot President Clinton. "That way," Khan said, "if the shot didn't kill him, he would die by poisoning."

Sitting in the hut on bin Laden's mountain in Afghanistan, I asked bin Laden if he had put out a contract on the president of the United States of America. He gave this answer: "As I said, every action elicits a similar reaction," he explained. "What does Clinton expect from those that he killed, assaulting their children and mothers?"

Bin Laden told me his first priority was to get the American military bases out of Saudi Arabia, the holiest of lands in Islam. "Every day the Americans delay their departure, they will receive a new corpse."

Bin Laden said that the American military would leave Saudi Arabia, regardless of the fact that the Saudi royal family welcomes the American presence. "It does not make a difference if the government wants you to stay or leave. You will leave when the youth send you in wooden boxes and coffins. And you will carry in them the bodies of American troops and civilians. This is when you will leave."

Civilians? Bin Laden looked up for a second when he uttered these words, which would echo around the world—because what I didn't know, and bin Laden did, was that an attack on American civilians was already in the operational stage, set to be launched in just a couple of months: "We do not differentiate between those dressed in military uniforms and civilians; they are all targets in this fatwa." Bin Laden argued that American outrage at attacks on American civilians constitutes a great double standard.

Bin Laden was claiming, in essence, that what we consider to be terrorism is simply the amount of violence required to get the attention of the American people. His aim was to get Americans to consider whether continued support of Israel is worth the bloodshed he promised. "So we tell the Americans as people," bin Laden said softly, "and we tell the mothers of soldiers and American mothers in general that if they value their lives and the lives of their children, to find a nationalistic government that will look after their interests and not the interests of the Jews.

The continuation of tyranny will bring the fight to America, as Ramzi Yousef and others did. This is my message to the American people: to look for a serious government that looks out for their interests and does not attack others, their lands, or their honor. And my word to American journalists is not to ask why we did that but ask what their government has done that forced us to defend ourselves." His last words to the camera were "It is our duty to lead people to the light."

Ali had been told to sit in the back of the room during the interview. When it was over, I went looking for him. "So, do we have a story?" I whispered when I found him. "Please tell me it wasn't just an hour of 'Praise Allah, Grace be upon him' and the rest."

"No," Ali said. "We have a very good story."

I asked Ali what bin Laden had said that would make this news.

"He was looking right into your face," Ali said, "and he was saying that you—you people, the Americans—would be going home from the Middle East in coffins and in boxes."

"He said that?" I asked, excited. "And while he was saying this, what was I doing?" Ali looked at me a bit oddly and said, "You were nodding like you agreed with his plan."

During the hour-long interview, bin Laden, assuming correctly that I did not understand a word he was saying, had taken to looking at his translator as he gave his answers. So, to keep his responses directed toward our camera, to make it look less awkward, I began to engage him in knowing eye contact and nodded thoughtfully. "So, Ali, you're telling me he's promising genocide, and I'm nodding like I agree?"

"Yes," Ali said, smiling. *Great,* I thought.

But we had our story, and on June 10, 1998, first on *World News Tonight* with Peter Jennings and then in a full half hour on *Nightline* with Ted Koppel, we introduced Osama bin Laden to the American people. The story caused a bit of a stir in government circles. The U.S. State Department put out a Worldwide Travel Advisory telling Americans traveling abroad to use caution because of the recent threat. Outside of that, bin Laden's fatwa did not attract much attention. To most people he was a nonentity. How could one man operating from a cave in Afghanistan try to take on the United States?

After our interview that chilly night in late May, bin Laden was once again surrounded by his men, leaving the way he came in, in a hail of celebratory gunfire. It was past two in the morning. This time, Rick shot the whole scene. But as we packed our gear, Mohammed Atef, bin Laden's military commander, and an aide came over to inspect our tape. Looking carefully at each scene of bin Laden arriving and leaving, they ordered any face not covered with a *kaffiyeh* to be erased. When I objected, they said the deal was simple: If we did not delete the faces, we would not leave with the tape. And so, into the night, they played and rewound, played and rewound. Over each face, Atef and an aide would confer. "He travels," one would say to the other, and we'd have to delete that second or two of footage.

One face in the crowd that night belonged to a man named Mohamed al-'Owhali. A day or two after the interview, al-'Owhali approached bin Laden and asked him for an assignment. He wanted an important job in the jihad. He was willing to sacrifice his life for the cause. Bin Laden counseled patience. But a few days after that he summoned al-'Owhali and revealed his mission to him: the suicide operation against an American target in Africa. Al-'Owhali was about to "travel."

CHAPTER 13

EMBASSY BOMBINGS

Bin Laden had been explicit about the timing of the next attack against a U.S. target. In our interview he had said "within the next several weeks." Having witnessed firsthand his penchant for self-dramatization, I figured he was going to stick to that self-imposed timetable. He had just put a face on a movement few Americans understood, and his future as a global figure depended on his ability to deliver on his threats.

What no one I knew could predict was where the strike would come. Bin Laden had talked about liberating the Palestinians, about forcing U.S. withdrawal from his native Saudi Arabia—"Every day the Americans delay their departure, they will receive a new corpse," he'd said. My guess was he intended to hit a U.S. target in the Middle East, most likely another military installation in Saudi Arabia itself.

The FBI's John O'Neill understood that something was coming soon.

On the Fourth of July, Jerry Hauer, a buddy of his who was director of New York City's Emergency Management office, was driving by O'Neill on a Manhattan street and pulled over to rag him about wearing shorts in public. O'Neill wasn't in a kidding mood. Leaning into the car, he said, "My friend's causing trouble again." Asked to explain himself, O'Neill said softly: "OBL. This guy's a problem."

Years later, it's still not clear how close any government agents ever came to disrupting a plot that resulted in the nearly simultaneous bombings of the U.S. embassies in Kenya and Tanzania on August 7. The first blast, in the Kenyan capital of Nairobi, injured some 4,500 people and killed 213, including 40 embassy employees. Another 11 lives were lost in Tanzania, where the lower casualty numbers owed mostly to luck: August 7 happened to be a national holiday, and the U.S. embassy in Dar es Salaam had been closed.

What has become clear with time is that facets of the East Africa plot had been known beforehand to the FBI, the CIA, the State Department, and to the Israeli and Kenyan intelligence services. The embassy attacks thus represented law enforcement's most egregious failure to date to protect the lives and interests of Americans and American allies against bin Laden's vicious holy war. Though, as any law enforcement official will remind you, intercepting 100 percent of all terror attempts is an impossibility, no one can seriously argue that the horrors of August 7, 1998, couldn't have been prevented.

It's hard to pinpoint the exact date bin Laden formed a cell in Kenya, but he had key associates stationed in Nairobi approximately five years before the embassy blasts. Bin Laden, then based in neighboring Sudan, was using Kenya as a staging area for his proxy war against the U.S. in Somalia, and he undoubtedly was anticipating a long battle over the future of East Africa. The Afghanistan veterans then pouring into the region had successfully turned back one superpower intrusion into the Muslim world, but that great victory hadn't come overnight.

Sometime before 1993 bin Laden dispatched Ali Mohamed, the former U.S. Army sergeant, to survey potential terror targets in Nairobi. Upon his return to Khartoum, Mohamed showed bin Laden photographs of the American embassy, the French Cultural Center and other key western targets, then watched as his leader drew a blue pencil line at the rear of the U.S. Embassy indicating where a truck could enter. The embassy had just become a target.

Even so, bin Laden was in no hurry to execute the embassy plot. As investigators would later find out, the Nairobi cell was one of many around the world. The U.S. embassy in Nairobi was just one target among hundreds. A careful, deliberate executive, bin Laden was willing to wait until the political climate and operational details were perfectly aligned before green-lighting any attack.

On the other hand, the Kenyan cell was never just any al Qaeda cell. One measure of its importance during the Somalia operation was that bin Laden sent his old Saudi friend Khaled al-Fawwaz, as well as the organization's top military official at the time, Abu Ubaidah al-Banshiri, to establish the cell's infrastructure. Al-Banshiri and al-Fawwaz arranged for apartments, cars, safe houses; they set up small businesses in and around Nairobi—whatever was necessary for a group of al Qaeda men and their families to blend into the local population. Then, in 1994, al-Fawwaz was transferred to London to serve as al Qaeda's director of worldwide media communications, and leadership of the cell was passed to three other veterans of the war in Afghanistan.

At least two of the three new cell leaders in Kenya arrived fresh from training and arming fighters for the warlords who were trying to turn back the U.S. humanitarian mission in Somalia. One of them, in fact—a slim Palestinian named Mohamed Saddiq Odeh—would later boast that he had provided the rocket launchers and rifles that brought down two Black Hawk helicopters and killed 18 U.S. soldiers in the infamous October 1993 firefight in Mogadishu. When Odeh moved to Kenya in 1994, he settled not in Nairobi itself, but 200 miles to the south, in the port city of Mombassa.

There he enjoyed the company of a new bride and the run of a seven-ton fishing boat that he generally used to sell other crews' catches at ports up and down the west coast of the Indian Ocean. Obviously, the ship also provided anyone so inclined with a convenient means of moving war-making materials in or out of the country.

The other two cell leaders began sharing a home in Nairobi sometime in 1994. Haroun Fazul, a native East African and former university student, had, like Odeh, recently been training fighters in Somalia. His boss, a 34-year-old father of five young children, had recently served a two-year stint as Osama bin Laden's personal secretary, and U.S. intelligence agents would come to be mesmerized by him, so much so that they seemed to lose sight of the most important reason to track the cell: to prevent it from doing harm.

To be fair, Wadih el-Hage did make an intriguing suspect. Born the only son of a Catholic family from Lebanon, he secretly converted to Islam at 14 and was disowned at the age of 18 after he revealed his secret to one of his sisters. The break had come just after el-Hage left the family home in Kuwait to study at the University of Southwestern Louisiana. Without his father's support, el-Hage could only afford about two classes a semester, but a Kuwaiti sheik who heard of the young man's plight soon stepped in to help pay the American school's tuition.

El-Hage's ties to the U.S. would grow stronger over the next two decades. But in 1981, the 21-year-old urban planning student put aside his books to lend his support to the American-backed mujahideen in Afghanistan. A withered right arm—the product of a botched operation at birth—limited el-Hage's effectiveness as a soldier. Even so, he quickly became a protégé of Abdullah Azzam, the father of the modern jihad movement, and he found various other ways to serve the cause. By some accounts, el-Hage served as a teacher or medic; on a later tour of duty, the soft-eyed warrior smuggled cash and supplies across the Pakistani border on a motorcycle. Throughout those years, he likely had frequent contact with another Azzam disciple, the young construction heir Osama bin Laden.

In 1984, el-Hage returned to the U.S. and entered into an arranged marriage early the next year with an 18-year-old American Muslim from Tucson. He completed his studies in 1986, and after briefly moving his bride and in-laws to Pakistan, he followed the whole clan back to Tucson. His wife's hometown, it should be noted, was home to one of the first al Qaeda cells in the U.S. The city's al-Kifah center, or Refugee Services Office, may even have predated Brooklyn's.

El-Hage apparently lived a quiet life in Tucson, working for low wages first as a truck driver, then as a city custodian. He kept up his overseas contacts, though, and soon after he became a U.S. citizen in 1989, he began popping up in the company of radical Islamic militants from Arizona to New York City.

The first hint to law enforcement of el-Hage's dangerous ongoing connections came in 1990, when it was learned he had escorted a suspect in the murder of a progressive imam on a visit to the victim's Phoenix mosque. Several members of Jamaat al-Fuqra, a radical Black Muslim sect, were eventually charged in the killing, and el-Hage's claim of innocence was allowed to stand. Still, investigators believed he had withheld vital information when he was questioned about the crime.

In early 1991, as investigators would later discover, el-Hage acquired two rifles and an AK-47 at the request of future World Trade Center bomber Mahmoud Abouhalima. Abouhalima, who had met el-Hage a few months earlier at an Islamic conference in Oklahoma City, later stated that he wanted the weapons to defend al-Kifah leaders in New York. Apparently, he never bothered to pick the guns up, but on the first day of March, Mustafa Shalabi, the emir of the Brooklyn al-Kifah office, was found shot and brutally bludgeoned to death in his home near Brooklyn's Coney Island. Police established that he had probably died about three days earlier.

Oddly enough, el-Hage had flown into New York the day Shalabi disappeared. El-Hage explained the coincidental timing of his arrival by claiming he had come to serve as the temporary leader of the Brooklyn office because Shalabi was planning to leave for Egypt. El-Hage's family later in fact told *Frontline* that el-Hage counted the victim as a good friend and may have been called in to calm a dispute that had pitted Shalabi against the blind sheik, Omar Abdel-Rahman. Abdel-Rahman had, almost since arriving in New York in 1990, questioned Shalabi's determination to continue pouring all of al-Kifah's money into Afghanistan despite the Soviets' withdrawal. Even members of Shalabi's inner circle, including Abouhalima, had joined the dissenters. None, however, were ever charged in Shalabi's murder. In fact, the crime has never been solved.

El-Hage left one other intriguing crumb during his New York adventure. Before catching his plane home, he paid a visit to El Sayyid Nosair, Meir Kahane's assassin, who was awaiting trial in a Lower Manhattan jail.

About a year later, while living in Texas, el-Hage received the offer of a lifetime. According to his wife, he jetted to Sudan to be interviewed, and returned with the news that Saudi millionaire Osama bin Laden needed a personal secretary and business agent and was offering $1,200 a month. "He seems fair," el-Hage allegedly reported. "Let's do it." A $14,000 salary apparently went a long way in Khartoum.

The job involved a lot of traveling. Over the next two years, el-Hage circled the globe, opening al Qaeda bank accounts, buying asphalt, seeking markets for Sudanese sesame seeds and corn, even purchasing a plane for transporting Stinger missiles from Afghanistan to bin Laden's current base country. Investigators believe he was finally transferred to Nairobi when al-Fawwaz, the original leader of the East African cell, began attracting too much attention.

El-Hage, along with his wife, his five children, and his subordinate Haroun Fazul, settled in a modest home near the Nairobi airport. El-Hage was, by all accounts, a model neighbor. Kids from the local Muslim academy were welcome at his home and his American wife became an active member of the school's PTA. How el-Hage earned a living, however, was a bit of a mystery. He and Fazul often worked at a computer in the house, and el-Hage handed out business cards identifying himself as the director of a private charity called Help Africa People. According to papers filed with the Kenyan government, the organization combated malaria by distributing mosquito control products, but U.S. investigators believe it was merely a cover for the cell's activities—meeting with foreign operatives, buying vehicles, transporting materials. El-Hage also maintained potentially profitable concerns on the side, including a gem-trading business that never seemed to realize its potential. Intriguingly, some of his business cards included the address of a Hamburg office building used by al Qaeda operatives who've since been linked to the 2001 hijacking attacks.

If the neighbors knew nothing of el-Hage's militant activities, the CIA already had much of his radical biography on file by mid-1996, when their debriefings of Jamal al-Fadl alerted them to the fact that al Qaeda maintained an important cell in Nairobi. Having gotten a glimpse of that file, investigators from the New York–based Joint Terrorism Task Force became convinced that flipping el-Hage was the best way to get to bin Laden. Of course, they felt they needed to gather more evidence against el-Hage before approaching him.

Kenya's police force was, by all accounts, riddled with corruption, so U.S. officials were wary of seeking a partnership. El-Hage's U.S. citizenship also presented an obstacle. Not only does the U.S. maintain strict regulations on monitoring in general, but there was remarkably little legal precedent at the time regarding the monitoring of U.S. citizens abroad. In the end, a special wiretap application had to be filed with the U.S. Attorney General's office, and the CIA finally was able to begin bugging el-Hage's Nairobi phone in early 1997.

The taps, unfortunately, yielded little useful information. Speaking in Arabic, el-Hage used a prearranged code to discuss sensitive matters. He referred to bombs as "weddings," for example, and to bomb makers as "engineers," and U.S. agents failed to decipher the code words until the "weddings" had already taken hundreds of lives. The CIA did know, from the numbers and locations el-Hage was calling, that he was speaking with bin Laden's people, and through them, most likely, to bin Laden. They knew as well that he made frequent trips to Peshawar and from there to bin Laden's new base in Afghanistan, usually returning with fresh influxes of cash. An al Qaeda document written in February 1997 describes one such pilgrimage in which el-Hage received instructions to begin military operations in East Africa. But as far as the law enforcement effort was concerned, little progress was made against al Qaeda in the first year that followed al-Fadl's windfall testimony.

A significant arrest shook things up in May 1997. Mandini al-Tayyib, bin Laden's brother-in-law and al Qaeda's chief financial officer, found his way into the hands of Saudi intelligence that month and in return for a promise of asylum agreed to share organization secrets on the condition that none of the information would be passed on to the U.S.

The Saudis honored their end of that unseemly deal. But when the British press broke the story that the Saudis had al-Tayyib in custody, then wrongly reported that al-Tayyib's secrets were being shared with the Americans, panic gripped the East African cell—as well as many of their contacts around the world.

Phone traffic increased dramatically: The CIA and NSA were picking up almost daily communications between el-Hage and al Qaeda members in Afghanistan, Pakistan, London, Germany and Mombassa. Many of the calls were tinged with desperation. *What was al-Tayyib saying? What should they do?* In one instance, while el-Hage was traveling in Afghanistan, Fazul felt compelled to explicitly warn a Hamburg operative, a man known as Abu Khadija, to stop calling because the lines were bugged. Hamburg kept calling anyway.

Once again, however, phone taps failed to turn up any smoking guns, and few, if any, incriminating statements. Certain they were under surveillance, cell members had become especially judicious about what they said, and at times even postured about their legitimacy and innocence.

Finally, on August 21, 1997, the FBI decided to act. As el-Hage was returning from Afghanistan, JTTF agents stopped him at the Nairobi airport.

Making it clear to him that al Qaeda's activities in Kenya were known to them, they strongly suggested el-Hage return home to the U.S. Meanwhile, another JTTF agent joined Kenyan police in a search of el-Hage's house in Nairobi. Using a fraud charge as a pretext—the police had traced the production of phony documents to his home—they confiscated el-Hage's date books, diaries and computer. They also told el-Hage's wife, who was present during the search, that it was no longer safe for her or her family to stay in Kenya.

The agents' purposes were threefold.

First, they wanted to get el-Hage back to the U.S., where they could keep closer tabs on him.

Second, they felt that with al-Tayyib cooperating, el-Hage might be more open to a "pitch"—an offer to make him a paid government informant. After all, el-Hage was a U.S. citizen and by then had seven children to support. Even if the first pitch failed, the government intended to put el-Hage in front of a grand jury, catch him lying, and then use the threat of prison to leverage his cooperation.

Most important, the task force wanted to disrupt el-Hage's cell and end its potential for violence.

But the plan failed on every count that mattered.

El-Hage did run: In September, he flew with his family into New York and was greeted at the airport by federal agents. They warned him that if he lied he could expect to spend the rest of his life in prison, then interrogated him into the night and brought him before a grand jury in the morning. El-Hage, though he admitted having worked briefly for bin Laden, didn't concede much else. He denied knowing anything about al Qaeda operations in East Africa, denied knowing any of the individual bin Laden followers he was asked about, and even refused to acknowledge authorship of a letter that he allowed looked as if it were written in his hand.

Prosecutors had sufficient evidence now to charge him with perjury, but he was cut loose instead and placed under close surveillance. El-Hage had been trained to be patient, however. Settling in Arlington, Texas, he took a job as the manager of a tire shop, and lived quietly with his wife and seven kids in a cinder-block apartment building located next to a tattoo parlor. The surveillance picked up nothing that would incriminate el-Hage or any other al Qaeda members.

In October, the FBI questioned him a second time. Again he lied about his al Qaeda contacts.

The hardest thing to understand in retrospect is why U.S. law enforcement did nothing else to disrupt the activities of the Nairobi cell. When el-Hage left Kenya, Haroun Fazul simply stepped into the vacant leadership slot and seamlessly resumed preparations for the embassy bombings. A garden-variety robbery crew would show at least as much resilience. Did the CIA and the FBI still not yet understand that an al Qaeda soldier was eminently replaceable?

Mary Jo White, the Justice Department's lead terrorism prosecutor at the time, says that her office continued to be concerned about the East African cell, but felt that it had been disrupted for the time being and no longer posed a greater threat than countless other pockets of anti-American militants around the world. Abu al-Banshiri, al Qaeda's chief military officer and director of East African operations, had died with 800 others in a 1996 ferry accident on Lake Victoria. The Kenyan cell's other founder, Khaled al-Fawwaz, had long since been transferred to London, and el-Hage, their successor, was strapped down in Texas where he wouldn't be able to twitch a muscle without U.S. intelligence knowing about it.

Yet Fazul had gift-wrapped the FBI a piece of evidence that all but cried out for further attention.

Shortly after raiding el-Hage's home in Nairobi, the Bureau dredged up from his computer's hard drive a number of troubling files. One of them contained a lengthy letter signed by Haroun Fazul, addressed to al Qaeda communications director al-Fawwaz, and dated a week before the FBI swooped in on el-Hage's home. Fazul may come across as a man who's easy to rattle, but he could hardly be categorized as a non-threat. He wrote to al-Fawwaz:

> We understood that there is a war and the situation is dangerous and anybody who is associated with [bin Laden] regardless of their position and nationality are at risk . . . My recommendation to my brothers in East Africa was to not be complacent regarding security matters and that they should know that there is an American-Kenyan-Egyptian intelligence activity in Nairobi aiming to identify the names and residences of the members who are associated with [bin Laden] since America knows well that the youth who lived in Somalia and were members of [bin Laden's] cell are the ones who killed the Americans in Somalia. They know that since Kenya was the main gateway for those members, there must be a center in Kenya . . .
>
> The fact of these matters and others leave us no choice but to ask ourselves are we ready for that big clandestine battle?
>
> . . . We, the East Africa Cell members, do not want to know about the operations plans since we are just implementers. We trust our command and appreciate their work and know that they have a lot of problems. But my advice here is for the practical part only since we started the project for "Re-establishing the Muslim State" as a collective effort and not an individual one; we are all part of it. So we are asking you for the sake of organizing the work, to tell us that there is a possible danger that may take place in a while due to a certain decision so we can prepare ourselves accordingly or [so that] we may go underground for a while since our presence might foil or complicate your plans that we know nothing of.

Not only does the eight-page letter admit to the existence of a Nairobi cell—and Fazul's participation in it; it also refers to a group of "partisans" in Mombassa, and talks about the imminent arrival of "engineers" in Nairobi.

In this sprawling, fevered document, Fazul also frets that Egypt, Kenya and the U.S. have launched a joint campaign to kidnap and kill cell members—perhaps because under the circumstances he can't imagine that they wouldn't have.

He vastly overestimated American resolve. Even with the letter and other documents in hand, the government failed to penetrate the rest of the cell, or arrest or detain any of its remaining members. When el-Hage was removed, the CIA wiretaps had to be removed too, meaning U.S. intelligence didn't even have nominal surveillance in place on Fazul.

Yet there were other warnings from independent sources.

In November 1997, a man named Mustafa Mahmoud Said Ahmed walked into the Nairobi embassy and informed intelligence officers about a plot to bomb the U.S. embassy. The CIA chose to disregard him. For one thing, U.S. officials received numerous tips about bomb plots every day. For another, they judged Ahmed an unreliable source. Not only did he fail a polygraph test, but he was also said to have made similar reports—reports that had not been borne out—to other embassies in Africa.

On the other hand, Ahmed was employed by one of bin Laden's Kenyan companies and may have therefore been in a position to know what he was talking about.

The U.S. government also chose to turn down repeated requests for more security from Prudence Bushnell, whom President Clinton had appointed ambassador to Kenya in July 1996. Bushnell, a career diplomat, knew that her embassy, located on the street at one of Nairobi's busiest intersections, presented a security nightmare, and she was not surprised when she was told that the State Department didn't have the budget to improve conditions. Still, she had been concerned enough about potential threats to short-circuit the chain of command and appeal directly in a letter to the secretary of state, Madeleine Albright.

As a former State Department official notes, Bushnell's request was one of scores that poured in from U.S. embassies around the world. Yet the climate in which these requests were made has to be considered. Since 1996, bin Laden had issued a series of escalating fatwas promising strikes against

U.S. targets, culminating in the May 1998 ABC interview in which he virtually guaranteed a terrorist action in the very near future.

Also, just months before the August 7 bombings, the Kenyan Intelligence Service warned the CIA about the imminent plot, according to Paul Muite, a prominent lawyer and legislator in Kenya. Muite says he was told by a top Kenyan intelligence official that the CIA showed the Kenyan report to Mossad, who were dismissive about its reliability, and that the CIA then chose to ignore it.

After an event like the Embassy bombings, these kinds of retrospective "signs" are not uncommon. Even one of the U.S. officials who were urging greater vigilance before the blasts has pointed out that Muite is a politician with an agenda and that his statements should be taken with a grain of salt.

Still, if there was only a particle of truth to Muite's allegations, the tip from Kenyan intelligence should have been a red flag to any U.S. official familiar with the existing files on the East African cell.

Inexplicable as the intelligence failure was, more baffling still was that al Qaeda correctly presumed that a major attack could be carried out by a cell that U.S. agents had already uncovered.

At about the time I was sitting across a table from bin Laden, Haroun Fazul had laid down cash for a six-month lease on a gated villa in Nairobi he shouldn't have been able to afford. The main residence had four bedrooms, three baths and a garage suited for bomb building. Best of all, the property was surrounded on all sides by a high wall and a hedge. Yet the landlady noticed that when her new tenant moved in with his wife and two young children, he was driving a Mitsubishi that he had to push to start. Furniture seemed to be beyond the family's means.

Approximately 2,000 pounds of TNT, aluminum nitrate and aluminum powder was carted into the villa's garage before final preparations began. The explosives were eventually packed into six wooden boxes and loaded onto a battered Toyota cargo truck. Tanks of oxygen and acetylene were also thrown in by the bomb makers on the widespread but mistaken assumption that the gases enhance an explosion.

Mohamed Odeh, al Qaeda's man on the Kenyan coast, has said he got word August 1 that he had less than a week to flee the country, so he bought an airline ticket and grabbed an all-night bus into Nairobi a couple days later.

Mohamed al-'Owhali, the 21-year-old Saudi who'd been a face in the machine-gun-toting crowd during my bin Laden interview, arrived alone in Nairobi on Sunday, August 2. After phoning Pakistan for orders, he was retrieved from the suburban Ramada where he'd checked in and was driven by Fazul to the Hilltop Hotel, a $10-a-night dive in the heart of Nairobi. Four men greeted him there, including another young Saudi, known as Azzam, whom al-'Owhali had met in Afghanistan.

The designated martyrs, Azzam and al-'Owhali, were briefed about their roles in the upcoming operation and informed of the twin strike planned for the Tanzanian capital and perhaps of at least one other planned attack that never materialized. The bombings were to be carried out Friday morning, August 7, between 10:30 and 11:00—a time frame selected because devout Muslims would be praying in the shelter of their mosques at that hour. After the plotters shared dinner, the martyrs were taken to the villa to look in on the truck and its payload. The bomb was now connected to a detonator that was in turn wired to several vehicular batteries and then to a button under the dashboard. Fazul led a tour of their targeted site the next day.

By Tuesday, when Odeh arrived from the coast and checked into the Hilltop, senior operatives were already beginning to leave the country. Odeh may have been the last one out, spending part of Thursday shopping for clothes before catching a 10:00 P.M. flight to Pakistan.

At about 9:30 Friday morning, al-'Owhali and Azzam boarded the cargo truck and, with Azzam driving, rumbled out from the villa toward busy downtown Nairobi and the U.S. embassy. Fazul led the way in a Datsun pickup while the martyrs behind him played Islamic tapes on the stereo and chanted religious prayers to keep their courage up. On Azzam's suggestion, al-'Owhali shed the light jacket he was wearing because it could slow him down when he tried to pull the handmade stun grenades from his waistband.

Shortly after the bombers set off, U.S. Ambassador Prudence Bushnell strolled into a 21-story glass office building just behind her embassy and rode the elevator to the top floor. She was skipping her own regular Friday morning staff meeting in order to sit down with Kenya's trade minister and brief him on an upcoming visit of the U.S. secretary of commerce. Beginning at about 10:00, the two dignitaries posed for photos and answered questions from the press for about 20 minutes, then narrowed their audience to a dozen or so aides and settled onto a sofa for tea.

At 10:30, Fazul peeled away from his comrades and Azzam and al-'Owhali rolled the Toyota up to the rear gate of the embassy. Back at the villa, they had rehearsed what was supposed to happen next: Al-'Owhali would jump from the truck, pull out a gun, and order the Kenyan guards to open the gate to the embassy's basement garage. Azzam would then speed down the ramp and detonate the bomb, collapsing the embassy from the inside and killing everyone on-site.

The plan demanded lightning speed and lockstep coordination. It would have neither. When al-'Owhali sprang from the passenger seat and began yelling at the guard, the gate didn't budge: Al-'Owhali had left his gun in the pocket of the jacket he had just abandoned on the passenger seat.

Improvising now, al-'Owhali grabbed one of the stun grenades, which had been intended for scattering pedestrians, and tossed it in the direction of the gatekeeper.

The explosion, no match for what was about to come, gave the guard a chance to run. But it would turn out to be just as lethal as the one-ton bomb waiting under the truck's tarpaulin, because it brought a great number of people to the windows—not just in the commerce minister's suite, but in all the nearby buildings—and exposed them to the steel and glass shards about to rip through their offices at 21,000 mph. Ambassador Bushnell, turning to the Kenyan trade minister, first asked if any construction projects were under way in the area, then moved to join her colleagues who were already peering out toward the rear of the embassy.

Azzam grabbed the 9 mm Beretta left behind by his partner and began firing at the embassy's windows. Al-'Owhali began to run. He later told authorities he had realized Azzam was positioned to detonate the bomb and reasoned there was no longer any glory in needlessly sacrificing his life. More likely, his instincts had taken over.

Azzam, however, had run out of options. He waited a few seconds for al-'Owhali to get clear and pressed the button on the truck's dashboard.

Bushnell felt the concussion and thought, "Bomb."

Then she was airborne.

When the ambassador came to, she was alone, sitting with her hands over her head as chunks of the ceiling tumbled down on her. She could hear the steady rattling of a tea cup. "This building is falling," she remembers thinking. "I'm going to die."

Bushnell's lip was split and blood was running down her suit. A man's body lay facedown near her. She assumed he was dead. It didn't yet occur to her that the embassy had been the target.

The back half of the embassy, however, was gone. Frank Pressley, the post's communications director, had been talking with an administrative manager named Michelle O'Connor on the first floor when the blast hit. He opened his eyes to see blood and human flesh on his office walls, a man's legs lying in the rubble, and Michelle O'Connor's decapitated body. Bones were sticking out of Pressley's own shirt.

Al-'Owhali, knocked down by the blast, got to his feet on Haile Selassie Avenue and made his way to a first-aid station. He had suffered cuts to his back, his hands and his forehead.

A young Commerce Department official found Ambassador Bushnell in the meeting room and together they searched the 21st floor for survivors before climbing over a blown-out door into a stairwell. As the two Americans descended, the stairway became choked with evacuees, and the injuries of those pouring in through the fire doors looked increasingly serious. Bushnell noticed there was more and more blood on her, but she couldn't find the injury. Then she realized the person following her was bleeding onto her back and into her hair. Lower still, the crowd's progress stopped in a blanket of thickening, noxious smoke, and Bushnell thought for the second time that morning that she was about to die.

She finally emerged into the smoky daylight, however, and as she caught sight of the crush of onlookers across the street, the young man from Commerce pushed her head down to keep the press from recognizing her. With her eyes lowered, she saw only random images of the horror around her: metal and glass debris on the sidewalk, the burned-out husks of over-turned cars, a charred body in the embassy parking lot, a burning bus, ghost passengers still seated in rows.

When she finally looked up, Bushnell realized for the first time that the embassy itself had been bombed. The exposed floors were sagging and filled with smoke.

She ducked into a hotel to clean up and then headed to the makeshift control center that embassy officials had set up a few blocks from the devastation. There, Bushnell listened to the early casualty estimates and learned that just seven minutes after the Nairobi explosion, an identical bomb had destroyed the U.S. embassy in Dar es Salaam.

A phone call came in from Secretary of State Madeleine Albright in Washington. "How could this have happened?" Albright asked her.

For the first time since the blast, Bushnell's horror turned to anger. There was too much history.

"I wrote you a letter," she said.

CHAPTER 14

THE SLEEPING GIANT AWAKENS

On August 20, 1998, America hit back. Less than two weeks after bin Laden's bombs rocked the embassies in Nairobi and Dar es Salaam, U.S. submarines stationed in the Arabian Sea off Pakistan's coastline launched 75 or so Tomahawk cruise missiles at two bin Laden–linked targets. The primary target was a complex of training camps in eastern Afghanistan, near Khost, where, according to CIA intelligence, bin Laden was meeting with his top aides. The second target was a factory in Khartoum that the CIA believed was producing chemical weapons for bin Laden. The attack demolished both sites and killed about 20 men, a handful of them members of al Qaeda.

But the mission was not a success. Intended to kill or at least send a strong message to bin Laden and his aides, the attack did neither. According to the CIA, its intelligence was off by a few hours, and bin Laden and his senior people escaped without harm. Nor, by all accounts, were bin Laden's troops intimidated, having spent years under bombardment in Afghanistan and places like Chechnya and Bosnia.

The attacks almost certainly caused bin Laden to heighten security arrangements, making the already elusive leader even harder to pin down. And while the attacks may have satisfied the administration's mandate for a measured response, they also seem to have convinced bin Laden that the U.S. had no stomach for the kind of ground war that would have posed a real threat to his operation.

But the U.S. lost the most on the public relations front. By going after *and* not getting bin Laden, the U.S. elevated his stature in the Arab world, in much the same way prosecutors inadvertently added to John Gotti's myth each time they tried and failed to convict him. In the wake of the U.S. attacks, mothers in the Middle East named their sons Osama, and al Qaeda's camps were flooded with new recruits.

Moreover, the U.S. lost face in the region. The long-range attacks allowed bin Laden to portray the U.S. military as a paper tiger lacking the courage to engage his holy warriors on the battlefield. The administration came under fire at home as well. Critics picked at the strike's ineffectiveness in general and the legitimacy of the Sudanese target in particular. Though senior Clinton officials maintain that their intelligence on the plant was accurate, even the CIA admits it was patchy, and the Sudanese were able to make a persuasive case in the media that the factory was engaged in the production of legitimate pharmaceuticals and that its owner had no links to bin Laden or any terror group. What's more, the Sudanese had captured two key suspects in the embassy bombings case and were negotiating their surrender to the FBI when the missiles struck, surprising both Sudanese and Bureau officials, and ending their talks.

However the attack was perceived, its planning and execution point up the implacable difficulties the administration faced in dealing with bin Laden and al Qaeda.

•   •   •

Administration officials had known right away that the Embassy plot had been orchestrated by bin Laden. On August 7, the day of the bombings, alert Pakistani immigration officials at Karachi Airport detained a tall man traveling with a Yemeni passport. There was nothing suspicious about his passport as such, but its photo showed a man with a full beard, and the passport's bearer, Mohammed Saddiq Odeh, who turned out to be the leader of al Qaeda's Mombassa cell, had shaved his beard a few days before so he wouldn't stand out as a religious zealot.

Odeh had left Nairobi the day before, stopping in Dubai en route to Karachi. Under questioning by immigration, Odeh admitted his participation in the Nairobi plot. He went on to describe the planning for the bombing at the Hilltop Hotel in Nairobi, even giving the address of the villa where the bomb was built and the names of the other bombers. Most important, though, he admitted to being a member of al Qaeda, under the leadership of bin Laden.

Then, on August 12, the Nairobi police received a tip that one of the bombers might be among the injured. The police tracked the information to a local hospital and discovered al-'Owhali with back wounds he'd received running away from the explosion. Later that week, under questioning by FBI agents, he too broke down and confessed his role in the bombing and his links to al Qaeda.

The trail became cold after al-'Owhali. Apparently, all the senior al Qaeda operatives—the men who engineered the bombs—had already left the region, probably for Afghanistan, prior to August 7. But the links to bin Laden were now firmly established.

As administration officials reviewed their options for retaliation against bin Laden, law enforcement stepped up other efforts to disrupt al Qaeda. During the first months following the embassy attacks, the authorities apprehended Khaled al-Fawwaz, the organization's communications director, who had been faxed statements heralding the bombings 12 hours before the explosions took place; Mamdou Salim, al Qaeda's religious leader and business manager, who would later stab a prison guard in the face while attempting to escape from prison; and Wadih el-Hage, bin Laden's former secretary and the one-time leader of the Nairobi cell, who was charged with 20 counts of perjury and 7 counts of conspiracy to kill Americans.

Meanwhile, the NSA reviewed the transcripts of calls made from the al Qaeda safe house in Nairobi during the months before the bombings, now managing to decipher some of the code words (among them "wedding" for bomb and "engineer" for bomb maker). They then combed through tapes of conversations within suspected cells around the world, looking for calls using the same code words.

Just days after the bombings, working with foreign police and intelligence services, the CIA began a series of other disruptions, breaking up cells in Uganda (where, informants divulged, the U.S. embassy had been a third target), India and Albania. Cell members were arrested locally and in many cases deported to their home countries, where often they were wanted for serious crimes. New evidence was gathered. A computer confiscated in the Albanian raid revealed that hundreds of targets around the world had already been surveilled and approved by al Qaeda's leadership. Several imminent plots—including a plan to bomb the U.S. embassy in the Albanian capital, Tirana—were stopped, no doubt saving hundreds, if not thousands, of lives.

But bin Laden and his top people remained at large, and national security officials worried that eventually a cell would slip past their guard, as happened in Nairobi. Many of these officials felt that in order to end al Qaeda's threat, the government had to go after its leadership, bin Laden in particular. Some of these officials went a step further. To really knock out a terrorist organization like al Qaeda, the U.S. would have to take on the governments that nurtured it, that provided it with safe haven and infrastructure. As Michael Sheehan, who became the State Department's counterterrorism chief in the wake of the embassy bombings, put it, "You have to drain the swamp."

Up until then, the administration hadn't taken bin Laden or al Qaeda all that seriously. As early as 1995, President Clinton had spoken about the threat of global terrorism before the UN General Assembly, and as late as June 1998, just two months before the embassy bombings, National Security chief Samuel Berger had told *Nightline* that "Osama bin Laden may be the most dangerous non-state terrorist in the world." But for the most part, the administration had dealt with bin Laden and his organization as a law enforcement matter. Even after U.S. prosecutors in New York's Southern District indicted bin Laden in early 1997 for conspiring to kill American soldiers in Somalia, the administration had made only perfunctory efforts to extradite him from Afghanistan.

Though his capabilities and intentions were known to the administration, bin Laden simply hadn't done anything that warranted their intervention. Bin Laden and al Qaeda had been linked, if only peripherally, to some horrific plots, but ones that either hadn't come to fruition or, if they had, hadn't exceeded the limits of what, according to the State Department's Sheehan, the government seemed to view as an "acceptable level of terrorism."

The 1993 World Trade Center bombing, for example, had been viewed by many in the government as a terrorist act that hadn't entirely come off. The Towers had withstood the impact of the explosion and the death toll had been only six. The building was operational again within weeks, and President Clinton never even felt compelled to visit the site.

The Landmarks plot to simultaneously blow up the UN, the FBI and the Lincoln and Holland Tunnels, a plot potentially as horrific as September 11, had been preempted and received scant attention at the national level.

Similarly, Ramzi Yousef's terrifying menu of aircraft downings and assassinations, and his plan for flying a small plane loaded with explosives into the CIA building in Langley, a preview of the September 11 plot, were either interdicted, or failed of themselves.

In truth, there had been numerous acts of terrorism against foreign targets on foreign soil throughout the 1990s, including a failed 1994 al Qaeda attempt to fly a hijacked airliner into the Eiffel Tower. (French commandos stormed the plane while it was refueling in Marseilles and killed the Algerian-born hijackers.) But none of these incidents had sparked any meaningful action by the U.S. government, and al Qaeda's fatwas and declarations of war had triggered little more than a security alert. Bin Laden simply hadn't done anything up until Nairobi that terrible, or as Sheehan put it, "Before the embassy bombings, Osama bin Laden was viewed within the administration as a gnat buzzing around a giant elephant's ear."

Now the giant elephant was awake. By this time, however, the U.S.'s options for retaliation were limited, and none of them that good. In the two years since bin Laden had left Sudan, he'd developed an almost unassailable base within Afghanistan. He'd poured money into the nation's parched economy, built roads and power plants and set up a network of camps and fortifications to house hundreds of terrorists-in-training as well as a private militia. Even more important, he'd forged an unbreakable bond with Taliban chief Mullah Omar, whom he'd first met and befriended during the war years. The two men became so close that each married a daughter of the other. In Sudan, bin Laden may have been an honored guest. In Afghanistan, he was family.

Severing those ties would not be easy for the U.S., given their already strained relations with the Taliban. The year before, in late 1997, after visiting an Afghani refugee camp, Secretary of State Madeleine Albright had chastised the Taliban for their despicable treatment of women. Hillary Clinton echoed Albright's criticism, and the U.S. had been the driving force behind UN-imposed sanctions on Afghanistan's Stone Age economy. Thus, U.S. envoys had limited wiggle room, and even less good will, in negotiating with the Taliban for bin Laden's surrender.

The administration's military options were only marginally better. A large-scale invasion of Afghanistan was felt to be politically untenable, and the Joint Chiefs recommended against a targeted commando-style attack as too risky. That seemingly left only one viable option: a long-range missile strike launched against bin Laden and his men from ships off the coast of

Pakistan, though that would require knowledge of bin Laden's whereabouts at least six hours in advance.

But then, even before Clinton's advisors had completed a review of their options, they were handed what they thought was an extraordinary opportunity to strike at bin Laden: the CIA's intelligence that the al Qaeda leader was about to meet with his top aides on August 20 at one of his training camps near Khost. Clinton's senior advisors unanimously recommended that the president order a missile attack on the site.

Clinton was in the midst of the Monica Lewinsky scandal. He'd testified before Congress in the days before the target date, admitting his affair with the young intern, and there was talk of his impeachment. Any decision he made on retaliation against bin Laden was likely to be viewed through a political lens: too mild a response, a sign of presidential paralysis; too strong a response, a case of "wagging the dog"—inflating a problem overseas in order to distract attention from his larger troubles at home. Nevertheless, Clinton approved the attack plans and added a second target, the Sudanese pharmaceutical plant.

Although the attacks failed to achieve their objectives, and despite the controversy over the second target, the pharmaceutical plant, few policy or opinion makers faulted the administration for the strategy behind the attacks. In fact, the *Times* and the *Washington Post* praised Clinton for his measured response to the East African bombings, and no other leader in Washington was calling in 1998 for a more strenuous response against bin Laden or his Taliban hosts.

Though Bill Clinton's hawkish critics now claim he was soft on terrorism, after the embassy bombings the Clinton administration actually waged a vigorous campaign against bin Laden, using all the viable military and law enforcement instruments at their command short of declaring war on the Taliban. The president soon doubled the counterterrorism budget, tripling the resources he allocated to the FBI and CTC. He issued a series of executive orders authorizing the CIA to use lethal force against bin Laden, his top deputies, and his aircraft. He repeatedly tasked the military to come up with a plan to neutralize bin Laden, and he permanently stationed two LA-class submarines in the nearest waters, in readiness to launch another missile attack.

Moreover, the Clinton administration actually had a counterterrorism policy. Until the mid-1990s, responsibility for counterterrorism had been divided among an alphabet soup of federal agencies. Then in 1995, the NSC's Samuel Berger signed up Richard Clarke, a bureaucratic "pile driver," to get them to work together. "I picked Dick to drive the counterterrorism train, even though I knew that at least once a month I'd get a call from some department head telling me I had to fire that guy," Berger says. "I picked Dick because I knew I'd get that call."

Clarke chaired a weekly meeting of senior security officials in the basement of the Old Executive Building to coordinate programs and hammer out policy recommendations; and every few weeks, Berger met with a handful of core cabinet officials, known as the Small Group, to make sure that Clarke's recommendations were given weight. During one six-week period in the fall of 1999, when the U.S. had been tipped off about the Millennium plots, Berger met virtually every day with the heads of the national security agencies to make sure "that everyone was on the same page." But the political and foreign policy concerns that had set the boundaries for the August 20 retaliatory strike stayed in effect, even deepening during Clinton's last year in office, and his efforts to capture or kill bin Laden were marked by frustration and dwindling options.

Three times during the final 29 months of Clinton's tenure, the CIA thought they had bin Laden in its crosshairs, and three times Clinton ordered final preparations for a missile launch, only to rescind those orders because the Agency couldn't verify its intelligence. The president's caution was well placed. On at least two of those occasions, the proposed target turned out to be someone other than bin Laden, according to a senior administration official. But even if it had been him, there's little guarantee that the missiles would have killed him, given the Tomahawk's relatively small footprint and the six-hour lag time from launch order to impact.

The problem, of course, was intelligence—not enough of it and not the right kind. The sightings had been based on signals intelligence or satellite surveillance. What was needed was human intelligence, someone on the ground close enough to bin Laden to identify him positively, and more important, to be able to predict his movements over the course of a day. Without someone like that, the Agency was just guessing, and with the stakes as high as they were, the U.S. couldn't afford another miss.

Frustrated, Clinton turned repeatedly to the Joint Chiefs to devise some form of limited action involving Special Forces. "It would be nice to drop a bunch of guys in black uniforms into one of bin Laden's camps in the middle of the night," he mused during one meeting with the military, a senior official recalls. "Wouldn't that scare the shit out of him?"

But the Joint Staff Chief Gen. Henry Shelton remained dead set against that kind of operation, which he deemed "going Hollywood." You couldn't just dump a small number of men into hostile, unfamiliar territory against battle-hardened fanatics defending their home ground without ample logistical support. You needed backup, a rescue plan in case something went wrong, as it often does. You needed more, not less, intelligence than that needed for a missile strike.

Shelton told Clinton the military could do the job, but continued to insist that it required a sustained, large-scale, multipoint offensive (on the order of the campaign waged after September 11). But neither Clinton, nor Shelton for that matter, felt the public would tolerate the loss of American lives likely to be incurred in that kind of an operation. Nor did Clinton feel he could sell an Afghan invasion to America's European allies, much less to the moderate Arab states whose cooperation, if only for logistical reasons, was vital. On another front, the Palestinian peace negotiations, which became Clinton's primary focus, depended on a relatively conflict-free environment to succeed. "Twelve Americans lost their lives in the embassy bombings," Samuel Berger told us. "You show me one reporter, one commentator, one member of Congress who thought we should invade Afghanistan before September 11 and I'll buy you dinner in the best restaurant in New York City."

Hamstrung by his lack of military options, Clinton turned to diplomatic solutions. His administration pressed the Saudis and Pakistanis, the Taliban's principal backers, to get the Taliban to give up bin Laden. But both countries had strong religious and cultural ties to the Taliban, and Pakistan had a vital strategic interest in having a strong ally on its western border. Although the Saudis eventually cut off government funding to Afghanistan after Mullah Omar rebuffed Prince Turki's entreaties on behalf of the U.S., they didn't place an embargo on private contributions.

The Pakistanis were even more ambivalent. Caught between his desire for Western aid and his military's fundamentalist sympathies, President Nawaz Sharif offered up an alternative solution in early 1999: a small commando force made up of Pakistani troops, trained and equipped by the CIA, to surprise bin Laden inside Afghanistan and kill or capture him. Just given the likelihood of security leaks, few officials in or outside of the administration gave the plan much credence, and it was dropped the following year when Gen. Pervez Musharraf seized power in a coup.

Meanwhile, the CIA launched a second front, hiring a mercenary group of Afghan fighters hostile to bin Laden and the Taliban, whom the administration called the Tribals. As part of the arrangement, the Agency slipped into southern Afghanistan in early 1999 and surveyed a deserted airstrip to be used in case the Tribals captured bin Laden or in case they themselves needed to be airlifted out. But the rendition idea was always a long shot. When the Agency presented the plan to the FBI at the Bureau's New York headquarters, an agent working with Alec station asked what the chances were of getting bin Laden back alive. "Slim to none," he was told.

The Tribals did engage bin Laden and his entourage in firefights on two occasions, according to their own reports. But the Agency wasn't able to confirm the attempts, and of course, bin Laden survived them.

As his second term wound down, Clinton asked for a report summarizing the efforts made to neutralize bin Laden so far. "Not good enough," he wrote in the margin of the finished report. "Unsatisfactory."

But Clinton was unwilling to expand the boundaries of military engagement set back in August 1998, especially now that he was focused on the peace negotiations between Israel and Palestine.

As a last-ditch effort, the administration resorted to a series of diplomatic bluffs, threatening military action against the Taliban. "If bin Laden or any of the organizations affiliated with him attacks the United States or United States interests, we will hold you, the leadership of the Taliban, personally accountable," the State Department's Sheehan warned the Taliban foreign minister in an April 2000 telephone call.

"If you have an arsonist in your basement, and he leaves your basement every night and burns your neighbors, and you're protecting him, you become responsible for his crimes," Sheehan added, according to the *Washington Post.*

It was a fitting analogy, but there was no starch in its conclusion. With the administration unwilling to take decisive military action, bin Laden remained, by default, mainly a law enforcement issue. The FBI continued to investigate and indict al Qaeda's senior operatives, and the CIA, working with local police and intelligence agencies, continued to identify and disrupt its cells around the world.

For a while, the strategy seemed to be working.

CHAPTER 15

POLITICS IN YEMEN, AND THE *COLE*

John O'Neill always wanted to be where the action was. So on New Year's Eve, as the year 2000 was being ushered in as a mega-event, O'Neill was not at the FBI's command center. He was standing dead center in the middle of Times Square in a dark overcoat watching the last minutes of one millennium pass into the next. Standing with O'Neill was Joe Dunne, the highest-ranking uniformed cop in the city. A giant at six-foot-six, the NYPD chief wore a mop of black hair, four stars on his shoulders and a line of medals over his shield. Dunne was one of the few cops who had been privy to all the JTTF activities leading up to this night, and like O'Neill, he wondered if the task force had missed something. The two men had a shared interest. O'Neill's job was to prevent a terrorist attack, and Dunne's was to clean things up if O'Neill's efforts failed.

As the ball began its slow descent, the crowd began the countdown.

"TEN! . . . NINE! . . ."

O'Neill knew that authorities in Jordan had two weeks earlier folded up an al Qaeda New Year's plot to blow up the Radisson Hotel in Amman as well as several Christian holy sites. O'Neill knew from his own contacts in Jordan that two of the main suspects in the Jordan plot had lived in the U.S. at one time. One had driven a cab in Boston. It was just another sign that bin Laden could get people in and out of the U.S. with little problem. It made O'Neill uncomfortable and he had said as much to me and others.

"EIGHT! . . . SEVEN! . . ."

In late December, Ahmed Ressam, an Algerian working for al Qaeda, had been captured trying to cross into the U.S. from Canada in a rented car with a trunkload of explosives. He would later admit his plan was to blow up Los Angeles International Airport on New Year's Day.

"SIX! . . . FIVE! . . ."

The FBI had found in Ressam's phone book the name Abdel Ghani Meskini, who turned out to be living right across the East River in Brooklyn. O'Neill had ordered the JTTF to place Meskini under surveillance. O'Neill knew right away he had enough to bust Meskini for helping Ressam, but he had had to learn if Meskini was the New York end of a bicoastal millennium bomb plot. The JTTF had listened to Meskini's phone until the last possible minute, but all the interesting conversations seemed to be in code. O'Neill had finally ordered the arrest at dawn on December 30.

"FOUR! . . . THREE! . . ."

O'Neill must have had an almost irresistible urge to close his eyes, put his fingers in his ears and hold his breath. New York on the millennium was almost too delicious a target. If his team had missed something, if the terrorists *were* going to strike, it would be right here, right now.

"TWO! . . . ONE . . . ! HAPPY NEW YEAR!"

The ball touched bottom, the 2000 sign began to flash, strobe lights popped, confetti flew, and the crowd went wild.

Just outside Times Square, I sat in a dark blue SUV with a full "live crew" monitoring the police radios. I was waiting for the first signs of an attack. An ABC News helicopter was hovering overhead ready to feed a live signal from my truck right to the studio from the scene of whatever disaster might come. But aside from some reports of shots being fired in Brooklyn, all was quiet.

Standing inside the "frozen zone" with the top brass of the NYPD, John O'Neill let out a deep breath. He hugged Joe Dunne, kissed him on the cheek and wished him a happy New Year. O'Neill pulled out his cell phone. Quickly he dialed the SIOC command center at FBI Headquarters in Washington to wish them a happy New Year, and then called the New York FBI operations center to do the same. The real reason for both calls was to find out "if anything had gone off" anywhere else. But aside from the noise of revelers, the world was fairly quiet in the first moments of 2000. O'Neill and another agent got into his black Mercury Marquis and drove slowly uptown with one ear on the two-way radio.

When I walked into Elaine's, the East Side watering hole, O'Neill was sitting at Table 1 with Elaine Kaufman herself.

"Is it safe?" I asked, only half joking.

"You know if I am sitting here, the city is safe," O'Neill said with his characteristic bravado. I noticed he had a glass in front of him, but it was soda. The city may have been safe, but at close to four in the morning, John O'Neill still wasn't about to have a drink.

On paper, things were good. The bombers of the East African embassies were in New York and about to go on trial (they would all be convicted and sentenced to life). Bin Laden cells in Albania, Italy and Germany had been taken out. The terrorist plans in Jordan and for the West Coast of the U.S. had been foiled.

But that night, all the bravado aside, it was clear that O'Neill knew—as good as his team was—they had been lucky too. O'Neill could sense the presence of the beast. He could see the glint of its eye in the darkness, nearly feel its breathing. He didn't know exactly where it was. But he knew it was near.

What O'Neill didn't know was that a militant cell on the southern tip of the Arabian peninsula was at that very moment making final preparations for a millennium attack of its own. Though luck would hold one more time, the FBI wasn't lucky enough to learn of its good fortune—and that would make all the difference.

January 3 was, that year, a much more important date on the Islamic calendar than New Year's Eve. It was the 27th day of Ramadan, the day the Koran was revealed to the prophet Mohamed, and that morning, a small group of men in Yemen backed a trailer down to the waterline of Aden Harbor and slid a 20-foot skiff into the surf. The boat, which was packed with at least several hundred pounds of explosives, immediately took on water and began to sink. And with it sank the third prong of bin Laden's millennium assault on America.

The bomb's intended target, an American destoyer named the USS *The Sullivans*, would refuel in Aden that day without incident, then continue on its way to the Persian Gulf to help enforce a U.S. embargo on Iraqi oil.

The suicide bombers, meanwhile, could do nothing but abandon their skiff and try to come up with a way to get the boat off the beach before someone discovered its cargo.

Several men who lived in a shack on the beach beat them to the draw. Seeing the fine boat, with its new engine, these locals reasoned that Allah, knowing January 3 to be "the day of destiny," had left the engine as a reward for their being good guys. So when the bombers returned the next morning, their boat was still there—half in, half out of the water—but the engine was gone. The terrorists would have to make some discreet inquiries around the beach and pay a ransom before they could recover the waterlogged engine. Meanwhile, it was back to the drawing board.

But unlike the millennium plans that had been foiled by law enforcement in Jordan and on the West Coast of the U.S., the Aden plot had been thwarted by the plotters themselves. That meant they could start over and try again.

During the ten months that passed between the failed attempt on the

USS *The Sullivans* and the deadly strike against the USS *Cole,* U.S. intelligence agencies would be awarded a number of warning signs. None were heeded.

Just two days after the debacle in Aden Harbor, al Qaeda operatives held a regrouping session in Malaysia. At least two men who became suspects in the *Cole* bombing were there, including Tawfiq bin Attash, bin Laden's head bodyguard. From the West Coast of the U.S. where the LA Airport plot had just been blocked, came two men, Khalid al-Midhar and Nawak al-Hazmi, who would help hijack an American passenger airliner in September 2001. Two years after the Malaysia meeting, Yemen's prime minister would claim that al-Midhar's travels in the interim had put him in Aden when the *Cole* lumbered into the harbor in October 2000.

The CIA knew about the Malaysia meeting in advance, thanks to a tap they had been running on a phone in Sana, Yemen's capital, since the embassy bombings. Would-be suicide bomber Mohamed al-'Owhali had called the number immediately after the Nairobi blast, and the CIA had since determined that the party at the other end was a significant al Qaeda operative. The CIA pressed Malaysia intelligence to monitor the early January meeting in Malaysia, so within weeks, the CIA had photos documenting what they would later learn was a planning session for the *Cole* and September 11 plots. The terrorists' host in Kuala Lumpur had been Yazid Sufaat, a former Malaysian army captain suspected of financing terrorist operations going all the way back to Ramzi Yousef's plot to blow up about a dozen airliners.

Sometime in the next few months another red flag was raised. A high-ranking official in an Egyptian jihad group who had turned informant passed along reports he had heard of an al Qaeda plot to blow up a U.S. warship. The warning, as it was passed on from the CIA to the FBI to navy intelligence, provided no details about the timing or location of the planned attack, and since navy vessels were already operating under a heightened state of alert in Middle Eastern ports, nothing came of the new information.

According to U.S. investigators, the leader of the Aden operation was Abd al-Rahim al-Nashiri, a top field operations man for bin Laden and the founder of the first al Qaeda cell in Saudi Arabia. Nashiri, also known as Mohammed Omar al-Harazi, is said to have been a cousin of the Nairobi suicide bomber known as Azzam.

After the botched attempt on the USS *The Sullivans,* Nashiri allegedly regrouped in Kandahar, Afghanistan, before directing the second round of preparations in Aden mostly from the United Arab Emirates. By June, he had the Aden cell back on mission.

The house at number 9 Jabal al Sakhra Street in Aden is a two-story cinder-block affair with an ornate blue door. It isn't much of a building. The room that served as sleeping quarters, with its felt rug and foam pads, offered little in the way of amenities. But the place had one perk that added to its charm and made it operationally essential to the man who rented it beginning in June. For $50 a month, it offered a spectacular view of Aden Harbor.

The new tenant paid four months' rent in advance. The FBI believes that he, and a second man who lived in the house, used the time to continue surveillance of U.S. Navy ships entering Aden Harbor. They could study how long it took the huge ships to enter the harbor and how long it took them to refuel. From the two windows in the front of the house, they could even see how close small boats were allowed to get to the battleships.

The two men wore beards, appeared to be in their late twenties and said little to their neighbors other than claiming to work among the harbor's fish-mongers. That was an explanation that made their comings and goings in the predawn hours seem normal. It was also an explanation that washed, if anyone noticed, with them owning a small boat. At least one of the men carried a well-worn copy of the Koran, yet neither he nor his friend were ever seen at the small white mosque just a few paces up the hill. Still, it's likely that both believed they were on a mission from God.

After the first boat-bomb sank, Nashiri arranged to get more money, about $5,000, and more help. The boat-bomb was reconfigured: It would not sink this time.

Several American warships came and went before the bombers were ready. Then, on October 12, 2000, ten months after the millennium attack had failed, the USS *Cole* pulled into Aden Harbor—a large, gray, 505-foot, billion-dollar sitting duck. Of course, the 294 sailors on board, most of them in their late teens or early twenties, had little or no idea how vulnerable they were aboard the mammoth warship. They did know that Yemen was supposed to be a dangerous place and that they were on "Condition Bravo," a heightened state of alert. That meant sailors were posted on deck with machine guns to ward off any civilian boat traffic.

As the *Cole* tied up at the "Dolphin," a mid-harbor fueling facility, the normal contingent of support boats moved about like flies on an elephant— the tugs that piloted her in, the garbage scow that would take her trash. The refueling operation would take a while. But then, from the starboard side, a small skiff came barreling toward the warship at full speed and a sentry on the quarterdeck thought momentarily about using his machine gun. The skiff cut its engine at the last moment, though, and it came about, bumping the *Cole* once lightly.

Looking over the rail, the sentry saw one of the two men wave before the blast knocked him back.

The explosion ripped through metal and man. Sailor Kathy Lopez, working in the huge ship's oil lab, had just watched her boss, Ensign Robert Triplett, exit the lab and close the door behind him. Triplett was killed instantly. Lopez's eardrum was punctured; her partner in the oil lab, Robert McTureous, found himself on the other side of the room. The *Cole* was rocking up and down, then pitching back and forth as flames and smoke roared from the gaping hole in her side. Lopez remembered thinking, "Did we do this? Did we make a mistake in the fueling process and cause an explosion?" But her thoughts turned quickly to survival. "I remember thinking I had to get out of there for my kids and my husband. There was no way I was dying on the *Cole*. I was getting out."

There were fumes, fuel, oil and water everywhere and live wires dangling and arcing all around Lopez and McTureous as they scrambled for safety. Lopez was sure they were about to be electrocuted, or caught in another flash of fire. McTureous arrived first at the 40-foot hole that had been blown into the side of the ship. The water below was thick with diesel fuel, but Lopez saw no choice. "I just pushed him out," she said. "I didn't even ask him. I was like, we gotta get out of here. And I pushed him into the water and we just swam out over away from the hull." The two sailors were eventually rescued by their crewmates. Lopez had been burned over 30 percent of her body.

The *Cole*'s sick bay was quickly overwhelmed and casualties began stacking up in a narrow passageway nearby. The hallway would later become known to the sailors as "the bloody aisle."

Seaman Carl Wingate had had the good fortune to oversleep and therefore hadn't been in the mess hall, where he would have likely been killed. Instead he was now working in the bloody aisle trying to save those he could. "They just kept bringing people in one at a time until the whole aisle was full," he said. "You actually had to walk over the people as you were going to the other side." The scene was nightmarish. Thirty-nine of the *Cole*'s sailors were hurt, some severely burned; 17 members of the crew were dead.

In Washington, the first word of what had happened to the *Cole* came in by way of a military attaché to the U.S. Embassy, who happened to see the explosion from the beach in Aden. The attaché used his cell phone to call the U.S. Embassy hundreds of miles away in Sana, feeding details to the duty officer as he watched the smoke billow from the ruined ship.

It was quickly determined that John O'Neill, as Special Agent in Charge of the National Security Division and the JTTF in New York, would lead the hunt for the bombers in Yemen, and so O'Neill immediately began to pull a team together. A military transport was ready. At the Navy, frantic efforts were being made to reach the *Cole,* but the bomb had torn through all of the ship's communications wiring. A team from the Naval Criminal Investigative Service would be the first investigators to reach the scene, though Yemeni officials would prevent them from getting to the ship itself until two days after the attack.

The scene was a mess. The traces of the bombers and their boat were tiny and everywhere. "On the decks, the type of evidence that was most found were pieces of fiberglass," said NCIS Special Agent Cathy Clements, who was charged with organizing and processing the crime scene. "There was a lot of fiberglass that was collected and swept into piles on the various decks. There were no body parts found on the top of the ship. There were small pieces of biological material that were found, yes, but not body parts."

Barbara Bodine, the U.S. Ambassador to Yemen, was flying into the country when the bombing occurred. She was no stranger to terrorism, having been the deputy ambassador in the State Department's Office of Counterterrorism, where her reputation was for being at once tough and something of an obstructionist, depending on whom you asked. A career diplomat then in her mid-forties, Bodine had a take-no-prisoners demeanor, and she immediately took charge. The State Department had sent in a FEST, or Foreign Emergency Support Team, including representatives from the State Department, Pentagon, FBI, CIA and other agencies meant to manage the crisis on the ground. They would all answer to Ambassador Bodine, who from the outset was adamant about one thing: There would be no U.S. "invasion" of Yemen. She told the FBI to keep the numbers of agents down—to say, 25 or 30—but the FBI, especially John O'Neill, had a different view. The murder of 17 U.S. servicemen was a big deal. The attack had killed more Americans than the 1993 World Trade Center bombing or even the bombings of the embassies in Kenya and Tanzania. In East Africa, hundreds of agents had been sent to work with the local authorities, and in each of the two countries a close working relationship had been forged.

From the first reports of casualties, O'Neill was furious. He knew what this was about: bin Laden. The beast had pounced, and just as quickly receded into the darkness again. O'Neill knew bin Laden's people were in Yemen. He felt that the clock was ticking. Leads needed to be run down quickly. Every minute was time for the plot's conspirators to get farther away. O'Neill didn't give two shits about ruffling feathers. Especially since he hadn't ruled out the possibility that the Yemeni president's half-brother, a high-ranking army general and known bin Laden associate, had played a role in the attack. He believed that cops were cops, and that if he had enough time with the Yemeni police, he would eventually break through to them and get them to work with him. O'Neill assembled a large contingent including investigators from the JTTF, agents from the Emergency Response Team, or ERT, and agents and civilian support personnel from the explosives section in Washington, from the photo unit. O'Neill would bring in about 150 agents, and in his mind, that *was* keeping the team small.

A foreign visitor enters Aden through an airport arrivals building that's nothing but a cinder-block hut with dim fluorescent light and a filthy floor. Our news crew, staggering in after a long flight, was swarmed by beggars. Every time one of us put a bag down, someone was trying to pick it up and take us to their car, a truck or someone else's taxi. The bosses had sent with us a couple of "fixers" who immediately proved their worth by ransoming back our passports from the airport officials who inspected them. We were then driven through the streets of Aden, watching as ramshackle huts gave way to junkyards and fleabag rooming houses. I was thinking as we approached each one, "Please, don't let this be where we are staying." But finally we rounded a corner, passed a strip mall and pulled through the heavily guarded gates of the Aden Hotel, which, all things considered, was pretty swanky. It was also the perfect place to be because it was the headquarters for the NCIS, the FBI, State, and the Marines, who would soon add 1,500 troops to the stepped-up U.S. presence in the harbor. In short, the Aden Hotel was either the safest place in town or the biggest target for any terrorist looking to ring up a few hundred American casualties. Frankly, though, the long flight had left me so tired, it didn't immediately occur to me to fear for my life.

Yemen is a nation armed to the teeth. Civil war had been a near constant for decades, and in 2000 the country literally had three times as many guns as people. It had also been a prime recruiting ground for the rebel forces in Afghanistan during the war with the Soviet Union, and thousands of bin Laden–trained troops had filtered back in. On top of that, the Yemenis were not the most accommodating hosts. From the moment the FBI and NCIS investigators arrived, they were held in virtual lockdown at the hotel, barred from visiting the ship even as Yemeni president Ali Abdullah Saleh initially voiced skepticism that the *Cole* explosion had been a bombing. Within one week, FBI director Louie Freeh was compelled to fly in to help persuade Saleh that the obstacles to the U.S. investigation had to go. Saleh then stood with Freeh for a press conference at which the FBI director stated that his agency and the Yemenis would act as partners on the case, though the FBI would be the "junior partner." To John O'Neill, that was already too true.

Even after Freeh's visit, Yemeni authorities would continue a pattern they'd established that first week of prohibiting the FBI from interrogating suspects. In fact, the Americans weren't even allowed to question witnesses.

It can't be said that O'Neill didn't try to fashion a healthy partnership, but the more he pressed for access, the less he got.

He tried all the tricks. He gave the Yemeni intelligence agents equipment, including handheld GPS devices. He also engaged in his usual joking. At one point he remarked to the chief of the Yemeni intelligence service that "getting information out of you is like pulling teeth." His counterpart looked alarmed, then angry. So O'Neill asked the man's translator to repeat the offending phrase in English. "If I don't get the information," said the go-between, "I will pull your teeth out." Another time, after tensions in the harbor had been eased by the U.S. military's decision to pull its warships farther offshore, a top Yemeni official who commented on the pullback had to puzzle through one of O'Neill's deadpan responses. "Not to worry," O'Neill had told him. "We still have the submarine in the harbor to keep an eye on things."

Not only did the FBI have difficulty getting information out of the Yemenis, the Yemenis were going out of their way to determine just what the FBI was finding out on its own. Each morning there would be a daily FBI briefing in the hotel's grand ballroom on the lobby level. More than a hundred FBI agents would be lined up, and O'Neill and the supervisors would run through the day's tasks and expectations. On a hunch, O'Neill had the room swept by his tech team one day. In short order, they came up with a transmitter. They were able to trace the signal to a room a few floors up. Drafting one of the bomb-sniffing dogs to play the role of "bloodhound," they crashed through the door of the room with the dog barking; the Yemeni agents jumped up on the bed, the desk and the couch, leaving all their listening equipment spread out before them. "Excuse us," one of the agents explained, "our dog followed the scent from this transmitter to your room. Did one of you guys lose this?" The point was made: Stop the funny business.

Despite the infighting, some progress, at least, was being made by both nations working the case.

Within days of the attack, the Yemeni Security Service had found and interviewed a crucial witness. He was a ten-year-old boy named Ahmed whose family resided on a middle-class block in "Little Aden," a neighborhood on the opposite side of the harbor from the bombers' lookout house. Ahmed lived to fish, and the day the *Cole* was bombed had been a school holiday, so Ahmed had been fishing off a small bridge in Little Aden when he saw the men drive the boat to a pier. Believing them to be fishermen, Ahmed wandered over to watch as a crane on the pier picked up the skiff and lowered it into the water. The men gave Amed a hundred Yemeni riales, or less than a dollar, to keep an eye on their trailer, then waved good-bye and motored off in their bomb-boat to blow up the *Cole*. Ahmed's story was passed on by his older brother to Yemeni authorities, who located the trailer and a Nissan truck parked under a bridge near the launch site. The vehicle was traced to a house on a quiet upper-middle-class street in al Burayqah, a neighborhood just a short drive from downtown Aden. Neighbors said the men who lived there would often play soccer with the local kids on a dusty street in the late afternoon. By day, however, they had kept to themselves, staying inside or working in the yard on what appeared to be a boat engine. During the last few days before the *Cole* bombing, the men were seen working at a frenetic pace. At first, the neighbors, who could not see into the yard, had been merely curious. Later they had complained about the noise. The neighbors said the men spoke with an accent common to the Hadhramaut region of Northern Yemen, bin Laden's ancestral homeland.

Yemeni security forces raided the house and found engine parts and the makings of the bomb itself. When the FBI's Evidence Response Team was brought in, those who had worked in Kenya on the embassy bombings were struck by the similarities between this safe house and the one in which Haroun Fazul's cell had built the Nairobi bomb. The Nairobi house had been a walled-in villa on a quiet residential street. The house had a wall in front and a fence running around the side, but the tenants had run a sheet of corrugated metal along the fence so that neighbors couldn't see into the yard. While the FBI technicians swept the house for fingerprints, coming up with latents, hair samples and DNA from toothbrushes, the Yemeni investigators had already located the owner of the house and obtained the names of the renters. Soon two men were in custody and were being questioned in the rough style favored by the Yemeni internal security service.

It didn't take long for the local investigators to extract enough information to round up four others. A Somali woman who'd sold the bombers the truck was held because she had allowed them to keep the truck registered in her name. Several government workers were rounded up on suspicion of issuing false ID to some of the suspects. At one point, more than a hundred people were in custody, though only six were actual suspects in the bombing. Many of the rest were witnesses. For instance, the ten-year-old boy who had fingered the bombers had been brought in for questioning and then held by Yemeni authorities so he wouldn't disappear. When it became clear that young Ahmed could not be held by himself, the Yemenis arrested the boy's father and held him as a material witness just so the kid would have some company. O'Neill mused, "If that is how they treat their cooperating witnesses, imagine how they treated the more difficult ones."

The Yemenis did provide mug shots to the FBI as suspects were apprehended, and O'Neill had rigged up a way to get quick profiles on some of
them. O'Neill had sent two of his men to keep company with the Egyptian
informant who had provided the early warning of an al Qaeda bomb plot
against a U.S. warship, and the informant was immediately able to identify
some of the photos O'Neill faxed out of Yemen. In fact, some investigators
contend that within 48 hours of the bombing, the link to bin Laden was firm
enough to justify a military response, if that had been the White House's
preferred course of action.

Jamal al-Badawi, the first suspect picked up by Yemeni authorities,
apparently even admitted to having trained in al Qaeda camps in
Afghanistan and to having fought in Bosnia with bin Laden forces in 1994.
He also allegedly confessed to buying the skiff for the bombing in Saudi
Arabia and to driving it down to Yemen to carry out the plot. He'd then
hooked up with Fhad al-Quoso, who was known in the close-knit circles of
al Qaeda as a well-trained operator.

The ringleader, Abd al-Rahim al-Nashiri, appears to have left Yemen
about 24 hours before the attack, following the pattern Ramzi Yousef had set
during the first World Trade Center operation. Nashiri had left instructions
with al-Badawi that al-Quoso should videotape the attack. It would have
made a devastating propaganda tool. The sight of the little skiff, bin Laden's
David against the *Cole*'s Goliath, with the bright orange fireball, martyrdom
and black smoke—it would have been brilliant television. And if Osama bin
Laden had demonstrated anything, it was his keen understanding of marketing terror. But on the day of the bombing, al-Quoso said he was asleep and
his pager did not wake him. He said the sound of the explosion did. He
missed the shot.

The FBI was getting transcripts of the interviews of these suspects, but
O'Neill and others believed they were being heavily edited. FBI agents were
allowed to pose questions, but only to Yemeni investigators, who would in
turn ask the suspects or witnesses. This was very different from the FBI
experience in Kenya and Tanzania, where they worked as full partners with

the locals. It was much more like Saudi Arabia, where the government was terribly hospitable, but when it came to protecting their turf, intractable.

Nothing was getting better between Bodine and O'Neill either. He wanted his people armed with MP-5s, the compact submachine guns that could make a difference if they wound up in a face-off with terrorists carrying AK-47s, but Bodine said no. O'Neill wanted Bodine to press the Yemenis harder; he felt she was more sympathetic to the Yemenis' sensibilities than to the FBI's needs.

I spent a lot of time with Bodine in Yemen. She *was* a tough cookie. But she was also articulating what appeared to be State Department policy: When dealing with a "moderate" Arab state, concerns about diplomacy trumped concerns about terrorism. She admitted being troubled about reducing the "American footprint" in Yemen, that the military and FBI personnel running around with all those guns were inflaming the public. Many Yemenis were talking about the "U.S. invasion" and looking to their government to curb it. Still, O'Neill felt that Bodine's job was not to sweat the sensitivities of the Yemenis but to run interference for him and help ensure the safety of his people. He was there to solve the murder of 17 U.S. servicemen and women, and if the Yemenis didn't like his style, he figured they'd just have to get over it.

The friction between O'Neill and Bodine degenerated into a bitter personal feud. O'Neill felt the ambassador was an obstructionist who was cavalier with the safety of his agents. Bodine, for her part, made it no secret among the members of the State Department support team that she thought O'Neill was a cowboy and a bull in her diplomatic china shop. She also thought that if her embassy staff could walk around the streets of Sana and Aden every day unarmed, why couldn't the FBI?

Around one in the morning on October 26, I walked into the Aden Hotel lobby, which was ordinarily busy almost 24 hours a day. Now it was deserted. There was no one at the pool tables, nor in the bar. It reminded me of those B westerns where the bad guys are expected to ride into town and everyone has gone to ground. Finally, I spotted O'Neill, who told me there was a bomb scare. (I would later learn that there was "credible information" that a truck-bomb was en route to the hotel right then.) When this information was discussed with the local authorities, the Yemenis judged that the security in place at the hotel's gate was adequate. Major Jim Western of the Marine Interim Security Unit did not agree. So he did what marines do—he improvised and adapted, moving two marine vehicles with roof-mounted 50-caliber machine guns to block the streets in front of the hotel. When the Yemenis protested that American forces shouldn't be doing that, Western simply offered that when Yemeni trucks with mounted 50-caliber machine guns showed up to relieve the marines, they would be more than happy to pull out. And that's exactly what happened. If there was a truck-bomb coming that night, it must have been clear to the truck's driver that he was not going to get anywhere near the Aden Hotel.

But the next day, most of the 200 or so investigators in Yemen were sent home. The remaining 50 or so were sent off to the *Tarawa,* an assault-helicopter carrier miles out of Aden Harbor.

On October 29, the USS *Cole,* with its gaping hole and what was left of the crew in dress-white uniforms, limped out of Aden Harbor. I stood on the shore watching. From the *Cole'*s PA system we heard "The Star-Spangled Banner" and then as the ship passed, the music shifted. It was Kid Rock, the white rapper, singing "American Bad Ass." Clearly this musical selection was the crew's choice. Many of them were little more than teenagers, and their message was clearly intended for the terrorists: We're American badasses; go fuck yourselves.

About a month later, O'Neill left Yemen a frustrated man. The government of Yemen had made it clear that the FBI was not going to run the case and the U.S. was certainly not going to be allowed to put the suspects on trial in an American courtroom. That, they said, would be against Yemen's constitution. Surely the Americans could understand.

For O'Neill, next to the Khobar case, the *Cole* investigation had to be the most galling. The links to bin Laden were everywhere. Each of the suspects being held in Yemen had admitted training in the Afghan camps run by bin Laden. Telephone records in Yemen showed that suspects in the *Cole* bombing had been in touch with suspects from the 1998 embassy bombings in East Africa.

Like the Khobar bombing, the attack on the USS *Cole* would go almost totally unanswered. Unlike the embassy bombings, there would be no missile attacks on bin Laden's camps, no attempts to invade Afghanistan. The Clinton administration was focused on trying to forge a Mideast peace accord, and President Clinton, who had struggled mightily for the second half of his administration to keep the focus on issues rather than on scandals, was trying to make a buzzer shot. He was hoping to earn a legacy that went beyond impeachment. That aside, according to a senior Clinton official, neither the FBI nor the CIA was ever able to tell the president that they had direct proof that the *Cole* was a bin Laden–ordered job, though now, in retrospect, it seems terribly obvious. In any case, even if there had been compelling proof that bin Laden was behind the *Cole* bombing, there was little chance that the Clinton administration would have launched an attack on any Islamic country while he was trying to get the Israelis and Palestinians to the peace table.

John O'Neill stayed on the case, often meeting with the parents of the 17 sailors who died. But because he had pushed so hard in Yemen and ruffled feathers, U.S. ambassador Barbara Bodine, in an unprecedented move, had O'Neill declared persona non grata in Yemen. And so he became the first FBI agent ever to be banned from a foreign country by his own government. He was not, of course, the first FBI agent to find himself in trouble for trying to do his job.

CHAPTER 16

ATTA

S heik Omar Abdel-Rahman stood in front of a three-judge tribunal in a Cairo courtroom. Behind him, in a metal cage, sat the 23 other defendants charged in the October 1981 assassination of Egyptian President Anwar Sadat.

Abdel-Rahman had been little known to most of his countrymen before Sadat was torn apart by machine-gun fire during an October 6 military parade. But several days after the assassination, the blind and bearded 43-year-old preacher had been hauled off in a tank and publicly accused of issuing the fatwa that had unleashed the killers. He was now a national figure, instantly recognizable in his long robe and fezlike red cap, wrapped by a white band marking him as a graduate of Cairo's prestigious al-Azhar University, the oldest university in the world and the Acropolis of Islam.

One of the judges put a question to the assassins' chosen spiritual leader that the conspirators had posed themselves.

"Is it lawful to shed the blood of a ruler who does not rule according to God's ordinances?"

The cleric narrowed the judge's query. "Is this a rhetorical question?" he asked.

Assured that it was, he concurred that death is an apt fate for such a ruler.

"What of Sadat?" asked the judge. "Had he crossed the line into infidelity?"

Abdel-Rahman hesitated, then refused to answer.

Before the trial ended in March 1982 with the acquittal of Abdel-Rahman and death sentences for five former army soldiers, a 13-year-old high-school student living in the Abdeen section of Cairo turned in earnest to prayer.

Whatever the actual trigger of his new fervor, young Mohamed el-Amir Atta would find in Islam a persistent argument against separating matters of politics from matters of faith. A long path lay ahead before he'd become fully indoctrinated in a global movement that advocated mass murder in the name of Allah. But if in taking the first steps along that path he followed the example of his namesake and father, he did so in the quiet of his home, in the company of a copy of the Koran and not much else. His faith grew, moreover, in a land where fervent Islamists had aided in toppling three regimes in as many decades, only to be disappointed each time by the new elite's inability to pull the great bulk of the nation's population out of poverty. His decision to begin answering the five daily calls to prayer coincided with the call by Sadat's murderers to adopt *shari'ah,* the Koran's system of divinely written law, as the foundation of a new theocracy.

From his bedroom window, Mohamed looked down on the rear yards of one of the poorest neighborhoods in an alarmingly overcrowded city. Coarse brick walls and shocks of white laundry met his gaze when he turned away from his Koran or his schoolwork. Some 4.5 million Cairenes, or three-quarters of the city's population, live on $180 a month or less, and in neighborhoods like Abdeen, many families live three to a room.

The Atta family, or the el-Amirs, as they were known, lived in relative luxury. They rented, at less than $10 a month, a double apartment—the entire floor of a building left over from the era of colonial rule. Mohamed, like each of his two older sisters, had a room of his own to which he could retreat, and from which he could sometimes make idle conversation with less shuttered backyard friends.

In the first several months after the name Mohamed Atta became known the world round, numerous reporters retraced his life path, seeking to understand. None gathered more insights than Terry McDermott of the *Los Angeles Times*.

As McDermott learned, the young Atta was afforded few other opportunities for socializing. A neighbor told the *Times* that the boy's walk from school had been timed, and if his return exceeded the necessary allotment, he was sure to be asked why. While his classmates loitered on the street, chewing pistachios and spitting out the shells, Mohamed spent his afternoons studying in his darkened apartment, sometimes indulging in chess.

Until the age of nine or ten, Mohamed had at least enjoyed the company of an extended family. He was born and raised in Kafr el-Sheikh, a sprawling settlement on the Nile Delta where street markets brim with citrus fruit, olives and other bounty of the rich Delta soil, but where even relatively wealthy families live on filthy cobblestone streets in modest concrete apartment buildings. Mohamed's father had no deep ties to the town; the senior Mohamed el-Amir Atta was the product of a poor village family. As a young man, though, he had earned a seat at Cairo University, and he moved to Kafr el-Sheik's modest provincial capital when a well-to-do fellow graduate from the town invited him to help open a law office there. The ambitious el-Amir soon wedded his friend's 14-year-old sister, Bouthayna, in an arranged marriage, and the partners' law practice thrived. Mohamed and his sisters thus were born into a family of relative influence, property and expansive prospects.

But Mohamed's father wanted something more. In 1978, he moved his wife and children south to Cairo, choosing the crumbling Abdeen District even though he probably could have afforded to settle in a newer, more middle-class neighborhood. Bouthayna's sister, Hamida Fateh, told the *Los Angeles Times* many years later that her brother-in-law's motive had been fairly transparent. "He wanted to be famous," she said.

In Cairo, the younger Mohamed also had a simple mission. His purpose was to excel in school, and his older sisters had amply marked the way. Both young women eventually won placements in prestigious programs at the Cairo University. One went on to become a botany professor; the other a cardiologist.

In a class of 25 other Mohameds at the Ahmed Oraby state school, the new kid from the provinces more than held his own. He consistently scored at the top of his class, though his academic successes exacted a price. He never joined his classmates on field trips to the beach, for example, and he often carried a sick note excusing him from participating in sports. Both tactics augmented the time he could give to his books.

Mohamed Kamel Khamis, a neighbor who ran an auto repair shop on the ground floor of Mohamed's apartment building, watched the comings and goings of the Atta family for many years. Sometimes the teenage boy would share a word, but never his parents. "His father was the most arrogant person I ever met," said Khamis. "He never talked to anyone."

Mohamed's mother, Bouthayna, resisted social interaction as well. As Terry McDermott reported, neighbors judged her a snob when she'd return from the market wheeling a cart laden with choice cuts of meat and other fine foods. She'd greet no one and refuse offers of help.

Most of the time, the family seemed to live inside their own bubble. "They were a close family. All five would go out and come back together," says Khamis. "You would never see them smile, ever. All of them—no one smiled."

In crowded Cairo, such behavior is not only unusual, it requires effort. For most Cairenes, the streets serve both as marketplace and parlor. Merchants and their donkeys shuffle past bearing sweet potatoes or dates. Tables, chairs and teapots are set out when friends drop by for a visit.

Every once in a while, young Mohamed would make an appearance outside his family's apartment as the evening sun cooled and the coffee shops filled with tobacco smoke and chatter. He might even engage in idle conversation with Khamis, telling the mechanic how he dreamed of becoming an engineer, how he hoped one day to build shining new cities in the desert.

Then the stern voice of his father would be heard calling, and Mohamed would rush back upstairs.

Sometimes the teenager's strong sense of purpose struck Khamis as an echo of the father's blatant narcissism. "Both of them had this conceit," he says. "Mohamed overvalued himself. Like when he was in secondary school, he acted as if he was in university." He greeted no one on his way home from school. "I felt this youth has a goal," Khamis says, "he is walking toward a goal."

That path didn't seem to have a religious end. By all appearances, the Atta family was moderate in matters of faith. Neither Bouthayna nor her daughters wore veils, and the skirts they wore barely fell below the knee. Neighbors can't recall seeing the family attending the neighborhood mosque. They remember well, though, the day the elder Mohamed el Amir replaced his old Fiat 132 with a flashy white Mercedes. During the Cairo food riots of 1977, such totems of wealth had been smashed and burned by the hundreds of thousands of students, civil servants, laborers and slum dwellers who took to the street in protest of proposed tax increases. A luxury vehicle still aroused resentment in a neighborhood where a good donkey was a luxury in itself.

Behind the Atta family's closed doors, Mohamed clung to his mother. Years later, when reporters called on his father after the September 2001 hijackings, the 65-year-old lawyer argued, in essence, that the son he knew had been too much of a sissy to be capable of such cataclysmic aggression. "I used to tell her that she is raising him as a girl, and that I have three girls, but she never stopped pampering him," he said. "He was so gentle. I used to tell him, 'Toughen up, boy!'" Even as a teenager, the *Sunday Times* of London reported, Mohamed would choose his mother's lap as his refuge when the tensions in the household erupted into fierce argument. His father nicknamed him "Bolbol"—Arabic slang for nightingale, or a small singing bird.

The elder Atta, speaking in the wake of the attacks, opened another window on his son's upbringing by offering the Western media his personal theory about how the World Trade Center towers had been destroyed. The

Mossad, he said, had carried out the attacks on America, framed his son and killed him. He branded the U.S. as "the root of terrorism."

However unprepared the 17-year-old Atta was for manhood, he entered the university with an academic record that promised great things to come.

Cairo University is enormous. With 155,000 students and 7,000 teachers, its campus devours acres of land on both banks of the Nile. As Terry McDermott reported, students who can afford cars often drive from one class to the next. First-year enrollees, all of whom qualify for seats solely on the basis of national test scores, are grouped by first name. In secondary school, there had been one class of Mohameds. At the university, there were three.

Mohamed el-Amir Atta did well in that crucial first year, according to McDermott. Degree programs typically require five years of study, and an aspiring engineer can be rerouted to a less prestigious department if he or she fails to keep pace with the competition. Atta not only met the standard during his preparatory year, he was funneled into architecture, the department into which the top engineering students were steered.

If the young scholar was thrilled with the direction his studies were taking, his father probably wasted little time impressing upon him, perhaps during their daily morning drive to the campus, that he would not be content with a son who was merely "a builder."

"We told him, 'Your sisters are doctors and their husbands are doctors and you are the man of the family,'" his father recalled later. "I told him I needed to hear the word 'doctor' in front of his name."

It may have escaped the elder Atta that contained in his son's professional ambition was a desire to improve not just his individual social standing but the world he saw around him. Somewhere in every architect beats the heart of a utopian, and the Egypt Atta had come to know during his adolescence cried out for social reform.

It also provided a philosophical template for revolutionary utopianism that the young Atta could hardly have overlooked.

•   •   •

Modern militant Islamism in Egypt traces its roots to 1928, when a schoolteacher named Hassan al-Banna founded the Muslim Brotherhood, a group dedicated to liberating Egypt from British rule and rebuilding an Islamic empire governed by divine law. By mid-century, membership in the Brotherhood numbered more than a half million, and when Israel declared statehood in 1948, the group's advance guard turned to violence. Cinemas showing Western films were bombed and British military barracks were attacked. Mass arrests and deportations followed, and al-Banna himself was shot dead on the street. The Brotherhood actively supported the operations of a revolutionary group of army officers who, following the assassination of a finance minister, overthrew British-backed King Farouk and ended almost 2,300 years of foreign rule. That officers' group was led by a lieutenant named Gamal Abdel Nasser; one of his captains, Anwar Sadat, had helped train the finance minister's assassins.

Over the next two decades, as President Nasser's pan-Arab socialist experiment folded into President Sadat's open-market system, the Brotherhood moved in and out of favor with both leaders. By the mid-1970s, the Brotherhood represented the moderate front of a swelling, semi-underground Islamist movement that had radicalized university faculties and established a network of "popular" puritanical mosques. Funding poured in from Saudi Arabia, allowing Islamist groups to build schools, day-care centers, and health clinics—filling needs neglected by the government. The Brotherhood even controlled, though briefly, several powerful banks and investment houses. But two more militant organizations may have held wider popular influence—Al-Gama'a al-Islamiyya (the Islamic Group), and al-Jihad (EIJ), the splinter group that had carried out Sadat's assassination and then was revived by a doctor and Cairo University professor named Ayman al-Zawahari. Both groups, incidentally, claimed Sheik Omar Abdel-Rahman as their spiritual leader.

The rough outlines of Islamist ideology would have been easy to ascer-

MILLER, STONE & MITCHELL | 245

tain even for a university student who didn't actively engage the issues. The
Muslim puritans hold that life's purpose is to manifest God's will, which can
be accomplished only by absolute compliance with shari'ah, or divine law.
Lives lived outside the divine law are considered offenses to God that
demand active resistance. For the puritans, jihad is not simply the internal
cleansing a believer undertakes in order to stay on the orthodox "straight
path"; it's a cleansing that must also be visited upon the unfaithful and the
unbelieving. "Prepare for jihad and be lovers of death," al-Banna urged his
followers. If Allah alone is sovereign, an attachment to life betrays an all-
too-human weakness, he believed.

Always, of course, the Islamist movement presents itself as a political
solution. Its central promise is a return to the righteous and prosperous
empire that Mohamed and his followers had founded 1,300 years earlier. It
supplies an answer to every humiliation Egyptians have suffered at the
hands of British colonialists, the Israeli army or American-style global cap-
italism. And its appeal grows each time the secular state fails its people.

During Atta's first year at Cairo University, police recruits, demanding better pay, rioted in the streets, torching several luxury hotels and nightclubs
that catered to Western visitors. These 1986 riots didn't compare in size to
the 1977 food riots, but it was the worst crisis of Hosni Mubarak's presi-
dency, and for only the second time in modern history, Egypt's army was
asked to advance against the civilian population.

If the upheaval had already inspired Atta to immerse himself in radical
Islamism, however, few of his classmates were aware of it. He was 100 percent student; an unremarkable face in the crowd. "Mohamed was there,
sharing all our fun times," classmate Waleed Khairy told the *Los Angeles
Times'* McDermott. "He would tell jokes, laugh. He was one of us."

He was also, at times, a bit withdrawn. When another classmate, Iman
Ismail, drew her whole class in caricatures, she placed Atta next to a sign
often posted at Egyptian military sites: COMING NEAR OR TAKING PHOTOS

PROHIBITED. Still, Ismail held him in high regard. "He was good to the roots," she told *Time* magazine.

"He was a little bit pure," countered Khaled Kattan, a third classmate. Atta could become incensed over the slightest injustice, emotional if an insect was killed in front of him.

Coursework, McDermott reported, seemed to be giving Atta all he could handle. Probably for the first time in his life, diligence wasn't enough to put him at the top of his class. He continued to excel at the nuts-and-bolts aspects of architecture—street plans, soil studies, the tensile strength of steel—but the department at that time placed a heavier emphasis on design and creativity. He struggled. "You would recognize him more as an engineer than an archi-tect," said Mohamed Mokhtar el-Rafei, who met Atta on their first day at the university and remained friends with him through graduation. "He was a very clever person in mathematics, physical structures; less good in design and the more artistic aspects . . . Maybe you could say he couldn't adjust himself to what was needed."

The challenge didn't bring out the best in Atta, according to another classmate. "One time something happened where he didn't get the grade he wanted, and he pouted," she told McDermott. "Somebody said to him, 'You're acting like a child.' Then he got very, very angry—proving the point: He really was a child. Spoiled."

Atta's final grades were respectable, but not strong enough to earn him a place in the university's graduate program. His father had always stressed the importance of mastering English and German so that study abroad would be an option. Now, leaving Cairo looked like it might be the only way for him to secure an advanced degree.

A photograph, apparently taken in 1990 at his graduation ceremony, shows the slim, five-foot-seven Atta standing post straight at the center of a crowd of jostling, jubilant classmates. They all appear to be shouting, and Atta, with a smile playing at the edges of his open mouth, clasps the shoul-der of a young man in front of him. The blocklike features and thick brow that the world would see 11 years later are recognizable, but there's a rounded, Charlie Brown–like simplicity to his youthful face as he smiles. A cute face, some of his female classmates later recalled. A baby face.

Atta was sensitive about such perceptions, according to McDermott. "I am grown up now," was a complaint Atta would often hurl at his family, who sponsored his journey to Germany two years later. In the meantime, he cruised around his beloved city in an 18-year-old yellow Fiat coupe his father had given him as a graduation gift, playing tapes of the Koran on the car's stereo.

He also landed a job at a local engineering firm. Years earlier, he had pulled out of a basketball league because it was run by the Muslim Brotherhood. Now he signed on as a member of the Engineers Syndicate, one of a handful of professional associations that the Muslim Brotherhood controlled.

Atta's father claims credit for orchestrating the dinner party that moved his only son to finally pack his bags and leave Cairo behind. "I almost tricked him," the senior Atta told the *Los Angeles Times*. Through a friend, he recalls, he had met a German couple who were developing a student exchange program that encouraged Egyptians to take advantage of free educational opportunities in and around Hamburg. When he opened his doors to the two retired high-school teachers, "Mohamed was the king of the evening, because he spoke German fluently."

Three weeks later, in July 1992, the 24-year-old aspiring architect walked into the couple's North Hamburg bungalow carrying a suitcase packed with expertly tailored leather jackets and bundles of Egyptian pounds. A spare room, rent free, was waiting for him.

He had never been on his own before, and one of the first questions he asked his hosts, according to McDermott, was the location of the nearest mosque.

Hamburg is a port city. Like most other port cities around the world, it extends particular courtesies to sailors. The bars are loud and plentiful. Prostitution and porn theaters thrive. To a pious man, it can be a bit overwhelming.

Atta's plan had been to enroll at Hamburg's University of Applied Sciences, but after passing the entrance exam he was denied admission and informed that the graduate architecture program was full. When his father promptly filed a discrimination suit, the school relented. Then, just weeks into his first semester, Atta dropped out and transferred to an urban planning program at the nearby Technical University of Hamburg–Harburg. He told his hosts that the architecture program would have forced him to repeat much of what he'd already learned as an undergraduate in Cairo.

Dittmar Machule, chairman of the Technical University's urban planning department, took an immediate interest in Atta. A Middle East specialist, Machule had adorned his office with maps and photographs of ancient Islamic cities, and he sensed in this taciturn Egyptian a shared passion. "He had deep, dark eyes," Machule later told Terry McDermott. "His eyes would speak. You could see the intelligence, the knowledge, the alertness." By 1994, the professor had convinced Atta to spend part of the summer at an excavation site in Syria outside Aleppo, a 5,000-year-old port city that boasts a famous *souk,* or marketplace, comprising miles of covered streets and twisting alleys. Atta's mind was made up: The remainder of his degree work would focus on the preservation of Islamic cities, and he would make Aleppo's souk the subject of his dissertation.

The academic work provided the basis of the few friendships Atta managed to form with non-Muslims during his eight years as a Hamburg resident. Beyond a small circle of like-minded planning scholars, his interactions with Westerners were at best businesslike. Often, they were weirdly antagonistic.

The retired couple who had initially invited Atta to live with them requested only six months later that he look for another place to stay. They told the London *Times* that they didn't appreciate the smell of the lamb chops he cooked or his refusal to eat any meals they prepared for him if the pans they used had ever touched pork. According to the *Los Angeles Times,* he played, once, with the couple's granddaughter, then tore into the girl's mother for bearing the child out of wedlock. He talked at length about religion with his Christian hostess, but frustrated her by forever insisting that his Islam offered the only true way. Small things about his presence made her uncomfortable. "He always gave me the impression that, although I was a woman, he respected my opinion," she said. "However, if I ever walked around the house without covering my arms, the atmosphere got very unpleasant."

Atta eventually departed on fairly amicable terms, and moved directly into a university complex called Centrumshaus. He soon took a part-time drafting job at a design firm called Plankontor, where he was a reserved but dutiful employee. But at Centrumshaus, among the German students he had already categorized as indolent and unserious, his isolation was complete.

Over the next five years, Atta had two roommates. The first lasted two years, the second hung in for three, but, as Terry McDermott reported in his lengthy profile of Atta in the *Los Angeles Times,* neither could stand to be in his presence by the time they parted ways.

The first roommate, an immigrant himself, made an effort to connect, inviting Atta once in the early days to join him at a screening of the Disney children's movie *The Jungle Book.* Kipling koans and singing bears apparently didn't agree with the quiet Egyptian. Before the film even started, Atta scowled at the audience's unruliness, muttering, "Chaos, chaos," as he huddled anxiously in his seat. On the walk back to the apartment, he said nothing, then ended the evening by slamming his bedroom door behind him.

(For a true believer, crude entertainments exemplify the barbarism, ignorance and chaos—or "jahiliyyah"—that a faithless society devolves to. When Atta was first exposed to Disney, he reacted as if he had fallen in the infidels' cesspool.)

Inside the small apartment, resentments mounted. Atta often padded through the kitchen in his blue flip-flops without acknowledging anybody else in the room. "We never shared food. We shared dishes," the roommate told the *Times*. Atta left his, unwashed, in the sink. Frequently, he made only the barest concession to the necessity of eating. He'd boil a pot of unskinned potatoes, mash them up, and eat a few warm mouthfuls. Then the potatoes and fork would go directly into the refrigerator, the roommate added, where they'd be on call throughout the week whenever a meal was required.

The second roommate whom the house manager paired with Atta was chosen because he was more laid-back. He too, though, found Atta's brooding nature almost unbearable, and his girlfriend bristled at the way Atta always averted his eyes and shut out her attempts at conversation. "It was a good day when Mohamed wasn't home," she told the *Times*.

To torture Atta, she talked her boyfriend into hanging a poster of a Degas nude above the toilet. When Atta finally requested its removal, the girlfriend put up a new picture in the kitchen. This one featured the Muppet character Miss Piggy in a revealing negligee. Atta let it go.

He did reveal a warmer side to a handful of Europeans. Centrumshaus's manager and his wife, for instance, accepted Atta's invitations to join him for tea at his apartment. He sometimes returned from Egypt bearing small gifts for the older couple. He was "perfect, without blemish, an exceptional young man," said Margritte Schroeder. And her opinion of Atta never changed. "Anybody who says he changed in later months is just trying to make themselves sound important," she told a London *Times* reporter in the fall of 2001. "I saw him here in early July and he was as nice as ever."

The non-Muslims who knew the most about his political mindset, however, were his teachers and colleagues in the Technical University's urban planning department. The same summer he visited Aleppo for the first time, Atta joined a group of classmates who were touring Istanbul. Among them was Volker Hauth, a devout German Protestant, who would travel with Atta a number of times before completing his degree in 1995. He was another Westerner whom Atta welcomed to his Hamburg apartment. "We were often there," says Hauth. "He would cook something simple, with chicken and rice, perhaps. We ate Arabic sweets a lot too."

Atta expressed strong feelings about politics, though he never worked himself into a rage.

"I knew Mohamed as a guy searching for justice," Hauth says. "He felt offended by this broad wrong direction the world was taking."

He was angered by the way Palestinian people are treated in Israel and the role the U.S. and its allies had played in the Gulf War, but he was most vehement about matters in his own country, including President Mubarak's suppression of Islamic fundamentalist groups.

"He was very critical of the Egyptian government," Hauth told McDermott. "He would say they showed the West a democratic face, but in fact, the intelligentsia of the country had sold out the poorer people," enriching themselves with Western handouts while the street peddlers suffered. "I would describe him as pro-democratic. That's how I saw him—a democrat within his religion."

On two trips the friends made together—one at the end of 1994, the other in the summer of 1995—Hauth glimpsed a side of Atta that surprised him, and witnessed a turning point in his friend's life that may have severed the thin thread that until then tied Atta to the main enterprise of modern culture.

Atta's first return trip to Aleppo introduced Hauth to an astonishing city. Or at least a piece of an astonishing city. The ancient souk itself was a honeycomb of tunneling limestone and evocative scents—spices, ropes, leathers. But elsewhere too, as McDermott noted, the streets carried wanderers 1,000 years back to a time when cities grew by different rules.

And then a monstrous hotel tower would appear at the next turn. Or a mini-mall. Or, as in the neighborhood Atta focused on, a 20th-century road would rip up the fabric of a 10th-century community and throw in a souvenir stand to boot.

Hauth told the *Los Angeles Times* Mohamed Atta was at home on these streets in a way he had never seen before. Interviewing shopkeepers, joking with children, navigating the municipal bureaucracy. On a side trip to Damascus, Atta even stepped up to lead prayers when he and his German friend visited a mosque. Hauth was stunned. Throughout the trip, he says, Atta was like "a fish in water."

There was even an attractive young woman, at the Aleppo city planning bureau, whom Atta seemed to connect with.

Her name was Amal. She was Palestinian, and she was observant enough of Muslim strictures that she took taxis to work rather than risk brushing against a man on a bus. But she was self-confident too and flirted with Atta during his almost daily visits to the planning office, often poking fun at his haughtiness. "All Egyptians are pharaohs," she'd say.

Atta clearly liked her too. Back at his hotel, however, Atta told Hauth that, regretfully, sharing his life with an "emancipated" Muslim woman was unthinkable for him. He didn't mention, apparently, that at some point he had discussed his interest in Amal with his father, nor that his father had been the one to forbid their union.

That second Aleppo visit nevertheless energized Atta, according to McDermott. The Egyptian headed back to Hamburg with Hauth, talking excitedly about his future, about how he would return as "an Arab to Arabia" to help build better communities.

Only a half-year later his dream was derailed during a three-month stay in Cairo. Atta, Hauth and a third student, Ralph Bodenstein, had won a grant to spend the spring of 1995 studying the renovation of two neighborhoods near Cairo's old city gates, Bab al-Nasr and Bab al-Futuh. What the three saw happening enraged them. Homes and workshops belonging to the poor were being torn down to make room for tourist parking and an open-air museum. Actors in peddlers' costumes were being brought in to replace the peddlers themselves. "We had a very critical discussion with the municipality," Bodenstein told McDermott. Atta, Bodenstein also told the *New York Times,* "said it was a completely absurd way of developing the city, to try to make Disney World out of it."

Adding to Atta's distress, McDermott reported, was the realization that Cairo's planning administration was a nest of nepotism. Jobs were handed down from generation to generation, and none was about to be handed to an upstart who sympathized with the fundamentalists. Suddenly, Atta's hope of pursuing his career at home rested on the long shot that an international organization would have a position for him. In his desperation, say his friends, he spoke increasingly bitterly about Mubarak's autocratic style of governing and about "the fat cats" who perpetuated Mubarak's reign.

"He lived in fear of being criminalized for his religious beliefs," Hauth told McDermott.

Perhaps his fears weren't misplaced. According to various reports, the Atta family home was under surveillance in 1995 because of suspected ties to Islamic militants.

When Hauth and Bodenstein left Cairo at the end of their three months, Atta stayed behind. Even to Hauth, with whom he'd often discussed religious matters, he mentioned nothing of joining the pilgrimage to Mecca that summer. But by the time he returned to Hamburg in early 1996, wearing a full beard and an exaggerated air of detachment, he had made not just one hajj, but two. The first, in June, was to the Grand Mosque, where he was among the youngest believers completing the journey all Muslims are asked to make once in life. The second, in February 1996, took him to Omrah shrine, which has a reputation for attracting a fair share of militants. Atta's father had financed—and helped secure the two visas for—both pilgrimages.

Upon his return to Hamburg, the 27-year-old planning student visited a radical mosque near the railroad station on April 11 to write out his will.

The will primarily details how his body should be handled after death. He wished to be dressed in three pieces of white cloth, and lain on his right side facing Mecca.

Four other instructions are worth noting:

I don't want a pregnant woman or a person who is not clean to come and say good-bye to me because I don't approve it.

The people who will clean my body should be good Muslims and I do not want a lot of people to wash my body unless it is necessary.

The person who will wash my body near my genitals must wear gloves on his hands so he won't touch my genitals.

I don't want any women to go to my grave at all during my funeral or on any occasion thereafter.

It closes with the following warning: "Whoever neglects this will or does not follow the religion, that person will be held responsible in the end."

CHAPTER 17

THE HAMBURG CELL

On the last day of October 1998, 30-year-old Mohamed Atta and two other graduate students signed a lease for a four-room apartment in a concrete slab of a building near their university. The accommodations were modest.

Just 625 square feet in all, the second-floor walk-up had a kitchen, bath and three small bedrooms. A pair of utilitarian-looking windows faced Marienstrasse, a narrow street crowded by similar working-class residences. Three months' rent was required up front, and real-estate agent Thorsten Albrecht reminded the young men that the return of their deposit was contingent on a final inspection.

When Albrecht returned 28 months later to close out that lease, the apartment was not only clean, its walls had been freshly painted white. Much else had happened in the interim as well. Said Bahaji, the fresh-faced 26-year-old who had handled all the bills and rent payments over those two-plus years, had been married for more than a year. He had also served a short stint in the German army, and he was expecting his first child within weeks. As for his old roommates, Ramzi Binalshibh was still kicking around, but Mohamed Atta had left for the U.S. in June 2000. Bahaji didn't mention that both had vowed to martyr themselves for an operation intended to kill as many Americans as possible.

U.S. investigators would eventually determine, several months after Atta and 18 other hijackers brought down four passenger planes and two of the world's largest skyscrapers, that the coordinated attacks of September 11, 2001, originated in a plan sketched out years before Atta, Bahaji and Binalshibh had even met. Some law enforcement officials also came to believe that at the time Atta departed Hamburg for America, the plot did not yet involve the hijacking of any passenger planes.

How much the operation was shaped or refined at 54 Marienstrasse may never be fully understood. But the apartment almost certainly functioned as the principal war room, billet and research center for the cadre of al Qaeda officers who carried out the deadliest terror attack in history. Most important, their Marienstrasse logistics base nurtured to maturity a cell that did not perish when three of its members martyred themselves in the World Trade Center mission. During the 28 months Atta's name appeared on the lease, 29 men of Middle Eastern or North African descent who were registered with German authorities cited the apartment at 54 Marienstrasse as their home address. In the end, only one of the three original roommates would die on September 11, 2001. The other two would disappear from Hamburg with only days to spare, leaving a trail of evidence that connected them to the very heart of the conspiracy.

Atta had left a clue about the nature of their activities from the very beginning. *Dar el Anser,* he wrote on each of the bank slips he used to transfer rent money to Said Bahaji. The phrase, which means "House of the Followers," appears to have been a tribute to a rented house outside Peshawar that Osama bin Laden had famously used as a logistics base in 1984. Bin Laden's "House of the Faithful" received, screened and deployed thousands of Muslim volunteers who were streaming through Peshawar to help chase the Soviet invaders out of Afghanistan.

European cities are built in circles. The old city and its monuments occupy the center, with prosperity and class descending as neighborhoods ripple outward. Northern cities especially have a habit of housing their immigrant populations in modern but bland blocks of flats on the city's periphery. Near the Technical University in Harburg, each row of houses has a simple playground, laundry room, parking lot and bicycle stand. The windows tell a story of lower-middle-class domesticity: small lamps glowing, neat rows of plants, valances strung at the top of the glass. Secrets are few; the sidewalks run so close to the buildings that a passing pedestrian could snatch the eyeglasses off any ground-floor resident who dared to let in some fresh air.

On the second floor of 54 Marienstrasse, red curtains quickly covered the windows, but neighbors in the building still noticed the glow of computers whenever the interior door opened. The "House of the Followers" had paid immediately to have at least two high-speed Internet connections installed.

Bahaji was the tech expert. A German citizen with a Moroccan father, he studied computer engineering at the Technical University. His talent for organization made him the natural point man for all communications between Albrecht and the tenants. It was to Bahaji that Atta signed over his personalized money transfers, and the other occupants who passed through did the same, even long after Bahaji himself left the apartment. Abdelghani Mzoudi, one of the later occupants, supplied a German online magazine with character sketches of many of the young men in Atta's circle. Bahaji, he said, was Mr. Reliable. "When you have an appointment with him," Mzoudi said, "he shows up."

Binalshibh seemed the opposite of reliable. A slight man with a fine nose and a broad, round forehead, he had had trouble holding jobs after leaving his native Yemen three years earlier, and his goal of attaining an economics degree had been stalled by his continuing failure to gain fluency in his language classes. He sat in on math lectures, but often used that time to read his Koran or catch up on his sleep.

Atta could have gotten to know his new roommates in any of several ways. In and around the university, Arab students tended to find one another. When Atta enrolled, there were only about 100 foreign students in the whole school, and more than half of them were ethnic Turks who had grown up in Germany. Arabs could be counted on one hand. "As a minority, you get to know each other fast," says Mzoudi. "In the student union you'd automatically steer yourself with your tray towards other Muslims."

For the past year, while Atta was still living at the Centrumshaus apartment, Binalshibh and Atta had also shared an employer. Atta's part-time job at the design firm Plankontor had ended in June 1997 when his bosses there informed him that a computerized drafting program had made his position obsolete. Several days later, Atta called one of the firm's partners to report that he believed he'd been overpaid on his final check.

He turned to menial work as an alternative, taking a position unpacking IBM and Phillips computers at a computer service company that recruited students for such tasks. Binalshibh too was toiling part-time at the company warehouse by the end of 1997.

For many of these young Muslims, however, life revolved around prayers at al-Quds Mosque. Located above a body-building parlor and a Vietnamese café on a seedy commercial thoroughfare, al Quds was home to the most fiery Islamists in Hamburg. Inside, anti-American rhetoric flowed freely. Outside on Steindamm street were porn parlors and hookers. Al-Quds wasn't the first mosque Atta visited when he arrived in Hamburg—most of the city's mosques serve Hamburg's moderate Turkish population—but it was the one where he settled.

Around this time, a secretive Muslim businessman named Mamoun Darkanzali began turning up in the lives of Atta and his new circle. While it's hard to draw lines connecting many of the hijackers to each other, almost all of them, at one point or another, could be linked to Darkanzali in Hamburg. FBI and CIA agents looking at phone records and money transfers in the months following September 2001 realized all roads lead back to Darkanzali. Darkanzali was not a new name to the FBI or CIA. He had been the business partner of Mamdou Salim, bin Laden's key financial advisor as well as his spiritual guide. When Salim was arrested in Germany just weeks after the embassy bombings and extradited to the U.S., Darkanzali, it appears, kept running the accounts they held jointly and doling out money to al Qaeda operatives.

After prayers, Atta and the others would often settle in at a nearby café or the local billiards parlor, freely venting their anti–U.S. feelings. At night, they'd frequently gather at 54 Marienstrasse. Eight or nine men would leave their shoes in the hallway and gather around the kitchen table, according to Albrecht, the real-estate agent. One neighbor told a reporter that before the red curtains went up, she saw a group of men drawing in a circle on the floor and then posting things on the walls. Mostly, the men seemed to be engaged in prayer.

"It would go on long and loud down there," said Violetta Sarnowski, a Polish immigrant in her early 30s who lived upstairs. "I could hear every word but could not understand any of it. It must have been in Arabic.

"They seemed like pretty normal people," she added. "Most of them were just like us."

The loudest and longest nights occurred when the kitchen gatherings were joined by a fat man who wore a white turban. Once, when the noise carried on until 2:00 A.M., Sarnowski asked if the talk could be toned down, but was disappointed by the lack of response. One afternoon when she was playing music in her apartment, Atta chewed her out, shouting in Arabic at her while she stood bewildered. "That was strange, because he could speak good German," she says.

The late-night prayer sessions may have been just that, but a similar scene that was playing out in a small house on the other side of the world offers some hint of the content of the Marienstrasse gatherings. In Puchong, Malaysia, a street vendor named Mohamed Sobri served sweet tea once a month when two dozen or more pious men gathered at his house to hear three clerics speak on a rotating basis. "They kept talking about jihad," said Sobri. "They would talk about the need to fight against the sinful things in the world." And they didn't just talk theory, he said. The third cleric in the lineup talked about revolutionary strategy, and about how to keep secrets. When the clerics' organization was broken up, authorities said the bin Laden–linked ring was planning to bomb Western embassies and U.S. Navy vessels in Singapore.

The man in the turban at the most boisterous meetings at 54 Marienstrasse is believed to be Mohammed Aydar Zammar, who was not just a prayer leader, but a veteran of the Afghan War who rarely let his listeners forget it.

Neighbors can't be faulted for accepting the gatherings as part of everyday life in Hamburg, but German intelligence has no excuse. As of the fall of 1998, the Marienstrasse apartment was officially under surveillance because Darkanzali was known to associate with one of Atta's roommates. Al-Quds Mosque was named as a surveillance target too. Whether either location was actually watched by Hamburg's state service unit is another question.

Three years later, a senior German intelligence investigator suggested that the subjects simply passed the smell test. "They had completely inconspicuous lives," he said. "Nothing they did gave us any cause to be suspicious."

Mohamed Atta had returned to Hamburg from Cairo that fall of 1998 exuding a sudden determination to wrap up his degree work. During the previous year and a half he had shown no progress toward completing his dissertation on Aleppo. He popped up again in Professor Machule's office, wearing a beard and seeming more remote than ever, according to the *Los Angeles*

Times. "Problems in the family?" Machule asked. "Yes, in the family, at home," Atta replied. "Please understand, I don't want to talk about this."

His parents, married some 45 years, were estranged during Atta's visit home, but that didn't explain the loss of an entire year. During that stretch, Atta did teach a series of multi-day seminars for the German think tank that had sponsored his study project in Cairo. But in early 1998, he had vacated his old Centrumshaus apartment completely for about three months, telling his suitemate he was making another pilgrimage. In the fall, having been forced to leave Centrumshaus, he holed up for several weeks in a small apartment shared by a large number of Arab men.

Some investigators suspect Atta used the three-month opening in his schedule earlier that year to train in an al Qaeda camp in Afghanistan. There have been reports that witnesses have placed him in one or more of the camps at about that time.

If Atta did attend the camps, his journey would have been made by invitation. Al Qaeda recruits didn't show up at the camps unannounced. They were selected and dispatched by bin Laden emissaries, and when they arrived in Peshawar or Karachi, in northern Pakistan, they could expect to sit for up to two weeks while their papers were verified, their backgrounds vetted and, if necessary, their beards allowed to grow.

The gatekeeper at Peshawar for most of the 1990s was a man named Abu Zubaydah. Though many trainees would hear directly from bin Laden during their weeks or months in the camps, Zubaydah became the most important person in their lives from the moment they met him. His entry interviews determined the type of training a recruit would receive. His exit interviews charged each "brother" with a mission.

If the mission was to build a cell and await further instructions, Zubaydah might well be the man who would deliver those instructions. Among bin Laden's inner circle, he was the one most adept at circling the globe, at slipping into new identities and crossing boundaries without gaining notice.

Ahmed Ressam, the bin Laden soldier convicted in the Los Angeles

Millennium bomb plot, detailed in trial testimony how the training process would unfold. Ressam, during his initial interview with Zubaydah, was given a letter to carry as he crossed into Afghanistan to the Khalden training camp. There, in the company of 50 to 100 other recruits, he learned how to fire handguns and rocket launchers, detonate explosives, sabotage power plants and military installations, assault buildings and carry out assassinations. Six months into his training he was moved to a new location and schooled in the use of poisons and lethal gases. Sources say Ressam has identified Atta and Binalshibh as among his fellow trainees.

Each day at the camps began with prayers before sunrise. Dried fruit was served before the morning's lessons, chickpeas and unleavened bread before the afternoon's. There was time too, for evening soccer matches, for denouncing America, and for exalting the glories of martyrdom.

A jihad "manual" that some trainees have carried out of the camps spells out the ideology the volunteers were drawn to. "Islam does not coexist or make a truce with unbelief, but rather confronts it," reads the introduction. "The confrontation that Islam calls for . . . does not know Socratic debates, Platonic ideals, nor Aristotelian diplomacy. But it knows the dialogue of bullets, the ideals of assassination, bombing, and destruction, and the diplomacy of the cannon and machine-gun."

Teamwork, willing submission to a leader, and, above all, secrecy were the ideals championed by the manual. Atta might have also noticed, on about page 66, that members engaged in a group mission should occupy apartments in groups of three. Mission commanders, it said, must exhibit intelligence, unflappability and patience.

Throughout the training, the instructors closely monitored each recruit's performance, paying closest heed to well-educated volunteers from Egypt and the Middle East.

The psychological screening could become intense. One former trainee, cited in a *Newsweek* report, alleged he was placed in a room and told to wait until someone came for him. Two and a half days later, he was told he had failed the test. The reason? He had parted a window curtain to look outside several times, each time indicating a "crack" in his fortitude.

An elect few of the trainees were deemed worthy of martyrdom missions and told to sleep on the idea for four or five days, an intelligence source told the London *Times*. If a nominee then accepted the offer, he was plunged into a new round of customized training. The lesser brothers, they could fight civil wars or hide package bombs at a Christmas festival. The ones who accepted suicide missions, they were the true elite among the faithful, members of "God's Brigade."

Jamal Beghal, the accused ringleader of a 2001 plot to blow up the U.S. embassy in Paris, stated in his confession that when he sat down with Zubaydah to be tasked with a mission, Zubaydah gave him the target—and a choice: He could load a van with explosives and ram the building, or he could send in a suicide bomber wearing the explosives on a belt or vest. Whichever he thought best.

Intelligence sources believe similar choices were laid before Atta, though his initial assignment may have been to prepare, and to wait.

Atta's last months as an urban planning student look like the preparations of a man waiting for death to tap him on the shoulder. He worked at his dissertation as if a large part of his legacy depended on it, and he founded a student prayer group, called Islam AG, at the university, that seemed to integrate his need to practice his religion faithfully and the capacity to gather new minds for jihad. The group's Web page, funded by the university, even provided an Internet link to the terrorist group Hamas.

Whenever Atta's martyrdom assignment was first revealed, the method of attack was probably fairly well decided.

Bin Laden operatives had, of course, tried before to crash a plane into a global landmark, when, in 1994, Algerian hijackers put a gun to the head of an Air France pilot and demanded he aim the airliner at the Eiffel Tower. Instead, he landed in Marseilles to refuel, and the terrorists were stormed by police.

Ramzi Yousef and his associates had dreamed up a variation on the air assault that seemed to hold more promise. If a small plane packed with explosives were used instead, al Qaeda could put one of its own in the cockpit. In fact, within a year of the attempt on the Eiffel Tower, Yousef's friend Abdul Hakim Murad was missioned to dive such a plane into CIA headquarters in Virginia. But that plot was foiled on the ground when the chemical fire inside Yousef and Murad's apartment in the Philippines caused neighbors to alert police.

The particular mistakes made in the Philippines could be easily avoided if a new plane and a new pilot could be lined up but al Qaeda leaders had apparently learned an even more important lesson. In the ever-growing jihad manual that its braintrust cranked out, the eleventh chapter outlines strategies for visiting holy war on Europe and the U.S. Pick sites with "high human intensity," like football stadiums or skyscrapers, it suggests, or symbols of great sentimental value, like the Eiffel Tower or Statue of Liberty. And don't settle for one strike at a time: "Four targets must be simultaneously hit in any of those nations so that the government there knows that we are serious."

Serious, but in another sense, sensible. Mounting four attacks at once greatly increased the odds that at least one plane would hit its target.

Of course, a four-prong aerial attack calls for four pilots.

Atta and Binalshibh could both take flight training. That would make two.

Among the frequent visitors to 54 Marienstrasse, investigators say, were the two other men who would answer the call.

Marwan al-Shehhi, a chubby and affable man from the United Arab Emirates, had worked with Atta and Binalshibh at Hayes Computing Service for about a year, and he and Atta were becoming close friends. They couldn't have been less alike. Atta was cold and humorless; al-Shehhi allergic to dark moods. "He was a funny guy who was always laughing and telling one joke after another," said Abdelghani Mzoudi. "I could only think that he and Atta were such good friends because they were such opposites." Al-Shehhi did have a pious side. The son of a Muslim cleric, he was inseparable from his father as a youth and would make the call to prayers whenever his father needed a stand-in. He could be pushed around. It's said he was forced back home into a marriage that lasted only two weeks, and that the same older brother who bullied him into that decision sent him off to Germany in 1996 to start working toward an aeronautics degree.

Ziad Jarrah seemed a far less likely candidate to be swept into a fanatical plot. "He was different," said Mzoudi. "A mixture of West and real Muslim. Sometimes you couldn't tell him apart from the Europeans."

There were many reasons Jarrah didn't seem to fit the profile of a fascist killer. None more powerful than the fact that he was in love.

In late 1998 into 1999, Jarrah was dividing his time between aviation studies in Hamburg and weekends with his longtime girlfriend in Griefswald. Neither the young woman he intended to marry nor the widow who let him a room in Hamburg suspected that the cheerful, outgoing and affluent 23-year-old they knew had anything but a long, happy marriage planned for his future.

Jarrah had met Aysel Senguen in the Baltic city of Griefswald about two years earlier, shortly after he and his cousin Salim arrived from Lebanon seeking education, opportunity and the best dance clubs in northern Europe. "I remember the first time we went to a disco here, we were laughing at how small and pathetic it was," says Salim, who now runs a restaurant in Griefswald. "Back home in Lebanon, discos are much more elegant, sprawling up several floors, and much more modern." Senguen, an attractive Turkish woman with long dark hair, was as forward-focused as Jarrah. She wore jeans and heels, and she was studying to become a doctor. They moved in together almost immediately, though they hid the arrangement from Senguen's conservative Muslim parents for years. The imam at Griefswald was another student, and he recalls Jarrah as "a weak Muslim" who had to be dragged to prayers when he did attend. But another man who knew him well says Jarrah was already hanging out in the prayer center late into the night, talking about Paradise.

Growing up in Lebanon, Jarrah had often dreamed of becoming a pilot. His father, a high-ranking official in the Lebanese social security administration, warned Ziad about the dangers of flying, but the family wasn't inclined to issue strict prohibitions. They sent young Ziad to the most prestigious schools in Beirut, which happened to be Christian, and they shielded their only son from the civil war ravaging the capital by driving each weekend to the Bekaa Valley oasis of Al-Marj, where he could play with his cousin and best friend, Salim.

The two cousins were 20 when they set off for Griefswald, where an uncle of theirs had lived for years, first as a Stasi agent and then as an exporter of medical supplies to Libya. The cousins parted ways only after Jarrah had mastered the German language, his fourth, and moved to Hamburg in 1997 to begin aircraft construction studies at the University of Applied Sciences.

For the two years he stayed, Jarrah earned above-average grades and the affection of his teachers and classmates. His landlady, Rosemarie Canel, trusted him so completely that she would leave him alone in her house for the summer. She even painted his portrait once, then gave the picture to him so he could make a gift of it to his mother. "I liked him very much. We understood each other very well," she says.

If he changed at all during his two years in her home, Canel says, he became somewhat more religious. He put a prayer rug in his room, and gave her a German Koran on his final Christmas there. He also spent an increasing number of weeknights somewhere else, telling Canel he had friends in Harburg, home of the Technical University, who put him up those nights.

By early 1999, Jarrah had apparently become a regular at both al-Quds Mosque and at the late-night gatherings inside 54 Marienstrasse. The "weak" Muslim still stayed with his girlfriend on weekends, but he was taking a strong interest in purifying the world.

In June that year, Atta turned in a draft of his Aleppo thesis. It was approximately 150 pages long, and along with its discussion of such arcane matters as building setbacks and height limits, it advocated preservation of the traditional ways that Muslims and Christians had lived together and propounded solutions for mediating between the new and the ancient, the secular and the sacred. "If you crossed out his name," Machule said years later, "it's the most neutral thesis you'll ever see."

It was quality work, but Machule thought Atta could use help polishing its German text before submitting the thesis for its final review. Though he knew Atta was uncomfortable near women, Machule asked Professor Chrylla Wendt to meet with Atta over the summer and go over the report chapter by chapter. Once a week, sitting side by side in Wendt's narrow office, they pored over the pages, talking at length about how to get Atta's thoughts across. With one chapter to go, however, Atta stopped at the office doorway, serious as always, and said he didn't want to continue the sessions. Wendt knew the physical intimacy of the work was difficult for Atta, but still she was surprised by his change of heart. "I had thought we had come quite close to each other," she said.

Wendt couldn't have known that funding mechanisms were already being established for the mission Atta would soon undertake. That July, his friend Marwan al-Shehhi opened a checking account in the United Arab Emirates at a branch of the international bank HRBC. Over the next 17 months, approximately $100,000 would flow through it.

Atta successfully defended his thesis at an oral examination in early August and was awarded a top grade. Machule, naturally, shook Atta's hand in congratulations, but when the professor's female assistant extended her hand to do the same, Atta simply ignored her. The final written version of the thesis also provided a surprise. Atta had added a new first page, which read: "My prayer and my sacrifice and my life and my death belong to Allah, Lord of the worlds."

A short return visit to Cairo left him depressed, according to people who saw him that fall. It was a strange response under the circumstances. His father had welcomed him home like a conquering hero, and what's more, had found him a bride. Atta soon met the young woman at a family gathering, and they seemed well matched. The woman's family approved of the groom, but insisted that their daughter not leave Cairo. So the young couple was merely engaged instead, and Atta headed back to Germany, ostensibly to begin work on a doctorate.

Machule saw Atta one final time that fall. The professor was tied up in conversation with another student when Atta appeared in the doorway, silent as he waited to be invited in. He stood there for almost ten minutes, then simply walked away.

Ziad Jarrah, after posting strong grades in his first two years in Hamburg, showed up for only one class that fall, then disappeared. Before the year was out, he, Atta and Binalshibh would all report that their passports had been stolen. Their replacement papers would show no records of any visits to Pakistan, Afghanistan or Iraq.

The operation was on.

S hortly after arriving in the U.S., Mohamed Atta paid a visit to a federal Farm Services Agency office in Homestead, Florida. Dressed neatly in Tommy Hilfiger clothing and smelling strongly of cologne, he asked if he might speak to someone about obtaining a $650,000 loan. He wished to purchase a twin-engine, six-passenger plane and convert it into a customized crop duster by removing its passenger seats and installing a large chemical tank.

The woman he met with had disappointing news. The U.S. Department of Agriculture does grant individual loans, she told him, but not for the purchase of crop-dusting planes. He might have better luck, she suggested, at the commercial bank on the building's ground floor.

Near her desk was an aerial photograph of Washington, D.C., that caught Atta's attention. She told Atta that one of the buildings was her former place of employment; the names written on the photo were those of friends and co-workers she had left behind when she moved to Florida.

Atta had another question.

"How would you like it," he asked, "if somebody flew an airplane into your friends' building?"

Some U.S. investigators have come to believe that if the federal government had granted Atta his wish on that day in mid-2000, the hijackings of September 11, 2001, would not have happened. Instead, the speculation goes, crop-dusting planes would have been used to crash into buildings, and the ensuing tragedy would have been on a much smaller scale. A used crop-duster can be purchased for about $30,000, which would seem to be within budget for an important al Qaeda operation. It seems now that Atta's U.S. mission was adjusted again and again over time, to address new obstacles and shifting strategic considerations.

There would be a certain comfort in thinking otherwise, in presuming that the September 11 attacks marked the culmination of a terror plot requiring years of dedicated planning. Certainly, the terrorists' planning was elaborate, and the plot's gestation period substantial, but a review of the operation's final 18 months reveals episode after episode suggesting the mission was capable of morphing into whatever shape would both ensure the survival of its cells and maximize its horror.

Bin Laden himself couldn't have been overly concerned with the particular form of the attacks. Weeks after the hijackings, he told friends and allies he hadn't anticipated that two flaming airliners would cause the collapse of the World Trade Center towers.

Atta may have at first believed he had come to the U.S. to pilot a crop duster, but he was not operating from a fixed blueprint. Nor was he operating alone.

In late 1999, at about the time the capture of Ahmed Ressam foiled the plot to bomb the Los Angeles International Airport, two Saudi Arabian men arrived at a large apartment complex in the heart of San Diego's large Muslim community. Neighbors say they seemed to have a local patron, a congenial but inscrutable businessman named Omar al-Bayoumi, who had not only driven the Saudis down from Los Angeles, but also paid the rent on their carpeted one-bedroom unit at the Parkwood Apartments. Their apartment was never furnished, and the two seemed to carry briefcases wherever they went, speaking incessantly on their mobile phones.

Khalid al-Midhar, the more aloof of the two, seems to have been al Qaeda royalty. The al-Midhar name is prominent in the recent history of Islamic militantism. In October 1999, the Yemen government executed Zein al-Abidine al-Midhar, the leader of the Islamic Army of Aden, for his role in the kidnapping of sixteen Western tourists and the murders of four. Khalid al-Midhar may or may not have had blood ties to the Islamic Army leader, but he had married into another Yemen family that had played a central role in the 1998 embassy bombings in Kenya and Tanzania. His father-in-law's phone also provided a critical communication link between the bombers who blasted a hole in the USS *Cole*.

Shortly after their arrival in San Diego, al-Midhar and his associate, Nawaf al-Hazmi, were apparently summoned to Malaysia for the January meeting that, according to one participant, had both the *Cole* bombing and the September 11 attacks on its agenda. Thanks to conversations the National Security Agency intercepted on the Sana phone in December, both the CIA and the FBI knew about the meeting in advance. The CIA had even managed to identify al-Midhar and al-Hazmi as two of the men expected to attend, though the names meant little or nothing to the CIA at the time. With help from a third country, however, it learned that al-Midhar had obtained a visa allowing multiple U.S. entries, making him an obvious candidate for surveillance. The Agency, which is barred from maintaining surveillance of individuals inside the U.S., passed the two names and details about al-Midhar's U.S. visa to the FBI by January 6 at the latest—but without asking the FBI to follow up. Meanwhile, the CIA had enlisted Malaysian intelligence to photograph the meeting's participants.

Al-Midhar and al-Hazmi stayed outside Kuala Lumpur in a condominium owned by microbiologist Yazid Sufaat, the former Malaysian army captain and suspected al Qaeda financier; on January 5, a camera captured al-Midhar meeting with Tawfiq bin Atash, the one-legged chief of security for Osama bin Laden. About a dozen men attended the secret multiday conference. Malaysian intelligence officers delivered copies of the pictures to the CIA within weeks, but inexplicably, the CIA seemed to have already lost interest in this mysterious gathering of al Qaeda associates. Investigators would learn later that at some point during the meetings, $35,000 changed hands.

When al-Hazmi and al-Midhar flew into Los Angeles on January 15, they sailed through Customs. Neither the CIA nor the FBI had bothered to alert Immigration officers by putting the duo on a terrorist watch list. Even more puzzling, when a third country later notified the CIA that al-Hazmi had, after a quick stop in Jordan, flown into Los Angeles International Airport following the Malaysia meeting, the CIA apparently failed to pass the tip on to the FBI, much less task them with finding out what he was up to. Given that Ahmed Ressam had been arrested less than three months earlier on his way to blow up LAX, it was an extraordinary oversight.

Al-Midhar or al-Hazmi would not have been hard to find. Almost immediately after their January return to southern California, they were made the guests of honor at a welcome-to-the-neighborhood party hosted by Omar al-Bayoumi. If the two globe-hopping al Qaeda operatives were trying to keep a low profile, they had a funny way of doing it. Of course, if they were trying to establish a new cell in San Diego, a party might have been as good a way to start as any.

By spring, both men had decided to begin pilot training. In April, al-Hazmi visited the National Air College flight school in San Diego and went up in a four-seat prop jet with a young instructor. Al-Hazmi was a small man with a courteous manner, and he carried himself with a self-assurance that suggested he might be a successful international businessman. He was interested in a training program that would earn him a license within a month, he said, and didn't seem at all fazed when instructor Arnaud Petit quoted him a $4,000 price. Petit, 23, decided to find out if his potential client would be fazed by the actual experience of flying a plane, and he was surprised at how adept al-Hazmi seemed when they took the four-seater up for an hour-long flight: "He was able to take off and land nearly on his own," Petit says. Even so, al-Hazmi was told he couldn't be taken on as a student until he brushed up on his English, which Petit estimated would take only a few weeks. "I thought he'd come back but he didn't," Petit said. "He was very excited after that first flight."

Al-Midhar and al-Hazmi instead sought out a cheaper option, signing up for training at a flight club, based at the same airfield, that had been founded by an Iranian-born pilot. The new instructor, however, didn't grade al-Hazmi's piloting talent as generously. In fact, he decided al-Hazmi and al-Midhar were both hopeless.

Al-Midhar was the worse of the two. Asked at one point to sketch the aircraft he was hoping to pilot, he drew its wings on backward. Up in the air, he seemed incapable of following directions: When instructor Rick Garza spoke, al-Midhar just nodded vaguely and said, "Very good, very nice."

Garza eventually concluded that neither student could speak English well enough to operate a small plane, let alone the big jets they dreamed of flying. "It was clear to me they weren't going to make it as pilots," says Garza. "It was like *Dumb and Dumber.*" So Garza showed them a stipulation in the FAA manual requiring English fluency for pilots and told them he wasn't going to take them up a third time.

The grounded conspirators apparently made no further attempts that year to earn their pilot's licenses, and when al-Bayoumi left the U.S. for London later in the year, finances for the two al Qaeda soldiers became a problem. For a brief period, al-Hazmi took a minimum-wage job at a car wash, manning the vacuum or filling out the towel brigade two days a week. Sometime in the middle of the year, responding to a notice posted in the local mosque, he and al-Midhar moved into a $300-a-month room in the home of one of the mosque's founders, a retired Indian-born professor named Abdussattar Shaikh.

Al-Midhar stayed six weeks in Shaikh's house before disappearing, apparently leaving the U.S. for the Mideast at around the time of the *Cole* bombing. al-Hazmi stayed on into December and convinced his landlord at one point to help him advertise on the Internet for a Mexican bride. The two men prayed together five times a day, but when Shaikh offered tutoring in English, al-Hazmi turned him down.

Following the failed bid for a crop-duster loan, plotting was probably not Mohamed Atta's primary concern during the second half of 2000. He might need a plane and a large quantity of chemicals when 2001 rolled around, but for the time being his task was to transform himself into a competent pilot of a multi-engine plane. He and his friend Marwan al-Shehhi, who had arrived in Newark at the end of May, rented apartments in the Bronx and Brooklyn briefly. Sometime in July, they scouted the Oklahoma flight school that Atta had e-mailed back in March, but they chose to settle in southern Florida instead, where they'd more easily blend in among the population and where they'd always be a short drive from Miami's international airport. At Huffman Aviation in Venice, they plunked down $10,000 each to begin a four-month training program on July 15. Two days later, Atta bought a red 1988 Pontiac Grand Prix to get around in.

The two terrorists at Huffman didn't exactly blend into their new surroundings. The affable al-Shehhi fared fine, but Atta had a knack for aggravating people. A couple who often rented a spare room to Huffman students could bear Atta's cold demeanor for only a week. When he greeted his hostess one day by saying, "It must be nice to sleep all day and do what you want," he was asked to pack and leave before nightfall. Atta and al-Shehhi tried harder with their next landlady. Along with their rent check, they presented her with cookies, and thus passed the next several months quietly in their own coral-colored two-bedroom house in Nokomis.

At Huffman, however, Atta rubbed just about everybody the wrong way. On one flight, he snatched a seat cushion away from fellow student Anne Greaves. When an infuriated Greaves turned to wrest it back, al-Shehhi lunged between the two, as if protecting Atta from any contact with her. "I remember thinking," says Greaves, "'What on earth could they be frightened of?'"

They certainly had no need to fret about money. Funding from overseas had been pouring in since Atta and al-Shehhi set foot in the U.S. From the United Arab Emirates, al-Shehhi received $4,790 in Manhattan on June 29. A joint account Atta and al-Shehhi opened at a SunTrust branch in Florida received $9,485 from the Emirates on July 19, $9,485 again on August 7, $19,985 on August 30, and $69,985 on September 18. Another $100,000 or so was sent to Atta in one lump sum that fall. It was more than two men needed, even though the cost of their pilot training ran to about $20,000 each by the end of the year.

The bulk of the funding seemed to have come from a bin Laden finance operative in the UAE named Ali Abdul Aziz Ali, alias Isam Mansour. But Ramzi Binalshibh, Atta's old Hamburg roommate, was also contributing. Between July and September, he wired undisclosed sums three times—first from Hamburg, the second time from the UAE, and the third from Hamburg again.

In fact, the pilots' plans seem to have had broad logistical support from overseas and its main elements—that it involved airplanes and would be directed against the U.S.—may have been known by a fairly wide range of al Qaeda personnel. Clearly, at least, the plan was not a secret shared only by the pilots in training and one or two puppetmasters in Afghanistan. That summer, for example, the Italian authorities recorded a series of conversations between two al Qaeda operatives—an Egyptian cell leader in Milan named Es Sayed and a Yemeni sheik known as al Hilal—that seemed to forecast the September 11 attacks. "I've been studying airplanes," al Hilal told Es Sayed on August 12, just after al Hilal had arrived at the Bologna airport from Yemen. "If God wills, I hope to be able to bring you a window or a piece of a plane the next time I see you."

"What, is there a jihadi planned?" Es Sayed asked.

"In the future, listen to the news and remember these words: 'Up above,'" al Hilal replied.

Es Sayed thought that al Hilal was referring to an operation in his native Yemen, but al Hilal corrected him: "But the surprise attack will come from the other country, one of those attacks you will never forget."

A moment later al Hilal said about the plan, "It is something terrifying that goes from south to north, east to west. The person who devised this plan is a madman, but a genius. He will leave them frozen [in shock]."

Was Atta that madman? Maybe. But most investigators believe the plot's mastermind was someone further up in al Qaeda's hierarchy. Atta soon was having enough trouble just seeing to it that four pilots would be ready for the operation.

Ziad Jarrah would soon join Atta and al-Shehhi in South Florida, but by mid-October, Atta must have realized his Hamburg associate Ramzi Binalshibh would never be joining the U.S. operation. Four times in five months Binalshibh had applied for a U.S. visa and four times he had been rejected. On October 24, another one of Atta's old roommates at 54 Marienstrasse, Zakariya Essabar, applied for a new passport, but Essabar's request for a U.S. visa would soon be turned down as well.

Another two candidates soon arose, however, in unexpected quarters. Zacarias "Zac" Moussaoui, a burly French-Moroccan who had been radicalized while working toward a master's degree in London, sent e-mails in September and October to the same Norman, Oklahoma, flight school that Atta and al-Shehhi had visited in July. Moussaoui, court documents would later charge, had trained at al Qaeda's Khalden camp in early 1998—about the same time Atta allegedly trained there. Moussaoui's October e-mail said that he would like a chance to become a flight instructor at the school and that he hoped to be in Oklahoma within two weeks. He did not keep to that schedule. Investigators say that during October, Moussaoui was in Malaysia as a guest of the microbiologist Yazid Sufaat, who gave the London graduate student $35,000 before sending him on his way. Moussaoui was back in London in early December, when Binalshibh himself flew into London two times in eight days. On December 9, the day Binalshibh arrived in London the second time, Moussaoui jetted to Pakistan.

What had happened in the interim to change Moussaoui's schedule? One theory held by investigators is that the plot itself changed course dramatically after an October 31 EgyptAir flight from New York to Cairo plunged into the Atlantic Ocean, killing all 213 people on board. Within weeks of the crash, U.S. investigators were telling reporters that the Egyptian co-pilot appeared to have sent the plane into its lethal dive intentionally. That news, the speculation goes, may have inspired September 11's plotters to begin focusing on the idea of using large airliners controlled by al Qaeda pilots to destroy ground targets.

The day before Moussaoui left London for Pakistan, a man who already held a pilot's license traveled on a student visa from Paris to Cincinnati; he was soon to make his way to Nawaf al-Hazmi's doorstep in San Diego. Hani Hanjour was no flying ace himself: When he called his old flight school in Scottsdale, Arizona, a month later seeking to enroll in training on multi-engine planes, his former instructor turned him down flat. Hanjour was a nice enough guy, the school's president said, but the diminutive Saudi had been a poor student, clearly not committed enough to become a professional pilot.

Nevertheless, Hanjour knew his way around U.S. flight training programs. He'd first entered the United States about a decade earlier, at age 18, and had dabbled in piloting for almost five years before finally securing a license overseas to fly small private planes.

Within weeks of his arrival in San Diego, he and al-Hazmi had both relocated to the Phoenix area, where they were taking lessons on a flight simulator at the city's Pan Am International Flight Academy. In a final phone call to his former San Diego landlord, al-Hazmi sounded excited again. Maybe he was going to be a pilot after all.

Atta and al-Shehhi were awarded their commercial pilot's licenses on December 21. Five days later (when German intelligence was smashing a Frankfurt cell suspected of plotting to bomb a Christmas market on the French-German border in Strasbourg), Atta and al-Shehhi took an astonishing risk in South Florida. Flying a Piper Cherokee they had rented from Huffman, the two unproven pilots touched down at Miami International Airport and were preparing to take off again when the plane stalled. Stranded on a causeway that led to a runway, they could come up with no way to revive the engine. But instead of notifying airport authorities, they simply flipped off the lights and abandoned the aircraft where it was, blocking ground traffic in one of the ten busiest airports in the nation. They were gambling that no penalties would be incurred or investigation launched. They bet right.

A little more than a week later, Atta and al-Shehhi were overseas. Atta had, several months earlier, told the loan officer in the Homestead, Florida, Department of Agriculture office that he intended in the coming months to make trips abroad to Spain, to Germany and to a third country. He was thus beginning to make good on his word when he flew into Madrid January 4. Al-Shehhi, meanwhile, headed to Morocco.

Investigators assume a series of meetings were held, at which either of two very different dramas could have played out. If Atta and al-Shehhi had dreamed up the multi-plane hijacking scenario long before, as many news outlets initially concluded, their January reports would have had to acknowledge that their half-year in America had been less than a perfect success. Atta and al-Shehhi were already fairly well prepared to aim an airliner at a target—they had even logged numerous hours on a Boeing flight simulator in late December—but Jarrah was several months behind them, having waited until October to begin his U.S. pilot training in earnest. Meanwhile, neither Binalshibh nor any replacement had emerged from the Hamburg cell to qualify as a realistic candidate for the fourth pilot position. Anyone who had contact with the West Coast operatives would have known that the candidate out there at the moment—Hani Hanjour—would also need a substantial amount of time to sharpen what skills he had. The January agenda, in that scenario, would logically have touched on how Atta and al-Shehhi could best serve al Qaeda while they bided their time, waiting for more pilots and for the gathering of the larger number of martyrs needed to hijack four planes. Arrangements for the hijacking pilots' "muscle" were made, investigators believe, during this trip.

Still possible, however, is a scenario in which Ramzi Yousef's idea of packing a small plane with explosives or other chemicals had not been ruled out. It is even possible that Atta and al-Shehhi were taken by surprise in 2001 when hijackings became central to their mission.

In any case, the two friends devoted the first several weeks after their return to the U.S. to activities that had little to do with the operation they ultimately carried out. They may have been simply gathering intelligence for the benefit of other al Qaeda operatives. They often acted, however, like two men might who didn't yet know what their target or their method of operation would be.

In late January, shortly before Hanjour and al-Hazmi were making at least a pit stop on the East Coast to secure a small apartment in a rundown section of Paterson, New Jersey, Atta and al-Shehhi decamped to greater Atlanta. On the last day of January, a flight instructor at Gwinnett County's Briscoe Field took them up for the routine check required of pilots seeking to rent planes for unattended flights. They stayed, during the next several weeks, at the Suburban Lodge in Decatur, and, significantly, they joined a local gym.

Not much is known about how Atta and al-Shehhi spent their time in Georgia, but in early March, two Middle Eastern men in a single-engine Cessna landed about 60 miles from Briscoe Field on a small airstrip in southeastern Tennessee. Danny Whitener, a 48-year-old junk-car dealer, was tending to his own plane when the taller of the two approached him. Whitener learned months later, from media reports, that the stranger's name was Mohamed Atta.

"Tell me about the factory I just flew over," Atta said. He was referring to a copper processing plant that was surrounded by dozens of round steel tanks and hundreds of rail tanker cars. Whitener said as far as he knew, the tanks were empty. "Don't tell me that," Atta shot back. Why, he wanted to know, would so many tanker cars be lined up alongside empty tanks?

"This guy was just arrogant," Whitener says.

But Atta was also right to doubt Whitener's word. The plant was in the process of shutting down its acid manufacturing operation, but the tanks still held as much as 250 tons of sulfur dioxide, enough to kill or seriously harm 60,000 people in the immediate area if the vapors were suddenly released. Atta also asked questions about the Ocoee River, which is dammed near the chemical plant to form a Tennessee Valley Authority reservoir. The Ocoee, he undoubtedly discovered, is a tributary of the Tennessee River, a major water source for several Southern states. The TVA, in turn, is the largest power provider in the United States.

Back in southern Florida later that month, Atta's interest in crop-dusting planes resurfaced. He arrived in a green van at South Florida Crop Care in Belle Glade and began pestering maintenance supervisor James Lester with questions. Crop-dusters are notoriously difficult for a novice to fly, and Atta pressed for all the information he could get. "He wanted to know how far the plane would fly, how much fuel the plane holds, what the capacity and the weight of the planes were," Lester says. Atta eventually made such a nuisance of himself that Lester had to push him away.

"All Atta said was, 'I want to sit in the airplane.' He kept insisting, 'I want to sit in the airplane.' So I shoved him and told him I had work to do."

Atta returned once during the spring, but even that wouldn't be the last Lester saw of him at the company's airfield.

Still, there were other indications that the main focus remained on the big jets. One clue came in mid-March, when al-Hazmi ordered delivery from the Ohio Pilot Store of flight deck videos for three Boeing airliners.

That same month, Chris Isham, the senior producer of the ABC News Investigative Unit, who had been a key player in landing the bin Laden interview for me, told me we had developed a new source of information. An ABC News freelancer who had extensive contacts in Afghanistan had an acquaintance who was working in a sensitive job for al Qaeda. This was someone who was inside bin Laden's camp. Isham flew to Peshawar to debrief the young man. Isham gave him a simple code name: "Max."

"Why is he willing to talk to us?" was the first question I had. "Why not the CIA or the FBI?"

"He tried that," Isham said. "He was a 'walk-in' to the U.S. consulate in Peshawar. He met with the CIA agents there a few times. They polygraphed him, learned he was telling the truth, then it all went to hell." Isham explained that Max was questioned extensively several times at the embassy. One day, while Max was not home, agents of the Pakistani ISI (Pakistani intelligence) came by his house asking questions about why he had been visiting the U.S. consulate. Max knew he'd been exposed and he was in trouble—at least with the Pakistanis and quite possibly with al Qaeda, since the ISI had extensive contacts with bin Laden's group. Max went into hiding.

Contacts in the U.S. intelligence community had confirmed to Isham that Max had in fact been a CIA "asset" and was now considered lost. Max was willing to tell us all he knew. All he wanted in return is the same thing he'd asked the CIA for. He wanted to defect from al Qaeda; he wanted to come to America. That of course meant visas and a lot of red tape and was not something we could pull off without official help. Isham met with the FBI's John O'Neill and laid out the story. How would the FBI like a confidential informant who has worked inside bin Laden's organization? It was a no-brainer, but O'Neill wanted to make sure it was cleared through all the proper channels, otherwise somewhere down the line he would be accused of leaking Max to us, instead of the other way around. O'Neill laid the case out to the U.S. Attorney's Office for the Southern District of New York. That was the office running all the prosecutions against al Qaeda.

Soon Isham and I were on a jet to Malaysia. We chose Malaysia because it was one of the few places an Afghani could enter without a visa. Max joined us at our hotel in Kuala Lumpur on April 9.

Max told us how he'd been recruited into al Qaeda. One day in 1999, Max got a visit in Afghanistan from Saif Rahman, the son of the blind sheik, Omar Abdel-Rahman. Saif talked to Max about joining al Qaeda. He said that he would be trained and paid. That his living expenses and food would be taken care of. It sounded pretty close to being a job to Max, though he says at the time he didn't know what al Qaeda or jihad involved exactly. Max told us that he, like all recruits, had to take a complex entrance exam. It involved what sounded like an IQ test. Those who scored high, like Max, were sent to bin Laden's intelligence training program. Those who scored lowest were sent to fight against the Northern Alliance on the front lines.

In intelligence school Max said he was trained by Saif al-Adel, who the FBI says is one of bin Laden's top military commanders. Max told us that al-Adel, while teaching a class on how to set up a target for a bombing, once touted his role in managing the embassy bombings. During their six months of training, the 15 or so members of Max's class learned how to scope out buildings, how to use hidden cameras, how to tail someone and how to detect when they were being tailed. Max learned that after a target was chosen and intelligence operators like him had supplied a package of photos and notes, another team, the bombing team, would take over an operation.

I asked Max if he had learned of any plans for future operations targeting America. He described a plan that was on the table when he was in the camps. The target was a commercial jetliner. The objective was to hijack a plane that was carrying a U.S. senator or ambassador and then try and use the dignitary as the bargaining chip to demand the release of the blind sheik from American prison. When we had finished with Max, we introduced him to Kenny Maxwell, the FBI supervisor who had run the hangar during the TWA Flight 800 case. Kenny was a smooth operator and had two agents go to work on debriefing Max and finding a way to deliver on the promise to bring Max to America.

Even after I got home, I kept thinking about the hijack plan. Could it really happen? Would it? Of course the plan Max described was very different than the one Mohamed Atta seemed to be working on in April 2001. But maybe the idea had simply evolved.

• • •

Much debate has arisen about what, in fact, Atta was doing in April 2001. By some accounts, Atta returned to Europe using a false passport. The Czech Republic's Interior Minister claims that Atta met that month with the Iraqi diplomat Ahmed Khalil Ibrahim Samir al-Ani, but other Czech officials have backed away from that assertion, telling the press only that counterintelligence agents had established that Atta and al-Ani met in Prague at least once.

Odder still than crossed reports about the Prague meeting is the account of a German taxi driver named Karl-Heinz Horst. Horst says that on April 20, he picked up three Arabic-speaking men in Furth, a city in southern Germany, and drove them 400 miles to Hamburg, where they were met by Atta at the main train station. Atta, Horst said, paid the $500 bill in cash.

What's known for sure is that by April 26, Atta was back in Florida. At 11:00 that night, he was stopped on a traffic violation by a Broward County sheriff's deputy and ticketed for driving without a valid license. Atta would skip a scheduled May court appearance, but he and Jarrah acquired licenses within a week of the stop to avoid future trouble.

Al-Shehhi at about this time flew to Amsterdam for a two-week journey that had him in Germany on May 2. For much of the next four months, Atta, al-Shehhi and Jarrah would seem to be taking turns crossing the continent or crossing the Atlantic Ocean.

The Hamburg cell was no longer alone in Florida. In the last days of April, the "muscle" of the operation had begun to arrive, and for a brief few weeks, Atta, al-Shehhi and Jarrah stayed within close proximity of each other, renting two residences in Hollywood while the new additions to their operation settled in. Seven arrived by the end of May, six more in June. Though all the newcomers were Saudis, they traveled, usually in pairs, from various cities around the world. With the return of al-Midhar to the U.S. on July 4—he obtained a visa from the U.S. consulate in Saudi Arabia, whose staff was still unaware of his terrorist links—all 19 future hijackers had nestled in for the final countdown.

Saudi Prince Turki al-Faisal would later theorize that bin Laden chose to fill out the hijack teams with Saudi operatives because he wanted the September 11 attacks to undermine the U.S.-Saudi friendship. Others have pointed out that al Qaeda may simply have decided that its North African operatives were poorly prepared to blend into American culture. The Algerian Ressam, after all, had been arrested because his answers to border officials raised suspicions.

Most of the latecomers spoke poor English, but they were not mere grunts. One of the first to arrive in the final wave was a doughy-faced college dropout named Waleed al-Shehri, who on April 28 checked into a Hollywood motel with another Middle Eastern man. Wail al-Shehri and his older brother Wail, who would arrive to join the conspiracy six weeks later, had grown up in western Saudi Arabia near the Yemen border in a large affluent family. Several of the al-Shehris' nine brothers reportedly worked for the Saudi armed forces, and their uncle may have been a director of logistics for the Saudi army. Wail had taken a different course. In fact, he had just begun a career as a phys ed teacher when mental illness forced him to take a six-month unpaid leave around the beginning of 2000. He soon talked Waleed into ditching his college studies to mount a pilgrimage to Medina, and the brothers secretly told friends that they hoped to find their way to Chechnya to join the Muslim fighters. Wail, the more charismatic of the two, gathered five other young men around him at a mosque in his hometown that spring and led them in making an oath to die for Islam. The al-Shehri brothers soon disappeared, as did at least three other local men who would participate in the September 2001 hijackings—Ahmed and Hamza al-Ghamdi, and Ahmed al-Haznawi. Intelligence sources are confident that Wail, at least, made his way to Afghanistan and al-Farouq, a training camp favored by Saudis, Palestinians, Iraqis and Jordanians. At al-Farouq, the imam who led prayers five times daily was a man named Abdulaziz Alomari whom al-Shehri would meet again in the United States.

Whatever Waleed al-Shehri's combat training had been, he and his roommate could not have been overly confident about their ability to commandeer a passenger jet, because on May 7, Ziad Jarrah stopped into a fitness center north of Hollywood and asked about the private street-fighting lessons offered by owner Bert Rodriguez. Jarrah was a logical candidate to serve as the group's in-house trainer. Being fluent in English, more athletic than al-Shehhi, and far more amiable than Atta, he could soak up Rodriguez's teaching without raising suspicion, and in time, he made clear to Rodriguez that he was sharing the information with other men, even practicing various close-quarter fighting tactics with them outside the gym.

Rodriguez, an intense man with a shaved scalp, carries the scars of a wild youth spent in the Williamsburg section of Brooklyn. He's been stabbed in the stomach and shot just above the heart, and he says he began studying martial arts not only to defend himself, but in order to pursue more confrontations in the streets. College taught him to think more philosophically about combat techniques, but in the spring of 2001 he still saw more value in disabling an enemy than in bowing to him at the end of a tournament. Though his Florida gyms had some 17,000 members enrolled, he limited his street-fighting classes to only 13 individuals, 10 of whom were police or corrections officers. Two were businessmen; Jarrah said he was studying to become a pilot.

Jarrah immediately impressed Rodriguez. "He was funny," said Rodriguez. "He had a real nice personality, a chuckling sort of voice and demeanor, very polite to the staff and me." But more than that, he was punctual, serious about the training, strong for a man of only about 180 pounds and astonishingly cool under assault. He bounced back from every blow, and kept his head even when Rodriguez did his best to frustrate him. The students didn't train on mats; they trained in stairways and narrow halls. They didn't train with padded gloves, they trained with baseball bats.

Rodriguez and Jarrah occasionally chatted about Buddhism and universal ideas shared by the world's major religions. Mostly, though, their conversations focused on fight scenarios.

"He wanted to know some of the techniques that just totally screw somebody up," says Rodriguez. "Like the minute that you grab them in a certain way, you break their wrist, their arm, tear their trachea, snap their neck." One day Jarrah said he had been having trouble with one of the techniques he was trying on his friends. "When you grab somebody you can choke them out in two seconds if you grab them right," Rodriguez says. "And if you don't, you'll be struggling with them. That was his problem."

Jarrah paid $1,000 for 20 lessons, missing sessions only when he had to travel out of town on "business."

Jarrah's next trip would be a mysterious four-day jaunt to Las Vegas, which was made all the more mysterious by the fact that Atta's sidekick, al-Shehhi, also seems to have made a solo trip to Nevada's largest city. On May 24, al-Shehhi flew from New York to San Francisco and from there on to Vegas, returning by the same circuitous route three days later. Jarrah appears to have been in Vegas June 7 through 10, and Atta hit the Strip at the very end of June. Investigators believe Atta's Vegas trip allowed him to hook up with al-Hazmi and Hanjour, who had spent the previous six days training in Phoenix on a flight simulator for a small multi-engine plane. But the reasons for Jarrah and al-Shehhi's visits are more puzzling.

Soon after departing Las Vegas, however, Jarrah and al-Shehhi each began functioning as the unit commander of a four- or five-member team. On June 23, Jarrah vacated his room in Hollywood, offering to pay the landlady for a broken coffee cup, and moved into a cottage in Fort Lauderdale-by-the-Sea that he would share with Ahmed al-Haznawi, one of the al-Shehri brothers' old associates. (Intriguingly, al-Haznawi showed up with an ugly lesion on his leg that, after examining the records of his treatment, some medical experts later determined was consistent with cutaneous anthrax.) Al-Shehhi went apartment hunting in Delray Beach in late June with Hamza al-Ghamdi, a beefy young man with a pronounced widow's peak who reportedly once served as a bin Laden bodyguard. Al-Shehhi did all the talking, according to real estate agent Gloria Irish; al-Ghamdi just

286 I THE CELL

glared at her. But al-Shehhi did rent an apartment in a gated community called the Hamlet, and al-Ghamdi took a $900-a-month place four miles away in a residential complex called the Delray Racquet Club. Atta's crew, which included the al-Shehris and a boyish-looking compatriot named Satam al-Suqami, set up in Boynton Beach.

By the end of June, the group had opened at least nine SunTrust bank accounts. The three known Florida teams each had at least one dedicated account accessible by debit cards handed out to all its members. In Delray Beach, a few regularly took advantage of free Internet access at the public library. Most of the men signed up at local gyms; some were indifferent about their conditioning, but Mohamed Atta, who worked out in grungy street clothes, hit the quadriceps machine with unusual energy. "Atta was working out intensely, spastically," said gym owner Jim Woolard. "He was crazy."

At the end of June, I was in Albuquerque at the annual conference of the International Association of Bomb Technicians and Investigators. I was there to speak about bin Laden. But the speaker before me, who was from the German Federal Police, was more interesting. He outlined in great detail, complete with color slides, the depth of what the cell in Frankfurt had been involved with before it was broken up the previous December.

The Frankfurt bust had initiated a new series of police actions against al Qaeda cells in Europe. On April 3, Italian police had raided a cell in Milan. Soon after, another cell had been taken down in London. John O'Neill was in weekly contact with the police and intelligence agencies in each country, and he judged that a lot of good work was being done. "Frankfurt led to Milan, Milan to London. We are getting a lot of intelligence from each one," he had told me. But the arrests also confirmed one of his great fears: al Qaeda cells were everywhere.

As the German official spoke, I was taking notes as fast as I could write. The chemicals, the explosives, the radio equipment that could be used for remote detonators—it was far more than had been in the papers. It signaled to me what O'Neill probably long knew: These cells were poised to strike all over the world.

My speech, which followed, was about the growing indications that bin Laden had plans to strike again, but this time in the United States.

At that time, U.S. authorities were divided over where bin Laden would strike next. Most officials believed that he was aiming at "soft" U.S. targets overseas, based on his past actions and electronic phone intercepts of al Qaeda members around the world. (In hindsight, at least some of these communiqués appear to have been part of a disinformation campaign.) Other officials, citing Ressam's failed Millennium plot to blow up Los Angeles International Airport, felt the next incident would take place on U.S. soil. But no one working on the problem seemed to doubt bin Laden's intentions to target Americans. A spike in phone traffic among suspected al Qaeda members in the early part of the summer, as well as debriefings of Ressam, who had begun cooperating with the government, convinced investigators that bin Laden was planning a significant operation—one intercepted al Qaeda message spoke of a "Hiroshima-type" event—and that he was planning it soon. Through the summer, the CIA repeatedly warned the White House that attacks were imminent, and director George Tenet—who seemed on a one-man mission to wake up the government— briefed National Security chief Condoleezza Rice in person on June 28. The FBI also warned local law enforcement about the possibility of attacks, and the National Security Council suspended all non-essential travel by its staff.

But despite the high state of alert, Atta and his many confederates continued to slip beneath the CIA's and FBI's notice. Moreover, when on at least two occasions Bureau field agents developed promising leads, their requests to follow up were either blocked or ignored by a sluggish, risk-adverse bureaucracy. In one instance, Kenneth Williams, a highly regarded counterterrorism agent based in Phoenix, noticed the emergence of a chilling pattern: A number of Islamic terror suspects he'd been following had begun applying for pilot training at a local flight school—too many to be a coincidence. Williams was no doubt aware that a cooperating witness testifying in the recent East African bombing trial had revealed that bin Laden was planning to send operatives to the U.S. for pilot training. Williams must also have known about the Ramzi Yousef plan to fly a small plane loaded with explosives into CIA headquarters in Langley. In any case, he was concerned enough to write a memo summarizing his fears and prescribing a course of action, which he sent to the Counterterrorism Section at FBI headquarters on July 10.

His letter began: "The purpose of this communication is to advise the Bureau and New York of the possibility of a coordinated effort by Osama bin Laden to send students to the United States to attend civil aviation universities and colleges." The memo then identified eight suspicious applicants and went on to recommend that headquarters begin to methodically investigate the possibility of a conspiracy. "Phoenix believes that the FBI should accumulate a listing of civil aviation universities/colleges around the country," Williams wrote. "FBI field offices with these types of schools in their areas should establish appropriate liaison."

None of the recommendations were heeded. According to FBI officials, what Williams was really asking for—a canvass of thousands of students at hundreds of schools and colleges across the U.S.—would have required too much manpower, especially at a time when the Bureau's terrorism units were already swamped by the *Cole* and Millennium investigations. FBI officials also point out that targeting Middle Eastern or Islamic men across the nation would have amounted to racial profiling under the Attorney General Guidelines, and would have subjected the Bureau to the risk of litigation or congressional censure or both.

Not doing anything, however, proved to be the greater risk. A CIA investigation undertaken six months after September 11 tied a number of the suspects on Williams' list to terrorist organizations, including al Qaeda, and suggests that a broad, timely inquiry might have at least led agents to the flight schools where Atta and his pals had trained. What's more, so many radical Muslims flocking to a single institution should have raised a few flags in the intelligence and aviation communities. But the memo was never communicated to the CIA or the FAA or any other agency. In fact, it was never even communicated to the top people in the Bureau's own counter-terrorism section.

While the FBI focused its resources elsewhere, Atta was in constant motion, weaving the final threads of the plot together. On July 1, the day he left Las Vegas, he rented a post office box in Delray Beach for three months. He flew that day from Vegas to Boston and then to New York, where he stopped over for two nights before returning to Florida. After four days among his fellow soldiers there, perhaps including the newly returned al-Midhar, he flew on July 7 to Madrid by way of Zurich. U.S. investigators believe Atta picked up a sum in the range of $10,000 during his Zurich stopover.

He arrived in Madrid around the time John O'Neill was in Spain to visit Spanish National Police Chief Juan Contino. O'Neill had been invited to give a speech on the need for international cooperation by police agencies to combat terrorism.

The first week of Atta's stay did not create much of a paper trail other than a car rental agreement he signed July 9 in Madrid. But the wife of the house manager at Atta's old student residence in Hamburg said she saw him at about that time and he was "as nice as ever." Other witnesses in Hamburg placed him at one of his old haunts in the company of al-Shehhi, which is possible if al-Shehhi had left the U.S. with a false passport. According to the *Sunday Times* of London, the head of the architecture workshops at the Technical University and a student in that department claim that they saw Atta, al-Shehhi and a third man in the workshops more than once, and each time the trio was inspecting a three-foot-square scale model of a building that looked like the Pentagon. Months later, the university reported the discovery that 60 to 80 slides of the Sears tower in Chicago were missing from its library.

Investigators speculate that final decisions on a date and targets were made in Spain. On July 16, Atta arrived in the seaside resort of Salou and took a $33 room in the same three-star hotel that days earlier had hosted John O'Neill when he made his speech to other counterterrorism experts. Two other Arab guests checked into the Casablanca Playa within 15 minutes of Atta, and the manager has said he had an intuition that they had come to meet with the grim Egyptian. The two men who followed Atta to the front desk carried U.S. passports that may have been forged, Spanish officials have said, and their identities have not been established.

Who gave Atta the final go-ahead for September 11?

Spanish authorities now believe that a man they were investigating prior to September 11 may have played a pivotal role in staging the attacks—and that there were hints to the September 11 plot in their own wiretaps. Imad Eddin Barakhat Yarkas, a 40-year-old family man in Madrid, had been under surveillance since 1997, and Spanish prosecutors say he was the leader of an al Qaeda cell in the Spanish capital. Yarkas, who's also known as Abu Dahdah, allegedly met, at some time or another, with Atta, and with Atta's ex-roommates Ramzi Binalshibh and Said Bahaji; his phone number was found among Atta's papers and in Bahaji's daybook, and he was carrying Darkanzali's phone number when he was arrested in late 2001. According to Spain's police chief, Juan Contino, Yarkas had advance knowledge, at the very least, that the World Trade Center and the Pentagon were targets.

Binalshibh was in the Salou area precisely at the same time as Atta. The slim Yemeni took a tourist flight from Germany into a small airport near Salou on July 9, then flew back to Germany on the sixteenth. He easily could have been the messenger communicating a final blessing to Atta's operation from higher up in the al Qaeda network, but as a financial operative, he would have had other reasons to join the meeting as well. Arrangements needed to be made to ensure the final stages were adequately funded, and that the martyrs had a way to return their excess funding during their final days. Binalshibh also had to worry about having the money and documents he and the other remnants of the Hamburg cell would need to slip out of Germany before the attacks.

Bin Laden himself has supplied clues as to who involved themselves in the plotting at the highest levels of his organization. Caught on a videotape speaking to friends and allies several weeks after the attacks, bin Laden attributed the operation to the group's "Egyptian family," which suggests that his partner in jihad, the physician Ayman al-Zawahari, or al Qaeda's military chief, Muhammed Atef, had direct oversight of the enterprise.

But some U.S. investigators believe that the man at the heart of the planning and execution of the September 11 attacks was none other than Ramzi Yousef's uncle, Khalid Shaikh Mohammed.

Mohammed, who'd been a fugitive since he was linked to the Bojinka plot in 1996, would not have traveled to Spain under his own name in July 2001. But he did not have to attend the final planning meetings to mark the operation as his handiwork.

Whatever his standing in the jihadi hierarchy had been in the fall of 1994 when he aided Yousef with Bojinka, Mohammed had secured a significant organizational role in the years since. He had returned that year to his native Qatar, where he then become the focus of a secret U.S. investigation that resulted in a 1996 warrant for his arrest. A rendition team was already on the way from Washington, when U.S. officials petitioned for, and received, Qatar's permission for his extradition. Mohammed—apparently tipped off to his imminent arrest—slipped away to Pakistan and from there to Afghanistan.

Once based at the home office in Afghanistan, Mohammed rose through al Qaeda's ranks and became one of bin Laden's chief money men, traveling extensively throughout Asia under a number of aliases to help channel funds to various far-flung operations.

Mohammed's financial transactions would, in the months following September 11, provide the paper trail that led investigators to suspect his central role in the U.S. plot—a suspicion that was later supported by interviews with captured al Qaeda official Abu Zubaydah. But the authorities have another reason to think that Mohammed is their man. Some investigators draw a straight line from the 1993 World Trade Center bombing through Ramzi Yousef's idea to crash a small plane into the CIA to the

September 11 attacks. Mohammed, in fact, had contributed his own funds to the original World Trade Center plot, and he'd been with Yousef about the time Yousef and his cohorts conceived of the aerial attack on the CIA.

Interestingly, during the same week that Atta was hammering out the final details of his plan in Spain, the CIA was preparing for a similar suicide attack from the air. President Bush was scheduled to attend the G-8 summit meeting in Genoa from July 20 to July 22, and Egyptian intelligence had warned the Agency that Islamic terrorists might try to crash an airplane into one of the host buildings. The CIA felt the threat was credible and tasked the military to ring the conference site with surface-to-air missiles. Clearly, the idea that Muslim extremists would fly a fuel-laden plane into a building was not a novel idea to the Agency.

But in July 2001, it was Atta's turn to bring Yousef's plan to fruition.

After his mysterious meeting at the Casablanca on the fifteenth, he changed hotels in Salou, drove the 355 miles back to Madrid and returned his rental car with about 1,200 miles added to the odometer. He flew back to the U.S. on the nineteenth. The same day, $10,000 from an "Isam Mansour"—i.e. Aziz Ali—was deposited in the United Arab Emirates.

One of Atta's pilots, Ziad Jarrah, was meanwhile taking life relatively easy. Jarrah, who had been in Germany visiting his girlfriend, Aisel Senguen, put off his own return to the U.S. until July 25, and the young couple talked about seeing each other again in late September at the wedding of Jarrah's younger sister in Beirut.

None of their previous separations had been for very long. A couple months after Jarrah had started his training, Senguen apparently flew to the U.S. to see him. In February, Jarrah had visited Bochum after spending three weeks in Lebanon to see his father through heart surgery. His daily phone calls to Bochum never stopped, though the tone of some of the conversations was not always as sweet as they once had been. "In the end, Ziad and I were fighting a lot," Senguen later told a German newspaper. "He wanted me to wear a head scarf. I wasn't allowed to listen to Western music, and I shouldn't go to parties anymore. All of a sudden, he wanted me to live strictly according to Islam." Another of Jarrah's sisters was to be married August 2, but Jarrah told Senguen and his family that he had to return to the U.S. to take his pilot's license test. On July 30, in fact, he earned his single-engine certification in Florida.

It was still July when John O'Neill, home from Salou, stood in my backyard on Shelter Island at a barbecue. I complimented him on the way things were going. "Bin Laden must be really frustrated," I said. "He hasn't been able to get off an attack since the *Cole* bombing. That must be driving him nuts."

O'Neill was having none of it. "They'll get one off," he said. "There is *always* going to be that one cell that slips by us."

CHAPTER 19

PREPARING FOR THE ATTACK

A ctor James Woods couldn't help noticing the four Middle Eastern men riding with him in first class on an August 1 flight from Boston to San Francisco. There were only a couple of other passengers up front that morning, and Woods makes a habit of watching people's behavior. It helps with his craft, he says.

These four men carried no hand luggage onto the transcontinental flight, which seemed odd, and odder still was the way they later ignored the female flight attendant, as if her presence didn't even register. His first impression was that they were either criminals or law enforcement, because there was a silent, unbroken line of communication tying them together that usually exists only between people engaged in a common mission.

Woods eventually concluded that the men were going to hijack the plane.

Woods hasn't discussed the specific evidence that led him to that conclusion and pledges he won't until he gets a chance to testify about the August 1 flight in court proceedings, but he says the clues were so obvious that he asked the flight attendant if he could speak with the pilot. When the first officer came out instead, Woods reported his suspicion, noting, "I'm very much aware of how serious it is to say the word 'hijack' on an American aircraft in flight."

The flight was extremely turbulent, but when the plane did land safely, both the first officer and the flight attendant reported the incident to the FAA—which had already been alerted by the White House to the likelihood that al Qaeda would attempt a terror strike that summer.

All four of the passengers from that day participated in the hijackings on September 11, Woods has been told, each on a different flight.

Also on August 1, Abdulaziz Alomari, the former Khalden camp imam, boarded USAir Flight 608 from Las Vegas to New York. Alomari told the flight attendant that he was a pilot and wanted to fly in the cockpit's jump seat to observe. When she asked to see Alomari's pilot's credentials, he admitted that he was just a student pilot but still very much wanted to ride in the cockpit all the way to New York. The flight attendant told Alomari to take his seat in the cabin, but promised to ask the pilots. When she came back to get him, he seemed very happy. He was allowed into the cockpit and spoke with the crew. He said he had lined up a job to fly for EgyptAir. But the more they asked him about his aviation background and flying hours, the more apparent it became that he was nowhere close to being qualified to fly a commercial aircraft. Alomari made a big fuss about being asked to leave the cockpit before takeoff. But the flight attendant told him the plane would not take off until he returned to his seat.

Halfway through the cross-country flight, it appears Alomari switched to Plan B. He was back on his feet, telling the flight attendant that he needed to get back in the cockpit right away because he was sure that he'd left a pen, which he claimed was of great sentimental value in the cockpit. He persisted until the flight attendant told him there was *no way* he would be getting back into the cockpit again, especially while the plane was in flight. But she promised the crew would look for his pen as soon as they landed. When the plane finally did land, however, Alomari was no longer interested in waiting around for his pen.

It is now clear to the FBI that Alomari's strange behavior was designed to test security and find out if someone carrying pilot's credentials could talk their way into the cockpit. The answer, he learned, was no. Now Atta and his men knew that if they were going to take over the cockpit of an airliner, they were going to have to go in with the heaviest force they could muster. Determining exactly how and when to take a plane was apparently the job of the four men on James Woods's flight.

That was one of the terrorists' great strengths: They worked together. They shared critical tactical information across units.

Unfortunately, the organizations charged with preventing terrorism were doing exactly the opposite. After half a summer of secret warnings about imminent terror strikes, the FBI, the CIA and even the White House were each giving heightened attention to al Qaeda and the threat imposed to U.S. security.

Ultimately, however, communication lapses old and new would render the efforts pointless.

Earlier that summer, concerned about a U.S. strike, President Bush asked the CIA to prepare a report on the domestic threat posed by al Qaeda. On August 6, the agency briefed him at his ranch in Crawford, Texas. Mostly a historical analysis of al Qaeda's methods, the report, among other things, said that bin Laden's organization had plans to hijack a plane and use the hostages to spring Sheik Omar Abdel-Rahman from U.S. federal prison. That matched precisely with the information "Max" had given ABC News.

By many accounts, Bush evinced a keener interest in national security than his predecessor, summoning the CIA for daily in-person briefings. But as of the summer of 2001, that interest hadn't translated into any significant changes in the government's counterterrorism policy. Bush's administration was no better at choking off al Qaeda's funding sources than Clinton's.

Attorney General John Ashcroft made terrorism a second- or even a third-tier issue, and as late as September 10, turned down a request from the FBI to increase its counterterrorism budget by $58 million. Nor did Bush's staff enhance the menu of failed military options employed by Clinton against al Qaeda. Defense Secretary Donald Rumsfeld was far more focused on building a missile defense shield than in getting bin Laden, and a promising program to equip unmanned surveillance planes with deadly Hellfire missiles begun under Clinton was allowed to languish while the CIA and the military wrangled over control of the project.

As the summer dragged on and it became increasingly clear that al Qaeda was going to strike against the U.S., possibly within the U.S., Bush tasked the CIA and the military to come up with a strategy to invade Afghanistan and neutralize bin Laden. The plan, completed on September 10, was lying on Bush's desk when Atta and his pals began their attacks.

The terrorists, for their part, spent their final weeks preparing sensibly for their mission. One day at the beginning of August, Abdulaziz Alomari and Ahmed Alghamdi secured fraudulent identification papers, which they would need to board commercial airliners, by paying a Salvadoran immigrant $100 to sign an affidavit on their behalf at a Virginia state motor vehicle office. With those papers in hand, Alomari and Alghamdi were qualified to sign affidavits the very next day on behalf of three other conspirators, Hani Hanjour, Khalid al-Midhar and Nawaf al-Hazmi. Throughout the rest of August, the plot's commandos worked out at gyms and the pilots rented small planes, often buzzing across the same territory each would navigate on the chosen day.

Among the connecting lines that don't fit an easy narrative are those that return Zac Moussaoui to the story in early August. Moussaoui, the French-Moroccan from London who had appeared eager to begin pilot training in the United States the previous October, had finally arrived at the Norman, Oklahoma, flight school in late February, following a two-month period in which he had disappeared into Pakistan. His hair and beard had grown out in the interim, and he was carrying at least $35,000 in cash when he arrived in America, $32,000 of which he deposited in a bank in Norman. His flight training was a disaster. Most students are deemed capable of flying solo after about 20 hours in the air with an instructor, but Moussaoui never gained that privilege and had paid for 50 hours before the school finally grounded him for good at the end of May. That didn't discourage him from making inquiries about starting a crop dusting company, in Oklahoma, from purchasing flight deck videos on June 20 for two models of the Boeing 747, or from proceeding with a plan to obtain extensive simulator experience in flying large airliners.

At the very end of July, Moussaoui's activities assumed an air of urgency. He made a flurry of calls from pay phones in Norman to a number in Dusseldorf, Germany, before Ramzi Binalshibh, during the first three days of August, wired him approximately $14,000 in money orders from train stations in Dusseldorf and Hamburg. Moussaoui arrived in Minneapolis, Minnesota, three days before his simulator training was supposed to begin at the Pan Am International Academy in nearby Egan. Having paid a deposit by credit card in early July, he covered the balance by reaching into a small satchel and pulling out $6,800 in cash.

Moussaoui's classroom instructor knew that affluent hobbyists sometimes signed up for simulator training even if they didn't have a license, but Moussaoui's decision to rush the training, and to ask so many questions about things like the protocol for communicating with air traffic controllers, created worry. At a routine staff meeting on August 14, the instructors soon were speculating how much damage a hijacker could do flying a 747 loaded with fuel. One of the flight school's managers volunteered to call a friend in the local FBI office, and that night, Moussaoui was arrested on visa violation charges.

The "overstay" charges were a pretext, of course, but the way Moussaoui refused to allow the agents to search his possessions, especially his laptop, increased the Minneapolis agents' suspicions; within days, French intelligence, responding to an FBI query, reported that Moussaoui had radical fundamentalist connections. When the Minneapolis investigators requested that headquarters seek a warrant to search Moussaoui's computer and other belongings, however, they were told they lacked probable cause—even in a secret national security court set up under the 1978 Foreign Intelligence Security Act (FISA) to hear just such requests.

The Minneapolis agents were stunned by headquarters' refusal to even submit their request for consideration. The circumstances of Moussaoui's arrest, the large cash payments he'd made to the flight school, his appearance and affect, his confirmed radical fundamentalist ties—these and other clues made the agents believe they were dealing with someone who might well be planning to use a large commercial jet in the commission of a terrorist act. One agent, it's said, even guessed at the September 11 scenario.

Initially, perhaps, headquarters had a reasonable argument. The French intelligence, in their view, did not meet the standard for a FISA warrant: namely, that the subject had to be acting on behalf of a state or foreign terror organization. Maybe too headquarters was wary of the chief judge of the FISA court, who had recently chastised the FBI for alleged improprieties in the way it applied for warrants.

But any reservations on the part of headquarters should have evaporated in late August when the French issued a second report confirming that Moussaoui had links to terrorist groups and was involved in activities connected to bin Laden. That, however, is not what happened. In fact, according to a memo later written by Colleen Rowley, the Minneapolis office's general counsel, headquarters seemed to go out of its way to undermine its agents' efforts to pursue a case against Moussaoui. Rowley wrote that the Washington supervisor who presented the petition to the FBI's lawyers amended it to its detriment and omitted the additional intelligence supplied by the French, effectively sinking its chances for a favorable review.

What was lost by this blunder will never be known. Right after September 11, providing even less information than was supplied in their original affidavit, Minneapolis agents obtained a warrant to search Moussaoui's belongings and found two knives, a pair of binoculars and a notebook in which was written two important German phone numbers and an alias that Ramzi Binalshibh was using. There was also a clue that seemed to hearken back to Atta's old crop-duster plot: a computer disk containing information related to the aerial application of pesticides.

None of these clues would have exposed the September plot, though the German connection was interesting. But if a vigorous investigation had turned up Binalshibh's wire transfers, they might have led agents to Atta and other flight schools.

Which brings up another oversight on the FBI's part. The unit that handled the Moussaoui matter—the Islamic Radicals Unit—was the same unit that dealt with the Phoenix memo. As mistaken as the handling of either matter alone appears in hindsight, the fact that both cases together didn't trigger a more proactive response—or any response, for that matter—now seems incredible. Once again, as with the Phoenix memo, headquarters made no attempt to communicate Moussaoui's arrest to other agencies, and when the Minneapolis agents out of desperation finally did inform the CTC at the end of August, they were reprimanded by their bosses in Washington.

No evidence has come out to suggest that Atta and his cohorts panicked when Moussaoui was arrested, though if Moussaoui was being groomed to be the twentieth hijacker on the four targeted planes, as some allege, Atta would have had plenty of opportunity to inform the affected team that they were expected to carry out the mission without a fifth member.

Another possibility is that Moussaoui's arrest shut down a separate element of the terror plot that has yet to come to light. After all, Moussaoui had maintained his distance from the other known conspirators in the U.S. and had been training incredibly intensely for a pilot who hadn't shown himself to be the equal even of Hani Hanjour.

Some of Atta's activities in August also hint at the possibility that the mission's parameters were still in flux when Moussaoui was taken into custody.

Personnel at the South Florida Crop Care in Belle Glade say Atta and

assorted associates visited the company's airstrip on several weekends leading up to September 11. Atta even touched down once in a small plane to
ask more questions of the company's staff.

Also, while the other pilots were training near their ultimate targets, at
that time Atta was still hundreds of miles from New York City and its Twin
Towers. In mid-August, he drove to a federal flight service station outside
Miami ostensibly seeking routine weather and route information for a flight
from Miami to Vero Beach. He also rented at least two planes north of
Miami during that period, one for 90 minutes and one that he flew for only
an hour but kept for four.

By far the strangest episode of the month, however, occurred inside a
drugstore in downtown Delray Beach, where several of Atta's associates
had become familiar faces. A SunTrust branch stood across the street, the
public library and its computers were two doors away, and there was a
bench outside the store where the brothers Wail and Waleed al-Shehri liked
to sit with sodas and candy when they were taking breaks from using the
Internet.

Atta, who was a less familiar figure in the neighborhood, didn't come
across as friendly.

"When I first saw him, I thought he was trying to rob the place," says
Gregg Chatterton, the pharmacist at Huber Drugs.

Atta and al-Shehhi had been hovering in the aisle stocked with women's
skin creams for a suspiciously long time when Chatterton finally
approached them, maintaining eye contact with a co-worker in case there
was trouble. Atta was nattily dressed in an autumn-colored shirt and the
kind of slacks not often seen in a store so close to the beach. Al-Shehhi had
a horrible cough.

First, though, Atta said he needed something for his hands.

When Atta held them up, Chatterton saw that the front of both hands
was red and swollen from the tip of the fingers to the base of the wrist.
There was no blistering, and the backs of both hands were normal.

"Have you been dealing with concrete or cement?" Chatterton asked.

"No."

Chatterton had seen workers from a nearby concrete plant get the same kind of hands when they failed keep their gloves on, but he could think of a lot of other activities that might irritate the skin that way and he couldn't easily recommend a remedy without first discovering the cause of Atta's symptoms. Atta, however, wasn't providing much information. During the long, fruitless interview that followed, it struck Chatterton more than once that Atta might be the operator of a cocaine lab.

"Have you been doing a lot of cleaning?"

Atta seemed insulted by that.

"Do you work with computers?"

"Yes."

"Do you repair them?"

Atta never did explain what he did with computers.

"Have you been using toluene?"

"I don't work with chemicals," Atta said.

That one had been a test, and Atta had revealed that he was familiar with a common ingredient of high-order explosives.

When he was running out of patience, Chatterton finally asked, "Have you been gardening?"

Atta harrumphed at that, as if the question again was an insult to his masculinity. Chatterton had had enough. Making no effort to hide his anger, the pharmacist rattled off a few options and was brushing past the two men on the way to his counter when Atta thumped him on the chest. Chatterton immediately flashed back to the thought that Atta was there to rob the store, but instead Atta said, "My friend needs something for his cough."

Chatterton gave al-Shehhi some medicine, but urged the ailing terrorist to visit a walk-in clinic because he had confessed to suffering night sweats. Al-Shehhi took a couple of referral cards and came back the next day to fill a prescription.

"*He* was nice," said Chatterton.

Only one piece of evidence that has emerged from the September 11 attacks fits with Atta and al-Shehhi's symptoms that day. On at least one of the planes, a hijacker claimed to be wearing a bomb. If in fact a bomb was carried onto any of the planes, it could have been the type of home-manufactured plastic explosive that some al Qaeda soldiers are trained to create from easily attainable ingredients like ammonium nitrate.

Chatterton's personal theory is only a little more satisfying. If Atta and al-Shehhi were regularly loitering around a crop-dusting facility, al-Shehhi could easily have developed a nasty cough from breathing in too many fumes, and Atta may have touched his hands on crop-dusting planes that hadn't yet been washed down.

But why would the leaders of an unprecedented hijacking operation be so obsessed at that late date with crop-dusting planes? Why would a remnant of Ramzi Yousef's plan still be keeping company with a riskier but potentially far more devastating plan of attack?

But the most perplexing questions about the events of that summer are reserved for U.S. national security officials. In the middle of August, prompted by repeated warnings that al Qaeda was about to strike, CIA director George Tenet ordered investigators to scour their files for any clues to possible upcoming attacks. At that point, the CIA apparently remembered al-Midhar and al-Hazmi, and after checking with INS, learned that both men were already inside the U.S. On August 23, they finally decided to alert the State Department, Customs, INS and the FBI, requesting that al-Midhar and al-Hazmi be placed on the terrorist watch list and asking the FBI to track the two men down.

Why they waited more than 17 months to inform the other agencies that al-Hazmi was in the country or that al-Midhar had obtained a multiple-entry visa for the U.S. in 1999 is unclear. The two Saudi terrorists attended flight schools, opened bank accounts and interacted with at least five other hijackers before September 11. FBI officials are convinced that routine surveillance of al-Midhar and al-Hazmi would have exposed the plot had the CIA only shared its intelligence on a timely basis.

The CIA's failure wasn't due solely to an oversight. Earlier in the summer of 2001, in fact, the Agency's reticence had created a surreal scene at the FBI's New York office. CIA officers had asked to meet on June 11 with JTTF investigators who worked the bin Laden desk. According to a government official familiar with the meeting, the CIA officers displayed four surveillance photos and, without explanation, asked what the JTTF knew about the men in the pictures. The task force agents identified several subjects, including Tawfiq bin Atash, as suspects in the *Cole* investigation. They even surmised that the photos were taken at the January 2000 Kuala Lumpur meeting, which they had learned about independently through their investigation of the *Cole*. But when they repeatedly asked their CIA counterparts for more information about the Malaysia meeting and its participants, the CIA officers stonewalled them, claiming the intelligence was too sensitive to be shared. The meeting degenerated into a shouting match.

By August 23, it was too late to locate the Saudis—though perhaps it shouldn't have been. A senior JTTF agent says the Bureau launched an "appropriate" search. (JTTF agents checked area hotels—al-Midhar had written Marriott in the address box of his July immigration form—and visited Choice Point, a public access database.) But the task force came up empty, a remarkable outcome given that both al-Midhar and al-Hazmi had obtained identity cards and credit cards and had even bought plane tickets, in their real names, just days after the Bureau began its search.

John O'Neill was not on the case. Shortly after returning in mid-July from Salou, Spain, he had told me one night at Elaine's that he was retiring from the FBI. One of the reasons was obvious: Over the past year, while O'Neill had been pressing the investigation of bin Laden, the FBI was investigating O'Neill. His problem: "the briefcase incident."

The year before, O'Neill had left his briefcase in a Miami hotel ballroom. The room was full of agents attending a conference. O'Neill stepped outside to take a phone call. When he returned to the ballroom, the agents had gone to lunch, the ballroom was empty and the briefcase was missing. In it was a classified report that broke down, in detail, every terrorism or espionage investigation being run out of New York's National Security Division. The briefcase was recovered by Miami police a few hours after it disappeared, in another hotel. A lighter and a cigar cutter were gone, but all the secret papers remained intact. They were even dusted for prints, but no one other than O'Neill appeared to have handled the papers.

Eventually, the Justice Department's internal probe of the briefcase incident cleared O'Neill of any criminal wrongdoing. As soon as he was off the hook, though, the FBI decided to open its own internal investigation of the incident.

"I just can't go through another year of being under investigation for something where all the facts are already known," he said of his impending retirement. "Give me my punishment and let's get on with the hunt for the bad guys. But not the death of a thousand cuts. It is time to end the bloodletting."

A couple of weeks later, O'Neill told me he had accepted a private-sector job that would be a lot less stress and a lot more money. That was never really what he wanted, but it would soften the blow of leaving the Bureau under a cloud. On August 19, the "briefcase incident" found its way into *The New York Times*. O'Neill had pissed a few people off from Washington all the way to Yemen. Now they were making him pay.

"What's the new job?" I asked.

"Director of security at the World Trade Center. I start in two weeks."

They bought their September 11 airline tickets two by two. Al-Midhar and Majed Moqed were the first, paying cash on August 25 to purchase one-way tickets for American Airlines' Flight 77 from Washington to Los Angeles. The al-Shehri brothers made reservations the next day for American's Flight 11 out

306 | THE CELL

of Boston. Nawaf al-Hazmi and his younger brother used the Internet on August 27 to book their seats on Flight 77. Of the rest, some paid cash, some used credit cards. Some visited travel agencies, others made their reservations by phone or on the Web.

Fifteen days before the hijackings, Jarrah, who would eventually fly out of Newark, checked in at a low-budget motel in Laurel, Maryland, for a three-night stay. He quickly changed his mind, however, signing out a day later and arguing with the front desk because the hotel granted a refund for only one of the other two nights. On the same day, Mohamed Atta flew from Baltimore to South Florida, where he, Jarrah and al-Shehhi would huddle one more time before the final phase of the operation was set into motion. Atta himself had waited until that day, August 28, to reserve a business-class seat on a September 11 transcontinental flight.

The mission requirements at this stage were relatively straightforward: Each operative presumably already had sufficient identification for boarding a domestic flight. He would also need a ticket, at least one weapon, a place to stay near his assigned airport of departure, a car or other means of getting to that shelter, transportation to the airport, access to adequate cash, a detailed knowledge of his role in carrying out the operation, and a means of maintaining communication at least with the team commander. Each pilot probably carried a copy of a "Boeing key," a universal key for opening the door of any Boeing cockpit.

The need of the men for spiritual support was not overlooked. At some point before the eleventh, copies of a handwritten five-page document were distributed among the hijackers to prepare each reader for martyrdom. Had it been composed by one of the martyrs? That was the early theory, though the pages easily could have been pressed into Atta's hands during the final weeks in any number of locations, including Western Europe, Florida, Nevada, and the New York or Washington areas. The document was meant to be reviewed by each man on his final night.

On August 30, Atta bought a utility tool that included a knife and, with

Jarrah, checked into the low-budget Longshore Motel back in Hollywood. They had laptop computers with them and said they would need Internet access because they were job hunting. Manager Paul Dragomir obliged, after he'd seen that they could get on the Web for free with their NetZero accounts, by running an extension wire from a phone jack in the office. Soon, though, he began worrying that his guests in Room 3 could be running up his phone bill with long calls to the Middle East, so he told them they'd have to work out of his office if they wanted the phone access.

An argument ensued, and Atta became insulting before Jarrah chimed in: "You don't understand—we're on a mission." Dragomir chuckled a bit at that idea, asking Jarrah if he meant a mission of Islam. "They said, 'No, we want to stay out of that,'" Dragomir remembers. They did demand a refund on the room, however, and drove away angry. Al-Shehhi, apparently, had already found a more accommodating motel up the coast in Deerfield Beach, and there they all reconvened.

On one of the first days of September, as the San Diego cell—Hanjour, al-Midhar, and al-Hazmi—headed north to Maryland and the Valencia Motel, a curious scene was playing out in Germany. Said Bahaji, carrying a suitcase and acting impatient, stopped by his father-in-law's house and announced he was leaving for a job in Pakistan but needed about $450 for the plane fare. On the 4th, he e-mailed his wife an "all's-well-in-Karachi" greeting, then disappeared completely. At almost the same time, Atta's other Marienstrasse roommate, Ramzi Binalshibh, also made for the border. Using an alias, Binalshibh received from the United Arab Emirates a wire transfer of some $1,500 before flying on September 5 from Dusseldorf to Madrid. He too vanished.

The hijackers, meanwhile, seemed to just be killing time. Four nights before the operation, on Friday, September 7, Atta and a few of his colleagues spent part of the evening in Florida at Shuckum's Oyster Bar in Hollywood. Atta drank cranberry juice and played alone on a video game while the other men downed mixed drinks and raised a fuss about the bill after al-Shehhi had sent his food back to the kitchen. Atta, who seemed to think the waitress took his friends to be deadbeats, pulled a fifty off a wad of bills and snapped, "I'm an American Airlines pilot. I can pay my bill."

The next day, Atta began shipping excess cash back to his paymaster in the U.A.E. He made two wire transfers totalling nearly $8,000 to Mustafa Ahmed al-Hisawi that Saturday. Waleed al-Shehri wired $5,000, apparently to the same man, on Sunday, and al-Shehhi finished off the process Monday with a $5,400 transfer from Boston's Logan Airport. On September 11 itself, some $16,300 was deposited into Mustafa Ahmed al-Hawsawi's Dubai bank account. Al-Hawsawi, arriving at the bank at a little after 9 in the morning Dubai time, removed more than $6,000 from an account belonging to hijacker Fayez Ahmed by using a check signed by Ahmed. He withdrew the remaining $1,361 in Ahmed's account using an ATM machine, and then flew to Pakistan.

By Saturday night, almost all the hijackers were in place for Tuesday's operation. Al-Shehhi was in Boston together with his and Atta's crews; Hanjour and the rest of the San Diego cell were with Majed Moqed in Maryland; and Jarrah's team had gathered at the Paterson, New Jersey, apartment. Only Jarrah was missing. Mistakenly, he had asked that his September plane ticket be mailed to his Florida address, so a long, panicky drive had been added to his duties. Shortly after Saturday midnight, he would be stopped on an interstate highway in northern Maryland for clocking 90 miles an hour in a 65-mph zone. Driving a Mitsubishi rented from the Newark airport, he produced a valid Virginia driver's license, accepted a $270 ticket, and continued on his way. Down in the vacated Florida apartment, a fold-out cardboard replica of a Boeing cockpit had been left behind.

Jarrah called his family in Lebanon on Sunday, promising he'd see them soon for his sister's September 22 wedding. He also sat down and produced a four-page farewell letter to his girlfriend, Aysel Senguen. "I did what I had to do, and you should be very proud of that," he wrote. "It is a great honor and you will see the result, everyone will be celebrating." In his closing, he urged: "Hold on tight to what you have, until we meet again." Then he miswrote her German address on the envelope. The letter would be seized by investigators after it boomeranged in the mail system.

Atta may have devoted much of his Sunday to gathering intel at Logan Airport. Surveillance cameras caught his rental car moving through the Boston air terminal at least five times during those final days, and a Massachusetts resident later said that two days before the hijackings she saw a man who looked like Atta, dressed in flowered gym pants and purple Nantucket T-shirt, intently jotting notes at an American Airlines gate.

On Monday, Atta and Alomari drove from Boston to Portland, Maine. They were scheduled to return to Logan the next morning in time to catch Flight 11 to Los Angeles, but why they risked the entire mission on the timely performance of the Portland commuter flight may never be entirely explained. Perhaps Atta wanted to be sure the chosen weapons would pass the security checks, or maybe the concern was that red flags would be raised at Logan if ten Middle Eastern men checked in for transcontinental flights all at the same time.

Other hijackers let their minds wander. One member of the Newark team passed part of his last afternoon at a go-go bar that featured "Jersey Style table dancing." That night, one or more of the hijackers in al-Shehhi's crew phoned Boston-area escort services seeking a prositute to have sex with four men. "It was over $400 and that was too much," a law enforcement source later told *The Boston Globe*. Ziad Jarrah, by all accounts, was faithful to his woman, but having recently convinced his parents to tag an extra $700 onto his September allowance, he spent extravagantly on his final night. He treated his colleagues to dinner at the finest of the four restaurants inside the airport Marriott in Newark and, more curiously, paid cash for seven rooms that looked out on the Lower Manhattan skyline according to some published reports. Only three operatives would be joining him the next morning on Flight 93.

Atta, by contrast, remained an ascetic. He and Alomari spent their final night on a featureless commercial strip on the outskirts of Portland, Maine. They checked into a Comfort Inn minutes away from the airport. They tarried no more than 15 minutes over a Pizza Hut last supper. They refueled their rented Nissan at a no-name service station and visited two ATMs. After 9:00, Atta shopped at a Wal-Mart for about 20 minutes, then retired for the evening.

A camera at one of the ATMs captured images of Alomari, the young imam, smiling at some private amusement while Atta stands stonelike behind him. The surprise is not that Atta is already dead but that the younger man in the foreground was so clearly still engaged in living.

The five-page document that Atta and Alomari probably consulted back in their hotel room asked that they sever all ties to the life of this world. It advised them to shower, to shave off all excess hair, and to apply cologne, and these simple rituals surely strengthened each man's sense of responsibility to the other warriors despite the many miles then separating them. But the manual's main thrust was to negate the present, and to transpose the actions the readers were about to take to an arena beyond nominal reality. In virtually all practical matters, the words and example of the prophet Muhammad were to govern their conduct, and, God willing, they would end their martyrdom mission not just in the outer circles of heaven, but "in the Highest Paradise, in the company of God."

Atta, if true to the instructions, would have blessed his body by reading verses from the Koran into his hands and rubbing his hands over himself. He would have repeated the ritual to bless his luggage, his clothes, his knife, his pepper spray, his ID, his passport and all his papers. He would also have prayed to God for victory and read two traditional war chapters from the Koran.

"Consider that this is a raid on a path," the instructions reminded him. "As the Prophet said, 'A raid on the path of God is better than this World and what is in it.'" This idea was crucial. During the last ten years of the Prophet's life, following his flight from Mecca in 622, he was engaged in building an Islamic state, and to do so, he endorsed the looting of nonfollowers provided that these "raids" were not enacted for individual enrichment, as had been the tradition, but that they advanced the cause of the community as a whole.

A variety of specific instructions stemmed from this notion that the hijackers were reenacting a particular historical drama. They were advised to tighten their clothes, or gird their loins, as "the pious generations after the Prophet" had done. "Do not forget to take a bounty, even if it is a glass of water to quench your thirst," the manual reminded. "If God grants any of you a slaughter, you should perform it as an offering on behalf of your father and mother, for they are owed by you." The chance to cut an innocent's jugular veins, in other words, was to be considered a test of faith and therefore a gift from God. The killer's knife was to be kept sharp so as not to cause undue discomfort to the victim. And finally, the manual urged, "take prisoners and kill them." The Prophet, allegedly, believed it foolish to waste energy on prisoners.

Many of the hijackers probably lay down that night still grappling with the prospect of their own imminent deaths. The manual had addressed the fear of dying with scattershot reassurances. Fatalism was one crutch offered: "Remember that anything that happens to you could never be avoided and what did not happen to you could never have happened to you." The rewards waiting in the afterlife, including "the women of paradise," were also dangled before them.

But the writer of the manual anticipated that fear would resurface in the airports and on the planes. The recommended solution was to submerge all other fears to the fear of God. "Fear is indeed a great act of worship," the manual said, and only God is worthy of it. A passage from the Koran was cited: "Fear them not, but fear Me, if you are Believers."

Atta and Alomari checked out of the hotel the next morning less than half an hour before their scheduled 6 o'clock flight. They had, if they were true to their instructions, once more washed themselves, and once more turned to Mecca to pray. The drive to the airport took less than ten minutes, and as the pale sky brightened, Atta and Alomari left their rental car in the airport parking lot and found their way to a US Airways counter.

A supplication was to be offered then, according to the manual:

Oh Lord, I ask you for the best of this place, and ask you to protect me from its evils.

Atta handed over two of his bags, which contained, among other things, his mission instruction manual and the will he'd signed in Hamburg more than five years earlier. He and Alomari both were carrying computer bags as they passed through security at 5:45.

Oh Lord, block their vision from in front of them, so that they may not see.

Nine of the 19 hijackers would have their bags subjected to close scrutiny that morning—six of them because a computerized screening system singled them out for the enhanced security checks, and three others because of irregularities in the identification documents that two of them held. Their knives, if discovered, had blades less than four inches long, which meant they were legal. Their responses to any questioning had surely been rehearsed.

During boarding for the Portland-to-Boston flight, passenger Vincent Meisner brushed his bag against Atta while passing in the aisle. Meisner apologized, but Atta simply hunched his shoulders and turned away. "I thought he just hadn't had his morning coffee yet," Meisner said later. They were due to arrive in Boston at 6:50, with Atta praying all the way.

At 7:20, boarding began at Boston's Logan Airport for passengers taking Flight 11 to Los Angeles. The connecting flight from Portland was late, so Atta and Alomari were among the last of 81 passengers to pass the boarding attendants. Atta's bags failed to make the connection in time.

Before you enter, make a prayer and supplications.

Atta settled into seat 8D in business class, with Alomari beside him. Further prayers and supplications were called for.

Moments before the plane's 7:59 takeoff, Atta pulled out his mobile phone and dialed someone inside another Boeing 767 that was about to take off for Los Angeles. The call, placed after all Flight 11 passengers had been asked to turn off their phones, lasted less than a minute, but it was long enough to signal to Marwan al-Shehhi that the operation was on.

When the confrontation begins, strike like champions who do not want to go back to this world.

Ziad Jarrah may have already been in the air on Flight 93 out of Newark when he made his last call to Aysel Senguen. In the message he left, there was nothing unusual about the words he chose, nor in the tone of his voice. He loved her, he said. But he always said that.

CHAPTER 20

AFTER THE ATTACKS

When the planes struck the Twin Towers, John P. O'Neill was on his second day as director of security for the World Trade Center. He came down from his 35th floor office to the Fire Command Station located in the lobby. A number of people I know saw him that day, in his blue pinstriped suit, fielding calls on his cell phone and trying to organize a plan. O'Neill had probably given some thought to the idea that for the next big attack, wherever it was, he'd be on the sidelines. I knew John well enough to know that he'd feel a tinge of frustration being out of the game. But maybe not on this morning. Granted it was his second day on the job as director of security, and the first day of his entire adult life as "a civilian," but the World Trade Center was his turf now. And it was the target. He was still in the game. As he walked he was seeing a lot of the faces of men from the NYPD, the FBI, the world he had just left. The very world he was now being pulled back into. From across the lobby of the North Tower, O'Neill spotted Wesley Wong, an FBI special agent he'd known since his Baltimore days. Wong was trying to set up communications for a temporary FBI command post in the lobby. O'Neill asked Wong what he was hearing.

"At this point it's a little chaotic," Wong said. "I'm trying to get some information." Just then Wong got through to the FBI New York Operations Center. "While I was on the line, John asked me if it was true that the Pentagon had been hit. I asked the Op Center and they confirmed it." The entire time, O'Neill was on his cell phone, relaying information. "He was still in charge. Calm, professional, just like the guy I'd known for 25 years," Wong recalled. As O'Neill turned to walk away, Wong remembered he'd missed the small gathering they'd had when O'Neill left the FBI just a few days before. "Hey," Wong called out, "I owe you lunch."

"Yeah," O'Neill said, with an ironic smile. "Give me a call when things calm down." O'Neill made a path through the lobby to the doors that would connect with the South Tower, where the second plane hit. He had to have known exactly what this was all about and who was behind it. He had been rehearsing for this moment for too long. He had agonized over every possible scenario. Perhaps every one *but* this one. Now John was hearing the thud of the bodies falling from above. He stepped outside to find a police command post. There were body parts everywhere.

For most of an hour, O'Neill shuttled in and out of the buildings trying to organize an approach to a rescue plan and then a crime scene search. In those moments, he called many of the people he cared about to tell them he was okay. Then the first tower fell, and John O'Neill vanished into the falling steel and white dust.

There is hardly any need to describe the irony. John O'Neill had spent the better part of ten years fighting terrorism and the better part of five trying to nail bin Laden. Now, Osama bin Laden had struck the two buildings in his care. Unwittingly—how could bin Laden have known?—he had killed his chief American nemesis. I called O'Neill's phone all that day . . . hoping . . . hoping for a miracle. I called all the next day too. We'd all heard about voids in the rubble that might hold survivors. We were all beginning to hear of people who'd turned up unconscious in hospitals in New Jersey and elsewhere, places that had been drafted to handle the injured. So, like many of his friends, I kept dialing the number. So did many others. Each time his voice would greet me *Hi, this is John O'Neill* . . . Several times I left messages. I knew it was stupid. At some point, the recording stopped. It was a new voice now, one of those phone-voice ladies who informed me that the party's mailbox was full. I was beginning to grapple with the idea that John was dead, but it still didn't seem possible. He had been larger than life, and almost singularly focused on one threat, one enemy. It was possible, I thought, he was still alive. *"Hi, this is John O'Neill"* . . . How could he die? And how could he die like that?

I had been on the air with Peter Jennings almost continuously for three days. We were only taking short breaks to go home, sleep for an hour or two, change and come back. Finally, on the night of September 14, I left the office and went to Elaine's. I walked in the door half-expecting to see John sitting at table 1. Instead it was Jerry Hauer, the former director of emergency management for New York City. It was Hauer who had lined up the Trade Center job for John, and he was one of O'Neill's best friends. We talked about John for a long time, and about all our other friends who died down there that day. And we drank. I have to say, it was one of the rare times I needed to.

I went home that night and accepted for the first time that O'Neill was dead. I got into bed and began to cry, alone, and loud. I couldn't stop. It had been four days since the planes had hit, and now for the first time I was being forced to deal with it, without the handy shield of professional detachment. Like so many people, I knew I was a wreck. I also knew that there was no time to deal with that. We all had to be back and focused in a very few hours. I knew it had to be worse for my friends who had been down there and made it out.

A few days later, somewhere in Afghanistan, Osama bin Laden was sitting in a safehouse describing to a Saudi sheik how he had tuned in to the radio on September 11 to listen to his handiwork unfold. Suliman Abu Gaith, bin Laden's chief spokesman, had come running in to tell him the news, but bin Laden already knew.

"After the first plane, they were happy, and thought that was it," bin Laden told his visitor, "I told them wait, wait. After a while they announced another plane has hit the World Trade Center (*laughter*)."

Bin Laden goes on to explain to his guest that he'd gotten more than he'd hoped for. "So if it hits the building here," bin Laden explained, gesturing with his hand, "the portion of the building above will collapse. That was the most we hoped for, the most we expected."

Bin Laden questioned the Saudi sheik who had come to visit. He wanted to know, how was all this playing back home in Saudi Arabia? The visitor assured him that in the mosques of Jeddah, bin Laden was a hero.

In New York, FBI Supervisor Kenny Maxwell, the agent who'd helped rebuild TWA Flight 800 out of the wreckage, had thought then that that job would be the most difficult job of his career. Now, he grappled with how to process the largest crime scene in world history. Even the concept of it was daunting. Barry Mawn, the top man in the FBI's New York office, told Mary Jo White, the chief prosecutor for the bin Laden cases, that he was not going to conduct a typical crime-scene evidence-collection at the site. "Why not?" she asked. "'Come with me,'" Mawn said he told her. "We were six blocks from the scene. She took one look around and she knew: It was just too enormous."

As it was, rescue workers would sift through the rubble and find a cop's gun, a woman's ring, a stack of engraved wedding invitations that would never be sent, their little white doilies caked in dust. The police and the FBI mounted a massive effort to collect as much evidence as they could, but the real goal was to locate and identify the dead.

As far as evidence was concerned—what for, really? There was no mystery. Airplanes had been used as weapons of mass destruction. The crime had been recorded on videotape from start to finish, and had been described by many of the hijack victims from their cell phones and by people inside the Trade Center. Their frantic calls to 911 were all on tape.

Even as the makeshift command post was being set up in an old warehouse on West 26th Street near the river, it occurred to Mawn that the FBI's priority now was probably not building a case against 19 dead hijackers. Or even bin Laden. It was already clear that on September 11, Osama bin Laden had gone from being the subject of a criminal investigation to the object of a military operation. In Washington, FBI Director Robert Mueller re-tasked his agents nationwide. The new priority? To do everything possible to prevent the next attack.

Three days after September 11, CIA Director George Tenet issued a directive to his head of operations, saying, in essence, the gloves are off. Do what you need to do. Many saw the memo as with one stroke ending 30 years of tentativeness and hand-wringing political correctness when it came to getting down and dirty against terrorism.

Rescue workers had found only a handful of the 3,000 victims by the time President George W. Bush addressed the nation on September 20. That night Bush told a for-once-united U.S. Congress and an anxious and angry America that the terrorists had finally gotten our attention, that now the sleeping giant was wide awake, and angry. Bush was very deliberate at first in denying bin Laden the war he no doubt craved, saying that this was not a conflict with the gentle people of Islam, but with terrorists and those who would protect them. For anyone trying to hedge their bets on this point, President Bush was emphatic.

"Every nation, in every region, now has a decision to make. Either you are with us, or you are with the terrorists." At this point there was applause. "From this day forward, any nation that continues to harbor or support terrorism will be regarded by the United States as a hostile regime." America had finally thrown down the gauntlet.

On September 21, the next day, rescue workers digging in the rubble of Ground Zero came upon the remains of John P. O'Neill.

On October 7, just as the bombing of al Qaeda camps and Taliban command centers was beginning, a courier delivered a videotape to Al Jezeera, the Arab television news network. On the tape, bin Laden can be seen sitting against a rock with his top people flanking him, defiantly telling viewers that the United States had it coming, and warning Americans that they will never feel safe until the Palestinians are too.

"And to America, I say to it and to its people this: I swear by God the Great, America will never dream nor those who live in America will never taste security and safety unless we feel security and safety in our land and in Palestine."

On November 10, as Northern Alliance and U.S. Special Forces prepared to take the city of Kabul, Osama bin Laden's cadre of guards readied his family to flee. At the Islamic Center of Jalalabad, bin Laden took the podium and rallied his troops. This was the fight bin Laden had been stirring for. However, as American coalition forces drove across Afghanistan, wresting control from the Taliban, most of the population cheered—this was clearly not the bloody, populist anti-American jihad bin Laden had no doubt dreamed of. Bin Laden's deputies began lining up the trucks and tanks that would transport bin Laden and his core group up into the mountains. In the ensuing chaos, bin Laden was apparently reluctant to leave, and continued pressing his case that he should stay and fight. Barbrach Khan, an Afghan miller, confirmed this to ABC News's David Wright.

"Osama was very upset," Khan said. "He kept wagging his finger saying he wanted to stay and fight. The deputy told him he must go quickly."

Clearly frustrated, bin Laden at last joined the caravan as it headed for the mountains near the Pakistani border. At one mountain pass, the convoy split, with one group headed for the dense Tora Bora mountains, and the other for the Milawa Valley, where bin Laden kept a secret summer hideout, complete with a pool and a playground for his children. Milawa took heavy U.S. bombardment during which the compound was destroyed and a series of al Qaeda hideouts and caves were uncovered. Bin Laden was last seen there on November 9, 2001.

By December of that year, bin Laden's forces had been traced to a network of caves at Tora Bora. The U.S. advisors stayed in the background while Northern Alliance troops went in after him, but bin Laden was able to escape. Ibn Sheik al Libby, one of bin Laden's ranking men who was captured there, told the FBI that bin Laden was in the Tora Bora caves throughout the battle. He said bin Laden had instructed him to take command of the battle, and then had fled.

The CIA felt al-Libby was holding back vital information. The CIA suggested that the FBI turn al-Libby over to the Egyptians, who have often been accused of using torture to speed up arduous interrogations. The FBI was opposed to the idea. If a suspect was tortured, then any statement he gave would be damaged goods in any American courtroom. The Bureau wanted to preserve al-Libby so he could testify in a trial. However, the CIA believed the criminal case was secondary to the need to answer two questions as quickly as possible: Where was bin Laden and what was he next planning against America?

In the end, CIA Director George Tenet and FBI Director Bob Mueller went head to head on al-Libby. Sources say the al-Libby matter was settled by the president, who said that al-Libby would be shipped to the Egyptians. It was a defining moment. The U.S. had drifted from the comfortable moral high ground that made things like torture unacceptable. Later, however, FBI sources complained to me that the Egyptians didn't learn any more from the prisoner than they had.

In February the CIA believed bin Laden was in the Logar province of Afghanistan. Agents had learned that bin Laden, with a very small group of bodyguards, perhaps just two or three, had walked into a village, spread some money among the elders and asked for help getting set up.

By March, with most of the major cities in Afghanistan under American or Northern Alliance control, there were still scant clues as to bin Laden's whereabouts. The Logar province information needed to be checked out.

But even with JTTF people on the ground in Afghanistan, it was not exactly like tracking a guy in the Bronx. You couldn't throw Tommy Corrigan in the back of a surveillance van and tell him to keep an eye out. You needed an armed team that would be ready to take on bin Laden and his people if they encountered them. You needed people who knew how to move in the tribal areas. In fact, the problem the CIA was having was, even the people they did have, operators from the Northern Alliance and other friendly tribes, could not just wander into a town in Logar without drawing a lot of attention. The minute they started asking questions or just hanging around, locals would begin asking, who are you, where did you come from, what are you doing here? If the answers didn't ring true, the bad guys would be coming out of the woodwork.

Around the same time, intelligence was indicating that not very far away from Logar, a group of al Qaeda fighters had tucked themselves into a mountain ridge near Gardez. When a small cadre of Special Forces troops choppered into the area they came under heavy, sustained fire. A Navy SEAL who fell from one of the choppers attempting to escape the gunfire ended up putting up quite a battle of his own, ultimately being killed by al Qaeda gunmen before reinforcements arrived. The battle of Gardez would rage for two weeks before it became a clean-up effort. Because the U.S. forces had met with such heavy resistance, some at the Pentagon and the CIA took that as a sign, just as they had in Tora Bora, that bin Laden might have been there. What else would they fight so fiercely for? But in the end, when they questioned the prisoners and searched the caves, they were told bin Laden had not been there, and they found no sign of him. What they did find, however, was disturbing. According to local tribesmen who had seen the caves, there were maps and weapons, as well as what appeared to be pictures of American cities and of landmarks and bridges. That meant not only were the al Qaeda fighters on the run and willing to fight, but that they were still in operational mode, looking at and planning for future attacks on U.S. soil.

Back in Washington, at the FBI and CIA, that seemed to fit in with a host of other bad omens. Before the September 11 attacks, the CIA and the

National Security Agency (NSA) had been monitoring communications between suspected al Qaeda telephones around the world, noticing a distinct increase in traffic. There was a lot of "chatter" on the lines. Most of the conversations were in code. What's more, the CIA and NSA were by charter not supposed to spy on Americans on U.S. soil. That was the FBI's job. As a result, in almost every case, calls between telephones in the United States and suspected al Qaeda phone numbers abroad were not monitored on the assumption that the U.S. party might be an American.

After September 11, an arrangement was devised to allow the NSA and CIA to intercept any call from a U.S. telephone line to a suspected al Qaeda telephone anywhere in the world. Instantly, a roving national security wiretap order would apply and the FBI could monitor the call. In addition, fast-response teams from the nearest FBI office would rush to the call's point of origin and try and observe the caller. Alarm bells started going off beginning in early March. The call level was high again, peaking to the same levels it had reached before September 11. If high levels of "chatter" signaled another attack, the FBI needed to know immediately who the al Qaeda operators here were. But when the fast-response teams got to the phones the callers were always gone. Calls from New York, San Francisco, Los Angeles, Miami, Boston and other cities, to numbers in Europe, Pakistan, the United Arab Emirates were all made on pre-paid calling cards that were untraceable.

No one with access to this piece of classified information liked the sound or feel of it. Bin Laden's last public communications had promised more attacks. The captured al Qaeda prisoners being questioned at the U.S. military prison at Guantanamo Bay, Cuba, were providing information, but it usually lacked specifics.

With bin Laden on the run, his communications largely cut off, there was one man who seemed the key to al Qaeda's ability to launch another attack, and that man was Abu Zubaydah. Since the embassy bombings case in East Africa, the FBI had known that Zubaydah was in charge of recruiting and placement for al Qaeda operators around the world. Running his show from Peshawar, Zubaydah knew the names, talents, and phone numbers of almost every man who had scored high marks in bin Laden's terror camps. He knew the leaders of the cells in Yemen, and Italy, France and Canada as well as in the United States. But as the controller of thousands of secret soldiers, a master of forgery and disguise, a man of a dozen different identities, Abu Zubaydah could make himself a very hard man to find.

The post–September 11 CIA was a very different animal from what had existed before the attacks. After Tenet's "take the gloves off" memo of September 14, bosses at Langley and officers in the field had taken the message to heart. "We were doin' shit we wouldn't have dreamed of a year before, or ten years before even," said one agent. Now, with some possible intercepts from suspect cell phones and a little human intelligence on the ground, the CIA was ready to move. Teams from the CIA's little-known Incidence Response Team (IRT) had been deployed in Afghanistan and Pakistan. The IRT was made up of former members of the SEALs, Delta Force, Air Force Special Operations Command and CIA officers with field experience. Since September 11, the IRTs had been all over Afghanistan and Pakistan, working with the locals booming in doors in the dead of night, capturing al Qaeda suspects and gathering documents and intelligence that would lead them to their next stop. Of course they were now backed up by a network that included the full resources of the CIA's intelligence-gathering apparatus, the vast electronic and satellite eyes and ears of the NSA, as well as the information being gleaned by the FBI and military intelligence. And then there was luck.

On a cool night in the last days of March, in the village of Faisalbad in northern Pakistan, a team of IRT operators and members of the FBI Joint Terrorist Task Force came to a stop on a quiet road just outside of town. Just ahead of the SUVs in which they rode was a line of pickup trucks filled with an elite squad of Pakistani soldiers under the command of a colonel. One more time, everyone checked their weapons, racked shells into the chambers, confirmed their individual assignments and rested their thumbs on the safety catches of their weapons. Then the trucks moved out, kicking up dust. As they turned the last corner, the headlights were killed and the trucks glided silently to a stop. The soldiers piled out and as the first member of the entry team leaped onto the fence to scale it, he got a shock, literally. The fence was electrified. The next man to hit the fence got the same message. One of the soldiers produced bolt cutters, breaching the fence and a gate. By now there were sounds from inside the house. The element of surprise was quickly fading. With a steel ram, the entry team boomed the door. It didn't budge. Again. BOOM. Nothing. The door was reinforced steel held fast by a series of dead bolts. BOOM, BOOM, BOOM, BOOM . . . the element of surprise was now a distant memory. Finally, the door gave. Now the house was alive with sounds of men's voices and feet. The first Pakistani soldier ran through the door. No sooner had he crossed the threshold than a man behind the door wrapped a piano wire around his neck and began to garrote him. The second soldier came through the door, got a glimpse of the scene and lit the al Qaeda piano man up with a blast of machine gun fire. He went down like a lump. Now soldiers went from room to room putting men down on the floor. A team ran up the stairs and onto the rooftop. A man was running. He was Pakistani, with glasses and a mustache. When the entry team caught up with him he spun around and grabbed one soldier's AK-47 with both hands, trying to twist it out of his hands. As the fugitive now had the barrel in his hands with the muzzle pointing just below his midsection, the soldier simply pulled the trigger, sending a short blast of bullets into the man's groin, legs and abdomen, ending a fierce struggle.

Abu Zubaydah fell down writhing in pain and quickly losing vast quantities of blood. Now, the CIA, IRT and FBI JTTF people entered the building. They took several prisoners. Two of Zubaydah's wounded bodyguards were loaded into one of the Pakistani military trucks. One was dead and the other was still alive, but barely. The Americans noted with interest but no particular emotion that there was no plan to rush the wounded gunmen to the hospital. That, they would get to after they completed their search. As for Abu Zubaydah, he was another matter. He possessed critical intelligence. Quietly, the CIA and FBI men gathered the papers from inside the house. Now the neighbors were watching the odd collection of Pakistani soldiers and American men in khaki cargo pants with bulletproof vests on their street. In a dusty caravan of SUVs and pickup trucks, the team vanished into the rising sun, leaving behind only dust.

The world was still a very dangerous place that morning, but it was also very different than it was six months before. A group of Americans, cops, FBI and CIA agents, had teamed up with Muslim soldiers in an Islamic country and taken a door because there was a terrorist behind it. In Afghanistan, al Qaeda and bin Laden were on the run. The U.S. military was now taking a lead role in any assault aimed at capturing bin Laden or routing his forces. FBI agents and New York City detectives from the JTTF were on the ground in Afghanistan going through al Qaeda documents and questioning prisoners. A CIA–FBI team had located bin Laden's chemical and biological weapons lab in a cinder-block building two miles south of Kandahar's airport. The scientist who ran it was captured in Pakistan and was cooperating with the FBI, and the CIA was gathering an incredible amount of information, much of it from sources they would have shied away from because they were unsavory just several months ago. Weeks after his capture, Abu Zubaydah was talking, but he was only giving vague hints as to what al Qaeda still had in store. Many of the agents questioning him felt he was not just holding back, but misdirecting them. Once again, quietly, discussions began about lending him to a friendly country practiced in using more physical means of extracting information.

"We were kicking ass and taking names, finally," said one JTTF agent who was in Afghanistan. "You know who would have loved this?" he asked rhetorically. "O'Neill would have *loved* this."

I n mid-2002, several months after the United States had blasted al Qaeda from its safe haven in Afghanistan, Washington began turning inward to explore how the September 11 attacks could have taken the American intelligence community by surprise.

At congressional hearings that summer, the directors of the FBI and the CIA had their feet held to the fire on issues of interagency cooperation and on internal coordination between the bosses and the field agents. President Bush soon agreed to appoint an independent panel to investigate the intelligence breakdown. Chaired by former New Jersey governor Tom Keane, who stepped in after Bush's original choice, Henry Kissinger, acknowledged potential business conflicts, the group commenced in early 2003 the hard work of determining What Went Wrong.

Perhaps, of course, no one could have anticipated the exact scenario that played out on September 11. Perhaps Hollywood has taught us to expect too much from our intelligence services.

Still, we spend roughly $30 billion a year on national security. It's part of the mandate of our intelligence agencies to think the unthinkable; to anticipate, rather than just react to events. The CIA, in fact, was specifically chartered after World War II to prevent another Pearl Harbor–type event from ever occurring.

The September 11 attacks did not arrive without warning. Nearly every aspect of the terrorists' operation that day had a precedent recorded in the existing U.S. investigative files on al Qaeda. Agents knew that bin Laden was training men in his camps to hijack planes. They knew that Ramzi Yousef had devised a plot to fly a plane filled with explosives into CIA headquarters in Langley, Virginia, and that an operative linked to al Qaeda had already hijacked a commercial aircraft in an attempt to dive-bomb the Eiffel Tower. They had intelligence indicating al Qaeda had intended to use planes to attack the July 2001 economic summit meeting in Italy. They had, in fact, taken that particular threat seriously enough that they had helped the Italian military set up batteries of surface-to-air missiles to thwart a potential assault. They had also heard chatter for months about bin Laden planning something big, a "Hiroshima"-like operation, and they certainly knew enough about bin Laden to understand the extent of his megalomania. He had been trying since the early 1990s, after all, to obtain chemical and nuclear weapons.

Much of this information had been made public. The federal government had even hired people to connect the dots. During the 1990s, a series of expert panels had been commissioned to predict future terrorist threats and assess the nation's ability to defend against them. As early as 1993, one Pentagon-funded report picked up on the threat of terrorists using airplanes as bombs. "Coming down the Potomac, you could make a left turn at the Washington Monument and take out the White House," wrote Marvin Cetron, the report's principal author. "Or you could make a right turn and take out the Pentagon."

In February 1997, a commission on civil aviation security chaired by Vice President Al Gore released a report recommending that the government fund substantial capital improvements related to airport security and that the FAA work with the airline industry to ensure that passengers be positively identified and subjected to more rigorous screening before boarding flights.

Then in 1998, following the embassy bombings in East Africa, Congress commissioned two more counterterrorism panels, one chaired by Paul Bremer, a former State Department counterterrorism chief under President Reagan, the other by former senators Warren Rudman and Gary Hart. The panels' findings, which were released beginning in June 2000, were virtually identical. The commissions recommended that Afghanistan be designated a sponsor of terrorism, that private sources of funding for terrorists be frozen, that there be a crackdown on student visas, that the CIA and FBI find better ways of sharing information and that the CIA reconsider the so-called "agent scrub" that had been discouraging its officers from recruiting unsavory characters as agency "assets."

All the panels were apparently ignored. Not one of their recommendations was signed into law or adopted as policy before September 11, 2001. Marvin Cetron's 1993 report, perhaps the most prescient of them all, wasn't even released. The report—which was based entirely on public, nonclassified information—was killed by none other than the State Department's acting coordinator for counterterrorism, Barbara Bodine, who would later lock horns with John O'Neill in Yemen. Cetron says Bodine told him its emphasis on Islamic terrorism would offend Arab sensitivities. He recalls her saying, "There's nothing we can do about it anyway. It's just too scary."

The Clinton administration did run an interagency working group on terrorism right out of the White House. But it's hard to say how much of President Clinton's attention the problem rated. In the summer of 1998, most Americans knew who Monica Lewinsky was, while relatively few had heard of bin Laden, even after the embassy bombers struck. Three years earlier, the TERRSTOP trial had played out almost simultaneously with the

O.J. Simpson murder trial. One courtroom drama received wall-to-wall media coverage, while the other received just a few lines. You can guess which is which. A president preoccupied with the threat of impeachment was not in a strong position to lead Americans into a war against a man they'd never heard of, in a country they didn't care about.

In its early days, George W. Bush's White House exhibited similar symptoms of paralysis and denial. "Before September 11, I couldn't get half an hour on terrorism with [Attorney General John] Ashcroft," says Tom Pickard, former deputy director of the FBI. "He was only interested in three things: guns, drugs and civil rights." It would take an event of the magnitude of September 11 to rearrange the priorities of the nation and its leaders. Or, as a Pentagon official told Marvin Cetron just before Cetron's report was shoved into the back of a drawer, "We can't manage a crisis until it's a crisis."

There is no doubt that a sense of urgency can make a significant difference. Had the FBI and the NYPD chosen to make a priority of preventing terrorist violence after the 1990 Kahane assassination, there may never have been a 1993 World Trade Center bombing. When preventing attacks *did* become a priority, the plot to bomb other New York landmarks was smashed before any lives could be lost. But an institution's ingrained priorities have a tendency to reassert themselves as time passes. By the summer of 1998, the fight against Islamic terrorism was back to square one. Documents had been found indicating bin Laden was planning an attack in East Africa. The American ambassador in Kenya was crying out for stepped-up security. Bin Laden himself had warned millions of American TV viewers during the May ABC interview that attacks would take place "within the next several weeks." So how was it that once again the FBI and CIA were taken by surprise when truck bombs struck the embassies in Kenya and Tanzania almost simultaneously?

Part of the responsibility of Paul Bremer's panel in the aftermath of the embassy attacks was to identify the institutional weaknesses of the U.S. intelligence agencies. The report he prepared for Congress stated, in essence, that the key to any counterterrorism policy is the ability to disrupt the terrorists before they act. "In order to disrupt terrorists," Bremer told us later, "you have to know about them and what they've been doing. And the only way to do that is to spy on them, and that means recruiting terrorists as informants."

Bremer, along with scores of other experts both inside and outside the CIA, had concluded that the Agency did not have enough spies on the ground, that it had become too reliant on third-country intelligence and electronic surveillance.

The cost had been dramatic. Hampered by a recalcitrant, risk-averse bureaucracy, the agency had failed to recognize the importance of the rise of Islamic fundamentalism, failed to anticipate the "blowback" from the Afghan War and had missed entirely the founding and formative early years of al Qaeda itself. By the time the CIA had gotten a handle on the organization, bin Laden was already ensconced in Afghanistan, out of easy reach of U.S. law enforcement. His training camps had already graduated hundreds, if not thousands, of jihadis, and had seeded them in Islamic communities around the world.

The FBI could hardly boast of a better track record. The fundamental weakness in Bureau culture during those same years was a tendency to be reactive, rather than proactive. It was focused, as it always had been, on making criminal cases rather than on penetrating terrorist groups to prevent the next attack. Driven by an appetite for headline cases and quantifiable stats, the Bureau prioritized leads according to how well the resulting evidence might stand up in court, and thus it often ignored or failed to analyze or act on otherwise valuable intelligence from other agencies. As we dug into the daily grind of FBI terror investigations, we bumped up against a kind of Golden Rule: Whenever the risks of collecting intelligence were weighed against the imperatives of making cases, the need to make cases won out. For example, the Bureau dumped Emad Salem during the run-up to the 1993 Trade Center bombing not because he was a poor informant—Louis Napoli felt Salem was one of the best he'd ever worked with—but because he wouldn't wear a wire and therefore was of limited value in collecting evidence for trial. Agents realized later that the information he had been providing might have allowed them to prevent the bombing.

Salem's dismissal was only the most flagrant example of the myriad ways in which the Bureau steered its agents away from intelligence-gathering. Tommy Corrigan and his partners at JTTF labored for years without support from their top bosses. Their surveillances were cut short, their requests for warrants and undercovers were rejected and they were drafted into doing street gang investigations. Only when the men they were chasing blew a hole in the Trade Center's basement did the pendulum swing the other way. Then came a drawn-out trial, however, and a frustrating investigation into the TWA Flight 800 crash that together tied them up for years.

On top of all these institutional faults, there was poor coordination and information-sharing between and even within the relevant national security agencies. The FBI did not have a Bureau-wide computer system until the mid-1990s, and old hands continue to use the old filing system today. FBI agents working on the bin Laden squad out of New York didn't know that the San Francisco office had interviewed Ali Mohamed about bin Laden in the spring of 1993 until Mohamed himself told them four years later. Then, when the New York agents tried to track down the reports of the San Francisco interview—the first known FBI intelligence that bin Laden was building an army to force U.S. troops out of Saudi Arabia—they discovered the reports had been lost.

As bad as communications were between the Bureau's field offices, they were even worse between the FBI and the CIA. Communications between the two agencies vastly improved with the establishment of the CIA's Alec Station in early 1996, but they were far from ideal—as the missed signals leading up to September 11 made clear. The CIA wasn't showing all its cards to the FBI. The FBI wasn't showing all its cards, either. Not even to its own agents. The Phoenix and Moussaoui memos were never considered together, in context, by anyone close enough to the street to put the two together. The INS was told a little, but too little too late. That's how two of the hijackers managed to get into the United States long after the CIA and

FBI knew they were terrorists. The president got a vague briefing on August 6, 2001, which stated the obvious: that bin Laden wanted to attack, and would probably try, soon. That is the way it was. Investigators and policy-makers were seeing different parts of the elephant right up until the morning of September 11.

Someday, students of history will ask: How was it possible that a man living in caves in a remote, backward country was able to declare war on the most powerful nation on earth?

One of the most important lessons we learned in the course of writing this book came from Neil Herman. He told us: Terrorism is cyclical. Left alone, it always comes back, usually in a bolder and more lethal way than before.

Osama bin Laden has been especially patient. He chose and planned his operations meticulously, spacing them out for maximum impact. He then built on his successes, and learned from his mistakes.

We also learned that the fight against terrorism cannot be waged from afar. It requires old-fashioned investigative shoe leather, human intelli-gence, and face-to-face encounters at every level of government. The first time Tommy Corrigan sat in an interview room with an Islamic terrorist and listened to him rant against Jews and Americans even as he consulted with his taxpayer-funded Jewish lawyer and tried to make a plea bargain deal with the U.S. government, Corrigan realized the story wouldn't end in Brooklyn. Neil Herman listened to what his agents were telling him, as did a small cadre of top officials, including John O'Neill, Mary Jo White and Richard Clarke. But as the message went up the chain of command, it inevitably lost a degree of power and urgency.

Despite the early efforts of the FBI to go after the Islamic militants bent on violence in Brooklyn and New Jersey, despite the CIA's life-saving disrup-tions around the world, the government came too late to bin Laden and was always one step behind him. When U.S. authorities had the opportunity to snatch him from the Sudan in 1996, they decided to wait until they had an indictable case against him, even though he had already been branded the world's most dangerous terrorist. When the same authorities had a chance to obliterate bin Laden's East African cells a full year before the embassy bomb-ings, they instead appeared to lose focus. And when a top-level informant warned the navy that al Qaeda was planning an attack on one of their warships a full year before the *Cole* bombing, the State Department brokered a deal with Yemen to refuel U.S. warships—with virtually no security provisions—in the Port of Aden, a well-known al Qaeda hotbed.

On May 31, 2002, more than eight months after the hijackers' attacks on New York and Washington, the work of cleaning up Lower Manhattan's Ground Zero was finished. In a moving ceremony, an empty stretcher, sym-bolizing the victims whose remains were never recovered, was carried from the vast pit. Then, laid out on the back of a flatbed truck, a multi-ton girder that had once stood at the base of the Towers was draped in an American flag and hauled up the long ramp from the hole. It was as if we were watch-ing a funeral for a pair of grand buildings and all that they once had sug-gested about American prowess and invincibility.

If anything else was put to rest that day it was the innocent belief that our government could surely protect us at home from any men so dark or deeds so evil.

Was that day also the funeral for the notion that "we can't manage a cri-sis until it's a crisis"? It better have been. The next wave of attacks could make September 11 a pale and distant memory.

ENDNOTES

CHAPTER 1

For this chapter, we interviewed dozens of government officials and ordinary citizens about their experiences of September 11, 2001, including Barry Mawn, the director of the New York office of the FBI, and FBI Assistant Director Tom Pickard, who managed the Bureau's Washington-based emergency operations center on September 11. In the end, we chose to focus on the stories of three individuals we interviewed: Michael Wright; Bernard Kerik, the New York City police commissioner; and Deena Burnett.

Some details involving the hijacked planes were drawn from the extraordinary television and newspaper coverage in the days following September 11. We're indebted to the *New York Times,* who obtained the air traffic controllers' logs from the morning of September 11 and published excerpts from them in an October 16, 2001, article by Matthew Wald with

Kevin Sack. Our descriptions of cockpit transmissions and attempts by officials to communicate with the hijacked planes and mobilize U.S. air defenses are based on the *Times* article.

We're also grateful to *Wall Street Journal* reporters Scott McCartney and Susan Carey, whose October 15, 2001, article told the stories of airline executives trying to cope with the September 11 crisis as it unfolded. Our portrayal of events and conversations taking place in the American and United command centers are based on McCartney and Carey's reporting.

New York 1 political reporter Andrew Kirtzman spent much of September 11 with Rudy Giuliani. Our depiction of the movements of the mayor and his staff was based on Kirtzman's excellent account, which appeared in the paperback edition of Kirtzman's book *Rudy Giuliani: Emperor of the City* (HarperCollins) and was adapted by the *Daily News* on October 21, 2001.

page 9: The Madeline Amy Sweeney–Michael Woodward exchange is from an FBI investigative document that was reported by Eric Lichtblau in the *Los Angeles Times,* September 20, 2001.

pages 10–11: The John O'Neill material is from our interview with Jerry Hauer, the former director of New York City's Emergency Management Office, who dined with O'Neill the night before the attacks.

pages 23–24: The Mark Bingham and Jeremy Glick exchanges are from ABC News interviews with the victims' families.

page 24: The Sandy Bradshaw and Todd Beamer material is based on an article by Kim Barker, Louis Kiernan and Steve Mills that ran in the *Chicago Tribune* on October 8, 2001.

page 26: The quotes from Giuliani are from the mayor's first televised interview of September 11, when he was questioned by New York 1 anchors Pat Kiernan and Sharon Dizenhuz.

CHAPTER 2

During the writing of *The Cell,* Neil Herman, Tommy Corrigan and Louis Napoli sat for hundreds of hours of interviews. Kenny Maxwell, John Liguori,

Chuck Stern, Frank Pellegrino, Jack Cloonan and other members of JTTF, past and present, were also extremely generous with their time. The material in chapters 2–7 is based on these investigators' recollections, case files and personal records, unless otherwise noted.

CHAPTER 3

pages 38–40: The reconstruction of Meir Kahane's murder is based on trial records; the recollections of onetime detective squad commander Eddie Norris; and the recollections and notes of Louis Napoli and Tommy Corrigan, the detectives who re-investigated the murder as part of a federal RICO case.

pages 40–46: The section dealing with the immediate aftermath of, and early NYPD investigation into, Kahane's murder is based on John Miller's notes and recollections, and our interviews of Norris.

pages 46 and 55: The story of the "missing" Nosair files is based on our interviews of Norris, Napoli and other FBI officials.

pages 47–55: Most of Nosair's biography was developed through our interviews with Napoli, Corrigan and Nosair's lawyer, Roger Stavis. New York *Newsday,* November 7, 1990, provided a window into Nosair's early years in the U.S. The Barbara Ausman quotes are from *Newsday.*

pages 49–50: The Abdullah Azzam quote is from a videotape of the First Jihad Conference recorded by author Steven Emerson.

pages 52–53: The Gorbachev and Uncle Charley's incidents, as well as the surveillances Nosair ran on Mubarak and a U.N. official, are from a confidential law enforcement source.

pages 53–54: Our main secondary source for the biographical passages on Sheik Abdel-Rahman was Mary Ann Weaver's *A Portrait of Egypt: A Journey Through the World of Militant Islam* (Farrar, Straus & Giroux, 2000).

page 55: The November 5 locker-room incident was reported in New York *Newsday* on November 8, 1990, by Karen Freifeld and David Kocieniewski.

CHAPTER 4

page 64: Former senior CIA officials Milt Bearden and Vince Cannistraro, as well as Tommy Corrigan, shed light on the tangled relations among Abdullah Azzam, Sheik Abdel-Rahman, Gulbuddin Hekmatyer and Osama bin Laden.

page 66: Our description of William Kunstler's original trial strategy is based on an interview with Ron Kuby, the late Kunstler's former law partner.

CHAPTER 5

Some details of the developing plot to blow up the World Trade Center were drawn from the testimony that Gil Childers, the lead prosecutor in the trial of the first World Trade Center bombers, provided at a February 24, 1998, hearing before the U.S. Senate subcommittee on terrorism.

page 78: Part of Ramzi Yousef's biography was drawn from *The New Jackals* by Simon Reeve (Northeastern University Press, 1999), still arguably the best book on Yousef.

pages 78–79: Laurie Mylroie advanced her theory about Iraq's role in the Trade Center bombing in an article called "The World Trade Center Bomb: Who Is Ramzi Yousef? And Why It Matters," which appeared in *The National Interest,* Winter 1995–1996.

CHAPTER 6

page 91: Yousef's methods relating to phone calls from his jail cell were described by Gil Childers in his February 24, 1998, testimony to a U.S. Senate subcommittee.

CHAPTER 7

pages 101–106: The discovery of the telltale truck part and the identification of the vehicle was related to us by Don Sadowy and FBI officials who were on the scene.

CHAPTER 8

The material relating to the hunt for and capture of Ramzi Yousef was based on our interviews with Neil Herman, who supervised the World Trade Center bombing case; Chuck Stern, who was the co-case agent for the WTC bombing case; Frank Pellegrino, who was the lead agent for the Manila Air case and the search for Yousef; and Gil Childers, the lead prosecutor in the WTC bombing case.

The New Jackals by Simon Reeve (Northeastern University Press, 1999) provided valuable background on Ramzi Yousef's movements as a fugitive.

pages 127–134: The history of the CIA in these pages was developed through interviews with Vince Cannistraro; Milt Bearden; James Woolsey, former CIA director under Clinton; and numerous other Agency officials, past and present, who wished to remain anonymous. Robert Baer, the former CIA field officer, was especially generous with his time, speaking to us in Lebanon, New York and Washington. Dewey Clarridge was interviewed by ABC News. Also, many fine articles provided context for our research, chief among them: "The CIA's Blind Ambition," Sam Tanenhaus, *Vanity Fair,* January 2002; "The Trouble with the CIA," Thomas Powers, *New York Review of Books,* January 17, 2002; and "What Went Wrong," Seymour Hersh, *New Yorker,* October 8, 2001.

CHAPTER 9

Law enforcement's gradual recognition that Osama bin Laden had links to Ramzi Yousef and that he was a terrorist worthy of the government's full attention was described to us during our interviews with Mary Jo White, the U.S. attorney for the Southern District of New York; Gil Childers; Neil Herman; Tommy Corrigan; John Liguori; Frank Pellegrino; Chuck Stern; Jack Cloonan; and other JTTF investigators. As a result of his investigation into the Manila Air case, Pellegrino became the lead agent in the search for Khalid Shaikh Mohammed.

pages 140–146: Ali Mohamed's biography is based in large part on a series of interviews with Jack Cloonan, Mohamed's FBI handler from the time the former bin Laden aide began cooperating with the government in 1997 until Cloonan's retirement in November 2002. Lt. Colonel Steve Neely also provided valuable insight in interviews with ABC News. Roger Stavis, El Sayyid Nosair's lawyer, was instructive about his client's relationship to Mohamed. Some of the Mohamed material was drawn from his army records and his October 20, 2000, allocution before Hon. Leonard B. Sand.

pages 146–148: Tommy Corrigan, John Liguori, Louis Napoli and Chris Voss, Siddig Siddig-Ali's handler, shed light on the TERRSTOP case.

pages 148–150: The CTC initiative to begin working with the FBI and to go after bin Laden was described to us during our interviews with Neil Herman, John Liguori, Tommy Corrigan and other FBI and CIA sources.

pages 149–150: The facts of the 1995 Riyadh bombing were widely reported at the time. A deeper exploration of the Saudi lack of cooperation with U.S. law enforcement is provided in Elsa Walsh's "Louis Freeh's Last Case," which ran in the *New Yorker,* May 14, 2001.

pages 151–153: The Sudanese attempts to improve relations with the U.S. and the ensuing negotiations involving bin Laden were described to us in interviews with former NSC chief Samuel Berger, former Sudanese ambassador Tim Carney, Milt Bearden and senior U.S. government officials. Other, excellent reports on this subject are to be found in "The Osama Files," David Rose, *Vanity Fair,* January 2002, and "U.S. Was Foiled Multiple Times . . . ," Barton Gellman, *Washington Post,* October 3, 2001.

CHAPTER 10

The Jamal al-Fadl material is from his February 2001 testimony in *U.S. vs. Osama bin Laden et al.,* and from Tommy Corrigan, Jack Cloonan and other JTTF members.

pages 157–159: Bin Laden's troubled relations with the Saudis were described in detail to us by Turki al-Faisal, the former Saudi intelligence chief.

Vince Cannistraro was also helpful in narrating bin Laden's life in the years after the end of the Afghan War.

page 159: Jack Cloonan, Ali Mohamed's FBI handler, described bin Laden's escape from Peshawar to Sudan. Mohamed was in charge of bin Laden's security for the move, dressing bin Laden in women's clothing as a safety precaution.

pages 159–165: Jamal al-Fadl shed light on bin Laden's time in Sudan in his February 2001 testimony. Cloonan and Corrigan were also instructive about that period. *Holy War, Inc.* by Peter L. Bergen (Free Press, 2001) has a very good section on bin Laden's activities in Sudan, especially regarding details of bin Laden's financial empire.

page 163: The characterization of the government's view of bin Laden before 1998 was based on a December 2000 interview with Michael Sheehan, the State Department's former counterterrorism chief.

page 164: The passage about al Qaeda's links to Iran and Hezbollah was based on our January 2002 interview with a CTC official and on the October 20, 2000, allocution of Ali Mohamed. Specifically, Mohamed said he arranged a meeting in Sudan between bin Laden and Imad Mugniyah, Hezbollah's chief in Southern Lebanon.

CHAPTER 11

pages 168–173: The details of the Flight 800 investigation and its impact on the JTTF were described to us by Neil Herman and Kenny Maxwell, the co-case supervisors.

pages 170–174: The John O'Neill material comes mainly from John Miller's notes and recollections. Lawrence Wright's profile of O'Neill in the January 14, 2002, *New Yorker* and Robert Kolker's December 17, 2001, *New York* magazine story were also helpful.

pages 172–173: The growing bureaucracy at the JTTF section is based on our interviews with Neil Herman and other FBI officials.

The section dealing with the origins of the Nairobi cell and the initial plans to bomb the U.S. embassies in Kenya and Tanzania was based on interviews with Jack Cloonan; Tommy Corrigan, who investigated Wadih el-Hage in the U.S. and Nairobi; Kenny Maxwell, who led the FBI investigation of the Dar es Salaam bombing; other JTTF members; and Ali Mohamed's October 20, 2000, allocution.

page 194: The anecdote about John O'Neill meeting Jerry Hauer on the Fourth of July was reported by Robert Kolker in *New York* magazine, December 17, 2001.

pages 196–200: The section dealing with Wadih el-Hage was based on our interviews with Cloonan, Corrigan, Louis Napoli, Neil Herman and other government officials. Our portrait of el-Hage also drew details from "Odyssey into Jihad," *Newsweek*, January 14, 2002; "Assault on a U.S. Embassy," Karl Vick, *Washington Post*, November 23, 1998; and "The Traitor Next Door," a lengthy profile of el-Hage by Mimi Swartz, which appeared in the April 2002 *Texas Monthly*.

pages 202–205: The failure by U.S. intelligence to anticipate, much less interdict, the embassy bombings elicited some of the most troubling questions in our writing of *The Cell*. We asked virtually every source we spoke to from top administration and intelligence officials to line investigators: What went wrong in East Africa? We never got a satisfactory explanation. Worse, some who should have known the facts seemed vague or evasive in their replies. But many others—among them Mary Jo White, Tommy Corrigan, Michael Sheehan and Prudence Bushnell—were candid, and while not necessarily agreeing with our conclusion that the bombings could have been prevented, helped steer us through the two-year period between el-Hage's flight to the U.S. and the August 7, 1998, attacks.

pages 204–205: The material dealing with Prudence Bushnell's request for added security is based on our interviews with Bushnell and a former top State Department official.

page 205: Paul Muite's statements are from an interview he gave to ABC News in 1998.

pages 206–207: Some details about Fazul's villa and its furnishings come from the November 23, 1998, *Washington Post* and the November 23, 1998, *U.S. News and World Report*. Some details about Mohamed al-'Owhali's movements in the days before the bombings come from the August 5, 2001, *London Observer.*

pages 207–209: The description of how the bombing was carried out is based on ABC News files. Descriptions from Prudence Bushnell's viewpoint are based on our interviews with the ambassador and on trial testimony she gave on March 1, 2001. The details about victims Frank Pressley and Michelle O'Connor appeared in the August 5, 2001, *London Observer.*

page 209: The phone call from Secretary Albright was described to us in an interview with Prudence Bushnell.

CHAPTER 14

page 211: The admission that intelligence about the Sudanese plants was "patchy" is from our interview with a senior CIA official.

page 211: The fact that the Sudanese were holding two embassy bombing suspects and were negotiating their surrender to the FBI comes from our interview with a U.S. official involved in the negotiations. (The suspects were later delivered to Pakistani authorities and released because of insufficient evidence.)

page 212: The description of the captures of Mohamed Odeh and Mohamed al-'Owhali are based on ABC News reporting. Peter Bergen also gives an excellent account of the arrests in *Holy War, Inc.* (Free Press, 2001).

pages 212–213: The arrests, disruptions and renditions of al Qaeda cell members in the aftermath of the embassy bombings were originally described to us by Tommy Corrigan, Jack Cloonan and other U.S. intelligence officials.

pages 214–220: The material dealing with the Clinton administration's campaign against al Qaeda—its view of bin Laden leading up to the twin missile strikes and its efforts at corralling him afterward—is based on our interviews with Samuel Berger, the president's second-term national security advisor; Michael Sheehan; former Nebraska senator Bob Kerrey; and other government officials. Gen. Henry Shelton spoke to ABC News in January 1999. Barton Gellman's reporting has been a valuable guide to us in this area, especially his December 20, 2001, *Washington Post* article, "Struggles Inside the Government Defined Campaign." James Risen's excellent work in the *New York Times* was also helpful.

page 219: The description of the CIA's rendition plan and its presentation to the FBI was based on our interview with a Bureau official who was at the meeting.

CHAPTER 15

The material in this chapter is based on John Miller's on-the-spot reporting and ABC News interviews with USS *Cole* officials and NCIS personnel.

CHAPTER 16

Hoda Hamid in Cairo and Hannah Cleaver in Hamburg provided the original reporting used in this chapter's portrait of young Mohamed Atta. Hamid and Cleaver interviewed a number of the individuals named, including: Atta's father, Mohamed al-Amir Atta; the family's Cairo neighbor Mohamed Kamel Khamis; professor Ditmar Machule of the Technical University of Hamburg–Harburg; and Atta's Harburg schoolmates Volker Hauth and Ralph Bodenstein.

We also owe a tremendous debt to other reporters who chased down details of Atta's life in the first months after the September 11 attacks. The *New York Times,* the *Wall Street Journal,* the *Washington Post, Time* magazine and the *London Observer* all published short profiles in the final months of 2001 that were invaluable. The *Sunday Times* of London added enormously to the known facts of Atta's life with a two-part profile that appeared

January 6 and 13, 2002. So far, though, the definitive portrait of Atta as a student is Terry McDermott's 9,000-word feature, "The Perfect Soldier," which was published by the *Los Angeles Times* on January 27, 2002.

For our material on radical Islamism and recent Egyptian history, we relied largely on Mary Ann Weaver's wonderful *A Portrait of Egypt: A Journey Through the World of Militant Islam,* and an essay by Jonathan Raban called "My Holy War" that appeared in the *New Yorker* on February 4, 2002.

Details and quotations that were drawn from these and other secondary sources are cited below.

pages 238–239: Details of Sheik Omar Abdel-Rahman's trial come from *A Portrait of Egypt* by Mary Ann Weaver. That Atta "turned in earnest to prayer" about this time was established by one of Hoda Hamid's interviews with Atta's father.

page 239: The description of the view from Atta's window draws on a photograph published by the *Los Angeles Times,* January 27, 2002.

pages 239–240: Many of the details in the descriptions of Atta's family apartment and of the family's background in the Nile Delta come from the January 6, 2002, *Sunday Times* of London and the January 27 *Los Angeles Times.* The details about young Atta's backyard conversations and the kids chewing pistachios are from the *Los Angeles Times.* So too is the quotation, "He wanted to be famous."

page 241: The neighbors' perception of Atta's mother and the conviviality of Cairo street life were described in the *Los Angeles Times,* January 27, 2002. The idea that he sometimes snuck out for chats with Khamis was reported in the *Sunday Times* of London, January 6, 2002.

pages 242–243: The senior Atta expressed views about his son and the U.S. at a news conference shortly after the September 11 attacks. Two of the quotations used here appeared in the *New York Times* on September 19 and October 10, 2001.

page 243: The description of Cairo University and Atta's early performance there relies on Terry McDermott's story in the *Los Angeles Times,* January 27, 2002. The quotation "We told him . . ." appeared in the *New York Times,* October 10, 2001.

pages 245–247: The students who called Atta "good to the roots" and "a little bit pure" were quoted in *Time,* October 8, 2001. Mohamed Mokhtar el-Rafei and the student who described Atta as childish were quoted in the *Los Angeles Times,* January 27, 2002. The photograph that's described was published together with that *Times* story. The vision of Atta cruising Cairo in his Fiat comes from the *Sunday Times* of London, January 6, 2002.

page 247: Atta's decision to drop out of a basketball league was reported by the *New York Times,* October 10, 2001. His decision to join the Engineers Syndicate was reported in the *London Observer,* September 23, 2001.

page 247: Atta's father was quoted describing his dinner party with the German couple in the *Los Angeles Times,* January 27, 2002. Most of the details about Atta's arrival in Hamburg come from the *Sunday Times* of London, January 6, 2002, though Atta's question about the nearest mosque was reported in the *Los Angeles Times* story.

pages 248–250: While Atta's clash with the University of Applied Sciences was reported in both the January 6, 2002, *Sunday Times* of London and in the January 27, 2002, *Los Angeles Times,* much of the description of Atta's early experiences in Hamburg draw on terrific details from the *Los Angeles Times* profile. Among them are the quotations about Atta's eyes and not doing dishes, as well as the anecdotes about the Disney movie, the mashed potatoes and Miss Piggy. The note about the lamb chops and the quotation about an "unpleasant" atmosphere are from the two-part profile that appeared in the *Sunday Times* of London, January 6 and 13, 2002; Margritte Schroeder's opinion of Atta appeared in the January 6 article.

page 250: Volker Hauth's description of Atta as "a guy searching for justice" appeared in the *Los Angeles Times,* September 27, 2001.

pages 251–252: The description of Atta's flirtatious relationship with the Palestinian woman in Aleppo is mostly drawn from the *London Observer,* September 23, 2001. Hannah Cleaver corroborated the general outline of the story in interviews with Volker Hauth.

page 252: The "Disney World" quotation is from the *New York Times,* September 18, 2001; the notion that Atta needed to find work with an international organization is from the October 10, 2001, *New York Times.*

page 253: An ABC News translation of Atta's will was used. The details about Atta's pilgrimages come from the *Wall Street Journal,* October 16, 2001.

CHAPTER 17

Law enforcement sources in the U.S. and Germany were invaluable in helping us piece together how various members of the September 11 cell came together in Hamburg and how their hijacking plot may have developed. Hannah Cleaver was again our main reporter on the ground in Hamburg; Hoda Hamid filled out some of the individual profiles with her reporting from the Middle East. The work of other ABC News correspondents gave us a running start. We drew as well from other broadcast and published reports, as indicated below.

pages 254–256: Most of the details in the chapter's introduction come from Hannah Cleaver's interviews with Thorsten Albrecht.

page 256: Abdelghani Mzoudi's characterizations of Bahaji and other of his friends are from an interview published by Spiegel Online.

page 257: The details about Ramzi Binalshibh's classroom performance are from the *New York Times,* December 13, 2001. The demographic breakdown of the technical university's student body is from the *Los Angeles Times,* January 27, 2002.

page 258: The description of al-Quds Mosque and its surroundings draws on reporting in the *New York Times Magazine,* October 28, 2001. Violetta Sarnowski's comments are from her interview with Hannah Cleaver.

page 259: The description of the Puchong, Malaysia, meetings are based on a report in the *Washington Post,* February 7, 2002.

pages 259–260: The conversation between Machule and Atta was reported in the *Los Angeles Times,* January 27, 2002, as was the information about Atta sharing an apartment briefly with several other men.

pages 260–263: Several secondary sources were used to flesh out the descriptions of the al Qaeda camps and Abu Zubaydah's role in the organization. Most useful was "Inside bin Laden's Academies of Terror," by Stephen Grey and Dapash Gadher, *Sunday Times* (London), October 7, 2001. Other articles appeared in the *Los Angeles Times* on October 21, 2001, and January 9, 2002; in the *New York Times* on February 14, 2002, in the *Sunday Times* (London) on January 13, 2002; and in *Newsweek* on October 22, 2001, and January 30, 2002.

The jihad manual, seized during a raid in Birmingham, England, was translated and used by U.S. prosecutors in the embassy trial.

pages 265–266: The portrait of Ziad Jarrah draws on reporting in the September 17, 2001, *Chicago Sun-Times,* the October 23, 2001, *Los Angeles Times,* the January 13, 2002, *Sunday Times* of London and "Beyond Belief," a special report presented October 1, 2001, by the Canadian Broadcasting Corp. The quotation about Lebanon discos is from the *Los Angeles Times,* October 23, 2001. The detail about Jarrah spending late nights at a Griefswald mosque is from an interview by Hoda Hamid with a confidential source. Rosemarie Canel's quotation is from the CBC broadcast.

pages 266–267: The descriptions of Atta's thesis work are derived from Hannah Cleaver's interviews with Machule and Wendt, and from reporting in the September 17, 2001, *New York Times,* the September 23, 2001, *London Spectator,* the September 25, 2001, *Newsweek,* and the January 27, 2002, *Los Angeles Times.* Machule's comment about a "neutral thesis" appeared in the *New York Times* story.

CHAPTER 18

Many of the dates and figures in this chapter that relate to the hijackers' movements and funding were made widely available by U.S. investigators. Our own sources provided a few additional details, and our researcher, Polly Blitzer, conducted dozens of phone interviews with civilians who had contact with at least one of the terrorists in 2000 or 2001.

pages 268–269: The anecdote about the Washington, D.C., photograph is based on our early 2002 interview with a confidential U.S. intelligence source. The details about Atta's clothing and cologne first appeared in the *Washington Post,* October 25, 2001. On June 6, 2002, ABC News's Brian Ross broadcast a much more detailed account of Atta's visit to the Farm Services Agency's Homestead office.

pages 269–273: Background on Khalid al-Midhar and Nawaf al-Hazmi and the descriptions of their activities in southern California draw on reporting by the *San Diego Union-Tribune,* the *Palm Beach Post,* the *Sunday Mercury* of London, the *Los Angeles Times,* the *Washington Post,* the *Record* (Bergen County, N.J.) and the *Chicago Tribune.* Omar al-Bayoumi's sponsorship role was reported by the *Sunday Mercury,* October 21, 2001, and by the *San Diego Union-Tribune,* October 25, 2001.

Details about al-Midhar and al-Hazmi's international travel were provided to us by confidential U.S. intelligence sources. Flight instructor Arnaud Petit was quoted in the Bergen *Record,* September 17, 2001; al-Midhar's "Very good, very nice" comment appeared in the *Chicago Tribune,* September 30, 2001; and Rick Garza's *"Dumb and Dumber"* assessment was published in the *New York Times,* October 16, 2001. The detail about al-Hazmi's job at a car wash is from the *Washington Post,* December 29, 2001.

pages 273–276: The flurry of activity described in these pages— including the flow of money and the movements of the hijackers Moussaoui and Binalshibh—has been detailed in public statements and documents released by law enforcement and intelligence agencies in the U.S., Germany and Italy. Our own intelligence sources reported the exchange of $35,000 in Malaysia and theories about Khalid Shaikh Mohammed's role in the plot.

Atta's remark to his hostess in Florida is from an interview she gave to Polly Blitzer. Anne Greaves's quotation is from the *Washington Post,* September 30, 2001. A transcript of the conversation between Es Sayed and al Hilal was released by German and Italian investigators.

page 276: Details related to Hani Hanjour's arrival in and Nawaf al-Hazmi's departure from San Diego draw on reporting by the *Los Angeles Times,* the *Wall Street Journal* and the *San Diego Union-Tribune.*

pages 276–279: Our account of Atta and al-Shehhi's movements from late December 2000 to early March 2001 is based on U.S. government statements and documents and on reporting by the *Wall Street Journal,* the Associated Press, *Newsweek,* the *New York Times,* the *Washington Post,* the *Miami Herald,* the *Atlanta Journal-Constitution,* ABC News, and other print sources.

Details about the stalled plane are from Polly Blitzer's interview with Huffman Aviation officials and from the *New York Times,* October 17, 2001. Atta's statement to the loan officer about his travel plans was reported by Brian Ross of ABC News on June 6, 2002.

Details about Atta and al-Shehhi's stay in Decatur were reported by *Newsweek,* December 12, 2001. The story about Atta in eastern Tennessee, including Atta's dialogue, was reported by Bill Pooley of the Associated Press on October 18, 2001. The fact that the chemical tanks had still been in use at the time was reported by the *Washington Post,* December 16, 2001.

James Lester's comments about Atta's visits to South Florida Crop Care appeared in the *Miami Herald,* October 21, 2001.

page 282: A useful chronology of Czech officials' statements about Atta's alleged meetings with an Iraqi agent appeared in the *Fort Lauderdale Sun Sentinel,* December 26, 2001. According to the *Prague Post,* Hynek Kmonicek, the Czech Republic's envoy to the United Nations in April 2001, still maintained as of June 2002 that Atta and al-Ani had met in Prague that April.

Details of the German taxi driver's story appeared in the *Wall Street Journal.*

pages 282–283: Many of the details about the backgrounds of the Saudi hijackers are drawn from a special report called "The Highway of Death" that appeared in the *Sunday Times* of London, January 27, 2002. Turki al-Faisal speculated about bin Laden's motive during an interview on the *Charlie Rose Show* in early 2002.

pages 284–285: Descriptions and quotations relating to Ziad Jarrah's combat training are taken from a Polly Blitzer interview with Bert Rodriguez.

pages 285–286: Following a September 16, 2001, story in the *Wall Street Journal,* the hijackers' movements in South Florida were widely reported. Jim Woolard's comment about Atta appeared in the *New York Times,* September 23, 2001.

pages 291–292: Background on Khalid Shaikh Mohammed was provided to us by Neil Herman, Tommy Corrigan, Frank Pellegrino and Jack Cloonan.

page 292: Jarrah's talk of bringing his girlfriend to his sister's September 2001 wedding was widely reported. We used published interviews of Aisel Senguen and of one of Jarrah's Florida roommates to piece together how often the young couple was together in Jarrah's final months.

CHAPTER 19

pages 294–295: Most of the details in the James Woods anecdote is from an interview Woods granted to Bill O'Reilly for the February 14, 2002, edition of Fox Television's *The O'Reilly Factor*. The Alomari story is from our interview with a U.S. law enforcement official.

pages 296–297: The section dealing with Bush's counterterrorism policies was based on interviews with senior FBI, CIA and government officials. Tom Pickard spoke to us about Attorney General John Ashcroft's lack of interest in terrorism issues and his rejection of the Bureau's request for additional counterterrorism funding prior to the September 11 attacks. Barton Gellman provided a more detailed account of the Bush administration's evolving pre-9/11 counterterrorism strategy in the *Washington Post* on January 20, 2002.

pages 298–300: The section dealing with the FBI's botching of the Moussaoui case is based on Colleen Rowley's May 21, 2002, letter to FBI Director Robert Mueller and interviews with Bureau officials familiar with the Minneapolis Office's external communications. The contents of Moussaoui's computer and the investigative leads they might have provided, had they been discovered, were described to us by an FBI investigator familiar with the case.

The detail about Moussaoui pulling $6,800 out of a bag is from the *New*

York Times, February 8, 2002. The material about Moussaoui's behavior at the Minnesota flight school and the instructors' response is largely based on reporting by the *Minneapolis Star-Tribune.*

page 301: The anecdote about Atta driving to a flight service station is from the *Miami Herald,* October 21, 2001. The detail about renting two planes during that period was reported by the *Palm Beach Post,* October 28, 2001.

pages 301–303: The scene in Huber Drugs is drawn from an interview Polly Blitzer conducted with Gregg Chatterton.

pages 303–304: Our description of the failed pursuit of al-Midhar and al-Hazmi is based on interviews with senior law enforcement officials. The June 11 CIA-FBI flare-up was described to us by an FBI investigator privy to the meeting. The details about the belated FBI search for al-Midhar and al-Hazmi are from the same investigator.

pages 306–313: Many of the details of the hijackers' movements in their final days were widely reported, and some released as FBI statements and documents. The details that came from particular secondary sources other than ABC News are noted below.

page 306: The notion that the hijackers had Boeing keys was put forth in the *Boston Globe,* November 23, 2001.

page 307: Details about Atta and Jarrah's stay at the Longshore Motel, including the quotations, appeared in the *Palm Beach Post,* October 15, 2001.

page 308: That Jarrah mistakenly had his airline ticket mailed to Florida was reported in the *New York Times,* September 23, 2001. That he had left a replica of a Boeing cockpit behind was reported by the *Pittsburgh Post-Gazette,* October 28, 2001.

page 309: The witness's account of Atta casing Logan Airport appeared in the *Boston Herald,* September 23, 2001. The camera evidence about Atta's car was reported the same day in the *New York Times.*

The detail about "Jersey Style table dancing" appeared in the *Times* on September 27, 2001; the details about calls to Boston-area escort services appeared in the *Boston Globe,* October 10, 2001.

Jarrah's spending spree in Newark was reported by the *Palm Beach Post,* October 28, 2001.

page 310: The contents of the five-page manual carried by the terrorists has been widely disseminated, but for guidance in interpreting the text we leaned on "Manual for a Raid" by Hassan Mneimneh and Kanan Makiya, an article that appeared in the *New York Review of Books,* January 17, 2001.

page 312: Vincent Meisner's comment about Atta not having had his coffee yet is from the *Wall Street Journal,* October 18, 2001.

INDEX

ABC News
  bin Laden interview on, 175–92,
    205, 279, 329
  Investigative Unit of, 176, 279, 296
  and the Millennium, 222–23
  Miller's work with, 13, 25, 30–31,
    175, 191, 316
  September 11 broadcast on, 1–3,
    13, 30
Abdel-Rahman, Omar
  in Afghanistan, 54
  arrest and trial of, 116, 146–48
  arrival in U.S., 53, 54–55, 63
  cells forming around, 50–51, 55, 63,
    65, 72, 75, 77, 80, 90–91, 96, 104,
    110–11, 112, 113, 115–16, 137
  early years of, 53

fatwa against U.S. issued by, 91–92,
    115–16
funding of, 137, 138, 148
influence of, 50, 71, 72, 73, 83, 90,
    110, 115, 140, 140–41, 143–44,
    146–47
and Landmarks plot, 147
in prison, 148, 296
and Sadat's assassination, 53–54,
    238–39
and Shalabi, 63–65, 198
son of, 280
and WTC 1993 participants, 90, 91,
    96, 116
Abouhalima, Mahmoud, 43, 77, 80, 84
  and bomb building, 65, 85, 91
  conviction of, 117

Abouhalima, Mahmoud (*continued*)
  and Kahane murder, 39, 44, 67, 96, 110
  in training camps, 50, 79
  travels of, 109, 111
  visit to Nosair by, 92
  and WTC 1993 bombing, 85, 92, 109, 111, 197
Abouhalima, Mohammed, 90, 109
Abu Bakr Mosque, Brooklyn, 74, 113
Abu Sayyaf army, 122, 138, 139
Achille Lauro, 129
Acosta, Carlos, 39–40, 41, 67
Adel, Saif al-, 281
Aden, Islamic Army of, 270
Aden Harbor, terrorism in, 224–37, 333
Advice and Reformation Committee (ARC), 163
Afghanistan
  al Qaeda in, 152–53, 156–57, 319–20, 325
  bin Laden in, 138, 145, 152–53, 156, 159, 176, 200, 214–16, 320–21, 325, 330
  civil strife in, 131, 138, 155
  economy of, 215
  fighting in, 50, 51, 65, 82, 137, 138, 150, 155, 158
  mujahideen in, 60, 64, 131, 143, 158, 196
  Northern Alliance forces in, 319–21
  refugees in, 64
  Soviet invasion of, 127, 130–31, 143, 156, 164, 187–88
  Stinger missiles in, 161, 198
  Taliban in, 131, 153, 180, 215, 319
  terrorist links to, 137–38, 198
  training camps in, 50, 77, 143, 146, 150, 155, 210, 215, 234, 237, 260–62
  Tribals in, 219
  U.S. covert aid to, 54, 64, 130, 143
  U.S. disregard for, 127, 131
  U.S. invasion plans for, 297
  U.S. retaliation in, 210–11, 215–16, 319
  veterans of war in, 194, 195, 211, 259
Afghan Services Office, 78, 113
Agriculture Department, U.S., 268, 277
Ahmed (Yemeni boy), 232–33
Ahmed, Fayez, 308
Ahmed, Mustafa Mahmoud Said, 204, 283
Aideed, Mohammed, 162
Aircraft Situation Display, 12
airplanes
  grounded, 16–17
  as missiles, 3, 37, 327
  transponders in, 9, 12, 24
Ajaj, Ahmad Mohammed, 77, 91, 108, 117
Akhtar (Afghan guide), 177–80
Albania, cell in, 213, 223
Albrecht, Thorsten, 254, 256, 258
Albright, Madeleine, 204, 209, 215
al-Farooq Mosque, Brooklyn, 49, 54, 58, 104, 155
al-Farouk training camp, 156, 283
Al Gama'a al-Islamiyya, 148, 164, 244–45
Al-Hijira company, 160
Ali (translator), 176, 177, 178, 180–81, 191
Ali, Ali Abdul Aziz, 274, 292
Alkaisi, Bilall, 38–40, 50, 55, 64, 76, 79
al-Kifah Afghan Services Center, 156
al-Kifah Refugee Services Center, Brooklyn, 49–50, 51, 52, 54, 60, 63–64, 78, 82, 86, 89, 90, 113, 138, 143, 149, 155, 156, 197–98

al-Kifah Refugee Services Center,
    Tucson, 197
Allied Signal, 85, 91, 92, 109
Alomari, Abdulaziz, 283, 295–96,
    297, 309–12
al Qaeda
    in Afghanistan, 152–53, 156–57,
        319–20, 325
    early days of, 31, 49, 145, 155–56,
        330
    escalation by, 36, 37, 213
    fatwas against U.S. by, 79, 215,
        274, 321
    founding members of, 156
    funding of, 122, 156, 225, 266,
        269, 271, 272, 274, 290, 292,
        296, 307
    informants about, 146, 154–57, 165
    investigative files on, 327
    in Kenya, 200, 201–4, 206, 212,
        213
    in London, 195, 202, 286
    in Malaysia, 225, 270–73, 304
    martyrdom in, 261–62, 306, 310–13
    media wing of, 163
    multi-plane hijacking scenario of,
        277
    recruitment into, 280–81
    in Somalia, 162
    standing army of, 160
    in Sudan, 157, 160, 164
    training camps of, 146, 155, 157,
        211, 234, 237, 260–62, 275, 281
    as umbrella organization, 36–37,
        137, 213–14, 220
    U.S. retaliation against, 319
    warnings about, 287–89, 295, 296,
        303
al-Quds Mosque, Hamburg, 257, 259,
    265
al-Taqwa Mosque, Brooklyn, 58, 60,
    61, 81–82, 104

Amal (in Aleppo), 251–52
American Airlines
    and the attacks, 8–9, 11–12, 16
    Flight 11, 8–9, 12, 305–6, 309,
        312–13
    Flight 77, 12, 18, 305, 306
"American Bad Ass," 236
Ames, Aldrich, 133
Amin-Shah, Wali Khan, 123, 134–35,
    138–39, 176, 189–90
Anderson, Colonel, 142
Ani, Ahmed Khalil Samir al-, 282
Anticev, John
    and Kahane case, 55, 63
    and Nosair's cell, 63–65, 80
    and Rashid, 83
    and Salem, 72, 74–75
antiwar movement, 128
Army, U.S., 141, 144
Arpey, Gerard, 16
Ashcroft, John, 297, 329
Atash, Tawfiq bin, 271, 304
Atef, Mohammed, 156, 162, 181, 184,
    192, 291
ATF (Alcohol, Tobacco and Firearms
    Department), 101
Atkinson, Bill, 105
Atlanta, Olympics bombing in, 172
Atta, Mohamed el-Amir, 239–53,
    273–79
    in Afghan training camp, 260–62
    bride arranged for, 267
    crew of, 286
    crop dusters investigated by,
        268–69, 273, 279, 300, 303
    early years of, 239, 240–42
    in Egypt, 251–53, 267
    in Engineers Syndicate, 247
    family of, 239–40, 241–42, 253
    final days of, 306–13
    financial arrangements of, 266, 274,
        308

Atta, Mohamed el-Amir (*continued*)
  flight training of, 263, 273, 276–77,
    278, 288, 300
  in Germany, 249–53, 256–60
  personality of, 249–50, 258, 263,
    264, 273–74, 279, 284, 301
  physical conditioning of, 286
  pilgrimages of, 253, 260
  political views of, 250–51, 252,
    258–59
  preparation of, 276–79, 281,
    300–303
  and radical Islamism, 245, 262
  in Spain, 289–90, 292
  travels of, 277, 282, 289–90, 292,
    306
  at university, 243, 245–47, 262,
    266–67
  in U.S., 255, 268, 275, 278, 282
  will of, 253
Atta, Mohamed el-Amir (father),
    240, 242–43, 246, 248, 252,
    260, 267
Attash, Tawfiq bin, 225
Ausman, Barbara, 48
Ayyad, Nidal, 76, 85, 91, 92, 107, 109,
    117, 137
Azzam (martyr), 206–8, 226
Azzam, Abdullah, 49, 50, 54, 64, 156,
    196–97

Badawi, Jamal al-, 234
Baer, Bob, 129, 132, 133–34
Bahaji, Said, 254–55, 256, 290, 307
Banna, Hassan al-, 244, 245
Banshiri, Abu Ubaidah al-, 156, 162,
    195, 202
Basit, Abdul, 78, 79
Bay of Pigs, 128
Bayoumi, Omar al-, 270, 271, 272
Beamer, Todd, 24
Bear, Tom, 99

Bearden, Milt, 130, 131, 137–38
Beghal, Jamal, 262
Bennett, Rick, 178–86, 192
Berger, Samuel, 214, 217, 218
Berlin Wall, fall of, 131
Bernstein, Schmulky, 41
Bey, Thomas, 61
Bhutto, Benazir, 120, 123
Binalshibh, Ramzi, 255, 256–57, 261,
    267, 277
  escape of, 307
  financial arrangements of, 274, 290,
    298, 300
  flight training of, 263
  travels of, 275, 290
  visa denied to, 275
Bingham, Mark, 23
bin Laden, Abu Abdullah, 157
bin Laden, Osama Muhammad
    al-Wahad
  in Afghanistan, 138, 145, 152–53,
    156, 159, 176, 200, 214–16,
    320–21, 325, 330
  and al Qaeda, 156, 160, 214–15
  ancestral homeland of, 233
  associates of, 138–39, 140, 145–46,
    149, 151, 156–57, 160, 162, 181,
    196, 197, 198, 200, 258, 260,
    271, 291, 317, 322–23
  and *Cole,* 229–30
  early connections of, 54, 137–39
  elusiveness of, 211, 216, 217,
    319–21, 322
  and funding, 64, 66, 79, 113, 122,
    137, 138, 146, 148, 152, 156,
    198, 215, 274, 291
  and Gulf War, 157–58
  as hero, 317
  indictment of, 163, 165, 174, 184,
    214
  informants about, 146, 165
  jihad organization of, 145, 158, 159

law enforcement case against,
148–50, 152, 214, 220, 318
Miller's interview with, 4, 175–92,
205, 279, 329
patience of, 332
popularity of, 159
public statements by, 4, 157, 163,
191–92, 290–91, 316–17, 319,
322, 329
in Saudi Arabia, 151, 157–59,
163–64, 174
and Somalia, 161–63, 194, 214
in Sudan, 145, 151–53, 157,
159–61, 164, 194, 215, 332–33
as suspect, 3, 29, 173–74, 176
training camps of, 50, 76, 78, 79,
146, 150, 176, 210, 215, 216,
237, 260–62, 281, 327, 330
war declared on U.S. by, 4–5, 150,
152, 174, 186–92, 193, 204–5,
212, 287
weapons of mass destruction sought
by, 164, 327
Yousef's links to, 138–39, 146, 176,
189
bin Laden family, 157, 158–59,
163–64
Bin Laden International, 157
Black Liberation Army, 34, 62
Black Muslim community
and Arab militants, 58, 60–63, 66,
81–84, 110–17
assassination planned by, 111–13
commando training for, 82, 111
hostage-rescue training for, 82–83
Black Panthers, 34
Blando, Sal, 40
Bodenstein, Ralph, 252, 253
Bodine, Barbara, 229, 235, 237, 328
Boeing flight deck videos, 279, 298
Boeing flight simulator, 277, 285
Boeing key, 306

Bojinka plot, 122–23, 124, 136–37,
138, 139, 168, 176, 225, 291
Bookstaver, David, 167
Borelli, Joe, 43–45, 46
Boser, Walter, 99
Bosnia, jihad in, 63, 83, 84
Boudin, Cathy, 34
Bradshaw, Sandy, 24
Bremer, Paul, 328, 329–30
Brinks holdup, 34, 35, 62
Buck, Marilyn Jean, 34
Buckley, James, 129
Burke, Mike, 107
Burnett, Deena, 17, 19–21, 23–24
Burnett, Tom, on United Flight (93),
17, 19–21, 23–24, 25
Bush, George W., 318, 326
Bushnell, Prudence, 204, 207–9

Calverton, New York, cell training in,
51–52, 57, 96
Canel, Rosemarie, 265
Cannistraro, Vince, 127, 130, 159, 176
Cantor Fitzgerald, loss of lives in, 29
Carlos the Jackal, 139, 151
Carney, Tim, 151
Carter, Jimmy, 130
Casey, Williams, 128
Cedeno, Jaime, 103–4
Cetron, Marvin, 327, 328, 329
Chatterton, Gregg, 301–3
Cheney, Dick, 22
Chesimard, Joanne, 34
Chicago Mob, 170
Childers, Gil, 125–27, 137, 146
Chile, CIA in, 127
CIA (Central Intelligence Agency)
and Afghanistan, 54, 64, 130–31,
143, 321, 323–25
agent scrub of, 328
Alec Station of, 150, 152, 219,
331–32

CIA (*continued*)
  and al Qaeda, 202, 204, 210–11,
    213, 220, 225, 287, 296, 320–25
  and bin Laden, 148–50, 152, 159,
    210, 216–17, 320
  change in focus of, 318, 323–25
  changing culture of, 127–28,
    131–33
  charter of, 327
  cluelessness of, 125–34
  and Cold War, 127, 128, 131–32
  and *Cole,* 225, 229, 237, 304
  congressional hearings on, 127,
    128, 133
  Counter-Terrorism Center (CTC),
    129, 148–49, 216
  Directorate of Operations (DO),
    126, 128, 133, 134
  and Egyptian fundamentalists, 54,
    111
  and executive order against political
    murder, 127
  and FBI, 124–27, 150, 271, 304
  human intelligence meltdown of,
    127–29, 134, 173, 218, 330
  Incidence Response Team (IRT),
    323
  interagency miscommunication by,
    297, 303–4, 326, 328, 331–32
  interference in foreign
    governments, 127, 131
  and Iran, 54, 128–29, 134
  and Kenya, 199, 200, 202, 204–5
  moles in, 133
  and Pakistan, 130, 323–24
  risk aversion in, 128, 129, 130, 131,
    133–34, 330
  terrorist activity monitored by,
    270–71, 287–88, 292, 303,
    321–22
  terrorist plot against, 123, 214, 263,
    288, 291–92, 327

  and war on drugs, 131, 132
  and Yousef, 119, 121
City Chemicals, 86
Clark, Don, 88
Clarke, Richard, 171, 217, 332
Clarridge, Dewey, 129
Clements, Cathy, 229
Clinton, Bill
  assassination plots against, 123,
    124, 176, 190
  counterterrorism efforts of, 150,
    211, 214, 216–20, 296–97, 328
  economy as focus of, 132
  and impeachment, 216, 295
  in Mideast peace talks, 237
Clinton, Hillary, 215
Cold War, 127, 128, 131–32
Coleman, Dan, 112, 148–49
Contino, Juan, 289, 290
Corrigan, Tommy, 29, 30, 31, 331, 332
  and al Qaeda, 36–37
  and Black Muslim investigation, 58,
    60–63, 81–84, 96, 110
  and Nosair's cell, 51–52, 57–63
  and TERRSTOP, 110–14, 147
  and WTC 1993 bombing, 79,
    86–90, 104, 107, 110–11
Coughlin, John, 16, 27
Cunningham, Dennis, 84

Dahdah, Abu, 290
Dahler, Don, 1–3
D'Amato, Alphonse, 72, 115–16
Darkanzali, Mamoun, 257–58, 259,
  290
Davis, Steve, 42–43
Defense Department, U.S., 145
Dembo, Bob, 97, 106
DIB Leasing, 104–5
Dinkins, David, 42, 67
DNA matching, 30
Downey, Ray, 16, 27

Dragomir, Paul, 307
drugs, war on, 131, 132
Dunbar, Carson, 70–71, 72, 74–75,
 84, 87–91
Dunne, Joe, 221, 223

East Africa, embassy bombings in,
 193–209, 216, 223, 229, 237,
 328, 329, 333
Egypt
 Atta in, 251–53, 267
 British rule of, 244, 245
 embassy bombing, 144
 food riots in, 242, 245
 intelligence service of, 71, 109,
  111, 112
 interrogations in, 320
 Islamism in, 53, 54, 140–41,
  244–45, 251
 jihad in, 64
EgyptAir crash, 276
Egypt Airlines, 141, 295
Egyptian Islamic Jihad (EIJ), 53, 141,
 144–45, 148, 156, 164
Egyptian Muslim Brotherhood, 78
Eiffel Tower, 214–15, 262, 263, 327
el-Amir (Atta) family, 239–40,
 241–42, 253
Engineers Syndicate, 247
Esposito, Joe, 2
Essabar, Zakaiya, 275
Es Sayed (Milan cell leader), 274–75
Europe, holy war on, 263

FAA (Federal Aviation
 Administration)
 on airport security, 328
 and the attacks, 12, 15, 24
 warnings to, 295
Fadl, Jamal al-, 154–57, 160–62,
 164–65, 166, 174, 199
Fahd, Saudi king, 158

Fahih, Saad al-, 177
Faisal, Prince Turki al-, 157–59, 219,
 283
FALN, 32, 33, 34
Farm Services Agency, Florida, 268–69
Farouk, king of Egypt, 244
Fateh, Hamida, 240
Fawwaz, Khaled al-, 163, 176–77,
 195, 198, 202–3, 212
Fazul, Haroun, 196, 198–99, 200,
 202–4, 205–6, 207, 233
FBI (Federal Bureau of Investigation)
 and al Qaeda, 202–4, 220, 280, 296,
  321–25
 and bin Laden, 148–50, 152, 176,
  200–201
 changing focus of, 318
 and CIA, 124–27, 150, 271, 304
 and Cold War, 32, 71
 and Cole, 225, 226, 229, 231–35,
  237, 288
 counterterrorism in, 35, 110–11,
  116, 121–22, 171, 173–74, 216,
  288–89, 297–300
 and Flight 800 crash, 166–73, 174
 focus on prosecution rather than
  prevention, 102–3, 124–25, 152,
  299–300, 317–18, 320, 330–31
 and interagency cooperation, 125,
  145, 150, 323–25, 326, 328,
  331–32
 interagency rivalry of, 33–34, 62,
  124–27
 Islamic Radicals Unit, 300
 and JTTF, 34, 35
 and Kahane case, 44, 45, 46, 55, 66,
  72
 and Moussaoui, 298–300
 National Security Division of, 171
 New York office of, 31–33, 84,
  113–14, 145, 214
 and Nosair's cell, 51, 72, 80

FBI (*continued*)
  and NYPD, 33–34, 44, 62, 84
  risk aversion in, 74–75, 87–91, 96,
    122, 287–89, 299–300, 330
  and Salem, 69–75
  Southern District, 147, 152, 214,
    280
  terrorist activity monitored by, 270,
    287, 303, 322
  urban gang investigations of, 84
  and WTC 1993 bombing, 79,
    87–90, 94–95, 96–97, 99–100,
    101–2, 105, 106–10, 172–73
  Young Turks in, 32
  and Yousef, 119, 121
Feehan, Bill, 16, 27
Fitzgerald, Patrick, 146
Ford, Gerald R., 127
Foreign Intelligence Security Act
    (FISA), 299
Forlani, Armaldo, 118
Forty Thieves, 61–63, 74
France, and Moussaoui, 298–99
Frankfurt, cell in, 286
Franklin, Irving, 39, 41, 67
Fraunces Tavern bombing, 99
Freeh, Louis, 174, 231

G-8 summit meeting, Genoa, 292, 327
Gabrowny, Ibraham el-, 77, 79, 96
  arrest of, 107–8, 116
  and bomb plots, 73, 83, 104
  funds obtained by, 137
  influence of, 86, 91, 92
  and Nosair, 49, 66, 70, 73, 80, 92,
    104, 115
  and WTC 1993 bombing, 107–8,
    110, 111
Gaith, Suliman Abu, 316–17
Galasso, Pat, 105
Ganci, Pete, 16, 27
"Gangster socks," 171

Garza, Rick, 272
Gawli, Sultan el-, 49
Germany
  Atta in, 249–53, 256–60
  cells in, 199, 200, 223, 254–67,
    276–77, 286
Ghamdi, Ahmed al-, 283, 297
Ghamdi, Hamza al-, 283, 285–86
Gibson, Charles, 2
Giuliani, Rudy, 8, 11, 16, 22, 25–27
Glick, Jeremy, 23–24
Glick, Lyzbeth, 24
Gonzales, Arturo, 9–10
Good Morning America (TV), 1–3, 13
Goodwill Games, 173
Gorbachev, Mikhail, 52
Gore, Al, 328
Gotti, John, 47, 133, 211
Gravano, Sammy "the Bull," 133
Greaves, Anne, 273–74
Ground Zero, cleanup of, 333
Guatemala, CIA in, 127, 133
Gulf War, 60, 79, 100, 157–58, 160,
    251

Haddad, Naji Owaida, 123
Hage, Wadi el-, 149, 196–202, 204,
    213
Haggag, Abdo Mohammed, 90, 112,
    113, 147, 148
Hamas, 100, 116, 144
Hamburg
  cell in, 199, 200, 254–67
  funding source in, 274
  safe house in, 256
Hampton-El, Clement (Dr. Rashid),
    83–85, 86–91, 104, 111, 113,
    115, 116
Hanjour, Hani, 276, 277, 278, 285,
    297, 300, 307, 308
Hanlin, Joe, 102
Harazi, Mohammed Omar al-, 226

Harrisburg, paramilitary training
    camp in, 90, 96, 104, 114
Hart, Gary, 328
Hauer, Jerry, 194, 316
Hauth, Volker, 250, 251–53
Hayes Computing Service, 263
Hazmi, Nawaf al-, 225, 270–73, 276,
    278
    final days of, 307
    flight training of, 271–72, 285, 303
    papers of, 297, 304, 306
Haznawi, Ahmed al-, 283, 285
Hekmatyer, Gulbuddin, 54, 64
Help Africa People, 149, 199
Herman, Neil, 28, 30–31, 37, 71, 332
    early years of, 32
    in FBI, 31–33, 103, 110, 124–26
    and Flight 800 crash, 168–70,
        171–73
    jihad investigation of, 84, 86, 88,
        89–91
    in JTTF, 30, 31, 34, 35, 57, 62, 97,
        172–73
    and Kahane case, 36, 55–56
    and pre-emptive cases, 147
    and WTC 1993 bombing, 97,
        98–100, 103–5, 108–11, 119–20,
        122, 136
    and Yousef, 119–27, 137
Hezbollah, 100, 129, 141, 152, 164
Hikind, Dov, 72–73, 115–16
Hilal, al (Yemeni sheik), 274–75
Holland Tunnel, 113, 214
Horst, Karl-Heinz, 282
HRBC, 266
Huffman Aviation, Florida, 273, 277
Hussein, Saddam, 100, 134, 157

Ibrahim, Kamal, 86, 92, 93
Ikegami, Hiruki, 118–19, 123
Imam Reza Shrine, 120
India, cell in, 213

INS (Immigration and Naturalization
    Service), 77, 139–40, 303
International Association of Bomb
    Technicians and Investigators,
    286–87
International Islamic Relief
    Organization (IIRO), 138
Iran
    CIA in, 54, 128–29, 134
    Hezbollah in, 164
    shah overthrown in, 54, 128–29, 130
Iraq
    and Gulf War, 60, 157–58, 160
    training camp of, 283
    and WTC 1993 bombing, 78–79,
        110
Irish, Gloria, 285–86
Isham, Chris, 176, 279–80
Islam AG, Hamburg, 262
Islamic Army of Aden, 270
Islamic fundamentalism
    basic ideology of, 245
    and Black Muslim community, 58,
        60–63, 66, 81–84, 110–17
    bomb plots of, 73–74
    in Egypt, 53, 54, 140–41, 244–45,
        251
    funding of, 155
    in Germany, 257, 262
    global jihad of, 49–50, 64, 159
    and Gulf War, 158
    informants about, 70–75, 144,
        154–57
    inter-branch cooperation in, 164, 330
    martyrs of, 261–62, 283
    militantism of, 31, 47, 49–50, 60,
        65–66, 71, 74, 129, 144, 329
    Nosair's adoption of, 48
    in Pakistan, 130
    Taliban, 180
    terror cells of, 50–51, 61, 120, 137,
        197, 270

Ismail, Iman, 245–46
Israel
    Arabs in, 41–42, 251
    creation of, 42, 244
    Kach party in, 41
    October War of, 72
    peace negotiations with, 218, 220, 237
    political figures sympathetic to, 115
    Six-Day War in, 47, 53
    targets in, 49
    U.S. support of, 157, 190
Italy, cells in, 223, 274, 286, 323

Jamaat al-Fuqra sect, 197
Janjalani, Abdul Rajak, 138
Jarrah, Ziad, 264–67, 275, 277, 282
    final days of, 306–13
    girlfriend of, 292–93
    pilot's license to, 293
    street-fighting lessons to, 284–85
    travels of, 285, 306
Jefferson, Lisa, 24
Jennings, Peter, 2, 13, 25, 30–31, 191, 316
Jersey City, cell formed in, 49–53
Jewish Defense League, 34, 38, 41, 66
jihad
    against U.S., *see* United States
    father of modern movement of, 196
    manuals of, 261, 263, 306, 310–13
    meanings of, 50, 245
Jihad Wal training camp, 155
John Paul II, Pope, 123–24, 172, 176
Jordan, 140, 223, 283
Josephs, Eddie, 34
JTTF (Joint Terrorism Task Force)
    beginning of, 31, 34
    and bin Laden case, 148–49, 199, 201
    Brinks case of, 34, 35, 62
    and CIA, 125, 304

domestic terror unit of, 32, 62
    expanded mission of, 173
    and Flight 800 crash, 168–70, 171–72
    informants sought by, 80
    jihad investigation of, 82, 86–91, 331
    and Kahane case, 36, 41, 44, 45, 55–56
    and NAFF case, 35, 36
    and Nosair's cell, 51, 58, 59, 62–63, 76
    in Pakistan, 323–24
    and pre-emptive cases, 35, 58, 86, 147
    and September 11 attacks, 30
    and TERRSTOP, 114–16, 145, 147, 173
    and WTC 1993 bombing, 96–97, 99, 104, 105, 106–9, 172–73, 331
    and Yousef, 120
Judge, Rev. Mychal, 16, 27
Justice Department, U.S., failure to see threats, 31, 202, 204–5, 329

Kach party (Israel), 41
Kaczynski, Ted, 122
Kahane, Rabbi Meir
    assassination of, 36, 38–46, 50, 55, 76, 83, 84, 96, 147, 198, 329
    body flown to Israel, 42, 67
    militancy of, 41
    murder case of, 42–46, 55–56, 57, 63, 65–67, 68, 72, 148
    stalking of, 55
Kallstrom, Jim, 169, 171
Karim, Abdul Basit, 78, 79
Kattan, Khaled, 246
Kaufman, Elaine, 223
Keane, Tom, 326
Kennedy, John F., 115

Kenya
  bin Laden's associates in, 146, 149, 213
  bomb building in, 205–6, 212, 233
  cell formed in, 194–96, 199–204, 205, 333
  as staging area, 194, 195
  U.S. embassy in, 194, 195, 204, 206–9, 210, 212, 229, 270, 329, 333
  warnings of plot in, 204–5
Kerik, Bernie, 11, 14, 16, 27
Khadija, Abu, 200
Khairy, Waleed, 245
Khalid ibm Walid training camp, 155
Khalifa, Mohammed, 138, 139–40
Khamis, Mohamed Kamel, 241, 242
Khan, Barbrach, 319
Khobar bombing, 237
Khomeini, Ayatollah, 128, 130
Khrushchev, Nikita, 71
Kissinger, Henry A., 73, 115, 326
Koppel, Ted, 191
Kunstler, William, 66–67, 80
Kuwait, and Gulf War, 60, 157–58

LaGuardia Airport bombing, 99
Landmarks plot, 63, 113–16, 147–48, 214, 329
Lebanon, 129, 163, 164
Lester, James, 279
Lewinsky, Monica, 216, 328
Lhota, Joe, 11
Libby, Ibn Sheik al-, 320
Lichstein, Terri, 175, 176
Liguori, John, 82, 86–90, 113, 148
Lincoln Tunnel, 113, 214
Lockerbie crash (1988), 35
Lombardo, Anthony, 102
London, cells in, 195, 202, 286
Long Island, Flight 800 crash near, 166–70, 174

Lopez, Kathy, 227–28
Los Angeles Millennium bomb plot, 260–61, 269, 271, 287
Lyons, Jimmy, 104

McDermott, Terry, 249
McGuire, John, 82, 87, 88–89
Machule, Dittmar, 248, 259–60, 266, 267
McNally, Tom, 57–62, 82, 147
McTureous, Robert, 227–28
Madrid, cell in, 290
Mafia, 164, 170
Malaysia, al Qaeda in, 225, 270–73, 304
Mansour, Isam, 274, 292
Marquis, Craig, 9
Masjid al-Salaam mosque, Jersey City, 49
Mawn, Barry, 317–18
Max (informant), 280–81, 296
Maxwell, Kenny, 169, 171, 281, 317
Meisner, Vincent, 312
Merlino brothers, 170
Meskini, Abdel Ghani, 222
Midhar, Khalid al-, 225, 270–73
  final days of, 307
  flight training of, 272, 303
  papers of, 297, 304, 305
  in U.S., 282–83, 289, 303–4
Midhar, Zein al-Abidine al-, 270
Milan, cell in, 286
Miles, Doc, 12
Millennium plots, 217, 221–23, 224, 260–61, 269, 271, 287, 288
Mills, Caren Ann, 48
Mohamed (prophet)
  and Islamic movement, 245
  words and example of, 310
Mohamed, Ali, 140–46, 195, 331
Mohammed, Khalid Shaikh, 122, 139, 291–92

Moqed, Majed, 305, 308
Morales, Willie, 33
Morgenthau, Robert, 55, 56, 57, 62, 67
Moussaoui, Zacarias "Zac," 275–76, 297–300
Mubarak, Hosni, 53, 72, 111–13, 147, 245, 251, 252
Mueller, Robert, 318, 320
Mugniyah, Imad, 152
Muite, Paul, 205
Munir, Ibrahim, 139
Murad, Abdul Hakim, 120, 123–24, 134, 135, 263
Murphy, Pat, 99
Musharraf, Pervez, 219
Muslim Brotherhood, 244, 247
Mylroie, Laurie, 78–79
Mzoudi, Abdelghani, 256, 257, 264

NAFF (New Afrikan Freedom Fighters), 35, 36, 58, 62, 147
Nairobi, *see* Kenya
Najim, Ismail, 91, 93
Napoli, Louie, 28–29, 30, 31
    and Kahane case, 55, 63
    and Nosair's cell, 57, 63–65, 80
    and Rashid, 83
    and Salem, 69–75, 84, 111, 113–16, 330–31
    and TERRSTOP, 110–11, 147
    and WTC 1993 bombing, 110
Nashiri, Abd al-Rahim al-, 225–26, 234
Nasser, Gamal Abdel, 244
National Islamic Front (NIF), 151, 157, 159, 161
National Security Agency (NSA), 121, 200, 213, 270, 322, 323
National Security Council (NSC), 287
National Transportation Safety Board (NTSB), 169

Naval Criminal Investigative Service (NCIS), 88, 228, 231
Naval Intelligence Service (NIS), 82, 87, 225
NBC studios, 97–98, 99, 106
Neely, Steve, 141–44
New Africa Republic, 34
New York City
    additional targets in, 14, 30, 45, 46, 63, 73, 113, 214, 329
    airspace of, 26
    Bank Squad in, 33, 34, 62
    Counterintelligence Squad in, 33
    JTTF in, *see* JTTF
    Landmarks plot in, 63, 113–16, 147–48, 214, 329
    Millennium in, 221–23
    police action in 1970s, 47
    Primary Day in, 8, 26
    survival of, 26, 135
    Times Square in, 221–23
    Twelve Jewish Locations plot in, 73–76, 78, 80, 83, 85, 90, 96, 104
New York 8, 35
New York Police Department (NYPD)
    Bomb Squad in, 97, 98–102, 116
    crime lab of, 102
    Detective Bureau of, 44
    "Don't make waves" in, 44–46
    and FBI, 33–34, 44, 62, 84
    and JTTF, 34, 62
    and Kahane case, 43–46, 55, 72, 96
    and WTC 1993 bombing, 97, 98–102, 107
NGOs (non-governmental organizations), 138, 149
Nixon, Richard M., 73, 115
NORAD (North American Aerospace Defense Command), 15, 18
Norris, Eddie, 43, 44, 45, 46, 55, 96
Northeast Air Defense Sector, 15

Nosair, El Sayyid
  associates of, 140
  background of, 47–48
  cell formed by, 49–53, 57–65, 72,
    76, 80, 90, 96, 104, 110, 111
  convictions of, 147–48
  document files of, 45, 46, 55, 65,
    137, 144
  hit list of, 45–46, 72–73, 115
  influence of, 65–66, 83, 85, 86
  jobs held by, 48–49
  and Kahane murder, 38–46, 55–56,
    65–67, 68, 72, 110, 148
  marriage and family of, 48
  multiple plans of, 52–53, 73, 116
  trial of, 46, 65–68, 70, 73
  visitors in jail, 70, 72, 73, 92, 108,
    115, 198

O'Connor, Michelle, 208
Odeh, Mohamed Saddiq, 195–96, 206,
    212
Office of Services, Pakistan, 49
Oklahoma City bombing, 172
Olympic Games, 172
Omar, Mullah, 215, 219
Omega 7 (anti-Castro), 34
O'Neill, John P., 325, 332
  and al Qaeda, 280, 286
  and the attack, 10–11, 29
  and bin Laden, 173–74, 193–94,
    293
  briefcase incident, 304–5
  and *Cole,* 228–37, 328
  early years of, 170–71
  and FBI, 170–74, 228, 304–5
  and Flight 800 crash, 171–72,
    174
  and Millennium, 221–23
  in Spain, 289–90
  at World Trade Center, 305,
    314–16, 318

Ong, Betty, 9
OSS (Office of Strategic Services), 128
Otis Air National Guard Base,
    Massachusetts, 15
'Owhali, Mohamed al-, 192, 206–8,
    212, 225

Pahlavi, Shah Mohammed Reza, 54,
    128, 130
Pakistan
  and arms to Afghanistan, 54, 130
  bin Laden's logistics base in, 255–56
  CIA in, 130, 323–24
  diplomatic negotiations with, 219
  Egyptian embassy bombed in, 144
  Inter-Services Intelligence Agency
    (ISI), 130, 280
  Islamic fundamentalists in, 130
Palestinian peace negotiations, 218,
    220, 237
Palestinian training camps, 283
Pan Am Flight 103, Lockerbie crash,
    35
Pan Am International Flight Academy,
    276, 298
Paris, U.S. embassy in, 262
Parker, Istiaque, 135
Pataki, George, 26
Pearl Harbor, 127, 327
Pennsylvania, fourth plane down in,
    18–21, 25
Pentagon, as target, 18, 20, 24, 290,
    315
Peshawar, logistics base in, 255–56
Petit, Arnaud, 271–72
Philippines Airlines Flight (434),
    118–19, 123
Picciano, John, 11, 14
Pickard, Tom, 329
Port Authority of New York and New
    Jersey, 98
Pressley, Frank, 208

Quoso, Fhad al-, 234

Rafei, Mohamed Mokhtar el-, 245
Rahman, Saif, 280
Ransom, Edwin, 58, 60, 81
Rapid Start database, 110
Rashid, Doctor (Hampton-El), 63,
    73–74, 83–85, 104, 111
Reagan, Ronald, 128
Ressam, Ahmed, 222, 260–61, 269,
    271, 283, 287
Rice, Condoleezza, 287
Robinson, Marcus, 61–63, 74, 82
Rodriguez, Bert, 284–85
Rowley, Colleen, 299
Rudman, Warren, 328
Rumsfeld, Donald, 297

Sadat, Anwar, 53–54, 141, 142,
    238–39, 244
Sadowy, Don, 101–3, 106, 110
Salameh, Mohammed, 50, 76
    apartment of, 77, 79, 85, 91
    arrest and conviction of, 104–5, 117
    and bomb making, 85, 91, 92, 108
    and Kahane murder, 43, 44, 55, 67,
        96, 110
    and WTC 1993 bombing, 85, 86,
        92–93, 96, 104–5, 107, 109–10,
        111, 122
Saleh, Ali Abdullah, 231
Saleh, Mohamed, 116
Salem, Emad, 69–75, 80, 83, 84–85,
    90, 96, 104, 111, 114–16, 147,
    330–31
Salim, Mamdou, 139, 156, 157, 160,
    161, 212–13, 258, 264
Salinger, Pierre, 169
San Diego, Muslim community in,
    270, 271
Sardone, John, 102–3
Sarnowski, Violetta, 258

Saudi Arabia
    al Qaeda in, 226
    bin Laden in, 151, 157–59, 163–64,
        174
    diplomatic negotiations with, 219,
        235
    explosion in, 149–50, 173–74
    and Gulf War, 157–58
    terrorists from, 283
    training camp for, 283
    U.S. troops in, 158, 159, 160, 173,
        190
Sawyer, Diane, 1
Scarfo, "Little Nicky," 170
Schlesinger, Alvin, 67, 72
Schroeder, Margritte, 250
Seaman, Michael, 29, 36
Sears Tower, Chicago, 289
Sebastian, Kris, 13
Secret Service, 18, 24
Senguen, Aysel, 264, 292–93, 308,
    313
September 11 attacks, 1–3, 8–27
    air tickets purchased for, 305–6
    estimates of deaths in, 26, 27, 29
    events following, 314–25, 326
    events leading to, 4, 47, 291–92
    predictions of, 3, 327
    preparation for, 51, 255, 269–86,
        294–313
    rescue efforts in, 26
Shaikh, Abdussattar, 272–73
Shakur, Mutulu, 34
Shalabi, Mustafa, 54–55, 82, 143
    and Abdel-Rahman, 54, 63–65, 90
    and al-Kifah center, 51, 52, 63–64,
        155, 156, 197
    death of, 64–65, 80, 83, 84, 149,
        197–98
    and Nosair, 52
Sharif, Nawaz, 219
Sheehan, Michael, 213, 214, 215, 220

Shehhi, Marwan al-, 263–64, 266
  final days of, 306–13
  pilot's license to, 276–77, 278
  preparation of, 273–78
  travels of, 277, 282, 285, 289, 306
  in U.S., 282, 284, 285–86, 301–3
Shehri, Wail al-, 283, 286, 301, 305–6
Shehri, Waleed al-, 283–84, 286, 301,
    305–6, 308
Shehri family, 283
Shelton, Henry, 218
Shinawy, Ali el-, 73–74, 83, 90
Shinn, David, 151
Siddig-Ali, Siddig, 90, 113–16, 147
Simpson, O. J., 329
Slotnick, Barry, 41, 42, 45
Small Group, 217
Smith, Richard, 57–58, 59–61, 66, 81
Sobri, Mohamed, 259
Somalia, 79, 161–63, 176, 188–89,
    194, 195, 203, 214
"Son of Sam," 44
South Florida Crop Care, 279, 300–301
South Yemen, holy war against, 158
Soviet Union
  Afghan invasion by, 127, 130–31,
    143, 156, 164, 187–88
  in Cold War, 127, 128
  collapse of, 131
  UN mission of, 41
"Star-Spangled Banner, The," 236
State Department, U.S., 119, 140, 141,
    151, 229, 235, 303, 328
Statue of Liberty, 263
Stavis, Roger, 48
Stern, Chuck, 77, 96–97, 100, 104,
    107, 109, 111, 135
Sudan
  al Qaeda in, 157, 160, 164
  anti-Western terrorists in, 151, 152
  bin Laden in, 145, 151–53, 157,
    159–61, 164, 194, 215, 332–33
  and chemical weapons, 164
  civil war in, 161
  training camps in, 146
  U.S. consulate in, 54
  U.S. retaliation in, 211, 216
Sufaat, Yazid, 225, 271, 275
Suqami, Satam al-, 286
Sweeney, Madeline Amy, 9

T & T Gunnery, 58–59
Taha, Ali Othman, 151
Tajikistan, CIA in, 133–34
Taliban, 131, 153, 173, 180, 215, 219,
    220, 319
Tanzania, U.S. embassy in, 209, 210,
    229, 270, 329, 333
Tayyib, Mandini al-, 200, 201
Tenet, George, 287, 303, 318, 320
Tennessee Valley Authority (TVA),
    279
Tepper, Len, 176, 177
terrorism
  "acceptable level" of, 214
  classic strategy of, 80
  cyclical nature of, 332
  diplomatic pressure against, 36,
    235
  economic sanctions against, 36
  funding of, 64, 66, 79, 113, 122,
    137, 148, 152, 156, 291–92, 298,
    307, 328
  global, 36–37, 121–22, 127–28,
    195, 198, 202, 213, 220, 286–87,
    330
  marketing of, 234
  nations supporting, 213, 219
  new kind of, 47
  not taken seriously, 56, 84, 87, 163,
    173, 204–5, 214–15
  as seditious conspiracy, 116
  state-sponsored, 36, 131
  war on, 318, 330, 332

terrorist attacks
disrupted plots of, 30, 35, 36, 194, 213, 214, 217, 222, 224, 262, 263, 271, 298, 329–30
fear as goal of, 80
flexible plans for, 281
four targets for, 263
jihad manual for, 263
predictions of, 3, 287–89
preparation for, 294–313
see also World Trade Center
terrorists
bin Laden's training camps for, 50, 76, 78, 79, 146, 150, 155, 215, 216
bomb plots of, 73–74, 91–93, 113–16, 122–24, 193–209, 224
chemicals obtained by, 85, 86, 91–93, 109
detonator caps for, 83, 84, 86, 96, 110
disinformation campaign of, 287, 322
final days of, 306–13
flight training for, 263, 273, 276–77, 278, 287–88, 300
"Gucci," 139
guns needed by, 58–59, 73, 74, 83, 111, 114
information shared by, 296
international conference of, 164
Islamic-ness vs. Western mien of, 80
in 1970s, 32–33
paramilitary training in U.S. for, 51–52, 57, 83, 96, 111, 114
passport scam by, 120, 267
physical description of, 9, 24
preparations by, 268–93, 294–313
street fighting lessons for, 284–85
watch lists of, 271, 288, 303
when to stop, 87, 330
TERRSTOP, 110–16, 137, 140, 145, 146–48, 172, 173, 328

Third World Relief Agency, 113
Torricelli, Robert, 133
TRADEBOM, 100, 103, 110, 114, 119–20, 137
Triplett, Robert, 227
Tucson, al Qaeda cell in, 197
Turabi, Hassan al-, 159, 164
TWA Flight 800 crash, 166–73, 174, 281, 317
Twelve Jewish Locations plot, 73–76, 78, 80, 83, 85, 90, 96, 104

Ubaidah, Yaya Abu, 82–83, 84, 87, 89–91, 113
Uganda, cell in, 213
Unabomber case, 122
Uncle Charley's, explosion in, 52–53
United Airlines
and the attacks, 16–17
Flight 93, 17, 18–21, 23–24, 25, 309, 313
Flight 175, 8, 12, 14, 15
United Arab Emirates, 226, 266, 274, 307, 308
United Nations, 41, 113–14, 115, 214
United States
cells formed in, 49–53, 57–63, 197
counterterrorism policy in, 217
embassy bombings, 129, 193–209, 212, 262, 270, 281, 328, 329
in Gulf War, 60, 100, 158, 160, 251
interagency miscommunication in, 145
jihads and fatwas against, 4–5, 50, 51, 58, 63, 65, 76, 79, 83, 90, 91–92, 100, 115–16, 137, 150, 152, 156, 160–61, 163, 174, 186–92, 193, 202, 204–5, 212, 215, 263, 274, 287, 321
national security expenditures of, 327

as nation of laws, 152, 199, 299, 320, 322
negative symmetry in, 131
as paper tiger, 163, 188, 211, 220
paramilitary training camps in, 51–52, 57, 83, 90, 111, 114
retaliatory options of, 210–11, 215–19, 237, 319
in Somalia, 161–63, 176, 188, 194, 203
US Air Flight 608, 295–96
USS *Cole*, 225, 226, 227–37, 270, 273, 288, 304, 333
USS *The Sullivans*, 224–25, 226

victims, jumping, 11, 26
victims' families, public sympathy for, 26
Villareale, Tony, 167
Von Essen, Thomas, 16
Voss, Chris, 112–13

weapons of mass destruction, 164, 317–18, 327
Weather Underground, 34
Wendt, Chrylla, 266
Western, Jim, 236
White, Mary Jo, 174, 202, 317, 332
White House
  bunker beneath, 22
  evacuation of, 18
  failure to see threats, 31, 329
  plane crash into, 132
  protection of, 24
  as target, 25
  warnings transmitted to, 296
Whitener, Danny, 278–79
Wilkie, Farr & Gallagher, 108
Williams, Dave, 101, 103, 106
Williams, Kenneth, 287–88
Wilson, Garrett, 81–85, 86–89, 111
Wingate, Carl, 228

Wong, Wesley, 315
Woods, James, 294–95
Woodward, Michael, 9
Woolard, Jim, 286
Woolsey, James, 132
World Trade Center attack (September 11), 1–3, 8–27, 314–18
  and collapse, 3, 22, 25, 37, 315
  crime scene of, 317–18
  devastation of, 10, 16, 18, 317
  dust and ash of, 22, 25, 29
  evacuation in, 15, 16, 17–18, 21
  Miller's responses to, 13, 25, 30
  preparation for, 4, 268–93, 294–313
  rescue efforts in, 15, 22, 26
  and sense of loss, 316
  suspects in, 29
  as target, 290
World Trade Center bombing (1993), 29, 94–117
  events leading to, 46, 56, 79, 85–93, 291–92, 329, 330
  funding of, 79, 122, 292
  investigation of, 99–100, 101–5, 106–14, 119–20, 172, 173
  Miller's activities related to, 97–98, 99, 100–101, 105–6
  and other plots, 46, 114–16, 126, 136–37, 291–92, 331
  purpose of, 80, 95, 96, 214
  re-creation of, 94–95
  suspects arrested in, 105, 107–9, 116
  terrorists involved in, 63, 78–79, 85, 90, 96, 104, 111, 119, 135, 137, 145, 189, 191, 197
  and TERRSTOP, 111–16
  as TRADEBOM, 100, 103, 110, 114, 119–20
  trial and convictions in, 117, 122, 125, 147–48
  as wake-up call, 136–37, 189

Wright, David, 319
Wright, Michael
  and the attack, 7–8, 9–10, 15
  escape of, 22–23
  evacuating the building, 15, 17–18,
    21
WTC, *see* World Trade Center

Yarkas, Imad Eddin Barakhat, 290
Yasin, Abdul Rahman, and WTC 1993
    bombing, 85–86
Yassin, Ahmed, 107, 109–10, 117
Yemen, 224–37
  civil war in, 230–31
  Cole explosion in, 227–29
  kidnapping and murder in, 270
  Miller in, 235–36
  Security Service of, 232–34
  U.S. investigators in, 228–30,
    231–32, 234–35, 236–37
Young, Dennison, 8
Yousef, Ramzi, 76–80, 278, 303
  arrest and trial of, 134–35, 171, 172
  arrival in U.S., 77, 80, 85, 108
  associates of, 85, 120, 121
  background of, 77, 78

and Bojinka plot, 122–23, 124, 137,
    138, 139, 168, 176, 225, 291
as bomb maker, 78, 79, 84–85, 86,
    91–93, 108, 118–20, 122–24,
    135, 136–37, 138, 168
car accident of, 92
and CIA plot, 123, 214, 263, 288,
    291–92, 327
computer of, 124, 137
escape of, 80, 120
at large, 117, 118–27, 137, 234
links to bin Laden, 138–39, 146,
    176, 189
name of, 78
personal qualities of, 77, 80
and WTC 1993 bombing, 80, 85,
    91–93, 96, 108, 110, 119, 135,
    189, 191

Zammar, Mohammed Aydar, 259
Zawahiri, Ayman al-, 144–45, 156,
    181, 183, 184, 185, 244, 291
Zindani, Abdul Wali, 64–65, 82–84
Zindt, John, 145
Zubaydah, Abu, 260, 261, 262, 291,
    322–23, 324–25